Italian Politics

ITALIAN POLITICS:
A REVIEW

Books in This Series

Italian Politics

The Center-Left in Power

EDITED BY

Roberto D'Alimonte
and David Nelken

A Publication of the Istituto Cattaneo

WestviewPress

A Division of HarperCollins*Publishers*

Italian Politics: A Review, Volume 12

Copyright © 1997 by Westview Press, A Division of HarperCollins Publishers, Inc.

Published in 1997 in the United States of America by Westview Press, 5500 Central Avenue, Boulder, Colorado 80301-2877, and in the United Kingdom by Westview Press, 12 Hid's Copse Road, Cumnor Hill, Oxford OX2 9JJ

A CIP catalog for this book is available from the Library of Congress.
ISBN 0-8133-3441-1 (hc)—ISBN 0-8133-3443-8 (pb)

The Istituto Cattaneo, founded in 1965, is a private, nonprofit organization. It aims to promote, finance, and conduct research, studies, and other activities that contribute to the knowledge of contemporary Italian society and, especially, of the Italian political system.

Istituto Carlo Cattaneo, Via Santa Stefano 11, 40125 Bologna, Italy

The paper used in this publication meets the requirements of the American National Standard for Permanence of Paper for Printed Library Materials Z39.48-1984.

10   9   8   7   6   5   4   3   2   1

Contents

Chronology of Italian Political Events, 1996

January

5   In Parliament, the debate over the future of the government commences. The parties take different positions: *Alleanza Nazionale* (AN) insists on a motion of no confidence, but Silvio Berlusconi disagrees and presses for reform; the *Ulivo* wishes to extend the Dini government, and the *Lega Nord* asks for the establishment of a constituent assembly.

6   The confrontation over government between the *Ulivo* and the *Polo* ends badly, with the former accusing the latter of promoting a crisis, and Berlusconi and the *Polo* complaining about the Center-Left's absurd requests. Inflation drops to 5.8%; GDP increases by 3.4% from the same quarter in 1994.

8   The Italian Presidency of the European Union begins.

10 The debate on the future of the government and the legislature is opened by Lamberto Dini's speech to the Chamber of Deputies; he emphasizes three possible solutions to the crisis: the establishment of a constituent assembly; a government for the duration of the European Presidency; or elections.
    Tommaso Buscetta again accuses Giulio Andreotti of being the central political figure involved with the mafia in the context of the Aldo Moro case, and the murders of Mino Pecorelli and General Carlo Alberto Dalla Chiesa.

11 A governmental crisis occurs, and Dini announces his resignation and goes to the Quirinale. PDS Secretary Massimo D'Alema's strategy thus fails, whilst *Alleanza Nazionale* leader Gianfranco Fini's hard line is rewarded. Prodi objects to the "broad agreement" idea: "it would be a mess".
    Silvio and Paolo Berlusconi are under investigation by the public prosecutor of Brescia for extortion and attempts at obstructing the political rights of Antonio Di Pietro, i.e. preventing the former magistrate from entering politics.

15 President of the Republic Oscar Luigi Scalfaro begins talks with the Presidents of the two Chambers at the Quirinale.

18 The trial of Silvio Berlusconi for alleged bribes paid to the *Guardia di Finanza* begins.

21 After the first day of talks with the Italian President, the possibility of an agreement on reforms fades, and the disagreement between Gianfranco Fini, who wants elections, and Massimo D'Alema, who favors the reappointment of Dini, harshens.

25 Center-Left candidate Valeria Onida and *Polo* candidate Carlo Mezzanotte are appointed judges to the Constitutional Court by the two Chambers of Parliament. They obtain 615 and 608 votes respectively.

27 The *Ulivo* rejects the *Polo*'s proposal, initiated by Mario Segni, for a "mayor of Italy".
    Salvatore Profeta, Pietro Scotto and Giuseppe Orofino are sentenced to life imprisonment for the Via D'Amelio massacre, in which Judge Paolo Borsellino and his escort were killed.

29 The "La Fenice" theater in Venice, one of the oldest in Italy, is destroyed by fire. It had been closed since August 1995 for renovations.

February

1   Parliament appoints Antonio Maccanico to form a government. He begins consultations and announces that the governmental program will center on reforms and the economy. Romano Prodi reacts negatively, Fini seems partially satisfied, and D'Alema agrees, but faces criticism from the *Popolari* and *Rifondazione Comunista* leader Fausto Bertinotti.
    Berlusconi and D'Alema reach a tentative agreement on a French-style presidential system, but they still disagree on how the government and the prime minister should be selected.

8   Parliament approves legislation on sexual violence, which is transformed from a moral to a personal offense, with 239 votes in favor, 39 against, and 15 abstentions.

14 Maccanico's attempt to form a new government fails. *Polo* and *Ulivo* blame each other for the failure.

15 Maccanico resigns and accuses the *Polo* of "having asked the government to act beyond its mandate."
    The Senate ratifies the law on sexual violence.
    The Brescia public prosecutor again requests that Di Pietro be put on trial.

16 President Scalfaro dissolves Parliament, and elections are scheduled for 21 April. The Parliament will reassemble on 9 May. *Par condicio* (equal access) is the central theme of the campaign.

17 The Court of Cassation (the ultimate court of appeal) upholds the sentences on the two previous Socialist mayors of Milan for illicit funding and acceptance of bribes. Paolo Pillitteri receives four years and six months, Carlo Tognoli three years and three months.
Mario Segni turns down the *Polo*'s offer and aims to recreate a centrist coalition.

20 Berlusconi reasserts his leadership of the *Polo*, which had been questioned by Fini in an interview; D'Alema courts Dini.

23 Roberto Spanò, a committal judge, acquits Antonio Di Pietro of charges of extortion and abuse of power, on the grounds of lack of evidence. Public prosecutors Fabio Salamone and Silvio Bonfigli announce they will appeal.
The *Lega* refuses a stand-down agreement with Prodi, who had asked for the closure of the Northern "Parliament".

24 Dini sides with the *Ulivo* but within his own autonomous movement, whilst Di Pietro declares his unwillingness to stand as a candidate in these elections until the judicial investigations against him are concluded.
The Rome public prosecutor charges Prodi with abuse of power, over the transfer of certain companies from the Cirio group to Fisvi whilst the *Ulivo* candidate for prime minister was president of IRI.

27 Maccanico introduces a new party called *Unione Democratica*, which will gather independents with Gerardo Bianco's *Popolari* in a joint electoral pact.

28 Dini officially sides with the *Ulivo*, and *Sudtiroler Volkspartei* and *Union Valdôtaine* are also close to an accord with the Center-Left. *Lega Nord* leader Umberto Bossi declares his decision to run alone.

29 Vittorio Cecchi Gori wins the TV and radio rights to football league matches over the next three seasons, with an offer of 213 billion lire per annum. Both the right and left criticize the Rai.
The CCD of Pier Ferdinando Casini and Clemente Mastella and the CDU of Buttiglione decide to present combined proportional lists under the old DC symbol (a cross-bearing shield).

March

5 Turin tradesmen organize a demonstration against the *fisco* (taxation system) and harshly criticize Prodi.
Fininvest decides, surprisingly, to forgo electoral advertising, claiming to

wish to "end the debate on the influence of commercial television". The Greens see it as a maneuver to reduce the visibility of the *Ulivo* and Dini.

7   Giorgio Fossa is appointed the new director of Confindustria, with 101 votes out of 145. The defeated candidates are the oil magnate Gian Marco Moratti and the industrialist Aldo Fumagalli.

10 A new protest by Milanese tradesmen against the *fisco*.
    Skirmishes continue over Prodi's candidature in the PPI proportional list. Following the criticism by Greens leader, Carlo Ripa di Meana, bishops also criticize the choice in the columns of the Catholic daily *Avvenire*.

11 Problems also for the *Polo*: the CCD and the CDU threaten to present their candidates separately in all constituencies. They argue that the number of safe seats for Catholic candidates is too low, leaving too much room for the "radical-libertarian culture" of Marco Pannella and Vittorio Sgarbi.
    Tension within the Center-Left over the candidacy of Ciriaco De Mita.

12 The head of the Rome committal judges, Renato Squillante, is arrested for corruption. The charges are based upon the revelations of Stefania Ariosto, the companion of Vittorio Dotti, leader of the *Forza Italia* deputies. *Forza Italia* Senator Cesare Previti is under investigation for the same charges.

14 Harsh disagreement within the *Polo*. Pannella, who demanded a number of constituencies "equal to those of the ex-DC", runs separately, whilst Sgarbi returns to *Forza Italia*.

17 Vittorio Dotti, companion of Stefania Ariosto, the main accuser of Senator Cesare Previti, is excluded from the *Polo* list of candidates, after Berlusconi's request that he resign the candidacy of the Milan 4 constituency, and his refusal to do so.

20 The *Polo* election campaign begins at the Palaeur in Rome, with the slogans "No Tax on BOTs [government savings bonds]" and "Stop the Communists".

21 The match between Cecchi Gori and the Rai ends; the director of the Fiorentina football club pulls out of the auction, and Rai President Letizia Moratti wins the rights to league coverage at the original price.
    Bertinotti promotes the taxation of BOTs, the *scala mobile* (escalator clause) and *equo canone* schemes, and says no to privatizations, severely embarrassing Prodi, Dini and D'Alema.

25 Confrontation within the *Lega* between Bossi and Pivetti. The Carroccio leader wants an independent Padania and secures a vote at Pontida on the Northern Constitution; meanwhile, the President of the Chamber of Deputies sees Padania's place as lying within Italy.
    The INPS (the national social security institute) is forced to reimburse 22,000 billion lire to pensioners after a ruling by the Constitutional Court.

29 The Conference on the revision of the Maastrict Treaty is held in Turin.

31 Di Pietro is acquitted of the charge of extortion in Brescia.

April

4 Rai President Letizia Moratti declares that she will resign together with the whole board of directors on 23 April, immediately after the elections and after presenting a balance sheet showing a profit of 68 billion lire.
A deficit of 10,000 billion lire appears in the balance of payments. The *Polo* accuses the Prime Minister of concealing the public deficit level.

6 Bruno Contrada, ex-number two of the Sisde, is condemned to ten years in prison for mafia involvement. Intensification of electoral debate on the tax system. Fini proposes the abolition of taxation at source for salaried employees and pensioners, but the *Polo* cautiously distances itself from this stance. Accusations of demagoguery come from the *Ulivo*.

9 Berlusconi appeals to Catholics to vote *Forza Italia*, eliciting criticism from the Church and embarrassing his own allies within the *Polo*. The *Forza Italia* leader then denies that the *Polo* manifesto includes the elimination of deductions from pay packets.

10 Prime Minister Dini affirms the necessity of passing an amendment to the budget, allowing the predicted deficit of 109,400 billion to be met.

12 The Higher Council of the Judiciary approves, almost unanimously, a document defending Gian Carlo Caselli and the Palermo magistrates after the accusations by *Forza Italia*, whose Council members provided the opposition.

14 The European Summit of Finance Ministers decides with an overwhelming majority upon "EMS 2", i.e., for a second wave of countries entering the EMU. The agreement allows their admission even if their national debt exceeds 60% of GDP, although the other parameters still remain applicable.

15 An electoral pact between Marco Pannella and Silvio Berlusconi: governmental seats in exchange for support in single-member constituencies. However, the CCD and the CDU reiterate the *Polo*'s position on drugs and abortion.

16 Former PSI Secretary Bettino Craxi is condemned to eight years and three months in prison as well as punitive fines amounting to over 50 billion lire. Barbara Pollastrini, former secretary of the PCI-PDS, is acquitted. These are the sentences passed by the Milan Court for bribes paid for work on the Milanese underground transport system. Francesco Paolo Mattioli (director of Fiat), Gianni Cervetti (an ex-PCI deputy) and Luigi Civardi (managing director of Cogielte) are also sentenced.

18 Eugenio Scalfari resigns as editor of *La Repubblica*. He is replaced by Ezio Mauro, editor of *La Stampa*.

21 The *Ulivo* wins the elections, obtaining an absolute majority in the Senate, but not in the Chamber of Deputies, where support from *Rifondazione Comunista* is consequently necessary. Prodi offers the Presidency of one of the Chambers to the *Polo*.

24 The Constitutional Court declares illegal the presence in the sentencing phase of a judge who has already presided in the accused party's bail hearing in the *Tribunale della Libertà*. As a result, many important cases risk being declared mistrials, including the one dealing with the Capaci massacre.

30 Prodi announces 18 months of austerity in an interview with the *International Herald Tribune* and replies to Bertinotti: "The *scala mobile* will not be reintroduced."
   Polo leaders meet to discuss the Center-Left's offer of the Presidency of the Chamber of Deputies.

May

3 A "trial saving" decree is prepared to prevent the release of 500 mafiosi after the ruling on incompatibility of judges by the Constitutional Court. Justice Minister Vincenzo Caianello receives the mandate from the Council of Ministers to hurry the law through Parliament with extreme urgency.
   Split in the CCD: Mastrella and 11 members stop work in open opposition to Pier Ferdinando Casini, who is proposing a merger with the CDU, which in turn will join with FI. Mastella says he wishes to safeguard the identity of the party, and looks to Di Pietro and Dini for support.

5 Bossi opens the new Northern Parliament in Mantua, in view of the forthcoming secession. Pivetti is cautious, and promotes institutional measures for gaining autonomy for the North.
   Di Pietro accepts Prodi's proposal and announces his participation in the government as Minister for Public Works.

6 The *Polo* proposes Francesco Cossiga for President of the Senate. The PDS immediately vetoes the move, regarding it as a provocation.

9 At the opening of the 13th legislature, the two alliances clash in voting for the Presidents of the two Chambers. Cossiga is rejected by the Center-Left and Carlo Scognamiglio is refused by the Center-Right. The *Ulivo* proposes Luciano Violante and Nicola Mancino.
   The trial against Erich Priebke begins in a military court in Rome. The ex-SS captain is accused of taking part in the Fosse Ardeatine massacre.

10 Nicola Mancino (PPI) is elected President of the Senate by 178 votes out of 314.
   The "trial saving" decree, which prolongs precautionary custody in case of retrial, is approved.

11 Luciano Violante is elected the new President of the Chamber of Deputies, with 316 votes in favor out of 609, and after three null ballots.

12 Arturo Parisi and Enrico Micheli are appointed as undersecretaries to the Prime Minister.

13 Bossi declares his willingness to support the Prodi government in exchange for a concrete commitment towards federalism. The Prime Minister reacts cautiously.
   The "government" of Padania is constituted with Giancarlo Pagliarini as Premier.

16 President Scalfaro asks Prodi to form the new government.

17 Prodi proposes a list of 20 ministers: nine from the PDS, three from the PPI, three from Dini's movement, one Green, one from the *Unione Democratica* (Maccanico) and three technocrats (Carlo Azeglio Ciampi, Antonio Di Pietro and Giovanni Maria Flick).
   Lawyers Giovanni Acampora and Attilio Pacifico are arrested, the latter placed under house arrest, in the Squillante investigation, and are charged with corruption of legal proceedings, together with Previti, for a bribe of 67 billion lire to pervert the IMI-Rovelli trial.

20 Giovanni Brusca, the mafia informant accused of being the executioner in the Capaci massacre, and the strangler of the son of mafia informant Santo Di Matteo, is arrested along with his brother Vincenzo.
   Inflation drops to 4.3%, and the lira drops to 1,008 against the German mark.

21 Forty-nine undersecretaries, amongst whom 18 are not members of Parliament, are appointed. The appointment of the undersecretary delegate to the Giubileo is delayed.

22 In his general policy statement in the Senate, Prodi promises to promote tax federalism, invites the opposition to participate in radical reforms, and asks for sacrifices in order to balance public finances.

24 Prodi and Di Pietro clash about the delegation to the Giubileo, which the latter claims in his capacity as Minister for Public Works with responsibility for urban areas.

29 The Prime Minister meets German Chancellor Helmut Kohl and announces the return of the Italian lira into the EMS by the end of the year.

31 The Chamber of Deputies carries a vote of confidence in the Prodi government by 322 votes to 299, out of a total 621.
Luciano Lama, prominent CGIL and PCI leader, dies in Rome.

June

5   Ignazio La Russa (*Alleanza Nazionale*) is elected president of the Committee for Pretrial Deliberation and announces that he is leaving his post of Previti's defense lawyer forthwith. The *Polo* also wins the presidency of the Electoral Committee, which goes to Elio Vito (*Forza Italia*). The 13 permanent committees of the Chamber of Deputies are controlled by the *Ulivo*.
Ernesto Pascale and Biagio Agnes are reappointed as the heads of Stet.

6   Having thrown out Tg5 and Tg1 reporters from the main square of Lodi during a rally, Bossi raises his sights and orders the presidents of the seven *Lega*-controlled provinces to oust their prefects.
Scalfaro states his opposition to the abuse of referenda and decree-laws "which by-pass parliamentary prerogatives" and declares that he will no longer countersign the resubmission of decrees.

9   Almost 250,000 people are called to vote in elections in 163 municipal elections (of which 33 in cities with more than 15, 000 inhabitants) and also for the provincial council of Caserta.

11 The results of the first ballot in the 163 municipal elections punish Bossi and the *Lega*, whose candidates are excluded from the second round (even in Mantua, the "capital" of Padania).
The appeal on the Banca Ambrosiana bankruptcy condemns Carlo De Benedetti, the president of Olivetti, to four-and-a-half years.

14 The governmental majority rejects the bill tabled by Rosy Bindi, the Minister of Health, for the introduction of a health contribution of 1.5% for pensioners with annual incomes over eight million lire. Criticism also emanates from the Vatican.

16 Elections in Sicily for the regional assembly and 25 municipal councils.

18 The *Polo* wins in Sicily, but FI only obtains half the number of votes of 21 April, dropping from 33% to 17%; AN remains at 14%, and the CCD and the CDU soar to 19%.

20 Prodi introduces a mini-budget of 16,000 billion lire (spending cuts accounting for 11,000, tax revenue for 5,000), added to which are the reduction of welfare payment taxation, 1,100 billion lire reduction in company investment, and the rationalization of public expenditure.

21 EU Summit of the 15 heads of state in Florence.

22 The EU Florence Summit, which marks the end of the Italian Presidency, breaks the deadlock on the "mad cow" crisis.
Chicco Testa is appointed the new head of Enel, replacing Franco Viezzoli; the managing director is Franco Tatò.

24 Abstention is the main trend in the second ballot of the administrative elections. Of the 1.6 million registered voters in the elections of 25 mayors and the president of the province of Caserta, only half turn out at the polls. The *Ulivo* wins in the North, the *Polo* in the South, in a repeat performance of the parliamentary elections.

26 The lira drops below the 1,000 level (998) against the German mark for the first time in two years.

28 Istat announces a rise in unemployment of 0.3 percentage points, to 12.3%. Notably, the South suffers a level of 22.2%.
The Dpef (the financial and economic program) is launched, proposing a budget of 32,000 billion lire in 1997, of which 21,000 will come from spending cuts, and an inflation level of 2.5%.

July

2 13th CGIL Congress opens in Rome under the banner of "No to the Dpef." According to European Commissioner Mario Monti, "with this budget, Italy will not be in the first wave of EMU".

3 The reform of the criteria for appointment to the managing council of the Rai is blocked by the Senate after a vote against it by *Rifondazione Comunista* and the *Polo*.
D'Alema and the ex-PSI Prime Minister Giuliano Amato draft a common program for the reunification of the left.

6 The government approves three draft laws proposed by Justice Minister Giovanni Maria Flick, which provide for the presence of the *giudice di pace* in the criminal system for minor offenses, a fixed-term hiring of retired judges over the age of 60 to reduce a backlog of over two million civil suits, and the regulation of video-conferencing.

7 At the Rome Fair, ex-Socialists of the Craxi period — Ugo Intini, Enrico Manca and Margherita Boniver — present the statutes for a new socialist party.

10 On four occasions, *Rifondazione* blocks the Dfep in a parliamentary committee, voting together with the *Polo*.

11 Agreement between the *Ulivo* and *Rifondazione* on the new guidelines for the Dfep: a 3% increase in 1997 for fixed-term contracts; an extraordinary three-year plan for employment, with investments amounting to 15,000 billion lire; and an increase in family benefits for the lowest income groups.

13 Silvio Berlusconi and Bettino Craxi are again sent to trial for 10 billion lire transferred from Fininvest foreign accounts to those of the ex-PSI leader. The government passes the Bassanini draft law for the reform of public administration. Maccanico proposes an accord between the government majority and the *Polo* within various committees, including the Rai watchdog committee.

18 The Council of Ministers passes a draft law on communications which institutes an "authority" and establishes anti-trust norms for publishing and TV.

19 Dialogue between the *Polo* and the *Ulivo* recommences, and the *Bicamerale* (a joint parliamentary committee) is established for reforms. The aim is to redefine the Constitution before June 1997.

20 The government approves the second phase of public administration reforms. The way is left open for the financial and teaching autonomy of schools.
The Greens brake Minister Di Pietro on the Bologna-Florence motorway extension.

24 The Governor of the Bank of Italy, Antonio Fazio, reduces interest rates by 0.75 percentage points, from 9% to 8.25%.

25 The approval of the Maccanico draft law on TV and the communications authority is delayed once more. The government has to implement urgent measures as a Constitutional Court ruling threatens to dissolve Mediaset.

27 The government unanimously approves the Bologna-Florence motorway extension.
The Council of Ministers approves the draft law on telecommunication systems regulation.

28 Foreign Minister Dini blocks the Bindi health reform on the adjustment of similar pharmaceuticals to the lowest price, on the grounds of its conflict with open competition. Harsh arguments occur within the government.

31 Prodi backs the 16,000 billion lire "mini-budget".
Irene Pivetti, who opposes the secessionist aspirations of the *Lega*, and Umberto Bossi publicly voice their disagreement.

August

1 The Prodi government wins a vote of confidence—on the 16,000 billion "mini-budget"—in the Chamber of Deputies by 319 votes (Center-Left and *Rifondazione*) to 284 (*Polo* and *Lega*).

2 A military court acquits ex-Nazi captain Erich Priebke of genocide because of mitigating circumstances, but finds him culpable of multiple homicide.

3 The law on voluntary financing of political parties through 0.4% of Irpef is blocked by Parliament.
The Council of Ministers approves seven draft laws proposed by Justice Minister Flick, in particular the appointment of a single *giudice di primo grado*, the decentralization of judicial services and the reorganization of the ministry, regulation of strikes by lawyers, the definition of disciplinary responsibilities and of areas of restriction for magistrates, and the acceleration of entrance examinations for the judiciary.

4 Irene Pivetti dissociates herself from Bossi and opposes the secession proclaimed by the *Lega* leader for 15 September.

6 Inflation drops again, to 3.6%.

21 Three possible cases in the pipeline against Bossi, by the Tolmezzo, Bergamo and Milan public prosecutors. He is charged with reconstructing the fascist party, defamation through the press, and slander against the President of the Republic.

22 Giovanni Brusca says that he has decided to cooperate with magistrates. The Palermo, Caltanissetta and Florence public prosecutors press for the implementation of security measures reserved for witnesses turning state's evidence.
Di Pietro steps forward for the leadership of a new central alliance with Dini and Pivetti in the next legislature, as an alternative to both leftist and rightist alliances.

24 Marco Pannella and Emma Bonino declare the end of the club experiment, and relaunch the Radical Party on the left.

25 The director of Fiat, Cesare Romiti, proposes the delaying of Italian entry into the EMU to foster employment. Deputy Prime Minister Walter Veltroni proposes instead the renegotiation of the Maastricht Treaty.

26 Prodi supports Maastricht after the declarations by Romiti and Veltroni.
The Deputy Commissioner of Police, Gianni De Gennaro, is skeptical about Giovanni Brusca's declarations.

28 The *Ulivo* and the *Polo* reach an agreement for a soft line of action on the TV
    decree-law. The government postpones by decree the expiry date of TV con-
    cessions to 31 January 1997.
    Foreign Minister Dini announces he has initiated the re-entry of the lira into
    the EMS.

29 Giovanni Brusca made up everything: the Deputy Attorney of Palermo,
    Guido Lo Forte, says that the aim of the confessions about the plotting was
    to discredit the president of the Chamber of Deputies, Luciano Violante, to-
    gether with Fiat director, Cesare Romiti.

September

2   Irene Pivetti launches the idea of a new party — a Social Catholic Center — to-
    gether with Fiat director, Cesare Romiti.

3   The European Commission gives its opinion on Bossi's proposal, according
    to which only Padania should be allowed to join the EMU: it is declared in-
    admissible.

4   Carlo De Benedetti resigns as director of Olivetti.

6   Rome's chief public prosecutor, Michele Coiro, is transferred to the head of
    the prison service, after a scandal involving Rome magistrates (the Squillante
    case and junior prosecutors). Minister Flick makes the appointment.

9   Friction between Romiti and Prodi. The director of Fiat says, "The govern-
    ment says a lot, but does little". The Prime Minister says, "Romiti should
    mind his own business".

11 The Turin city council's proposal to liberalize soft drugs splits the parties,
    even internally. The PPI, part of the PDS, *Alleanza Nazionale*, CCD and part of
    Forza Italia are oppose the proposal; *Rifondazione*, part of the PDS and of *Forza
    Italia* are in favor.

12 At the source of the River Po, at the celebration of "Three Days of Padanian
    Independence", Bossi symbolically declares Padania's independence from
    Italy. Pivetti, skeptical about the project, is definitively expelled from the
    Lega.

14 The Catholic Church, in the person of Cardinal Camillo Ruini, President of
    the Italian Episcopal Conference, condemns the *Lega*'s intention to secede.

15 *Tangentopoli* re-erupts: the La Spezia public prosecutor orders the arrest of
    the managing director of the state railways (*Ferrovie dello Stato*), Lorenzo
    Necci.

16 The provisional government of Padania is appointed, but the huge demonstration announced by the *Lega* is a failure.

18 Francesco Storace (*Alleanza Nazionale*) is appointed president of the Rai watchdog committee.

24 For the first time, a "European tax" is mentioned. Minister Ciampi foresees the need for an extra 40,000 billion for the budget.

27 Prodi and Bertinotti reach a compromise on the budget: fewer spending cuts, more taxes. Gianni Agnelli publicly criticizes this decision. The projected revenue from the "European supertax" is 12,000 billion lire.

October

5 The PDS and *Rifondazione*'s opposition to the budget harshens.

8 The head of the PDS group in the Senate, Cesare Salvi, criticizes Milan magistrates on the *Mani Pulite* investigations: "Too many vague enquiries and hasty actions by the public prosecutor." The PDS is split on Salvi's position.

9 Prodi and D'Alema are divided on the *Mani Pulite* issue: the first is unreservedly supportive; the second has doubts about the investigators' methods.

12 The Bertinotti-Bianco axis freezes the *Bicamerale* on reform. The reason is the nomination of the prime minister: the two are opposed to the idea of direct elections, as proposed by the *Polo*.

19 The Prodi government names the new heads of the secret services after a general structural overhaul. They are Francesco Berardino (CESIS), Vittorio Stelo (SISDE) and Gianfranco Battelli (SISMI). According to the *Polo*, PPI, and the Greens, "the appointments were too hasty."

22 Inflation drops to 3.1%.

23 The chief public prosecutor of Florence, Pier Luigi Vigna, is the new national anti-mafia prosecutor.

26 The government majority reaches an agreement on the budget: reduced rate of Irep; the lower income groups are spared. Businessmen, however, strongly contest this solution.
200,000 youths demonstrate, under the auspices of *Sinistra Universitaria*, against the limitation of university enrollments.

28 Opposition between D'Alema and *L'Unità*: the newspaper defends the *Mani Pulite* group of magistrates against criticism from the PDS secretary. This is

the first time that disharmony has arisen between the head of the party and the newspaper.

30 Permission is again sought to send to trial Marcello Dell'Utri, *Forza Italia* deputy and ex-managing director of Publitalia (Fininvest), for mafia involvement.

November

1 Prodi and the PDS are split over relations with the *Polo*. The PDS says: "More dialogue is needed if the *Bicamerale* is to work with the government". The Prime Minister retorts, "I refuse to take lessons on reform from D'Alema".

4 Minister Ciampi announces having made further moves towards the lira's re-entering the EMS.
   News that the *Guardia di Finanza* is investigating the activities of Minister Di Pietro when he was a magistrate and of the entire *Mani Pulite* group, after the declarations of Francesco Pacini Battaglia.
   Giuliano Vassalli (a Socialist) is nominated by the Parliament as the new president of the Constitutional Court. Scalfaro nominates Piero Alberto Capotosti, Fernanda Contini Contri, Guido Neppi Modona, and Gustavo Zagrebelsky as other members.

9 As a consequence of the *Guardia di Finanza*-Di Pietro affair, the heads of the *Guardia di Finanza* remove the Florence GICO commander, Lieutenant-Colonel Giuseppe Autuori, the head of the agents who investigated Necci and who are now also pursuing Di Pietro on the evidence of Pacini Battaglia.

10 The Center-Right demonstrates against the budget: half-a-million people (according to police estimates) march in Rome alone, but many other Italian squares are also crowded.

11 The *Polo* chooses the hard line and deserts the Chamber of Deputies during the vote on the budget.
   The merger of Stet and Telecom is announced by Ciampi.

12 The first definitive sentence by the Court of Cassation on Craxi: five years and six months for corruption in connection with the Eni-Sai affair. Other "excellent" sentences are meted out to Sergio Cusani (4 years), who goes to jail, to the ex-administrative secretary of the DC, Severino Citaristi (5 years and 6 months), and to Salvatore Ligresti (2 years and 4 months).

14 Minister Di Pietro resigns from government amid continuing accusations from the *Guardia di Finanza* and the public prosecutor of Brescia.

16 The Chamber of Deputies approves the budget. The *Polo* does not participate in the vote. The government confirms the Eurotax at 11,500 billion lire.

19 The elections for 120 municipal councils and one province (a million registered voters) indicates continued Center-Left strength in the first round, with
a modest drop for the Center-Right and feeble results for the *Lega*, which declares that it will not support any candidate in the second round. The *Polo*,
however, can claim a clear victory in Trieste.
At the *Movimento Sociale Fiamma Tricolore* (MSFT) Congress, Pino Rauti is confirmed as plenipotentiary secretary-general. In his own speech, Rauti
strongly criticizes *Alleanza Nazionale* and sympathizes with Bertinotti.

21 Paolo Costa, rector of the University of Venice, is named as Minister for Public Works. He is a technocrat from the Catholic camp, chosen in order to
calm the disenchanted North-East.

22 Licio Gelli sees his cases closed with a no guilty verdict on the P2 freemason
lodge case: statute-barring of charges of illicit favors for money and cal-
umny; the sentence condemning him to 17 years is thrown out without the
possibility of appeal to the Court of Cassation; the case against the procure-
ment of classified documents cannot be tried due to extradition problems.

23 Eight-hour general strike and demonstration in Rome by metal-workers to
obtain the renewal of contracts, which expired in June.

24 The lira rejoins the EMS: its central parity with the mark is fixed at 990.
Luigi Manconi is appointed the new spokesman for the Greens, replacing
Carlo Ripa di Meana.

25 The Rome public prosecutor requests that Prodi and the board of directors of
IRI be put on trial for the crime of conflict of interests in the sale of Cirio-
Bertolli-De Rica to Fisvi (1993).

28 Luigi Berlinguer, Minister of Public Education, presents the draft law reforming state exams. The new rules should come into force in June 1998.

December

1 Mario Segni's *Cobac* announces that it will start to collect the requisite 50,000
signatures needed to present the proposed law on the election of the constituent assembly.

4 Ottaviano Del Turco, member of *Socialisti Italiani*, is appointed as president
of the Parliamentary Anti-Mafia Commission.
Split between governmental majority and the *Polo* on the initial law concerning Irep, regarded by the Center-Right as a condition for its re-entry into discussions and the vote on the budget.

6 Raid by the *Guardia di Finanza* on the homes and offices of Antonio Di Pietro,
under the mandate of the Brescia public prosecutor.

8   Scathing attack by the President of Confindustria, Giorgio Fossa, on the government, following the parliamentary vote approving the amendment by *Rifondazione* freezing the minimum wage.

15 Giuseppe Dossetti, aged 83, one of the fathers of Italy's Constitution, dies.

16 Agreement between the government, the *Ulivo* and the *Polo* on TV broadcasting authorizations, which are extended until June 1997.

19 The Senate approves the budget.

20 The government continues with its appointments: General Sergio Siracusa as Commander of the *Carabinieri*, General Rolando Mosca Moschini as Commander of the *Guardia di Finanza*, and General Francesco Cervoni as Commander-in-Chief of the Army.

21 Federmeccanica blocks the latest attempt by Minister of Labor Tiziano Treu to break the deadlock on the renewal of the metal-workers' contracts: an increase of 200,000 lire per month.
    The law on the public financing of parties is approved. Citizens will decide if and to whom the 0.4% will be paid at the moment of income declaration.
    In December, inflation remains at the level of the preceding month: 2.6%.

22 Final approval of the budget, which provides for a 62,500 billion lire maneuver, by the Chamber of Deputies.
    Split in the Parliamentary group of *Rinnovamento Italiano*, led by Minister Dini. The president of the group, Diego Masi, and another 10 deputies (out of 25) decide to split from their colleagues. They are members of the *Patto Segni* and of *Socialisti Italiani*.

26 Dini, Bianco and Maccanico announce the birth of a centrist federation within the *Ulivo*, capable of dialogue with the centrist groups in the *Polo*.

30 The "end-of-the-year" decree is passed, amounting to 4,300 billion lire: the mini-budget of the government envisages, amongst other things, incentives for the purchasing of new cars. The implicit aim is to restart negotiations on the metal-workers' contracts.

1

Introduction:
A Year of Difficult Dialogue

Roberto D'Alimonte and David Nelken

Nineteen-ninety-six was a year rich in novelty. After the "stalled transition"[1] of 1995 many things began to change. The most obvious of these changes was the ending of Dini's unelected government of technocrats, supported by a heterogeneous group of supporters in Parliament and its replacement by Romano Prodi's government, a coalition of the parties which had won the general election of 21 April 1996. But what will probably be remembered as an even more important change was the new climate of dialogue amongst the main political forces which had emerged in this period of transition between the two Republics. From 1993 until the end of 1995, by contrast, there had been a frontal conflict between the two main forces of Center-Left and Center-Right, a conflict so sharp that it had split the *Partito Popolare Italiano* (Italian Popular Party, or PPI), when it was obliged to choose with which side to ally itself.

This conflict had blocked political progress because of the way each side delegitimated the other, with a rhetoric reminiscent of the cold war. And the new electoral laws, in the absence of any underlying agreement, made things worse. Approaching the political transition as a zero-sum game made it impossible to find that minimum common denominator on which to construct a new political system, and explains why no political reform apart from that of the electoral rules had emerged after the old system had entered into crisis.

In 1996, *despite the general elections*, cooperation again became part of the political game. The initiative of PDS Secretary Massimo D'Alema and *Forza Italia* leader Silvio Berlusconi to reach mutual agreement had begun already before the fall of Dini's government and was concretized in their efforts to form a government supported by both the main political alliances. Dialogue continued even after Antonio Maccanico gave up the attempt to realize this broad-based government. Even the elections, despite the aggressiveness of the campaign, were conducted in a different spirit from the preceding one. There was little resort, unlike in the previous election campaign, to the use of arguments or metaphors intended to question the legitimacy of one or other of the forces competing to govern the country.[2] But it can be said that the outcome of the elections certainly complicated the dialogue. This had begun behind a veil of uncertainty because the opinion polls provided no security about who was likely to win or lose an eventual contest, and the future roles of government or opposition had not yet been assigned. Without elections therefore the agreement over who should form the government and how the political institutions should be reformed could be considered the same question. The elections, by removing all these uncertainties, created the conditions for separating the issue of who should govern from the larger question of institutional reform.

But this had not been an easy task. The *Polo per le Libertà* found it difficult to accept the separation of these issues; many of those who made up the *Ulivo* coalition, on the other hand, feared that any kind of collaboration with the *Polo* could delegitimate the actions taken by the government and lead to its fall. There was a fear of the country returning to its previous habits of seeking transversal collaboration behind a front of apparent competition. Given the background, it was a minor miracle that discussions continued and in the summer produced a limited and provisional agreement on the way to proceed to political reform, that is, through the creation of a joint two-chamber commission (the *Bicamerale*) rather than a constitutional assembly. The opposition of Fini and Mario Segni was not enough to block this accord.

The period of greatest difficulty came in the autumn. The 1997 budget had given the opposition the opportunity to gain popularity at the expense of the government. Both the size of the maneuver and the way it was so heavily biased towards increasing the amount of tax collected rather than cutting back on expenditure drew criticism from the *Polo per le Libertà*. This expressed itself in the large scale protest meeting at Rome and the subsequent decision to abandon Parliament so as not to take part in the vote on the budget. But the Left too had its moments of hesitation and rethinking about the wisdom of dialogue, provoked in particular by the agreement over Berlusconi's private television channels and the decision to allow Mediaset to continue to benefit from its concessions until the sector was comprehensively reorganized. But, in reality it was the danger of combining institutional questions and other problems (such as the reform of the system of justice or television concessions) which created suspicions, both within and outside the Center-Left, that this dialogue could or would lead to improper compromises.

D'Alema chose to respond to these suspicions in an article in *La Repubblica* in the course of an exchange of opinions with Eugenio Scalfari, its then editor, over the alleged suicidal tendencies of the Left. The PDS leader repeated his view that the only strategy open to his party in this period of transition was to seek to overcome the crisis of Italian society by means of a patient and difficult reciprocal legitimization of both major political forces. Only in this way would it be possible to arrive at the common definition of a framework of rules capable of allowing Italy to function as a "normal" democracy.[3] In this way, notwithstanding the various tensions, for example the way the *Polo* had walked out of Parliament over the budget, or the unease on the Left, the dialogue went ahead. In January 1997 by a large majority Parliament approved the law introducing the *Bicamerale* commission for political reform of which D'Alema became president.

The Elections: From Parties to Coalitions

The failure of Maccanico's attempt to form a broad-based government was quickly followed by the dissolution of Parliament and new elections. It is still not entirely clear why his efforts failed. Certainly there were many who actively wished for a general election to be held. *Alleanza Nazionale*'s leader Fini, for example, feared the implications for his party of the increasing convergence between D'Alema and Berlusconi, and hoped to emerge from elections with *Alleanza Nazionale* as the largest party on the Center-Right, as the opinion polls were suggesting. Likewise the *Partito Popolare Italiano* was far from enthusiastic about the new climate of agreement, especially as regarded the plan to introduce a form of semi-presidentialism on the French model; they also insisted that Prodi had entered the political ring the previous year in order to make the elections possible rather than in order to postpone them. In the most clear-cut case, Fausto Bertinotti of *Rifondazione Comunista* had been aiming at elections ever since the fall of Berlusconi's government.

On the other hand, there were also those who did not want elections. Berlusconi and D'Alema above all, but also all of those inside or outside the parties who argued that going to elections without having first achieved a reform of the political system would not resolve the question of who should govern and how. And, after all, many were convinced that the elections would not produce an outright winner. The two most likely results were considered to be either a divided Parliament with the Senate going to the Center-Left, and the Chamber of Deputies to the

Center-Right, or else a hung Parliament with Umberto Bossi's *Lega Nord* as the arbiter of any would-be majority coalition. If these outcomes had come about, all that would have happened is that Italy would have returned to the blocked political situation which Maccanico had been working to overcome. In any case those in favor of elections prevailed over those who wanted a broad agreement, and perhaps were right in thinking that the time was not yet ripe for an accord which would cover not only institutional reform but also the other troublesome issues which had arisen in the transition from the "First Republic", such as the reform of the courts, anti-trust legislation, and television and telecommunications holdings.

So the elections arrived and produced their unexpected results; in fact they yielded more than one surprise. The first was that the much despised new electoral system had managed to produce a winner, that is to say a majority which corresponded to one of the competing coalitions. The second surprise was that the same forces emerged as winners in both chambers of Parliament. In fact, the coalition formed by the *Ulivo* and *Rifondazione Comunista* obtained 50.8 percent of the total number of seats in the Chamber and 53.0 percent in the Senate. From this point of view the electoral system had even functioned better than in 1994, when the winning Center-Right coalition did not manage to obtain a majority. The third surprise was that the Center-Left won and thus, with the arrival of the Left in power, Italy was to have a real alternation between the forces competing to govern. But this Left would have to take its place within a larger coalition, and one more biased towards the Center than that proposed to the electorate in 1994.

Thus at first glance it might seem as if the 1996 elections had consolidated the transformation of the Italian party system into a well functioning bipolar pattern. In reality, however, this is not how things stand. True, the elections produced a majority, but it is equally true that, as in 1994, it was an imperfect majority. In 1994 the two "poles" organized under Berlusconi had obtained more than 50% of the votes only in the Chamber, failing to do so in the Senate. But above all the government then put together was the result of two alliances which had presented themselves to the electorate with competing programs. Similarly in 1996, if one looks more carefully, one will see that the majority in the two chambers was not the same. The parties which formed the *Ulivo* coalition and those most closely allied to it obtained a majority in the Senate, but in the Chamber of Deputies the support of *Rifondazione Comunista* was crucial to their majority. Thus, strictly speaking, even this time it would not be correct to say that the government corresponded to the popular will expressed in the elections. The parties of the *Ulivo* coalition and *Rifondazione Comunista* had not presented themselves to the electorate with a common program. They had formed merely a tactical electoral agreement based on abstention from competing in single member constituencies so as to avoid competition which would have been mutually damaging, especially for the *Ulivo*'s hopes of obtaining an overall majority. But could it fairly be said that those who had voted for the *Ulivo* felt themselves to be voting for a government which would have to be sustained by *Rifondazione Comunista*? This doubt did not however prevent Prodi from putting together just such a government.

But the imperfections of Italian bipolarism do not end here. These elections confirmed two other aspects of the transition period which keep Italy from arriving at a well functioning bipolar system. The first of these is the role of the *Lega Nord*. It must be premature to speak of bipolarism when there remains a third pole capable of getting 8.2 percent of the majoritarian seats in the Chamber and 7.8 percent in the Senate. These figures show unmistakably that the *Lega* is much stronger than the third pole (*Patto per Italia*) was in 1994. It is true that the seats gained by the *Lega* do not count this time, because they did not help to form a parliamentary majority; certainly if the same thing happens in the next election we could speak of a bipolar system in practice. But can we be sure that it will happen again?

The question of why the *Lega* had the success it did is discussed in Diamanti's chapter in this volume. Here we will limit ourselves to observing that the *Lega* of 1996 was very different from that which presented itself to the electorate in 1994. Whereas the first was a party which, all things considered, located itself along the left-right political divide, the second removed itself from this axis and placed itself along another axis labeled "unified state vs. secession from the state". In this way Italian political space returned to being bi-dimensional. But the *Lega* is also a third pole which is located along a dimension which is inaccessible to the other parties. The more it emphasizes this strategy and has success with it, the more the hopes for bipolarism will depend on the contingency of election results. For now all we can note is the considerable extent in 1996 to which the *Lega* did stress the theme of succession, so defining itself a party different from all the others .

But the main obstacle on the road towards bipolarism remains the fragmentation of the party system. Despite the essentially majoritarian electoral system, despite the cut-off limits for parties, and despite the disappearance of many former political groupings, today the number of parties is greater even than under the old proportional election system. The only real difference respect to then is that now we also have coalitions. The *Progressisti* and the *Ulivo* coalitions and the Center-Right "Poles" are the only real novelties in Italian politics over the past few years. Their importance is such that their success or failure determines whether elections are now won or lost. And in fact, it was in this way that the *Ulivo* coalition managed to deliver electoral victory even though the parties which formed it were supported by a minority of the population (see Chiaromonte's chapter in this volume[4]). Good coalitions are therefore more than the sum of the parties which form them, though it is not clear in the end whether this something more is merely added value in electoral attractiveness or whether it represents the nucleus of new political actors. The impression we have is that (unfortunately) coalitions are pushed to the front during election campaigns but become less important after the elections when the parties move back into the limelight. In sum, the coalitions have not substituted the role of the parties. And whether there are three or four or, instead, eight or nine parties makes a big difference as far as the functioning of a bipolar system is concerned.

It as an open question why there should still be such a high level of fragmentation in the party system. Is it a result of the persisting element of proportionality of the electoral system, or is it rather the fault of the parties who turned the majoritarian system into a proportional one in the way they divided the seats amongst themselves? Or is it caused by the fact that the voters have not yet internalized the rules of a majoritarian system and continue to vote for parties and candidates who are certain losers instead of voting strategically according to the logic of the "least worse" choice?[5] Whatever is the explanation it is a fact, in the light of the events of 1996, that the Italian political transition is characterized by a high number of parties and sub-parties and that the relationship between parties and coalitions is a major unresolved problem. Nor will this problem be resolved just by simplifying the political situation if the parties continue to ignore the fact that, in order to work well, a majoritarian electoral system needs to rely on auxiliary mechanisms which are inspired by the same philosophy. This is certainly not true, for example, of the recent law on party financing, which was approved in December, by a large majority with record-breaking speed, according to which funds are allocated according to rigorously proportional criteria.[6]

In conclusion, the 1996 election gave the country a government but did not resolve the problem of how to build up a "normal" bipolar system. The election did not even interrupt the cross-party dialogue between PDS and *Forza Italia*. But they did change the context making a broad-based government less likely and forcing the two main political forces to find a new formula with which to continue their dialogue.

The Government: From Coalitions to Parties

At the moment of its installation the Prodi government found itself facing three challenges: (1) the transformation of an electoral coalition into a coalition capable of governing; (2) the relationship with the opposition; (3) participation in the project of creating a European Monetary Union (EMU).

Crucial for the first of these challenges was the fragmentary nature of the parties who supported it and above all the position of *Rifondazione Comunista*. The effectiveness of any government depends on the number of parties which sustain it; the more they are, the more difficult it is to reconcile the interests of the coalition with those of the single parties which make it up, each of which has its own electorate to satisfy. The consequent search for "visibility" and the need to show one's distinctiveness reduce the cohesion of the coalition and its capacity to act as a government. Government policies, like the division of electoral colleges, tends to be worked out on proportional principles. And this is all the more likely where coalitions are extremely heterogeneous from an ideological standpoint. The Berlusconi government had fallen victim to this syndrome. In the case of the *Ulivo* the difficulty was even greater because of the radical stance of the *Rifondazione Comunista* and its ambiguous relationship with the government.

From the beginning the nature of this relationship had been unclear. When there had been a vote of confidence in Parliament the *Rifondazione Comunista* had voted in favor of the government, but their political programs did not coincide. And this reflects the divisions within the Italian left, its unresolved dilemmas which are discussed by Hellman in his contribution to this volume. These dilemmas were made even more acute by the dynamic tendency towards bipolarism. Thus the question arises: What sort of government does Prodi lead? Can we speak of a majority government even if it rested on the external support of *Rifondazione Comunista*, or must we treat it as really nothing more than a minority government? It is not easy to choose. Prodi's government never took on the characteristics of one or the other of these two alternatives. It was unlike the first in not having a political program, at least for the midterm, which could unite all the parties which supported it — given that *Rifondazione Comunista* had always refused this option preferring to make *ad hoc* agreements with the government over each single issue. But it was also different from the second type of government, in that it was unable to rely on changeable majorities for different issues, or, in other words, the possibility of choosing allies from the right as well as the left. There were various reasons why this never happened, even if such a possibility was theorized. In the end throughout the year the only person with whom Prodi could do business was Bertinotti.

All of this could not fail to sow dissension within the *Ulivo*. And here the government had to deal with another of its weaknesses — the nature of the coalition which supported it. Was the *Ulivo* an electoral coalition or something more? Here we return to the subject of the relationship between coalitions and parties raised earlier. This relationship oscillated between the desire of some to see the *Ulivo* develop into the basis for a future party, even if of a federal character, and the caution or unwillingness of others to contemplate such a prospect. It goes without saying that the choice between these prospects had important implications for the stability and — even more importantly — the effectiveness of the government. Differences of policies or programs seem less important in the first scenario but are exacerbated in the second. It needs to be added that the hypothesis of the *Ulivo*'s becoming a party depends also on some reinforcing of the center-leaning parties to balance the presently preponderant strength of the PDS. In the course of the year various attempts of this sort were made, but all ended in failure. The center-leaning parties of the Center-Left coalition remained divided. Indeed, at the end of the year they were further fragmented when the *Socialisti Italiani* and a part of those forming the *Patto Segni* left the group of *Rinnovamento Italiano* led by former Prime Minister Lamberto Dini.

In terms of the daily functioning of the government the other major problem concerned the relationship with the opposition. A bipolar party system does not only require electoral arrangements which encourage bipolarism but also parliamentary rules and practices which are inspired by the principle that those forces which win the election should be given the chance to govern. The job of the opposition is to provide a critical function so as to stimulate the government to improve its performance. We are still very far from following such a model of conduct in Italy, even if there have been some small steps taken in that direction. At the beginning of the legislature the majority parties decided that they would allow the opposition to appoint one of their number to be the President of the Senate as well as to chair some of the parliamentary commissions: the aim here was precisely to introduce conditions for a relationship with the opposition based on an underlying shared framework. But after agitated and confused negotiations regarding who should actually take on these roles, the *Ulivo*'s offer as regards the Presidency of the Senate was not taken up (this went to Nicola Mancino of the *Partito Popolare Italiano*, one of those supporting the majority, whilst Luciano Violante of the PDS became President of the Chamber of Deputies). However the *Polo per le Libertà* did at least gain the chance to appoint the presidents of a number of special bicameral commissions, as well as numerous vice-presidencies of legislative commissions.[7]

Not that this concession improved the atmosphere of collaboration in Parliament. The *Polo* in fact made considerable use of a number of obsolete parliamentary regulations in order to obstruct the work of the government. Parliamentary obstructionism was a constant factor in the relationship between government majority and opposition right up to the point at which the protest led by the *Polo* in Rome against the government's budget actually led them to stage a walk-out from the Parliament. The opposition's veto power was reinforced when the Constitutional Court passed a sentence forbidding the previously common practice of repeatedly renewing temporary government decree-laws, thereby short-circuiting parliamentary debate. In view of the large number of such decree-laws inherited from the previous Dini-led administration and the determined obstructionism of the opposition, the Prodi government certainly faced considerable difficulties. But none the less it did succeed in getting an important part of its program through Parliament; in particular, it succeeded in achieving approval for its budget to which were attached the last hopes of joining in the project for a common European currency.

But the events which accompanied the passing of the budget for 1997 were strange and turbulent. The story begins in the summer when Parliament was presented with a document setting out the economic and financial package which the government proposed in order to reach the 1997 EU targets. This document gave the impression that it would be possible to bring the country into line with the financial parameters set at Maastricht for inclusion in the common monetary union without any special efforts and, in particular, without having to reduce the costs of the pensions system or engage in a more general reform of social security provisions. The amount set as a target, all things considered, was quite modest (a reduction of 32,500 billion lire in public spending). Such a budget would certainly not have enabled the country to arrive anywhere near the required goal of a relationship of 3 percent between the public deficit and GDP by the end of 1997. But it would have avoided a clash with *Rifondazione Comunista* and the labor unions on the one hand and the opposition on the other, which would have threatened to reveal the contradictions of the government's strategy. In short, caught between the limits on its powers due to the weakness of its parliamentary majority and the constraints of the Maastricht parameters, the government had deceived itself for a while into thinking that it could ignore the second of these constraints so as to not have to face the first. The expectation—which turned out to be erroneous—was that other countries—especially Spain and Portugal—would have found themselves in the same position as Italy so that the other European partners would have granted a limited extension for arriving at the target parameters or even allowed Italy to enter the monetary union in breach of the criteria.

This scenario—which Mario Monti, the Italian commissioner at Brussels judged to be too optimistic already that same summer—collapsed altogether by September when it became clear that Spain and Portugal were determined to satisfy the Maastricht parameters by 1997 and that the other European countries were unwilling to discuss modifications in the period allowed for satisfying the criteria, and even less willing to admit Italy with reduced requirements. Thus at this point the government found itself obliged to accelerate the process of cutting public spending and to set itself the objective of really arriving at the 3 percent target by the end of 1997. In this way the size of the economic savings to be made in 1997 went up from 32,500 to over 60,000 billion lire.

This reopened the conflict within the majority, between the majority and the opposition and between the government and representatives of social interests outside Parliament. Above all, the weakness of a government without a cohesive parliamentary majority re-emerged dramatically. Once again *Rifondazione Comunista* made its weight felt forcing Prodi to put aside any plans to reform the pension or social security systems if he wished to continue to have its support. Despite the pragmatism of the PDS and the pressure brought to bear by Dini's group, all the difficult political decisions were put off in the budget and instead resort was made to increasing the amount of money gathered in taxes with the introduction of another tax on earnings (the "Eurotax"), whose incidence falls mainly on the middle or upper tax brackets.

The reaction of the opposition was to be expected: the size and nature of the economic maneuver, together with the ample recourse made of delegated powers, gave them the possibility to put the government in difficulty by voicing the widespread discontent generated by the budget, especially amongst the middle classes. As we have noted, this culminated in the well-attended protest in Rome and the opposition's decision to abandon the Parliament. Confindustria, representing the business community, through its leader Giorgio Fossa, promptly aligned itself with the line taken by the *Polo per le Libertà*, attacking Prodi with a degree of severity rarely shown toward a government in office. The budget was nonetheless approved in the set time, and in November the lira rejoined the exchange rate mechanism of the European Monetary System. Meanwhile inflation continued to fall, as did interest rates. Yet the debate concerning the 1997 budget did not serve to clarify the relationship between the majority and *Rifondazione Comunista*; thus the future of the Prodi government remained uncertain. The showdown had only been postponed.

Towards a "Normal" Justice System

This volume does not include a contribution on the justice system (other than the description of the Andreotti trial in the chapter by Allum). This could be said to reflect the reduced importance of *Tangen-*

topoli as it entered its fourth year and the re-emergence of the political sphere in its own right. But it would be a mistake to think that this meant that the relationship between the politicians and the judges was now back to normal. Throughout 1996 this problem was never far from the center of debate and remains one of the great unresolved anomalies of the Italian political system. Amongst other things, after *Tangentopoli* it became a central symbolic issue as far as the correct functioning of a democracy is concerned. The judges had helped bring about the current political crisis through their anti-corruption campaign, but the way out of the crisis also seemed to require a reform of the justice system which would need to be set in motion by politicians, some of whom had their own special interests to protect. In this difficult and complex situation it was difficult to find reforms which would reflect a point of equilibrium between the fears of those who saw in the activity of the investigating magistrates the risk of a "judicial democracy"[8] and those, on the other hand, who worried about the real dangers of reducing the independence of the judiciary.

But despite this in 1996 some interesting novelties were registered even in this delicate terrain (which were significant both at a symbolic level and for their practical implications). Though we should say that we are talking here mainly of signals, of mere proposals, which emerged in the course of the intermittent dialogue between the PDS and *Forza Italia*. Two topics were central: the search for a "political" solution to *Tangentopoli* and the reform of the judicial system. But alongside these issues there were also others which got mixed up with them: the investigations initiated by the La Spezia prosecutors into the activities of Francesco Pacini Battaglia (the so-called *Tangentopoli 2* scandals); the skirmishes surrounding Antonio Di Pietro and the investigations into his affairs conducted by the GICO of the Florence *Guardia di Finanza*; the fight against organized crime; and the role of the *pentiti* (repentant mafiosi).

The inability of the politicians to bring *Tangentopoli* to a close after five years is evidence of the awkward relationship between politics and justice. It was an unequivocal sign, for example, of the absence of popular legitimacy of the previous governments. In fact, up until Prodi the majority of recent governments were guided by politicians who were themselves under judicial investigation or by politicians appointed because of their technical qualifications, such as Dini, without the legitimacy which comes from an electoral mandate.[9] The advent of the Prodi government should have changed this situation, but in reality even this elected government moved with considerable caution for a number of reasons: the failure of previous attempts to close *Mani Pulite,* the fear of being accused of throwing in the towel and then being obliged to retreat as in the case of previous governments, the continuing popularity of the

Mani Pulite judges, and, not least, continuing differences of opinion within the government and within its main component (the PDS).

Only as the year ended did the situation begin to unblock itself. Flick, the Minister of Justice, came forward with a reform project, similar to those he had proposed before becoming minister, the express intention of which was to end *Tangentopoli* so as to avoid the crimes of corruption it exposed falling into the statute of limitations.[10] This was to be achieved essentially by enlarging the possibility for plea bargaining in return for an admission of guilt and restitution of misappropriated sums. This new form of plea bargaining was to be extended to all crimes which fell within the prescribed maximum penalties, not only to those being dealt with in the course of the *Tangentopoli* investigations. In this way it was hoped to avoid the impression of special treatment for the politicians and other influential people caught up in the corruption investigations. Not least of the benefits of this bargain was the provision that those who took advantage of it could serve their sentence under house arrest rather than in prison. Judges were given considerable discretion in adjusting the penalty in terms of the bargain entered into by the accused. Cases excluded from this plea bargaining were those which were said to be the source of serious social alarm; significantly, this definition was not extended to cases of corruption.

As can be easily imagined, Flick's proposals generated a variety of reactions. To some it seemed a reasonably deft attempt to solve a problem which others had fumbled. Others considered it unsatisfactory. The judges in general were happy with this proposal. Ferdinando Zucconi Galli Fonseca, the General Prosecutor of the Court of Cassation (the ultimate court of appeal), at the opening of the judicial year in 1997 spoke favorably of the trade-off reflected in Flick's project, i.e., between ensuring the certainty of punishment and accepting a reduction in its entity. He added that it was illusory to rely on the providential arrival of the public prosecutors as the main method of dealing with corruption; what was needed rather was to combat its causes by improving the efficiency of the public administration, simplifying legal regulations and making other forms of control more effective.

During 1996, however, the absence of a political or legal solution meant that *Tangentopoli* continued its course. By the end of 1995, 875 cases related to political corruption had been initiated; the majority of accused had been convicted at least at the first trial stage. But it is difficult to estimate how many cases are still in the early stages of investigation and even harder to imagine the extent of corruption itself. The Venetian magistrate Carlo Nordio (noted for his investigations of leading members of the PDS in relation to alleged illegal party financing received from the "red" cooperative movement) argued that less than 5 percent of cases of corruption had been unturned. What brought this point home to public attention was the tapping of Pacini Battaglia's telephone conversations, which led to what came to be known as *Tangentopoli* 2. Pacini Battaglia, former owner of the Karfinco Bank in Geneva and trusted financier of the Socialist Party, had interests in arms, energy, construction, and trains (the last three of these were especially important in allowing him to act as a mediator between the world of politics and business). The contents of his conversations raised the specter that many of the corruption systems attacked by *Tangentopoli* were still in place. It also exposed the problem of how individuals such as Paccini—and Lorenzo Necci, the powerful head of the *Ferrovie dello Stato* who was very well-connected to leading politicians across the political spectrum—had managed to survive the earlier investigations unscathed.

For those who felt that this proved that the judges still had a lot of work to do, there were many others who thought that the more important issue from a political point of view was to find a way of reforming those aspects of the legal system which had allowed the judges to become overweening in their powers. The most central and sensitive of these issues was the need to ensure greater separation between the role of judge and that of public prosecutor. The *Polo per le Libertà* had long made it known that it was in favor of a complete separation. The surprise was that some leading members of the PDS, for the first time since *Tangentopoli* exploded, also began criticizing the judges.

The PDS move towards a renewed emphasis on the rights of the accused created some consternation. Pietro Folena, the youthful PDS spokesmen for justice, argued that the current combination of roles impaired judicial impartiality, and this position was also taken still more forcefully by Cesare Salvi, the PDS parliamentary group leader in the Senate. These claims had no basis in the party's manifesto, as many internal critics were quick to point out. But the meaning of these signals was clear. On this subject, as on others, the PDS was narrowing the difference between its ideas and those of the Center-Right so as to improve the chances of fruitful dialogue across the board. So much so that the whole question of reforming the justice system became caught up in 1997 in the work of the *Bicamerale* commission and thus part of the general negotiations regarding the reform of the Constitution itself. This had the consequence of slowing down and in some cases even blocking the parliamentary progress of Flick's various reform projects.

The Period of Transition Continues

The year 1996 ended with the approval of the budget, and 1997 began with the approval of the *Bicamerale* commission for political reform. But the two decisions were the result of two different parliamentary majorities. The first was limited to the parties making up the *Ulivo* coalition, together with *Rifondazione Comunista*. The second included all the forces of the *Polo per le Libertà*—including those such as *Alleanza Nazionale*, who right until the end would have preferred to follow the route of creating a constitutional assembly. The coming months will show whether this method of relying on different majorities will stand the test of time; it will not be easy to overcome the inevitable tensions that will arise in the course of governing the country (for example in reforming the welfare state) and in the collaborating in the *Bicamerale* (in the definition of new institutional rules). The political game here is complicated, and it is difficult to forecast whether the conflictual elements will eventually win out over the advantages to be gained by cooperating. Amongst the various factors that will influence the outcome, one of the most important is admission into the European Monetary Union. What should be underlined is that in 1996 the main political forces started to seek agreement on how to overcome the period of transition; this itself ought to offer some guarantee of stability. Yet it would be foolhardy to deny that it would be all too easy for the heterogeneous coalition which emerged from the April 1996 elections to fail to hold together.

What would then be the result of the political crisis which would result? We could imagine three possible outcomes: new elections, the transformation of Prodi's administration into a minority government, or the birth of a broad-based government. On the other hand, Prodi could manage to continue to govern with the current majority through 1997, so as to arrive at the EMU decision at the end of 1998. But the serious doubts about this are a certain sign that the electoral rules introduced in 1994 are not sufficient to assure the smooth functioning of a bipolar democracy. In the meantime we shall see if the dialogue over political reform continues and, above all, whether the reforms which emerge from these talks take us nearer or further away from such a model.

Notes

1. This is the expression used by M. Caciagli and D. Kertzer in the edition of *Italian Politics* which deals with the events of 1995 (*Italian Politics: The Stalled Transition*, Boulder: Westview Press, 1996).

2. The differences are well described in P. Segatti "I programmi elettorali e il ruolo dei mass media" in S. Bartolini and R. D'Alimonte, eds., *Maggioritario ma non troppo. Le elezioni politiche del 1994* (Bologna: Il Mulino, 1995) and in G. Sani and P. Segatti, "Programmi, media e opinione pubblica", in R. D'Alimonte and S. Bartolini, eds., *Maggioritario per caso. Le elezioni politiche del 1996* (Bologna: Il Mulino, 1997).

3. *La Repubblica*, 23 December 1996.

4. See R. D'Alimonte and S. Bartolini, "Come perdere una maggioranza: la competizione nei collegi uninominali", in R. D'Alimonte and S. Bartolini, eds., *Maggioritario per caso, op. cit.*, pp. 237-284., and S. Vassallo, "Struttura della competizione e risultato elettorale", in P. Corbetta and A.M.L. Parisi, eds., *A domanda risponde. Il cambiamento del voto degli italiani nelle elezioni del 1994 e del 1996* (Bologna: Il Mulino, 1997), pp. 21-79.

5. A more "optimistic" interpretation of the process of transition is proposed in the introduction by P. Corbetta and A. M. L. Parisi to the volume they edited, *A domanda risponde, op. cit.*

6. Law no. 2 passed on 2 January 1997, concerning "the regulation of voluntary contributions to political movements and parties".

7. Specifically, they obtained the Parliamentary Commission for Information, Security and State Secrets (Franco Frattini, *Forza Italia*); the Parliamentary Commission regarding Criminal Procedures against its members (Ignazio La Russa, *Alleanza Nazionale*); the Parliamentary Commission for Guiding and Supervising Radio and Television Services (Francesco Storace, *Alleanza Nazionale*) and the Parliamentary Commission for Supervising Bank Deposits and Loans (Giovanni Pace, *Alleanza Nazionale*).

8. See C. Guarnieri and P. Pederzoli, *La democrazia giudiziaria* (Bologna: Il Mulino, 1996).

9. See D. Nelken, "Stopping the Judges", in M. Caciagli and D. Kertzer, eds., *Italian Politics: The Stalled Transition, op. cit.*, pp. 187-204.

10. *Ibid.*, pp. 200-201.

2

The General Elections of 21 April 1996

Alessandro Chiaramonte

At a distance of only two years from the first elections to be held under the new, predominantly majoritarian, electoral system in 1994, Italians returned to the ballot box on 21 April 1996 to elect a new Parliament. Three events during the preceding legislature were chiefly responsible for the Parliament's dissolution and the calling of early elections:

1) the collapse of the Center-Right coalition which won the 1994 elections and the fall of the Berlusconi government in December of that year following the *Lega Nord*'s withdrawal from the parliamentary majority;

2) the resignation in January 1996 of the Dini-led technocratic government which had replaced Berlusconi (without having any agreed parliamentary majority), under the combined pressure of *Rifondazione Comunista*, which opposed its economic policies, and the *Polo per le Libertà*, which accused the government of being an expression of those parties wanting to overturn the result of the 1994 elections: the Center-Left, which had lost, and the *Lega Nord*, which had "betrayed" the legitimate outcome;

3) the failure of Antonio Maccanico's attempt to form a broad government coalition to revise the second part of the Constitution along semi-presidential lines and to introduce administrative decentralization.

The early dissolution of Parliament and calling of new elections certainly came as no surprise, even to those political forces in favor of prolonging the legislature. Nonetheless, it resulted in an acceleration of the process of political redefinition then taking place. The parties had to turn existing agreements and ongoing negotiations into an electoral strategy which would maximize their chances of success, and those of the coalition to which they belonged.

Tickets, Lists, and Parties: The Definition of Alliances and Strategies

Following the change in the electoral system, and the more or less direct political consequences produced by the *Tangentopoli* corruption scandal, three main coalitions had formed and faced each other in the 1994 elections: the *Progressisti*, an alliance of left-wing parties—*Partito Democratico della Sinistra* (Democratic Party of the Left, or PDS), *Rifondazione Comunista* (Refounded Communists), the *Verdi* (Greens), the Socialists, *La Rete* (Network) and *Alleanza Democratica* (Democratic Alliance)— the centrist *Patto per l'Italia* (Pact for Italy, comprising the *Partito Popolare Italiano* and the *Patto Segni*) and the *Polo*, an alliance of conservative-leaning forces centered on *Forza Italia* (Go Italy, or FI) and minor allies such as the *Centro Cristiano Democratico* (Christian-Democratic Center, or CCD) and the *Unione di Centro* (Union of the Center), but divided geographically between the *Polo per le Libertà* (Freedom Alliance) together with the *Lega Nord* (Northern League) in the Central and Northern Italy and the *Polo del Buon Governo* (Alliance for Good Government) with *Alleanza Nazionale* (National Alliance, or AN) in the South.

As already mentioned, the fall of the Berlusconi government less than a year after the election opened a new chapter in the process of coalition-building made necessary by a majoritarian electoral system. On the one hand, the alliance between the *Lega Nord* and the other parties of the *Polo*, which had already appeared under strain during the 1994 election campaign and continued to be difficult throughout their common experience of government, had been definitively broken. On the other, the political forces which had opposed Berlusconi and which went on to support Dini (along with the *Lega Nord*) were collaborating in the construction of an alliance which was put to the test successfully in the regional elections of April 1995 and consecrated immediately afterwards by the formation of the *Ulivo* (Olive Tree), a center-left coalition *without* the Communists of *Rifondazione Comunista* which, with Romano Prodi as leader and candidate for premier, advanced its claim to govern the country.

At the general election of 1996, therefore, the two principal contenders were the *Polo per le Libertà* (minus the *Lega Nord*) and the *Ulivo*, both coalitions composed of a large number of lists (for the Chamber of Deputies) and parties (Table 2.1), although less than there had been in 1994.[1] The *Polo* comprised the same political forces which had stood at the regional elections the preceding year. The only difference was that Rocco Buttiglione's *Cristiani Democratici Uniti* (United Christian Democrats, or CDU), a breakaway from the *Partito Popolare Italiano* and incorporated in *Forza Italia*'s list in the regional elections of 1995, had now agreed a common list with the CCD for the proportional element of the

Chamber of Deputies, partly in order to pull the coalition—considered to be leaning too far to the right—towards the center. As in the past, politicians from minor movements such as the *Federalisti Liberali*, Raffaele Costa and Luigi Negri the most noted among them, and the *Partito Federalista* with Gianfranco Miglio, found room under *Forza Italia*'s electoral wing. Agreement between these parties and the *Lista Pannella-Sgarbi* proved more difficult and was not reached until the latter had already presented candidates in opposition to the *Polo* in a number of seats (particularly numerous in the Senate), creating a situation where votes would be unavoidably wasted.[2]

TABLE 2.1. Lists and Parties Composing the Principal Tickets in the Majoritarian Electoral Districts

Ticket	List	Parties
Progressisti 1996	*Rifondazione Comunista*	*Rifondazione Comunista*
Ulivo	PDS-*Sinistra Europea*	*Partito Democratico della Sinistra* (PDS), *Comunisti Unitari, Cristiani Sociali, Laburisti, Lega Autonomista Veneta, La Rete*
	Partito Sardo d'Azione	*Partito Sardo d'Azione*
	Federazione dei Verdi	*Federazione dei Verdi*
	Pop.-SVP-PRI-UD-*Prodi*	*Popolari* (PPI), *Partito Repubblicano Italiano* (PRI), *Unione Democratica* (UD)
	Lista Dini-Rinnovamento Italiano	*Lista Dini, Socialisti Italiani* (SI), *Patto Segni, Movimento Italiano Democratico*
Lega Nord	*Lega Nord*	*Lega Nord*
Polo per le Libertà	*Forza Italia*	*Forza Italia* (FI), *Federalisti Liberali, Partito Federalista*
	Alleanza Nazionale	*Alleanza Nazionale* (AN)
	CCD-CDU	*Centro Cristiano Democratico* (CCD), *Cristiani Democratici Uniti* (CDU)
Lista Pannella-Sgarbi	*Lista Pannella-Sgarbi*	*Lista Pannella-Sgarbi*
Movimento Sociale-Fiamma Tricolore	*Movimento Sociale-Fiamma Tricolore*	*Movimento Sociale-Fiamma Tricolore* (MSFT)
Lega d'Azione Meridionale	*Lega d'Azione Meridionale*	*Lega d'Azione Meridionale*
Sudtiroler Volkspartei	(*Pop.*-SVP-PRI-UD-*Prodi*)	*Sudtiroler Volkspartei* (SVP)
Pour la Vallée d'Aoste	–	*Pour la Vallée d'Aoste* (PVA)

Essentially, the main political forces within the *Ulivo* coalition were
the PDS, the *Partito Popolare Italiano* and the Greens. They were joined at
the last minute by the *Lista Dini-Rinnovamento Italiano* (Dini List-Italian
Renewal) movement which had recently formed around the personal
figure of the outgoing prime minister. A number of minor (and
"homeless") movements—Enrico Boselli's Socialists (SI), the *Patto Segni*
and Sergio Berlinguer's *Movimento Italiano Democratico* (MID)—joined
forces with *Rinnovamento Italiano*. Although there were only four lists for
the proportionally assigned seats in the Chamber of Deputies within the
Ulivo coalition, the parties and movements comprising them were a
great deal more numerous. Something of the complexity of the forces involved in the center-left coalition is revealed by the exact designations
used by the two main lists: PDS-*Sinistra Europea* and Pop.-SVP-PRI-UD-
Prodi. The first contained members of the *Comunisti Unitari* (Famiano
Crucianelli), the *Cristiani Sociali* (Pierre Carniti) and *Laburisti* (Valdo
Spini) as well as of the PDS for both proportional and majority places. *La
Rete* presented its own candidates for single-member electoral colleges.
The second list, headed by Gerardo Bianco's *Partito Popolare Italiano* and
including individuals chosen directly by Romano Prodi, also including
the Republicans (PRI) of Giorgio La Malfa and Maccanico's *Unione Democratica* (UD). Despite appearing as part of the list's official designation,
the *Sudtiroler Volkspartei* (South Tirol People's Party, or SVP) was not part
of the *Ulivo* but a partner of the *Partito Popolare* only in the proportional
segment for the Chamber of Deputies and stood its own candidates
(with *Popolare* support) in the majoritarian electoral districts for both the
Chamber and the Senate in Trentino-Alto Adige. Attempting to widen
its support as far as possible, the *Ulivo* also made agreements with lo-
calist movements such as the *Lega Autonomista Veneta* (Venetian Autonomy League) and the *Partito Sardo d'Azione* (Sardinian Action Party) in
various regions.

In order to avoid a mutually damaging competition between their
candidates, the *Ulivo* and *Rifondazione Comunista* reached a stand-down
agreement for the majoritarian districts shortly before the deadline for
presenting candidates. The agreement had two main points: (1) it was
expressly declared that it was purely electoral; (2) there was a clear predominance of *Ulivo* candidates in the allocation of seats. The fact that
two separate programs for government were presented and that *Rifondazione*'s majoritarian candidates ran under the *Progressisti 1996* symbol
rather than the *Ulivo* made clear that the agreement sprang from electoral necessity and had no political implications. As far as the allocation
of districts was concerned, 27 for the Chamber of Deputies and 17 for
the Senate were assigned to *Progressisti 1996* (relatively few compared
with the votes they could expect to win, but most of them were safe

seats), the rest going to candidates from the *Ulivo* coalition (Table 2.2). The stand-down agreement failed to work in only three cases: in the Valle d'Aosta, for both Chamber and Senate, and in Irpinia for the Chamber. In the latter case, the candidature of a former secretary of the *Democrazia Cristiana*, Ciriaco De Mita, backed by the *Popolari* despite opposition from its coalition partners (who refused to allow De Mita to use the *Ulivo* symbol but did not present a rival candidate), goaded *Rifondazione Comunista* into presenting a candidate.[3]

TABLE 2.2. Number of Candidates Presented in Majoritarian Electoral Districts by Each Major Ticket

Ticket	Chamber of Deputies				Senate			
	North	Central	South	Total	North	Central	South	Total
Total	180	80	215	475	87	40	105	232
Ulivo	175	69	202	446	84	35	96	215
Progressisti 1996	5	11	11	27	3	5	9	17
Rifond. Com.	1	0	1	2	1	0	0	1
Polo per le Libertà	180	80	215	475	86	40	104	228
Lista Pan- nella-Sgarbi	7	1	21	29	35	29	58	·122
Lega Nord	176	53	0	229	87	40	0	127
MSFT	17	17	145	179	52	14	99	165

Source: Elaboration of data supplied by the Ministry of the Interior.

Given its strong territorial roots in central areas of the North, the *Lega Nord* was potentially the most dangerous of the other political formations involved in the majoritarian component of the elections. Having broken away from the *Polo*, the *Lega* had talks with a number of leading center-left politicians in an unsuccessful attempt to find common ground for an alliance. The decision to run alone (and only in the North) represented a notable risk for the *Lega* in terms of the numbers it could expect to get into Parliament but gave it the opportunity to present itself to the electors (both its own and others) as distinct from, and an antagonist of, both the *Ulivo* and the *Polo* and the ill-concealed unwillingness of both of its opponents to back radical reform in the direction of a federal state was emphasized by the *Lega* during the election campaign. In contrast to 1994, the *Polo* had a competitor to its right in 1996 in the shape of Pino Rauti's *Movimento Sociale-Fiamma Tricolore* (Social Movement-Tricolor Flame, or MSFT), which successfully gathered the enough signatures to present its candidates, particularly in the South (Table 2.2). The MSFT carried on the *Movimento Sociale Italiano* (MSI) tradition when the latter began the transformation which led to the formation of *Alleanza Nazionale*, a party Rauti swiftly abandoned. There were also numerous local lists, *Pour la Vallée d'Aoste* (PVA) and the *Lega d'Azione Meridionale* (Southern Action League) being those (along with the SVP) with the best chances of winning at least one seat. On this occasion too, so-called "do-it-yourself" lists presenting independent and personalistic candidacies in single electoral colleges were present.

TABLE 2.3. Average Number of Candidates per Electoral District in 1994 and 1996

	Chamber of Deputies		Senate	
	1994	1996	1994	1996
North	4.4	3.5	7.8	6.7
Central	4.3	3.1	5.4	5.2
South	4.7	3.2	5.5	5.4
Italy	4.5	3.3	6.3	5.8

Source: Elaboration of data supplied by the Ministry of the Interior.

Although the principal electoral coalitions were once again rather heterogeneous, the choice was less fragmented than it had been in 1994. As Table 2.3 shows, the average number of candidates for uninominal seats dropped throughout the country between 1994 and 1996, for both the Chamber of Deputies and the Senate. The parties had a better idea of the rules of the new electoral game and had defined their electoral strategies more carefully. In 1994, for example, there had been two center-right candidates in every district in the North (one from the *Polo* and one from *Alleanza Nazionale*) and in the South, in the Abruzzo and Campania 2 districts, the collapse of the agreement behind the *Polo del Buon Governo* led to candidates from FI and AN confronting one another. The *Progressisti* coalition also suffered from internecine conflict, in Sicily and Sardinia. In 1996, on the other hand, if the support of the *Partito Popolare Italiano* for the SVP in Trentino-Alto Adige and the three districts in which the stand-down agreement between the *Ulivo* and *Rifondazione* failed are excluded on one side, and the last-minute and contradictory agreement between the *Polo* and the Pannella-Sgarbi List on the other, the two main coalitions remained free of internal division. This and the fall in the number of minor candidates explains the less fragmented electoral situation in 1996 compared with the previous election. However, only the actual result would tell whether this minor fragmentation would lead to a more bipolar political situation after the polling stations had shut.

The Result: the Vanquished and the Near-Victors

The result from the ballot box was less ambiguous than many in Italy's history but needs to be analyzed carefully (Tables 2.4 and 2.5 give the results for the Chamber and Senate, respectively). The 1996 election undoubtedly saw the *Polo per le Libertà* beaten. The fact that the various lists composing the *Polo* obtained more votes (44 percent, including the Pannella-Sgarbi List) than the *Ulivo* and *Rifondazione Comunista* (43.4 percent) in the proportional quota for the Chamber of Deputies is of little relevance. Victory did not go to the *Ulivo* coalition, however, which failed to obtain a majority of seats in either the Chamber (45.2 percent) or the Senate (49.5 percent), but to the *Ulivo* and *Rifondazione Comunista*. An alliance which had been purely electoral thus became the sole basis for a parliamentary majority. In truth, the *Ulivo*, which had presented itself to the electorate as a candidate for government without *Rifondazione Comunista* (despite the stand-down agreement), could have formed a majority in the Senate with the two elected representatives of the SVP.[4] In the Chamber, however, they could not do without the Communists, also because any possibility of agreement with the *Lega Nord* had foundered during the election campaign. Thus, the *Polo* may have lost the 1996 election, but the *Ulivo* did not win it outright.

In essence 1996 was a repeat of 1994. Thanks to the majoritarian/proportional mix in the electoral system no parliamentary majority which directly expressed the will of the electorate was produced (counting only the uninominal districts the *Ulivo* coalition would have taken more 50 percent of seats).[5] In 1994 *Forza Italia* and its leader, Silvio Berlusconi, had to try and hold together two political formations (the *Lega Nord* and AN) who had not even been allies during the election campaign. In 1996 two groupings which had marked the political distance between them by producing separate programs for government would be forced to form a parliamentary majority.

Nevertheless, a government with a clear political complexion had been produced. That had been far from certain going according to eve-of-election predictions. In fact, on the basis of opinion poll results, many had been expecting a stalemate between the *Polo* and the *Ulivo*, with the *Lega Nord* holding the key to any majority in Parliament. This would almost certainly have led to the formation of a technocratic government of the kind led by Lamberto Dini during 1995, or a broad coalition for institutional reform of the kind Maccanico wanted—but failed—to get off the ground prior to the election. In any case, the election result could not have been worse for the *Lega*: it did not hold the pivotal role within the political system, nor could it claim to be the principal antagonist of a broad coalition government. Paradoxically, the *Lega* had actually done a

TABLE 2.4. General Results for the Chamber of Deputies (Tickets, Lists, and Parties)

Tickets/Lists, and Parties	Votes				Seats					
	Majoritarian Segment		Proportional Segment		Majoritar. Segment		Prop. Segment		Total	
	No.	%	No.	%	No.	%	No.	%	No.	%
PDS-*Sin. Eur.*			7,897,044	21.1						
PDS					124	26.1	24	15.5	148	23.5
Com. Unitari					6	1.3	2	1.3	8	1.3
Cristiani Soc.					4	0.8	0	0.0	4	0.6
Laburisti					6	1.3	0	0.0	6	1.0
La Rete					5	1.1			5	0.8
P. Sardo d'Az.			37,974	0.1	0	0.0	0	0.0	0	0.0
Verdi			937,684	2.5	15	3.2	0	0.0	15	2.4
Pop.-SVP-PRI- UD-Prodi			2,555,082	6.8						
PPI					58	12.2	3	1.9	61	9.7
UD					5	1.1	1	0.6	6	1.0
PRI					2	0.4	0	0.0	2	0.3
L. Dini-Rinnov. Ital.			1,627,191	4.3						
Lista Dini					8	1.7	2	1.3	10	1.6
Patto Segni					6	1.3	2	1.3	8	1.3
Socialisti Ital.					3	0.6	4	2.6	7	1.1
MID					1	0.2	0	0.0	1	0.2
Ulivo Indep.					4	0.8	0	0.0	4	0.6
Ulivo Total	15,762,460	42.3	13,054,975	34.8	247	52.0	38	24.5	285	45.2
Progressisti 1996	982,248	2.6	3,215,960	8.6	15	3.2	20	12.9	35	5.6
Rif. Com.	17,996	0.0			0	0.0			0	0.0
Ulivo +*Rif. Com.* Total	16,762,704	44.9	16,270,935	43.4	262	55.2	58	37.4	320	50.8
CCD-CDU			2,190,019	5.8						
CCD					13	2.7	6	3.9	19	3.0
CDU					5	1.1	6	3.9	11	1.7
Forza Italia			7,715,342	20.6						
Forza Italia					81	17.1	37	23.9	118	18.7
Fed. Liberali					4	0.8	0	0.0	4	0.6
Part. Fed.					1	0.2	0	0.0	1	0.2
All. Nazionale			5,875,391	15.7	65	13.7	28	18.1	93	14.8
Polo per le Libertà Total	15,027,275	40.3	15,780,752	42.1	169	35.6	77	49.7	246	39.0
L. Pannella-Sgarbi (LP)	74,314	0.2	701,033	1.9	0	0.0	0	0.0	0	0.0
Polo+ LP Total	15,101,589	40.5	16,481,785	44.0	169	35.6	77	49.7	246	39.0
Lega	4,038,511	10.8	3,777,786	10.1	39	8.2	20	12.9	59	9.4
SVP	156,973	0.4			3	0.6	0	0.0	3	0.5
Lega d'Az. Mer.	82,279	0.2	72,152	0.1	1	0.2	0	0.0	1	0.2
PVA	37,428	0.1			1	0.2			1	0.2
MSFT	633,385	1.7	338,721	0.9	0	0.0	0	0.0	0	0.0
Others	491,264	1.3	553,586	1.5	0	0.0	0	0.0	0	0.0
Total	37,304,133	100	37,494,965	100	475	100	155	100	630	100

Source: Elaboration of data supplied by Ministry of the Interior and party secretariats.

TABLE 2.5. General Results for the Senate (Tickets and Parties)

Tickets and Parties	Votes		Seats					
			Uninominal		Proportional		Total	
	No.	%	No.	%	No.	%	No.	%
PDS			77	33.2	11	13.3	88	27.9
Comunisti Unitari			0	0.0	0	0.0	0	0.0
Cristiani Sociali			3	1.3	0	0.0	3	1.0
Laburisti			2	0.9	1	1.2	3	1.0
La Rete			1	0.4	0	0.0	1	0.3
Lega Autonomista Veneta			1	0.4	0	0.0	1	0.3
Partito Sardo d'Azione			1	0.4	0	0.0	1	0.3
Verdi			14	6.0	0	0.0	14	4.4
PPI			22	9.5	5	6.0	27	8.6
Unione Democratica			1	0.4	0	0.0	1	0.3
PRI			0	0.0	2	2.4	2	0.6
Lista Dini			3	1.3	1	1.2	4	1.3
Socialisti Italiani			4	1.7	1	1.2	5	1.6
Patto Segni			1	0.4	0	0.0	1	0.3
MID			1	0.4	0	0.0	1	0.3
Ulivo Independents			2	0.9	2	2.4	4	1.3
Ulivo Total	13,448,392	41.2	133	57.3	23	27.7	156	49.5
Progressisti 1996	940,980	2.9	11	4.7	0	0.0	11	3.5
Rifondazione Comunista	5,682	0.0	0	0.0	–	–	0	0.0
Ulivo+Rif. Com. Total	14,395,054	44.1	144	62.1	23	27.7	167	53.0
CCD			8	3.4	7	8.4	15	4.8
CDU			7	3.0	3	3.6	10	3.2
Forza Italia			23	9.9	24	28.9	47	14.9
Federalisti Liberali			0	0.0	0	0.0	0	0.0
Partito Federalista			1	0.0	0	0.0	1	0.3
Alleanza Nazionale			28	12.1	15	18.1	43	13.7
Polo per le Libertà Total	12,187,498	37.3	67	28.9	49	59.0	116	36.8
Lista Pannella-Sgarbi (LP)	511,689	1.6	0	0.0	1	1.2	1	0.3
Polo+LP Total	12,699,187	38.9	67	28.9	50	60.2	117	37.1
Lega	3,394,527	10.4	18	7.8	9	10.8	27	8.6
L'Abete-SVP-PATT	178,415	0.5	2	0.9	0	0.0	2	0.6
Pour Vallée d'Aoste	29,536	0.1	1	0.4	–	–	1	0.3
MSFT	748,759	2.3	0	0.0	1	1.2	1	0.3
Others	1,191,117	3.6	0	0.0	0	0.0	0	0.0
Total	32,636,595	100	232	100	83	100	315	100

Source: Elaboration of data supplied by Ministry of the Interior and party secretariats.

great deal better than any pre-election forecasts suggested it would. No one had imagined that it could take more than 10 percent of the proportional vote, and even less that it could win 39 seats in the Chamber and 18 in the Senate running alone.[6] Nevertheless, even this was not enough to hold the balance of power in Parliament.

Moving from the various tickets to individual parties, the PDS was the strongest party within the *Ulivo* coalition and indeed the strongest party, both in terms of votes and seats. The PPI was a long way behind, although its candidates did win many marginal seats, particularly in the

North. The *Lista Dini-Rinnovamento Italiano* movement reached its objective, passing the 4 percent cut-off point for the proportional quota in the Chamber of Deputies, something the Greens failed to do, just as they had in 1994. The careful allocation of seats among the various minor forces within the *Ulivo* coalition allowed them to elect representatives. On the other side *Forza Italia* reaffirmed its primacy within the *Polo*, despite predictions it would be overtaken by *Alleanza Nazionale*. The CCD-CDU list also exceeded expectations, taking nearly 6 percent of the vote. As will be seen in more detail below, however, the positive overall result obtained by the *Polo* in the proportional segment was set against a negative outcome in terms of votes and, even more, in terms of seats in both the Chamber and the Senate as a result of the distortion produced by the electoral system. Therein lies the key to the *Polo*'s defeat and (to a great extent) to the victory of the *Ulivo-Rifondazione Comunista* alliance.

The Reasons Behind an Unexpected Outcome: Why the Defeat of the *Polo* Explains More than the Victory of the *Ulivo*

Having briefly discussed the result and the political consequences of the election, it remains to understand why things happened as they did. True, the pre-election forecasts were not completely overturned (no one was betting on a victory of the Center-Right), but the most credited idea, that the vote would split more or less equally, suggested that the *Polo* would gain more seats than the *Ulivo-Rifondazione Comunista* alliance. There were two reasons for this. Firstly, the Center-Left had a strong concentration of votes in the central, "red" regions of the country. While this meant they could inflict humiliating defeats on competitors there, it also meant a "waste" of votes which would have been of more use to them where the contest was closer.[7] Secondly, in 1994 the left had struggled to carry the votes it received in the proportional lists across to majority voting in the colleges, while the opposite had been true of the right. Had the same thing happened in 1996, and the enlargement of the left-wing coalition (which in fact became a center-left coalition) suggested it would, the expected tie in votes in the proportional segment would have been transformed into an advantage for the *Polo* in the single-member districts. In reality the result turned out as it did not because the two main forces were not substantially even in voting for the proportional segment, but because they performed differently to expectation in the uninominal electoral districts.

Separate ballot papers for the Chamber and the availability of data for both the majoritarian and proportional vote at electoral district level allows the performance of the various tickets to be analyzed in both of these areas. Table 2.6 shows the average difference between votes received in the electoral districts and in the proportional segment (calculated on numbers actually voting) for each formation and also, for the *Ulivo-Rifondazione Comunista* and the *Polo*-LP alliances, according to the party of the candidates in the districts.[8] The variations between North, Center and South are also given.

TABLE 2.6. Average Difference Between Majoritarian and Proportional Segment Votes for the Chamber of Deputies by Ticket and Geographical Area (% of Actual Voters)

Tickets and Parties	North		Central		South		Italy	
	% Var.	No.	% Var.	No.	% Var.	No.	% Var.	No.
PDS	+1.0	58	+0.4	43	+3.3	84	+1.9	185
Comunisti Unitari	+2.5	1	-0.2	3	+1.5	3	+0.9	7
Cristiani Sociali	+0.9	2	+1.7	1	+3.0	4	+2.2	7
Laburisti	+1.5	2	+1.4	3	+4.0	8	+3.0	13
Lega Aut. Veneta	+1.5	1	–	–	–	–	+1.5	1
La Rete	+0.5	3	–	–	+3.7	8	+2.8	11
P. Sardo d'Azione	–	–	–	–	+1.6	1	+1.6	1
Verdi	+0.2	14	+0.5	5	+3.7	8	+1.3	27
PPI	+1.8	64	+1.8	7	+4.1	58	+2.8	129
Unione Democratica	-3.2	2	–	–	+4.1	5	+2.0	7
PRI	-2.0	1	+2.0	1	–	–	0.0	2
Lista Dini	+0.5	6	+0.2	3	+0.7	5	+0.5	14
Patto Segni	+0.8	7	-1.0	1	+2.8	5	+1.4	13
Socialisti Italiani	+0.9	8	-1.0	1	+1.5	3	+0.9	12
MID	–	–	–	–	+4.2	6	+4.2	6
Ulivo Independents	+2.7	2	+0.8	1	-0.7	1	+1.4	4
Rifond. Comunista	-7.6	5	-6.2	11	-8.1	11	-7.3	27
Ulivo Total	+1.2	174	+0.6	69	+3.5	202	+2.2	445
Ulivo+Rif. Com. Total	+1.0	179	-0.4	80	+2.9	213	+1.6	472
CCD	-2.8	13	-0.9	7	-5.7	21	-4.0	41
CDU	-3.5	12	-0.7	13	-4.0	15	-2.8	40
Forza Italia	-3.2	102	-1.6	33	-5.2	88	-3.8	223
Federalisti Liberali	-2.6	8	–	–	-14.5	1	-3.9	9
Partito Federalista	-2.8	1	–	–	–	–	-2.8	1
Alleanza Nazionale	-3.3	43	-1.2	27	-5.0	90	-3.9	160
Polo Total	-3.2	179	-1.3	80	-5.1	215	-3.7	474
Lega Nord	+1.7	175	+1.1	53	–	–	+1.6	228
MSFT	+1.5	17	+2.4	17	+3.0	145	+2.8	179

Note: The number of cases for the parties of the *Ulivo* coalition is less than the number of the coalition as a whole because the political allegiance of some candidates was not ascertainable.

Source: Elaboration of data supplied by Ministry of the Interior.

The figures clearly demonstrate that the greater heterogeneity of the Center-Left compared with 1994 and with their Center-Right opponents was not a handicap, or at least was not perceived as such. In any case, *Ulivo* candidates in the majoritarian electoral districts systematically gained more votes than the proportional lists which backed them (+2.2 percentage points, on average), demonstrating their capacity to attract support from outside their own political area, particularly in the South (+3.5 percentage points). This was not true of *Rifondazione*'s candidates, running as *Progressisti 1996*. They suffered a massive defection of votes (averaging 7.3 percentage points), in all probability those of more moderate *Ulivo* voters. On the other side, the *Polo* lost a considerable number of votes in the districts, unable to maintain the levels of support obtained by its component lists in the proportional segment. This loss of votes, an average of 3.7 percentage points in every district, was particularly marked in the areas where the coalition was strongest: the North (– 3.3 percentage points) and the South (–5.1 percentage points). Moreover, the loss was systematic and independent of the political identity of candidates. This suggests that it was due to the coalition itself rather than the quality of candidates.[9] The *Lega Nord* was the principal beneficiary of this defection in the North, and was thus able to win a number of districts it would have lost had it obtained only the votes it received in the proportional segment. In the South it was the MSFT and, in part, the *Ulivo* itself which benefited.

The difference in performance between the competing formations in the majoritarian vote for the electoral districts explains how relative equality in terms of (proportional segment) votes was translated into a clear superiority of the *Ulivo-Rifondazione Comunista* alliance in terms of seats won. However, it remains to explain why candidates of the Center-Left took more votes in the majoritarian districts than the lists supporting them this time when just two years earlier this had been the case for their Center-Right opponents. The different composition of the coalitions and the events which took place between the two elections would seem to have changed voters' attitudes.

The political forces making up the *Ulivo* coalition had certainly done everything in their power to avenge the defeat of the *Progressisti* and *Patto per l'Italia* in 1994. This was demonstrated by the political and tactical decisions taken in the intervening two years and immediately before the election. Stated briefly they had: (1) formed the *Ulivo* itself, bringing together a major part of the left and the center (who had lost running separately in 1994) but excluded *Rifondazione Comunista* in order to make their candidacy for government more credible; (2) designated their candidate for the premiership well ahead of the elections and chose a man who, while he was certainly not "new", was known to be of the political center; (3) accepted, and therefore guaranteed the election of, candidates from minor movements close to the center-left, avoiding the possibility of rival candidatures; (4) prevented a dispersal of left-wing votes by stipulating the stand-down agreement with *Rifondazione Comunista* and, at the same time, (5) succeeded in allaying the fears of more moderate voters by getting across the message that it was an alliance of necessity and would have no implications in the formation of a government. These decisions undoubtedly influenced the outcome of the elections. However, the impression remains that the *Ulivo* coalition would not have won without the fragmentation of the Center-Right and the perception among voters that the *Polo* was less united than previously.

TABLE 2.7. Effective and Potential Uninominal Seats on the Basis of a Hypothetical Alliance Between the *Polo* and Other Political Formations

Effective and Potential Uninominal Coalitions	Chamber of Deputies				Senate			
	Polo	*Ulivo* +RC	*Lega*	Others	*Polo*	*Ulivo* +RC	*Lega*	Others
Based on Majoritarian Segment								
Polo	169	262	39	5	67	144	18	3
Polo+*Lista Pannela-Sgarbi*	172	259	39	5	75	137	17	3
Polo+MSFT	205	228	37	5	93	119	17	3
Polo+*Lega*	272	198	—	5	123	106	—	3
Based on Proportional Segment								
Polo	237	205	29	4				
Polo+*Lista Pannela-Sgarbi*	263	180	28	4				
Polo+MSFT	249	193	29	4				
Polo+*Lega*	318	153	—	4				

Note: Seats in the "*Polo*" column sums those of the *Polo* and its hypothetical ally.

In the MSFT and (even more importantly) the *Lega Nord*, the Center-Right coalition which prevailed in 1994 had lost two important elements, now among its most direct competitors. In terms of seats competition with these two parties cost the *Polo* dearly. The first part of Table 2.7 shows what the division of seats in the electoral districts would have been for both the Chamber and the Senate had the Center-Right coalition been broader.[10] The *Polo* would have won had it still been in alliance with the *Lega Nord*. Even if it is deemed illegitimate to consider the *Lega Nord* part of the Center-Right, given the failure of the earlier alliance and the particularity of the views it represents, the presence of the MSFT on its own cost the *Polo* 36 seats taken by the *Ulivo* in the Chamber (it would have won 205 instead of 169) and 26 in the Senate (they would have taken 93 rather than 67). In other words, if MSFT voters (including those of one *Polo* list which defected in the electoral district vote) had had no choice but to vote for the *Polo*, the *Ulivo-Rifondazione Comunista* alliance would not have had an absolute majority in the Chamber. Had that been the case, it is not difficult to imagine a very different political situation than the actual one arising.

The fragmentation of the Center-Right and the internal competition which resulted does not explain everything, however. In fact, if the *Polo* had maintained its proportional segment vote in the electoral districts, the result would have been reversed also. As the second part of Table 2.7 shows, where the proportional vote is taken into account in a hypothetical distribution of uninominal seats the *Polo* would have won without any allies at all. An alliance with the Pannella-Sgarbi List would have ensured an absolute majority of the representatives elected. If this did not happen, as the hemorrhage of votes already mentioned proves it did not, this can only be because the *Polo* failed to hold up (relatively speaking) *as a coalition*.[11] In other words, it is plausible to suggest that the voters who deserted the *Polo*'s candidates in the majoritarian electoral districts did so 1) because they believed the ideological differences within the coalition would impede united action, 2) because they wished to reject the coalition's leader (Berlusconi)[12], or 3) because they did not believe the coalition would guarantee governability.[13] In the latter case, this judgment may have derived from a retrospective verdict on the Berlusconi government and on the *Polo*'s attitude to Dini and Maccanico. Each of these motivations probably played their part. Whichever of the three was most significant, however, there is no doubt that the object was to punish the *Polo* as a whole. These were the circumstances in which the *Ulivo* coalition, which appears to have been able to offer (at that particular moment, at least) greater dependability and political credibility, conceived its victory.

Composition of Parliament and Imperfect Bipolarism: What Prospects?

In a transition period such as Italy is presently experiencing, one election follows closely on the heels of the last. The election of 1996 was the third in the space of four years, and the second held under the quasi-majoritarian electoral system introduced in 1993. It is worth asking at this point whether the result of the ballot box reveals that simplification of the party system or tendency towards bipolarism which was expected to stem from repeated application of the new rules. This is not a simple task for two reasons. Firstly, it is well known that different methods exist of counting parties (and/or political groupings). In the Italian case, moreover, the mixed electoral system means that it is difficult to determine exactly what constitutes a party, the political unit to be counted. Let us look more closely at the problem.

Table 2.8 shows the composition of Parliament in 1994 and 1996 in a number of different ways. It adopts two distinct criteria for counting parties. The first is based on the arithmetic sum of the political actors present (simple count), the second on their relative "weight" (weighted count).[14] In addition, it uses five different political units. The first three — parties, lists and tickets — have already been discussed above in relation to Table 2.1. Here political groupings and post-election parliamentary groups are also included. The latter is self-explanatory. The former refers to electoral alliances (which may be implicit or partial as well as formal) between two or more tickets. Thus, both the *Ulivo-Rifondazione Comunista* alliance in 1996 (based on a stand-down agreement) and the alliance between the *Polo per le Libertà* and the *Polo del Buon Governo* and its variants (based on territorial differentiation) would be considered as a *single grouping* in the specific sense described above.

TABLE 2.8. Breakdown of Chamber and Senate Composition According to Type of Unit and System of Counting Political Formations (1994 and 1996)

		Parties[a]	Lists[b]	Tickets[c]	Groupings[d]	Parliam. Groups[e]
Chamber 1994						
Simple Count	No.	20	13	6	3	7
Weighted Count	Eff. No.	7.6	6.2	3.7	2.2	6.4
Senate 1994						
Simple Count	No.	21	14	6	3	9
Weighted Count	Eff. No.	8.1	6.9	3.7	2.5	7.1
Chamber 1996						
Simple Count	No.	24	11	4	3	8
Weighted Count	Eff. No.	7.3	6.2	2.7	2.4	6.2
Senate 1996						
Simple Count	No.	25	13	4	3	10
Weighted Count	Eff. No.	7.1	6.2	2.6	2.4	6.2

[a] Parties obtaining at least one seat.
[b] Proportional lists for the Chamber (and a hypothetical reaggregation on that basis for the Senate) which obtained at least one seat in either the proportional or majoritarian segment of the vote.
[c] Tickets obtaining seats in more than one constituency.
[d] Electoral alliances obtaining seats in more than one constituency.
[e] Excluding the residual "mixed" group.

Comparing 1994 and 1996, the impression is of relative stability. The number of party units present in 1996 remains extremely high, reflecting the ongoing process of decomposition and recomposition of political forces. The same is true of the lists represented, although their number diminished slightly as a result of improved electoral strategy (after numerous lists failed to make the 4 percent cut-off in 1994). Continuity is also evident in relation to political groupings. Although the make up of each had changed, the Center-Left and Center-Right were still there, contrasted by a third significant force: *Patto per l'Italia* in 1994, the *Lega Nord* in 1996. The number of parliamentary groups was also essentially unchanged. The only significant difference which emerges between 1994 and 1996 was the reduction in the number of tickets. This was largely a result of the *Polo's* greater compactness. No longer allied to the *Lega Nord*, the *Polo* could present a single ticket throughout the country.

Following the 1994 election it was said that "the political units which the facts oblige us to use in future to classify the structure of the party system will tell us what overall effect electoral reform has had on political strategies".[15] Even in the wake of the 1996 election the answer to this problem has yet to emerge. Certainly, the party system is still highly fragmented and is likely to remain so in the future. The parties, as the term has been understood here, may well disappear, absorbed into wider formations such as the electoral lists. Aided by the electoral system for the Chamber of Deputies, which offers them visibility and reinforces the maintenance of distinct identities, the latter may well become the basic units of the party system (they already are to a great extent). This would appear to be confirmed by the fact that, on a weighted basis, the number of lists and the number of parliamentary groupings is almost identical. If this were to be the case, the new party system would be just as fragmented as the old.

On the other hand, alongside this element of continuity with the past, the new electoral system has produced a contest revolving around two political poles and their respective leaders. It is an imperfect bipolarism (and indeed it has been necessary here to distinguish between tickets and groupings in order to elucidate the different kinds of alliance between political formations). This was probably inevitable in the current transitional phase. There is undoubtedly a long way to go before a fully bipolar system emerges. One obstacle is represented by the large number of political parties, which undermines the cohesion of the coalitions formed for the majority vote in the electoral colleges and thus impedes the birth of a true bipolarism. A further unknown is the role to be played by third forces such as the *Lega Nord*. As far as can be seen at present, a bipolar system is not impossible to achieve. Much will depend on the way in which the tensions between the aggregating and centripetal logic of a uninominal system and the disaggregating and (potentially but not necessarily) centrifugal logic of a proportional one are resolved. However, much will also depend on harboring no illusions that by itself a new, and imperfect, electoral system can resolve them.

Translated by John Donaldson

Notes

1. A "ticket" refers to a coalition of parties/lists or a single party/list whose candidates all stand under a common designation (or explicitly recognize a common political identity) in the majoritarian electoral districts. "Lists" refer to those political formations (composed of one or more parties) which compete for the proportionally assigned seats in the Chamber of Deputies. A "party", finally, refers to a formally organized political entity which participates in the process of selecting common candidates for the majoritarian ticket to which it belongs, when it is not a grouping in its own right.

2. The divisions of North, Central and South used in Table 2.2 and subsequent tables are composed as follows: North=Valle d'Aosta, Piemonte, Lombardia, Trentino-Alto Adige, Veneto, Friuli-Venezia Giulia, and Liguria; Central Italy=the traditional "red" regions, i.e., Emilia-Romagna, Toscana, Umbria, and Marche; South=all remaining regions.

3. Although De Mita's candidacy was under the symbol *Democrazia e Libertà*, the votes he received and his election are here counted as being in favor of the *Ulivo*. The liaison created by the *Partito Popolare*, the fact that their partners in the coalition did not stand candidates in opposition to him and that he later joined the *Democratici Popolari per l'Ulivo* parliamentary group all suggest the legitimacy of doing so.

4. If life senators were also counted (they are not here) the *Ulivo* would probably have an absolute majority even without the SVP.

5. As can be seen from Tables 2.4 and 2.5, the *Ulivo* coalition won 52 percent of majoritarian seats in the Chamber of Deputies and 57.3 percent in the Senate.

6. For an analysis of the results obtained by the *Lega* at the regional level see the tables in the appendix to this volume.

7. In other words, where the votes obtained are more or less equal, the coalition which has the largest surplus of votes in the districts in which it wins comes off worst.

8. The *Ulivo* and *Rifondazione Comunista* are considered jointly in this case because although, it was not explicitly declared, the stand-down agreement implied that their respective electorates would vote for each other's candidates. The *Polo* and *Lista Pannella-Sgarbi* are also treated as a single actor since, despite the fact that the latter stood separate candidates (very few for the Chamber of Deputies, in reality) the alliance formed immediately prior to the election foresaw support for the candidates of the *Polo*. The average difference between votes received in the majoritarian and proportional segment of the election is calculated on those actually voting to take into account voters whose ballot was spoilt or left blank in one of the two segments.

9. For an essentially similar view, see R. D'Alimonte and S. Bartolini, "Come perdere una maggioranza. La competizione nei collegi uninominali", in *Rivista Italiana di Scienza Politica*, vol. 26, no. 3, 1996.

10. Obviously these should be taken as broadly indicative figures. Had the party line-up really been different the response from voters would have been different as well.

11. It has already been noted that the quality of its candidates is not a sufficient explanation for the poor showing of the *Polo* in the majoritarian districts.

12. These two hypotheses have been suggested by R. D'Alimonte and S. Bartolini, *op. cit.*

13. P. Natale, "Mutamenti e stabilità nel voto degli italiani", in R. D'Alimonte and S. Bartolini, eds., *Maggioritario per caso. Le elezioni politiche del 1996* (Bologna: Il Mulino, 1997).

14. The simple count (No.) always involves setting limits which are to a certain extent arbitrary (specified in this case in the notes to Table 2.8). However, it provides additional information to that provided by the weighting of party influence. The latter uses Laasko and Taagepera's effective party index, in the column labeled "Eff. No." (see M. Laasko and R. Taagepera, "'Effective' Number of Parties: A Measure with Application to West Europe", in *Comparative Political Studies*, no. 1, 1979, pp. 3-27). A third, qualitative criterion also exists: Sartori's rules for counting on the basis of the coalition and/or intimidatory power of the parties (G. Sartori, *Parties and Party Systems*, Cambridge: Cambridge University Press, 1976). This is taken into account to a certain extent in the simple count thresholds for tickets and groupings.

15. R. D'Alimonte and A. Chiaramonte, "Il nuovo sistema elettorale italiano: le opportunità e le scelte", in S. Bartolini and R. D'Alimonte, eds., *Maggioritario ma non troppo. Le elezioni politiche del 1994* (Bologna: Il Mulino, 1995), p. 57.

3

Forza Italia:
Old Problems Linger On

Patrick McCarthy

In April 1996 *Forza Italia* (FI), or more precisely the *Polo per le Libertà*, of which it was the largest part, was defeated in the parliamentary elections. The elections dominated the year: FI spent most of January and February trying to avoid them; next came a bitter campaign and a mixed result, creditable for FI but disappointing for the *Polo per le Libertà*.

Back in opposition, FI was forced, once again, to rethink its organization, its strategy and — albeit timidly — its entire identity. So 1996 was much more than a year of defeats. At the end of 1995 an observer of FI concluded that it had entered the second phase of its existence. A period marked by success in the 1994 elections had given way to a period of opposition to which FI was less suited. The movement oscillated between a hard and a soft line: for most of 1995 it anathematized the Dini government and demanded elections, while from December 1995 until March 1996 it sought to reach agreement with its great enemy, the PDS, on a neutral or else broadly-based government and on constitutional reform.[1]

This view seems to me entirely correct provided it is set in the context of the underlying dilemma of FI.[2] Wrongly perceived as the mere creation of TV, *Forza Italia* was and remains the latest incarnation of Italian populism, revolving around the two poles of Berlusconi, the charismatic leader, and "the people" represented by the clubs. The novelty of FI was the role of the Fininvest corporation, which was the motor of the political movement. This also created a dilemma: would FI become a center-right party of modern capitalism, inserting itself into the space opened up by the process of change, begun in 1992? Or would it be a clan, whose prime aim was to defend the interests of its leader and his company?

The answer is that FI would try to do both. The economic triumphs of Fininvest had been inseparable from Berlusconi's place in the old political order, although his ability as an entrepreneur should not be underestimated. When that order collapsed, leaving Berlusconi with a mountain of debts, he entered politics to fight on behalf of Fininvest. Despite the novelty of "the corporation as political party", his battle may be understood as an example of clan warfare. Clans are a traditional feature of Italian politics: the DC currents were, in part at least, clans. But they were also groups that had programs, represented broader interests and sought to govern. Similarly Berlusconi represented the worldview of many frustrated Northern Italians.

In 1994 voters who wanted to be rid of the over-worked, over-intrusive state could identify with FI, which declared that it would both rein in the state and improve public services by introducing private-sector efficiency. FI was perceived as a vehicle for change. The populist cult of the great entrepreneur allowed it to be both a clan and a force for modernization. Certainly Berlusconi saw no contradiction between saving himself and saving Italy!

But the way in which Berlusconi went about his two tasks created a contradiction. During his spell in government he spent too much time and used up too much political credit trying to reshape the Rai and to rid himself of the Milan magistrates. Ironically Berlusconi made fewer changes in the Rai personnel than the Center-Left has done. But he was perceived as waging a war on behalf of Fininvest, while the public debt and the health of the lira were neglected.

In 1995 there was a debate within FI about strategy, but the contradiction of identity did not surface until the end of the Dini government. Before that FI was divided between the exponents of hard and soft opposition. At the Dini government's vote of confidence on January 25, many FI parliamentarians wanted to vote yes out of fear that their electorate would not understand why they were opposing a prime minister who had held a key post in the FI-led government of 1994. But Berlusconi imposed abstention. His language grew harsher in 1995, and he repeated that Italy could no longer be considered a democracy. When the budget came to parliament in December, he called for a no confidence vote, but it failed because a number of FI and *Alleanza Nazionale* parliamentarians did not turn up.[3]

Retrospectively this was not merely the start of a softer opposition but a sign that FI was shifting into its role as the political arm of Fininvest. Preparations were underway to launch the media segment of the corporation, which meant primarily the three TV networks and Publitalia, on the stock market. If successful, this move would relieve Berlusconi of his debts and lessen or disguise his conflict of interest problems.

To help him, a group of state-owned banks, including Istituto Immobiliare Italiano (IMI), agreed to buy shares in Mediaset and to guarantee a capital increase. The private bank, Credito Italiano, which was part of Enrico Cuccia's empire, refused to join the group. It is not unreasonable to see a link between the half-hearted no confidence campaign and the action of the banks.[4]

When the Dini government came to its natural end on 30 December 1995 Berlusconi surprisingly did not press for immediate elections. Our hypothesis, which we cannot prove and which we present as a possible explanation of Berlusconi's shifts over the next nine months, is that FI was now a clan. Once more this did not abolish its identity as a political movement. But it did mean that FI had two sets of priorities.

Although the signs of this double identity are most evident at the summit of the movement, all segments of FI are effected. If FI were to become the party of liberal capitalism, its parliamentary group would have to gain greater autonomy of its leader and its base would have to participate in decisions. Charismatic populism is suited to crises but cannot replace the participation of elites and members, especially when they are relatively well-educated.

Berlusconi seemed to understand this. In 1995 a change took place in the organization of the clubs: the full members were allowed to elect a committee and a president who became part of the political movement proper and joined the assembly of FI members at the constituency level.[5] But while this could have represented a first step towards democratizing FI, it was in fact a way of bringing the clubs under more direct control. The other constituency and regional delegates of the political movement were appointed from above so the few club representatives would have scant influence.

Power remained in the hands of the charismatic leader and those members of his court to whom he listened. At the top was a coordinating committee, which had no official status and was little more than Berlusconi's group of collaborators: Marcello Dell'Utri, Gianni Letta and others. This control from above was essential if FI were to be the political arm of Fininvest. There is no reason why an ordinary club member should chose to devote his free time to defending the antics of the teenage pop star Ambra Angiolini. Still, control from the top is an integral part of populism and does not prove that FI existed to defend Fininvest.

An analysis of *Forza Italia*'s activity in 1996 must begin with that surprising shift from demanding elections to cooperating with the PDS in order to avoid elections, as well as to set up a neutral government and to reform the constitution. We must then glance at FI's performance in the election and its new phase of opposition. This last section will re-examine the various segments of the movement as well as its leader.

Silvio and Massimo: Best Friends

The most vicious language that Berlusconi used in his 1994 campaign was reserved for Massimo D'Alema.[6] Yet a curious complicity had emerged between the two leaders even as they adopted opposing positions towards the Dini government. When that government fell, complicity almost became alliance.

Did the head of *Forza Italia* have the support of his followers for his policy of collaboration with the enemy? According to Gianni Pilo, the majority of FI militants were opposed. Certainly Vittorio Feltri, the editor of Paolo Berlusconi's newspaper, *Il Giornale*, was not in favor, and neither were hard-liners like Antonio Martino, Pietro Di Muccio, Fabrizio Del Noce and others. However Pilo's polls found that 84 percent of FI voters supported their leader's initiative, as did Vittorio Dotti and the doves in the parliamentary group.[7] Indeed, one suspects that many Italians preferred the new reasonable Berlusconi to the intransigent critic.

So Berlusconi did not lack strictly political reasons for his abrupt shift of strategy. Polls showed him that the Center-Right coalition might well lose the election and that FI might run behind *Alleanza Nazionale*. Moreover, the constitutional changes that were mooted suited Berlusconi and his party. They went in the general direction of strengthening the executive either by direct election of the prime minister or by some version of the French constitution. Nor did Berlusconi and D'Alema lack common interests. The PDS leader also feared losing the election and had scant confidence in Romano Prodi. D'Alema's long term plan was to accentuate the right-left split and weaken the center. Probably D'Alema also felt that Berlusconi was a vulnerable opponent who should be propped up.

This vulnerability was the second reason for Berlusconi's quest for a general agreement. As a party leader he could not but see the disadvantages of his choice: it made him seem inconsistent and it was bitterly opposed by his ally, Gianfranco Fini. Yet he plunged ahead. It cannot be coincidence that Berlusconi was now called to stand trial on charges of bribing the *Guardia di Finanza*. Although he dismissed the magistrates as politically motivated and asserted his role as the owner of A.C. Milan by chatting with the courtroom spectators about his players[8], he must have thought that he needed protection against the many other charges that were being brought against him. To face them with a hostile Center-Left government in power would be folly.

In short, the clan chieftain, in return for making concessions to D'Alema as well as to President Scalfaro, sought advantages for himself and his company. A rough list of his demands might be: an amnesty for *Tangentopoli* or at least a friendly minister of justice, or the depenalization of certain offenses; help from state-owned banks to launch Mediaset; favorable treatment if and when Stet and IRI were privatized and the third portable telephone contract awarded; assistance with the Constitutional Court's ruling that Fininvest give up one of its three TV networks by August 1996.[9] But Berlusconi had asked for too much, and D'Alema could not give him enough.

There were many reasons why Maccanico's attempt to form a government failed. Fini remained hostile because he believed in the polls that showed *Alleanza Nazionale* outdistancing FI and gaining as many as 22 percent of the votes in an immediate election. Nor could he welcome a pact from which *Alleanza Nazionale* would be omitted. Prodi preferred elections, and Berlusconi could not have been the only leader who was hungry for ministries. But one reason why FI opted for the ballot box was surely that it had failed to strike a deal favorable to Fininvest. Silvio's friend, Massimo, refused to be seduced.

Elections: FI Holds While the *Polo per le Libertà* Loses

FI's parliamentary group not only existed chiefly as a reflection of its leader but it lost two prominent members, Raffaele Della Valle and Vittorio Dotti, who had resisted the hard line that Berlusconi had imposed in 1995. Della Valle, a deputy speaker of the Chamber of Deputies, gave up politics, although in a Parthian shot he blamed the *Polo per le Libertà*'s defeat on its "truculent and arrogant language".[10] Dotti's departure was one result of the Stefania Ariosto affair. Since he was her long-standing companion, he could hardly not have shared her knowledge of the acts of corruption she claimed to have witnessed in Cesare Previti's circle. He must also have realized she was collaborating with the police. When Berlusconi offered him a choice between denying Ariosto's assertions and giving up his seat, Dotti's position became impossible.

Della Valle had tried to give the FI parliamentarians some independence. Sharing the view that FI should not, like traditional Italian parties, acquire a bureaucracy that did nothing but expand its own power, he argued that the parliamentarians constituted the link with the voters and hence had a legitimate right to elect the FI leaders. Della Valle had also attacked Biondi's decree.[11] Dotti was a Fininvest lawyer and his clashes with Previti could be seen as a mere reflection of their struggle to obtain business from the company. It was, however, symbolic that, when Previti was appointed chief coordinator of FI by Berlusconi, Dotti suggested that a vote be held to ratify the appointment and Previti refused.[12]

In the election campaign the FI candidates were mere foot-soldiers. Berlusconi made decisions from which there was no appeal. In Bologna the ex-minister, Giorgio Bernini, a local man, thought he had received assurances that he would head the FI list. He learned from the newspaper that Gianni Pilo had been parachuted in to replace him. Fininvest employees continued to receive preference. Safe seats were found for Marcello Dell'Utri and Massimo Maria Berruti to afford them protection in their legal battles. Nicolò Querci, Berlusconi's secretary, entered parliament.

In this context it is hard to accept Gianni Pilo's argument that FI lost the elections because, whereas in 1994 its candidates were chosen on merit by Dell'Utri, in 1996 they were the survivors of battles in smoke-filled rooms dominated by the regional coordinators.[13] After all, the coordinators had been chosen by Berlusconi and his Fininvest advisers only one or two years before. If they had become, as Pilo suggests, indistinguishable from the old political class, this was because FI was a traditional clan.

Anyway, the *Polo per le Libertà*'s defeat cannot be blamed primarily on FI. It obtained 20.6 percent of the vote, compared with 21 percent in 1994 when it was running with the CCD. Since the joint CCD-CDU vote amounted to 5.8 percent, it is reasonable to suppose the defection cost FI 2-3 percentage points. This would account for FI's decline in such colleges as Lombardy 1, which includes Milan, where it polled only 1.2 percentage points less than in 1994. FI's losses were heaviest where the *Lega* was strongest: in the Veneto 1 and 2 FI fell by 7 and 6 percentage points, while the *Lega* rose by 6 and nearly 10 percentage points. This does indeed imply that FI, perceived in 1994 as offering a new solution to the old political problems, had become, two years later, a part of those problems.

In Central Italy losses were limited to 1.1 percentage points in Tuscany and 2.3 in the Marche, while in Umbria FI went up 1.2 percentage points. The gains, which allowed FI roughly to equal its 1994 national score, came in the South. In part it was merely a matter of organization: in Puglia, where FI had failed to get on the ballot in 1994, it polled 24.6 percent, while in Basilicata it jumped from 11.8 to 18.2 percent. But FI made modest gains in regions where the economy was faring relatively well—it rose by 1.6 percentage points in the Abruzzo—and recorded modest losses in the poorest regions—it dropped by 0.8 points in Calabria. In the South FI was still perceived as an agent of modernization, although there were other reasons for its success.

FI gave way to the PDS as Italy's largest party, but it was a mere 0.5 percentage points behind. It reaffirmed its presence throughout the country: it was weakest in the Center where the left is strongest—the PDS stood at 28.6 percent—and where the better organized *Alleanza Nazionale* —with 22.3 percent—offered a stronger challenge than FI with 15.7 percent. In the North FI ran closely behind the *Lega*—20.1 to 20.5 percent—

and ahead of the PDS (18.6 percent) and *Alleanza Nazionale* (11.0 percent). The South gave FI a clear although not overwhelming victory: 22.3 percent to the PDS's 20.9 percent and *Alleanza Nazionale*'s 19.2 percent. In the Islands FI's triumph was overwhelming: 29.7 percent to the PDS's 17.6 percent and *Alleanza Nazionale*'s 13.5 percent. Fini's dream of overtaking FI vanished as *Alleanza Nazionale* reached only 15.7 percent nationally.[14]

Some FI members feel their movement might have done even better if it had come to an agreement with Pannella earlier and if in its propaganda it had used its own symbol more and the logo of the *Polo per le Libertà* less. Complaints about how badly the campaign was run are not limited to Pilo. Indeed, his criticism of the regional coordinators may be interpreted as one more sign of the conflicts and confusion.

Under these circumstances FI's fairly good national result demonstrates that there is a continued need in post-1992 Italy for a center-right party that appeals to the values of the private sector. The cultural space FI fills is indicated by a glance at the attitudes of its supporters: 74.1 percent of them favor lower taxes and fewer services, whereas the figure for the PDS is 45.9 percent; agreement between the social partners is cited as a prerequisite of economic reform by only 37.2 percent of FI supporters, whereas 72 percent of PDS followers think it essential; 74.8 percent of FI voters favor the direct election of the head of state or government, which has the backing of only 32.7 percent of PDS voters. These are classic differences between Center-Right and Center-Left in Europe. Similarly, when asked which area most needs reform, 41 percent of FI supporters reply that it is taxation and a mere 29 percent cite health. The figures for PDS supporters are 26 and 40 percent.[15]

A glance at the social and professional backgrounds of the FI parliamentary candidates enables us to flesh out this profile: 22.9 percent of FI's Chamber of Deputies candidates were entrepreneurs, whereas the figure for the *Ulivo* was 6.9 percent; lawyers constitute FI's second largest group—15.2 percent, a statistic which stands in marked contrast to the percentage of judges, 2.9 percent. University teachers are drawn to the left, and the *Ulivo* has 11.9 percent of them. Free professionals were drawn to FI and made up 14.8 percent of its Chamber of Deputies candidates. The *Lega* had many more—28.6 percent—but the *Ulivo* was way down with 8.9 percent. This profile shows a party strong in the private sector and among the self-employed, with a particular liking for entrepreneurs.[16]

However FI cannot fill this cultural space on the center-right if it moves too far right. There are two indications that it—or more precisely its leader and the coalition he led—did so. The first is that the Center-Right gained fewer of the centrist Catholic voters, who in 1994 had voted for the PPI-*Patto Segni* alliance, than did the Center-Left: 38 percent to 59 percent.[17] The second indication is that the sum of the votes won in the proportional segment by the parties of the Center-Right was greater than the votes won by the *Polo per le Libertà* in the "British" segment of the election.[18] Since it is probable that here people vote for a project, a style and a government—even if Pilo maintains that 8 percent are influenced by the candidate her/himself—one may suggest that Prodi and the *Ulivo* were more convincing than Berlusconi and the *Polo per le Libertà*.

To unearth the reason, one might remember Della Valle's remark about the Center-Right's arrogant language. The Center-Left spoke of combining innovation with solidarity, and Prodi, while hardly inspiring, was reassuring. By contrast Berlusconi tried to ride the current of anti-statism, that the Turin shopkeepers had revealed. He was virulent in his remarks about the Milan magistrates, and his hard-line followers, such as Previti, talked of taking no prisoners if they won the election.[19] There were signs too that Berlusconi's charisma was fading: he was less happily narcissistic than in 1994. His seductive smile was flashed on and off and, when it was off, he looked grim.[20] It is likely that enough voters found Berlusconi extremist to swing the election to Prodi. The *Polo* rather than FI went down to defeat.

After the Election: FI Battles with Mediaset

Having lost, Berlusconi gradually moved to a softer position and sought to salvage from electoral defeat gains for himself and his companies. This stranded FI: it had established no independence of its leader, whose charisma, while still strong, was flagging and who now treated it as a bargaining-chip. During 1995 it had begun to learn how to organize for opposition by developing spokesmen and teams of experts on the various policy issues. But more work was required.

FI's troubles became apparent in the Sicilian regional elections of June. Where it had gained 32.2 percent in the general elections, it plunged to 17.1 percent. Conversely the CDU-CCD, which had won 8.1 percent in the earlier election, now jumped to 18 percent. Of course local elections rarely follow national patterns, and FI had fewer notables among its candidates. But at least one reason must have been that the Sicilians changed their minds about FI after it lost the parliamentary elections. There is an old Southern tradition of not wasting votes on candidates who will not be able to offer rewards. The DC had been reliable in the past and might be so in the future. Berlusconi spent ten days on the island and drew big crowds of people who did not, however, vote for him. FI's Sicilian regional coordinator, Gianfranco Miccichè, a Dell'Utri protégé, offered his resignation, which was not accepted.

The Sicilian elections were hardly encouraging. If FI was plagued by old problems.[21] the solutions seemed obvious, perhaps deceptively obvious. FI needed more internal democracy and leaders who were not tied to Fininvest. Domenico Mennitti, who had played a role in the creation of the *Polo per le Libertà* in 1994, called for the abolition of the President's Council. He proposed a party congress to pass judgment on proposals for reshaping FI's organization and its policies. These proposals were to be circulated and amended by the base in advance of the congress.[22]

Faced with a nascent protest, Berlusconi dragged his feet and agreed that a congress be held on 27 March 1997. In the meantime he turned to a new face: Franco Frattini, who was young, intelligent and an ex-minister. The decision to designate a problem-solver rather than to analyze the problem is typical of the personalized company culture of Fininvest. Frattini's proposals were impeccable: FI must be reformed from below, and congress delegates must be elected.[23] But Frattini himself did not last long, which is also typical of companies that personalize issues. For the same reason Frattini staged a comeback and became president of the parliamentary committee on control of the secret services.

One problem to be tackled was the financial situation. In 1995 FI reported an income of approximately 15 billion lire, of which 13 billion lire represented the public financing of the elections. Spending amounted to 39 billion lire but, since 19 billion lire is accounted for by "general expenditure" and "other activities", it is hard to know where the money went.[24] Until now Berlusconi has bailed out his movement, and in 1995 he bore part of the cost of renting FI's expensive headquarters at the ill-named Via Dell'Umiltà.

The deficit caused the ousting of Domenico Lo Jucco, ex-Publitalia and responsible for FI's finances. He was replaced by Giovanni Dell'Elce, ex-Mondadori, whose task is to make FI self-financing. The leadership claims there are 300,000 sympathizers and wants each of them to pay 100,000 lire a year. FI has forty provincial offices and wants to cover the entire national territory, which means increasing the number to 103. Both goals are ambitious, and the figure of 300,000 seems implausible.

What are the implications of the financial problem? A drive towards self-financing means a more autonomous party: a member who pays a fee will want input into decisions. Berlusconi must know this; so does one conclude that he is at last ready to grant FI its freedom? If so, is he edging out of politics, or does he perceive that only a revitalized FI can bring him back to power? Or does he simply hope to maintain control, while paying less? Perhaps he himself does not know. The strain of the some sixteen legal actions that are pending against him and of launching Mediaset leaves him less time and energy for politics.

He has given his blessing to another restructuring of the organization to be undertaken by Claudio Scajola. An ex-Christian Democrat who was mayor of Imperia from 1990 to 1995, Scajola, like Frattini, has no ties to Fininvest. He is flanked by four collaborators on a National Coordination Committee: Dell'Elce, Mario Valducci of Diakron, who is responsible for local government, Rocco Crimi, who is to set up some twenty departments responsible for the various fields of policy and organization, and Paolo Buonaiuti, a journalist who is in charge of communication.

A draft of what the new FI will look like is being circulated. It is bolder than its 1995 predecessor but remains ambiguous. This time all those who join the movement must join a club—although the reverse is not true—and they must pay their dues, which are fixed here at L 50,000. They should be aware that they are not joining a party based on ideology or class but one that has two distinctive traits: it is "at the service of the electorate and it has come together around the person and the message of Silvio Berlusconi".[25] This is vintage populism that reaffirms the two poles of the leader and his people, and it is quite different from parliamentary democracy. The individual member or parliamentarian subordinates himself to the leader and to the mythical *gente*.

Yet the member[26] has more input than before. The new FI is to have five levels: national, regional, provincial or city, electoral constituency and village. The method of choosing officials is a mixture of election from below and co-option from above, with more "election" than previously but with the emphasis still on "co-option". Thus at the constituency level the council, itself elected by an assembly of all members, elects delegates to the provincial assembly which in turn elects the provincial coordinator and his "team". The provincial coordinators sit on the regional council, but the regional coordinator is not elected by them; s/he is appointed by the national leadership. The national congress meets every three years to elect a president who is flanked by a presidential committee. Of its fifteen members, counting the president, seven are chosen by him, three are members by virtue of their offices as head of the FI groups in the Senate, Chamber of Deputies and European Parliament, and four are elected. This ensures a majority for the president who can rely on eight votes, including his own. So members are encouraged to be active up to the provincial level, whereas regional and national decisions are left to the leadership.

There is not much to be learned from Berlusconi's writings on political parties. He has condemned all pre-1992 parties as "Leninist" and praised but not defined "the American model". He has referred to a "Catholic-Liberal tradition", which seems little more than an appeal to the Catholic voters to abandon Prodi.[27]

After the election FI offered little constructive opposition.[28] Here again parties that lose elections need to turn inward and rethink their strategy. *Alleanza Nazionale* was also introvert. But one cannot avoid the question of whether FI's immobility is linked with the kind treatment Mediaset has received from the government. We offer a possible but unproven interpretation.

Berlusconi has devoted much time to his entrepreneurial activities and legal difficulties. If the latter are still unresolved, he has met much success with the former. Over the summer Mediaset was launched. The price of a share was set at 7,000 lire and rose on the first day to 7,377 lire; 245,000 new shareholders came forward. The company's brochure stated that four of the twenty-one directors were facing legal charges and that the Constitutional Court had ruled that Mediaset possessed too large a chunk of the Italian television market.[29] However, the *Economist* described the Mediaset offer as unsuited to widows and orphans but as a potentially lucrative investment.[30]

The Center-Left government contributed to this triumph. Antonio Maccanico, Minister of Post and Telecommunications, which includes responsibility for TV, produced a law that met the requirements of the Constitutional Court, but only barely. It did seem to make Berlusconi give up one network, but it specifically allowed him to transfer that network to cable or to satellite. It also cut his share of publicity but allowed him to meet the requirement—at least temporarily—by reducing the number of advertisements on one channel only. A final decision on how to meet the Constitutional Court's ruling that no single group could have more than 25 percent of the total TV business was postponed until mid-1997. This could have been interpreted as suspending a sword of Damocles over FI's leader for the period when the budget goes through parliament. There was no mention in Maccanico's law of conflict of interest.

Future treatment of Mediaset is likely to be equally generous since the authority set up to regulate TV is to consist of a president nominated by the government, along with eight members chosen by parliament. Clearly some of the eight will be FI supporters. Best of all there is to be no restriction placed on Mediaset's candidacy to build the third portable telephone system.[31]

The magistrates have been less forgiving. The various legal proceedings against Fininvest are going ahead. D'Alema had made speeches about the need to restore politics to its rightful place by defining more clearly the magistrates' sphere of activity.[32] But the Lorenzo Necci-Pacini Battaglia revelations, which have lain bare corruption in the railways, where Necci was in charge, but also in many other parts of the public sector where Pacini Battaglia distributed largesse, may curb the PDS's enthusiasm for this project. Even so, the help that Berlusconi has received from the government is intriguing. Is it merely the latest example of the historic embrace of state and industry? Is it a new phase of the Silvio-Massimo friendship, designed to produce constitutional reform as well as a profit-making Italian company? Or is it an unspoken—or secretly spoken?—agreement that FI will not complicate the life of a weak government more than it absolutely has to?

Here again there are solid political reasons why FI might be helpful: to diminish *Rifondazione Comunista*'s influence over the government and to prepare for a Center-Right coalition in which FI could obtain ministries. But such reasons do not preclude FI's other role as the political arm of Fininvest. The contradiction between FI as clan and FI as the party of modern capitalism is still present. Perhaps it cannot be resolved as long as Berlusconi remains leader. But then FI has yet to show it can survive without Berlusconi: that is why the "obvious" solutions may not work and why the new identity has still to be found.

There are hints that Berlusconi may withdraw from everyday politics, perhaps becoming the movement's president. This would allow other leaders—Antonio Martino, Giuliano Urbani, Frattini or Scajola—to emerge. It would reduce the elements of populism in FI culture and make FI a center-right party like the UDF (*Union pour la Démocratie Française*) in France. Other possible scenarios are that FI might break up in a general realignment of Italian politics or that the collapse of the present government could bring FI back to power. The fluidity of the political situation in the autumn of 1996 makes prophecies risky.

Various recent events have highlighted Berlusconi's strange position. Francesco Cossiga made a series of speeches refusing—and hence seeking—the leadership of the *Polo per le Libertà*. The press granted him a day of fame and then forgot him, but until when? Meanwhile Berlusconi, sensing the challenge, proposed an alternative budget which would stimulate the market, and the *Polo per le Libertà* used systematic parliamentary obstruction to slow down passage of the government's budget. But Berlusconi continued to support D'Alema's plan for a joint Senate-Chamber of Deputies committee on institutional reform. Once more *Alleanza Nazionale* is displeased, but Berlusconi is forming an ever more important bond with D'Alema. FI and the PDS look on bewildered.

Berlusconi testified at one of Dell'Utri's trials and depicted the head of Publitalia as a Franciscan monk utterly uninterested in money. At the same time Franco Di Carlo, the latest repentant mafioso, described the close ties that supposedly linked Dell'Utri and Berlusconi to Stefano Bontade. On October 29, the Palermo magistrates decided there was enough evidence to try Dell'Utri, although not Berlusconi, on the charge of complicity with the mafia.[33] The next day the House of Lords threw out Berlusconi's appeal that documents about dummy companies that he allegedly controlled should not be turned over by the British police to the Italian magistrates. The Lords did not take seriously Berlusconi's claim that he was a political victim. Meanwhile, it was discovered that Berlusconi's office had been very clumsily bugged. One awaits the next installment...

It has become obvious that FI cannot move forward until Berlusconi leads or leaves it.

Although all interpretations and any mistakes are my own, I wish to thank Emanuela Poli who has been generous with her knowledge of *Forza Italia* and Gianfranco Pasquino who read this chapter and suggested improvements.

Notes

1. M. Maraffi, "*Forza Italia*: From Government to Opposition", in M. Caciagli and D. Kertzer, eds., *Italian Politics: The Stalled Transition* (Boulder: Westview Press, 1996), pp. 119-135.

2. See our "*Forza Italia*: The Overwhelming Success and the Consequent Problems of a Virtual Party", in P. Ignazi and R.S. Katz, eds., *Italian Politics: The Year of the Tycoon* (Boulder: Westview Press, 1996), pp. 37-55.

3. *La Repubblica*, 15-16 December 1995.

4. For the accusation that the banks helped Mediaset for political reasons and for a reply by Gianni Zandano of San Paolo di Torino see *L'Espresso*, 7 January 1996, pp. 50-56. Eugenio Scalfari called the whole incident "comic opera": *La Repubblica*, 17 December 1995. Yet some state-owned institutions like the Istituto Nazionale delle Assicurazioni (INA) refused to back Mediaset, while Comit, which was part of Enrico Cuccia's empire, agreed (*La Repubblica*, 19 December 1995).

5. M. Maraffi, *op. cit.*, p. 153.

6. *Panorama*, 4 February 1994, p. 32.

7. For Gianni Pilo's polls, see *La Repubblica*, 16 January 1996. Vittorio Feltri expresses his view in *Il Giornale*, 3 January 1996. For a list of the hard-liners see *L'Espresso*, 14 January 1996, p. 41.

8. *La Repubblica*, 18 January 1996.

9. According to Antonio Maccanico, who was supposed to be prime minister of the new government, these were the issues which caused the breakdown of the talks (*La Repubblica*, 14 February 1996). Maccanico later denied this version, but such denials are not always to be taken literally.

10. *La Repubblica*, 27 April 1996.

11. A. Gilioli, *Forza Italia* (Bergamo: Ferruccio Arnoldi Editore, 1994), pp. 51 and 218.

12. *Ibid.*, p. 220.

13. G. Pilo, *Perché il Polo ha perso le elezioni* (Rome: Newton & Compton Editori, 1996), pp. 59 and 135.

14. Unless otherwise stated, election statistics are taken from *Il Corriere della Sera*, 24 April 1996. All the figures quoted above indicate the proportional vote

for the Chamber of Deputies.

15. Censis, *Dal voto al Governo: le aspettative degli italiani* (Rome: Fondazione Censis, 1996), pp. 6 and 32.

16. *Il Sole-24 Ore*, 1 April 1996.

17. Censis, *op. cit.*, p. 51.

18. G. Pilo, *op. cit.*, p. 100. Pilo estimates that of the 1,400,000 who switched, 570,000 went to the *Ulivo*.

19. For Previti see *La Repubblica*, 16 April 1996. For a longer but still incomplete analysis of the language of the elections, see our forthcoming "The Discourse of Serenity: a Linguistic Victory in the 1996 Italian Elections", in L. Cheles and L. Sponza, eds., *The Art of Persuasion: Political Language in Italy from 1945 to the Present* (Manchester: Manchester University Press, 1997).

20. For Berlusconi's TV performance, see G. Pilo, *op. cit.*

21. E. Galli Della Loggia, *Il Corriere della Sera*, 7 June 1996.

22. *La Repubblica*, 9 June 1996.

23. *La Repubblica*, 10 June 1996.

24. S. Gilbert, "Forza Italia, obiettivo autofinanziamento", *Il Sole-24 Ore*, 11 September 1996.

25. "Sintesi delle linee guida della struttura organizzativa del movimento Forza Italia", p. 1.

26. The Italian word is *socio* rather than *iscritto*, the term used by the despised old parties.

27. S. Berlusconi, "E ora al lavoro per un'Italia di liberi e forti", *Ideazione*, vol. 3, no. 5 (September-October 1996), p. 5; "La mia vera Forza Italia", *Panorama*, 22 August 1996 p. 29.

28. *L'Espresso*, 11 July 1996 p. 57.

29. Mediaset s.p.a., *Nota Informativa Sintetica*, submitted to Consob, 10 June 1996, pp. 1-3.

30. *Economist*, 22 June 1996 p. 77.

31. For various interpretations of the law see *Il Giornale* and *Il Corriere della Sera*, 18 July 1996.

32. D'Alema chose the conclusion of the national Festa dell'*Unità* to invite the magistrates "to respect the principles and the rights that characterize a lawful state" (*L'Unità*, 23 September 1996).

33. *La Repubblica*, 12 October 1996.

4

The *Lega Nord*:
From Federalism to Secession

Ilvo Diamanti

The year 1996 represented a turning point for the *Lega Nord* and its political strategy. The *Lega* definitively changed character, transforming itself from an versatile and heterogeneous political actor, a "great chameleon" as Giovanni Pajetta described it,[1] into one with a project so specific and distinctive as to make any kind of political mediation difficult: "secession" and the creation of an independent state in northern Italy. This change in character came about and was reinforced in two stages which created very different climates of public opinion.

The first stage coincided with the election of 21 April, in which the *Lega* scored an unexpected success. With nearly four million votes, more than 10 percent of the total, the *Lega Nord* was the largest party in the North and fourth in Italy as a whole. This result relaunched the *Lega* in Italian politics after a period of decline. Above all it pushed the problems and demands which the *Lega Nord* articulated to the fore.

The second stage also coincided with a specific date. The *Lega* called demonstrations along the length of the River Po for 15 September, to coincide with its "proclamation of the independence of the Padanian peoples". The initiative aroused a great deal of attention and caused apprehension among observers and other political forces. The enormous coverage devoted to the event gave it a media dimension quite out of the ordinary, but participation was actually far less than had been expected and, as a consequence, there was a decline in interest in the *Lega*, demands for secession and the underlying causes of such demands.

So there were two dates and two events with very different impacts on politics and society: from emergency to dismissal; from emphasis on the secessionist threat to disregard for the tensions which had riven northern Italy in the preceding years. It was almost as if, on 15 September, the question of the *Lega* and of the various problems associated with it had simply sunk into the Po. This attitude, switching directly from dramatization to underestimation without any intermediate stages, has accompanied every phase of the *Lega Nord*'s developments. So far, it has allowed the *Lega* to recover each time it appeared in crisis. At the same time, it has impeded any solution—or even a reliable definition—of the problems and demands embodied by the *Lega*. In this article we shall try to reconstruct the background and the evolution of these events and at the same time to shed light on the additional issues and problems they have raised.

Between Protest and Secession:
The *Lega Nord* and the Crusade of 21 April

At the April 21st elections the *Lega Nord* stood behind the banner of secession. During the election campaign the party's leader, Umberto Bossi, presented the vote as a referendum on independence for the North. To vote for the *Lega* was to vote against the national parties and groupings and for the autonomy of the northern Italy. In other words, he sought to harness the various sources of dissent and tension present in the North through the call for independence, highlighting those aspects of the "northern question" which remained unresolved and unrepresented and which had favored the growth and strength of the *Lega* in the first place: the desire for local administrative autonomy, the inefficiency of the public administration and machinery of state, the tax question, representation for the productive middle classes, etc.[2] Moreover, the *Lega* sought once again to intercept voters who identified with neither of the two main groupings and their candidates. "Secession" from the two main political fronts was associated with and reinforced the call for independence from Rome. Bossi presented his party as a means of keeping undecided voters away from "Rome and the two main political formations" which he defined, without much originality but efficaciously, as "Roma-*Polo*" and "Roma-*Ulivo*".

Overall, then, the situation was very different to 1994. The *Lega* was standing with a project for independence, an aggressive language and no allies. And this time round they were not aiming for participation in government. Indeed, they seemed likely to lose a large number of votes and an even larger number of representatives in Parliament. The most generous estimates in the weeks leading up to the vote gave the *Lega* twenty deputies and under ten senators, largely thanks to the proportional recovery mechanism.[3]

However, the *Lega* was gambling on a further unraveling of the politi-

cal system and, in the short term, a Parliament without no stable majority or government capable of addressing the country's main problems. The *Lega Nord* would thus be in position to play a decisive role despite electing a smaller parliamentary group.

Too Great an Electoral Success

If the *Lega Nord* approached the election with very different expectations and political positions than in 1994, the result also came as a surprise, even to the *Lega's* leadership. At the same time, it produced elements which contradicted Bossi's hopes. The *Lega's* electoral success was
certainly notable, and the parliamentary group elected was far larger
than anyone had expected: the *Lega* took almost four million votes in the
contests for the Chamber of Deputies and Senate, more than 10 percent
of the electorate, and elected a total of 90 parliamentarians. This was the
high point of the *Lega Nord's* brief but intense political biography and relaunched it as a major player in the Italian political game. The electoral
success faithfully followed the script proposed by the *Lega's* leader.
Around 4-5 percent of its votes came from the hard core supporters who
had followed the *Lega* and its leader through thick and thin, up to and
including the secession idea. An only slightly inferior number originated
from protest and dissatisfaction concerning specific questions: taxes,
lack of state reform, frustrated desires for autonomy, etc. Finally, a
smaller quota of the *Lega's* votes (around two percent) came from floating voters, moderates unable to decide between the two major political
groupings and who translated that indecision into votes for an avowedly
"outside" third force.[4]

The result was less satisfying for the *Lega* and its leaders in other respects, however, placing strict limitations on the "mission" the *Lega* had
set itself during the election campaign and, more generally, on its current political strategy.

Firstly, while certainly conspicuous, the *Lega's* presence in Parliament
was not decisive. Contrary to the *Lega's* expectations the election had a
winner, the *Ulivo* coalition, which could form a government, although
dependent on the "critical" contribution of *Rifondazione Comunista*. This
diminished the *Lega's* possibilities of acquiring bargaining or coalition
power, using Rome to amplify the resonance of its action in the North at
the same time as it sought to foster territorial and economic division. Immediately after the election, Bossi made no attempt to hide his dissatisfaction in this respect. It was evident, in fact, that the *Lega's* electoral
success was responsible not only for the defeat of the *Polo* but also for reducing its own influence in Parliament.

Secondly, the *Lega*'s unexpectedly large parliamentary presence had negative as well as positive aspects. The question of the organization's internal coherence, which had caused the leadership a great many problems in the past, resurfaced. The geographical concentration of the *Lega*'s representatives had been pushed towards the North-East of the country, but its political center of gravity remained the Lombard group and its leader, Umberto Bossi. This imbalance had (even quite recently) caused internal conflict. Only two years earlier, in 1994, the founder and leader of the Venetian League (*Liga Veneta*), Franco Rocchetta, had been "excommunicated" and forced out of the *Lega* after attempting to organize opposition to Bossi's leadership in the Veneto. The return of such personalities as the retiring President of the Chamber of Deputies, Irene Pivetti, to the internal political life of the *Lega* was a further threat to cohesion. What is more, in the critical passage from a federalist party drawing potential support from a number of directions to a movement organized and mobilized for the very precise objective of secession, homogeneity and internal cohesion would be crucial.

The vote of April 21st also highlighted the persistence of the principal impediment to the *Lega* in fulfilling its "mission": its heterogeneous electoral base and, even more, its entrenchment in the foothills of the North. Although the *Lega* presented itself as the party of the whole of northern Italy, calling explicitly for independence, its success depended on its original strongholds. Moreover, as already noted, the "secessionist" segment of its electorate remained small.

New Votes, Ancient Roots

For a more precise picture of the problems created for the *Lega* by its own electoral success in 1996 it is useful to examine what is most significant in this respect: its territorial implantation, central for both its identity and political demands. Where were the *Lega*'s strongholds in the April election? Where they always had been. The areas where the *Lega* recorded its electoral successes in 1996 were little different from those in which it had been most powerful during the period it began to acquire political visibility, between 1983 and 1987.[5] Looking at the 40 electoral colleges in which the *Lega* did best in the majoritarian segment of the vote, obtaining an average of 40.2 percent of votes cast, the picture is a familiar one: 3 districts in Friuli (2 in Pordenone and 1 in Udine), 15 in Veneto (virtually all the districts of Belluno, Treviso and Vicenza, some in Padua, Verona and Venice), 21 in Lombardia (all the districts of Bergamo and Sondrio, others in Brescia, Varese and Como) and, finally, one in Piemonte (Cuneo).

These provinces follow the line of the foothills from Friuli, across the

Veneto bordering on the Trentino, up again through upper Lombardia
and finally pushing into Piemonte. In essence, these were the same areas
from which the phenomenon of the *Lega* had sprung and developed
since the 1980s. Rather than a new surge, therefore, one might speak of
growth around the *Lega's* traditional bases. It is also interesting to note
that support for the *Lega* rippled out into areas contiguous to this line,
dissolving as peripheral provinces were reached, particularly on the
other side of the Po (particularly in Tuscany and Romagna). This had
also been the case in the previous phase of expansion between 1990 and
1993, when the provinces bordering the *Lega Nord's* original strongholds
had been invested by a wave of support, only for the wave to ebb after
1994.

The April 21st result thus had deep roots. Those surprised by it demonstrated their unfamiliarity with recent political history or their unwillingness to understand its significance.

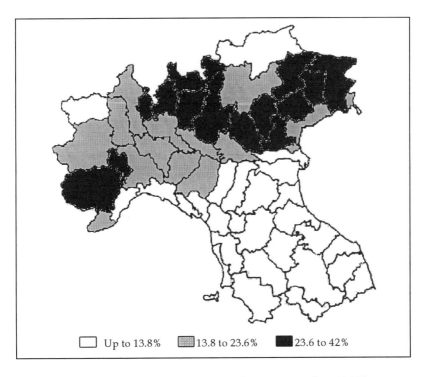

FIGURE 4.1. Electoral Map of the *Lega Nord's* Success in the 1996 Elections
(% of Votes Received by the *Lega Nord*)

The *Lega*: An Electoral Map

To better understand the nature of conditions favoring its implantation and growth, the electoral districts where the *Lega* was present in the
majoritarian vote on 21 April 1996 have been divided into three groups
on the basis of the level of support reached. At the extremes are the districts in which support for the *Lega* was highest (the 46 districts in which
it took more than 34 percent of the vote) and lowest (the 44 districts in
which it took less than 10 percent). The very large intermediate group
(139 districts) includes those in which support was less than in the first
group but nevertheless significant. In this way it is possible to distinguish a number of environmental characteristics favoring or inhibiting
support for the *Lega*.

The first point can be grasped without any recourse to statistics. It is
enough to look at the map in Fig. 4.1 to see that the *Lega* struck roots and
flourished in the northernmost areas of the country, peripheral to the
major urban concentrations (Milan, Turin, Genoa and Venice) and outside the special status regions (with the partial exception of Friuli, where
its support nevertheless remained limited).

TABLE 4.1. Electoral Districts Classified on the Basis of the *Lega Nord*'s Showing in 1996
Chamber of Deputy Elections (Majoritarian Segment): Socio-economic and Political Characteristics

| | Lega's Showing | | | |
	Low	Average	High	Total
% Votes Received in 1996	3.9	19.6	12.8	20.7
Districts: No.	44	139	46	229
%	19.2	60.7	20.1	100
Urban Districts (%)	45.5	41.7	8.7	35.8
Socio-economic Characteristics:				
% Employed in :				
Commerce	37.3	40.3	54.8	42.7
Industry	23.7	22.6	19.1	22.1
Services	39.0	37.1	26.1	35.3
Unemployed (as % of Labor Force)	10.6	10.1	7.8	9.8
Business Units per 1,000 Residents.	84.4	73.7	80.5	77.1
% Votes Received in 1992 Election by:				
Democrazia Cristiana	23.7	23.0	32.1	25.0
PDS	28.2	14.7	7.4	15.8
Rifondazione Comunista	8.7	6.0	3.1	5.9

Source: Elaboration by the Laboratory for Political and Social Studies of the University of
Urbino of data supplied by the Ministry of the Interior and Istituto G. Tagliacarne.

However, a socio-economic and political profile of the three zones delimited by levels of support for the *Lega* (Table 4.1) also supplies important information. In particular, it shows that the *Lega*'s electoral success was highest: a) in small and medium centers (less than 10 percent of the electoral districts in which it did best were in provincial capitals compared to 50 percent of those in which it did worst); b) where the level of industrialization was high, in terms of both businesses and employees, and the tertiary sector small (public and private services); c) where unemployment was low.

The *Lega* gave visibility, therefore, to those small entrepreneurial areas of the North which had experienced rapid development in the preceding two decades, particularly in recent years. However, economic considerations are not in themselves sufficient to define the electoral geography of the *Lega*. Other areas of the country had similar characteristics: those parts of central Italy where the left was traditionally strong and in which the *Lega* made no impression. In the foothill regions, on the other hand, there was a profound change in voting patterns. This deserves attention precisely because it is the political background which appears to be the other factor involved in the electoral results obtained by the *Lega* (Table 4.1). In fact, the *Lega*'s electoral support was: a) highest where the Christian Democrat presence had been strongest. In the districts where the *Lega* was strongest, the Christian Democrat vote had remained around 34 percent in 1992. Where the *Lega* was weakest it had been around 24 percent; b) lowest where electoral support for the parties which emerged from the crisis of the Italian Communist Party (the PDS and *Rifondazione Comunista*) was highest.

In other words, the *Lega* grew in the traditionally white areas of small enterprise and diffuse urbanization. These very precise connotations had been with the *Lega* from the beginning. However, they were now even more marked than in the past. This is clear if the electoral districts where the *Lega* stood in 1996 are grouped according to the difference between the votes they received in that year compared with 1994 (Table 4.2).

It is evident that the *Lega*'s success was based on exploiting the circumstances which had always favored it. The largest increases in the *Lega*'s vote (more than 8 percent) came in a group of 38 districts in which the average employment in industry was 54 percent. Support for the *Lega* fell in line with levels of industrial employment. In the 87 districts where the *Lega*'s vote declined compared with 1994 (these were numerous: 87 in all), only 33.5 percent of employment was in industry. The same pattern can be observed regarding the number of businesses and the incidence of the industrial sector. The similarity of the political background in the areas where the *Lega* was growing and its original heartland is also evident. The Christian Democrats had averaged 34.3 percent

of the vote in 1992 in the electoral districts which saw the largest increases in support for the *Lega* and only 20 percent where the *Lega*'s vote
dropped (though not significantly for the most part). The *Lega* consolidated around its original heartland, building up a new electorate where
it had already laid roots. It thus came to "dominate" where it was already "strong", among the small, independent producers and employees
of areas with a highly developed small enterprise sector, the same areas
which had once been strongholds of the Christian Democracy. The *Lega
Nord* would thus appear to have replaced the Christian Democracy in
these areas.

TABLE 4.2. Electoral Districts Classified by Variation in the *Lega Nord* Vote Between 1994
and 1996 Chamber of Deputies Elections (Proportional Segment): Socio-economic and Political Characteristics

	Falling	Stable	Moderate Growth	Strong Growth	Total
1994-1996 % Variation in Votes	-0.9	+1.6	+4.7	+11.4	+3.0
Districts: No.	87	54	61	38	240
%	36.3	22.5	25.4	15.8	100
Urban Districts (%)	57.5	33.3	31.1	2.6	36.7
Socio-economic Characteristics:					
% Employees in:					
Commerce	24.6	22,0	22.0	19.2	22.5
Industry	33.5	44.0	45.2	54.3	42.1
Services	41.9	34.1	32.8	26.4	35.4
Unemployed (as % of Labor Force)	10.5	10.1	8.9	7.6	9.5
Bus. Units per 1,000 Residents	79.2	74.4	78.8	81.0	78.3
% Votes Received in 1992 by:					
Democrazia Cristiana	20.0	20.2	26.5	34.3	24.0
Partito Socialista Italiano	12.5	12.5	12.1	10.3	12.1
PDS	23.7	18.5	11.2	7.5	16.8
Lega Nord	10.8	14.5	19.9	22.1	15.7
Movimento Sociale Italiano	4.4	4.5	3.5	2.7	3.9

Note: Falling=decrease; stable=0 to 2.5% increase; moderate growth=2.5 to 8% increase;
strong growth=increase greater than 8%.

Source: Elaboration by the Laboratory for Political and Social Studies of the University of
Urbino of data supplied by the Ministry of the Interior and Istituto G. Tagliacarne.

The Political Class:
Three Profiles and Three Types of Social Background

The particularity of northern Italy in socio-political terms revealed by
the 1996 election is confirmed, and if possible accentuated, when analy-

sis moves from the electorate to the elected. Three particular types emerge, with different socio-economic backgrounds and political and institutional experience (see Table 4.3).

TABLE 4.3. Age, Education, and Profession of *Lega Nord*, *Ulivo*, and *Polo* Parliamentarians Elected in 1996 Elections (Chamber and Senate; % Values)

	Lega Nord	*Ulivo*	*Polo*
Age:			
Less than 40 Years Old	31.4	6.5	12.8
40–49 Years Old	44.2	40.6	31.2
50–59 Years Old	20.9	40.1	33.3
60 Years Old or Older	3.5	12.9	22.0
Level of Education:			
Secondary School Diploma	29.0	21.2	15.3
University-level Degree	71.0	78.8	84.7
Profession			
Employed Worker	23.1	19.9	5.2
Self-employed Worker	14.1	0.5	2.2
Entrepreneur	9.0	3.9	15.6
Liberal Professions, Management	46.2	29.1	54.8
University Professor, Magistrate	2.6	18.4	16.3
Politician	1.3	27.2	5.2
Other	3.8	1.0	1.7
Total	100	100	100
Number of Parliamentarians	86	217	141

Sources: Il nuovo parlamento italiano, XIII legislatura (Rome: Vama Edizioni, 1996); *Il "chi è" del nuovo parlamento,* supplement to *Panorama,* no. 19, 15 May 1996; data and elaboration of the Laboratory for Political and Social Studies of the University of Urbino.

Looking at age, the *Lega's* parliamentarians were undoubtedly the youngest, with 31 percent under 40 years of age and only 3 percent over 60. Those elected for the *Ulivo* coalition were concentrated in the intermediate age group (40-60 years of age). Those of the *Polo* were more evenly distributed, but the main peak was in the oldest group, 22 percent of its parliamentarian being over 60. Turning to social background, the *Lega's* representatives were the least educated, the *Polo's* the most. However, the difference between the various formations in this respect was not great and generalization is best avoided. In fact, more than 70 percent of the *Lega's* members of Parliament had a degree and most of the rest were in possession of at least a diploma. This bears little resemblance to the stereotype of the *Lega's* leadership prevalent in political journalism and public opinion, a stereotype the *Lega* itself has sometimes sought to convey. For the *Lega*'s leader, Umberto Bossi, and many militants, bluntness of language and violent political discourse has, to some extent, constituted a deliberate communication strategy, marking the boundaries between "us" ("the ordinary people", "the people of the North") and "them" ("Rome", "the corrupt political class").

Moreover, as Table 4.3 shows, the *Lega*'s representatives really did reflect the structure and tendencies of the North, and the northern foothills in particular, far more closely than those elected for the other two formations. The *Lega* had the highest proportion of employed workers (whose "weight" was greater in the *Lega* than in the *Ulivo* coalition), small entrepreneurs and the self-employed, as well as a sizable contingent from the liberal professions. Professional politicians, on the other hand, were few within the *Lega*'s ranks and most numerous among those elected for the *Ulivo*. The *Lega* continued, therefore, to provide a "channel" for the productive social classes: the "emergent" small-producing bourgeoisie and employed workers of the private sector. It also confirmed its propensity to promote generational change, a propensity less in evidence in other political groupings.

TABLE 4.4. Previous Political Positions Held by Parliamentarians of the *Lega Nord*, *Ulivo* and *Polo* Elected in 1996 elections (Chamber and Senate; % Values)

Previous Position	Lega Nord	Ulivo	Polo
Parliament	51.2	57.1	49.6
Local Administration	22.1	43.8	19.1
Party Machine	16.7	30.9	24.5

Sources: *Il nuovo parlamento italiano, XIII legislatura* (Rome: Vama Edizioni, 1996); *Il "chi è" del nuovo parlamento*, supplement to *Panorama*, no. 19, 15 May 1996; data and elaboration of the Laboratory for Political and Social Studies of the University of Urbino.

Similarly, the profile of the *Lega*'s parliamentarians in terms of previous political experience (Table 4.4) confirms the *Lega*'s extraneousness to the two traditional channels of political recruitment: party organizations and local administration. Taken together, the data suggests a profile consistent with the idea of a "local political party" successfully advanced by the *Lega* in the past,[6] giving political visibility to areas with a dispersed economic structure and to emergent social categories. This was in marked contrast to the larger entrepreneurs and professionals of the *Polo* and even more to the professional politicians, powerful presence of magistrates and university professors and the importance of previous political and administrative experience among candidates of the *Ulivo* coalition, marking its affiliations with the traditional political system. On the other hand, institutional presence and "political competence" were important factors in the *Ulivo*'s success. The coalition had presented a reassuring image, stressing its ability to govern and familiarity with the "state machine". For these very reasons, however, the *Ulivo* appears the furthest removed from the realities and social transformations of northern Italy among the various political formations. The *Polo* (as the "map of the vote" demonstrates) embodied that part of the North which coincided with "centers of services and intangible goods". The *Lega* appears deeply rooted in the foothills, which produced most of its elected representatives, and the social structure of which, based on the dependent and independent strata of the small enterprise sector, it reproduced. The *Lega*, like the strata from which its sprang, had little propensity to follow the typical career path of the "professional politician".

Secession: From Tactical Threat to Strategic Objective

Electoral geography and the profile of the *Lega*'s elected representatives help to demonstrate that its success depended on its ability to identify with a very precise and particular territorial context. However, this same identification was reflected in the *Lega*'s difficulties in penetrating traditionally hostile environments: urban areas, big industrial units and the service sector. It also serves to show that Bossi's project for representing northern Italy, to "liberate Padania" by presenting the *Lega* as an independence movement, faced a number of evident difficulties: "Padania" simply did not exist; and politically the *Lega* represented an important but bounded part of the North.

Paradoxically these limitations emerged more visibly and acutely thanks to the electoral success of April 1996. It was to conceal and overcome these problems, to go beyond the foothills and accentuate the cohesion and identity of his electoral base, that Bossi further accelerated the independence strategy immediately after the election, transforming "secession" from a tactical threat into a strategic objective.

In other words, he chose "the division of the country, the end of Italy as a unitary state"[7] as the aim to be reached. From a "promised land", Padania was transformed into a "real nation" which had to be given visibility. Bossi was trying to "unify" the geo-political map of northern Italy, still divided by the "real" orientation of voters, through communication and political action. He gave increasing space to initiatives which marked a distance from central institutions. The so-called "Parliament of Mantua" (in which the *Lega*'s members of parliament and local administrators met periodically) was flanked by a series of organs which challenged legality as well as Italian national identity in an increasingly open manner. A Committee for the Liberation of Padania was set up, along with the "Green Shirts", sometimes presented as a "stewards service", sometimes as an autonomous "militia" for the *Lega* (and implicitly for the whole of the North).

The event which allowed Bossi to redefine the *Lega*'s position, however, transforming its organizational structure and identity and recovering a distinctive space within the Italian and northern political system was undoubtedly the proclamation of the birth and independence of the "Padanian nation" and the accompanying itinerant demonstrations along the River Po, from its source to the Adriatic. Posters throughout northern and central Italy proclaimed the event's aim as "the self-determination of the Padanian peoples" and called on people to participate "for the freedom of *your* land, to be master in *your* house" (original emphasis). Thus we are dealing with a rite designed to promote a sense of identity and collective self-awareness around three dimensions: territory, community, property.

However, it was what came before, the process preparing and accompanying it both internally and externally, rather than the demonstration itself which sealed the *Lega*'s change of direction. The demonstration quickly seized center-stage in political debate and captured the imagination of the public thanks to the quite extraordinary coverage given by the mass media. In the two weeks leading up to the demonstration of September 15th the press, radio and television gave more space to it than to any other national or international question, political or otherwise. This gave plausibility to the underlying reasoning behind the demonstration, legitimating the secessionist idea, although every investigation had demonstrated that only a minority in northern Italy and indeed of the *Lega*'s own supporters (as studies by Poster-Limes, Ispo, Directa and Cirm confirmed) were in favor of such a move. At the same time, the fact that it could be discussed seriously, and discussion was indeed serious, gave Padania a certain institutional "reality".[8] Like the threat of secession, Padania was the object of pronouncements by all the major political forces and offices of state.

The "preparation" of the demonstration also allowed Bossi to modify the *Lega*'s internal organization and presence on the ground rapidly and profoundly. Most importantly, it provided so strong and exclusive an identity as to render communication and debate both within the *Lega* and between it and the outside world very difficult. This allowed the *Lega*'s leader to unify and regain control of an organization and rank and file which had become overly heterogeneous and contradictory. Disagreement with this perspective became incompatible with continuing membership of the *Lega*.

This was confirmed by the case of Irene Pivetti, whose dissent on the question of secession led to her "banishment". The Pivetti case was probably quite consciously managed by the *Lega*'s leadership in order to "make an example". The preparation of the September initiative also served to "reconstruct" the *Lega*'s organization: mobilizing militants, involving sympathizers, making approaches to other social groups, revitalizing existing sections and opening new ones. During the summer the towns of the "deep North" became the theater for *Lega* mobilization and propaganda. This was all the more significant and apparent because it took place in the context of a political desert, abandoned by the other parties, which had become so "light" in structure as to have lost any local visibility. In the vacuum left by the fall of the mass parties, and the Christian Democracy in particular, the *Lega* resumed its penetration, now as a "secessionist movement" rather than a political party.

The Independence Demonstration on the River Po

The hue and cry surrounding preparations for the River Po demonstration contrasts starkly with its outcome and even more with the silence surrounding the *Lega* and its initiatives in the period which followed. Estimates of participation varied widely. However, there is no doubt that it remained well below both the "promises" made by the *Lega*'s leader and the most prudent estimates of observers and other political actors. A figure of around 200-250,000 people along the River Po has been claimed, with 30-35,000 in Venice for the "proclamation of independence". This was poor given the expectations generated by Bossi (who had announced that over a million people would be present and that there would be an uninterrupted human chain along the entire course of the River Po) and by the media.

It was the broad base of support the *Lega* enjoyed in its strongholds, those people who voted for, and were possibly sympathizers of, the *Lega Nord* without making a continuous commitment, which failed to participate. As reporters following the demonstration commented, only the "hard core" of the *Lega* was present on the banks of the Po. The *Lega* had once more failed to impose itself as the representative and promoter of the broader "northern question" rather than of only one part of the North.

It is possible that the "media promotion" the *Lega* itself sought was in part responsible for the demonstration's failure. The media circus and the dramatization of the event by other political forces, state institutions and the magistracy (who opened investigations into the "Green Shirts" and into the legality of threats to national unity) altered the symbolism of the secessionist demonstration. It ceased to appear like a "day out" and took on a more disquieting aspect; the march had become a serious political and judicial confrontation, no longer a festive occasion but a threat. As already noted, however, potential *Lega* voters were moderates who had once formed the base of the traditional governing parties. They did not like risks. On the contrary, they chose the *Lega* because it exasperated and amplified the fears and motivations they preferred to whisper in their everyday life and own surroundings.

The indications which emerge from the "proclamation of Padanian independence" are therefore contradictory. If it was meant to give visibility and affirmation to the social foundation of Padania as an entity it certainly did not succeed. On the other hand, the intense political debate and extensive media coverage undoubtedly legitimized the issue of secession and made the "northern question" central to political debate. Moreover, it is also true that the *Lega* successfully transformed itself into a secessionist movement, maneuvering its identity and membership in that direction.[9]

This transformation further polarized the *Lega*'s internal organization, the leader on one side, militants on the other, stifling dissent and tightening internal control. This was possible because "reformists" and "federalists" within the party (mainly local administrators, but also some territorial units such as the Veneto region) were marginalized during this phase. However, this very situation could generate tensions, as has happened, not surprisingly, in Veneto.

The *Lega* presents itself today as a secessionist movement. That it will be successful in its "mission" appears unlikely, nor does the "geo-politics" on which that mission is founded—the unification of the North and its resentments towards the state under the *Lega*'s banner—appear very plausible. The "promised land" of Padania would therefore seem as distant as the possibility of secession and, implicitly, the strategy of reuniting the North in its feelings of malaise and disaffection towards the state.

The Abiding Problem

It should not be assumed, however, that the failure of the September 15th demonstration somehow measures the strength of the foundations on which the claims of the *Lega* rest. Secession may have proved to lack solid backing, but the idea that the problem of the *Lega* has ceased to exist would be without foundation. The motivations which led to the *Lega* and its initiatives being taken seriously during the summer, before the secessionist demonstration, have not changed in character or intensity.

Support for the *Lega* has not fallen greatly, and the ill wind blowing in Rome's direction from the North has certainly not ceased.

Measurements of party preference and political orientation reveal that support for *Lega* remains at similar levels to the April 1996 election. Moreover, the climate of opinion upon which it built its success has consolidated. A panel-based telephone poll (repeated on the same sample, therefore) by Ispo, a Milan research agency, shortly after the "proclamation of Padanian independence" showed little change in support for the *Lega* since the previous June.[10] Support for the *Lega* fell by a little over one percent, well within the range of statistical error, and most of this fall had in any case taken place between June and July. It should also be noted that opinion polls tend to "underestimate" support for the *Lega*. It remains an unacceptable choice in many circles, and not everyone is willing to confess such support. Bearing all this in mind, the poll would seem to suggest that its "secessionist" initiatives have not greatly modified the *Lega*'s influence. Moreover, the same poll reveals a significant but disquieting picture of attitudes towards public institutions and social organization.

Firstly, it points to a generalized failure of confidence in central institutional and governmental organisms: Parliament, the government and the Prime Minister in particular. The President of the Republic has resisted better, but began with less popular support anyway. Regardless of the events of the period in question this reflects, at least in part, "normalization" after an initially favorable climate of opinion when a new government takes office. However, it is interesting to note that this process took place at a faster rate in the North, and in the among the foothills in particular, than in Italy as a whole. The number of people polled who pronounced themselves very or fairly pleased with the Parliament had fallen by 9 percentage points since June in the foothill regions compared with 6.5 points in the North as a whole and 5 points at national level. Support for Romano Prodi had fallen by 4.1 points (analogous to the fall in both the North and in Italy); support for the government by 6 points, while in the North as a whole and at national level the fall was around 4.5 points. A marked loss of confidence in the press was also registered, with a fall of 8 points in the area of foothills, 4 points in the North and 2 points at national level. Moreover, delegitimization invested all institutions and organizations in the foothill districts, including those which appeared to be holding up elsewhere: the magistracy, the trades unions, the Church, and even the European Union. Thus, there were unequivocal signs of a climate of intense disaffection with the public sphere and of civic disorientation showing no signs of subsiding and which forcefully highlighted the territorial fractures between the North and the rest of Italy and, even more strongly, between the foothills and the rest of the North.

The *Lega's* advance, then, was halted by the march on the River Po, and it emerged reduced in strength. But the climate of disaffection with the public sphere and the state (tending at this level to absorb and explain any problem, no matter how locally rooted and well-entrenched in the model of development of the North and its foothill districts) remains. Padania does not exist, and secession is unlikely. However, the problems and tensions which gave rise to talk of a "northern question", favoring the outcome of the April 21st election, have not been exhausted. They are still waiting to find representation and solutions. If the *Lega* has failed to achieve that, it is also true that no other political force has so far been able to take its place.

Translated by John Donaldson

Notes

1. G. Pajetta, *Il grande camaleonte* (Milan: Feltrinelli, 1994).

2. For a closer examination of the questions dealt with here, see I. Diamanti, *Il male del Nord. Lega, localismo, secessione* (Rome: Donzelli, 1996). For a broader treatment of the whole phenomenon of the Lega Nord, see I. Diamanti, *La Lega* (Rome: Donzelli, 1995, new ed.). Finally, on the secessionist demonstration on 15 September, see I. Diamanti, "Dietro al fantasma della Lega", in *Il Mulino*, no. 5, 1996, pp. 879-877.

3. See P. Scaramozzino, "La Lega risica (e forse rosica)", in *Il Sole-24 Ore*, 12 March 1996, p. 2.

4. This is suggested by polls conducted by Swg of Trieste and Ispo of Milan.

5. A reconstruction of this phase can be found in I. Diamanti, *La Lega, op. cit.* To understand the logic behind the initial phases of the *Lega's* growth, however, it is useful to consider the interview given by Rocchetta to Marc Lazar: "L'Italie existe-t-elle?", in *Politique Internationale*, Winter 1992-1993, pp. 129-152.

6. See V. Belotti, "La rappresentanza politica locale delle Leghe", in *Polis*, no. 2, 1993; G. Riccamboni, "La zona bianca", in I. Diamanti and R. Mannheimer, eds., *Milano a Roma* (Rome: Donzelli, 1996).

7. See U. Bossi, *Il mio progetto. Discorsi sul federalismo e Padania* (Milan: Sperling & Kupfer, 1996) p. 158.

8. The "secessionist" question has also been the object of reflection and debate at international level. See C. De Flores and D. Petrosino, *Secessione* (Rome: Ediesse, 1996), particularly Petrosino's article, "Democrazie di fine secolo. L'epoca delle secessioni?".

9. See, for example, the "conversion" to independence of two leaders of the *Lega* in the Veneto, interviewed by M. Maugeri ("Come nasce un secessionista", *Il Sole-24 Ore*, 11 September 1996, p. 8), whose political-cultural backgrounds are far removed from "northernism": Manuel Dal Lago, ex-leader of the Liberals (PLI) and Ettore Beggiato, ex-leader of the *Union del Popolo Veneto*, an ethno-

regionalist, therefore, but not Padanian.

10. A telephone poll conducted weekly on a panel of around 4,000 individuals, representative of the national population by Ispo-Cra Nielsen.

5

The Italian Left
After the 1996 Elections

Stephen Hellmann

The year 1996 marked a truly historic moment for the Italian left, and above all for its major party, the *Partito Democratico della Sinistra* (PDS). The general elections witnessed the victory of a center-left coalition, the *Ulivo* (Olive Tree), that received its major inspiration and support from the PDS, the direct descendant of the Italian Communist Party (PCI), which had systematically been excluded from a governmental role from 1947 until the end of the so-called "First Republic." Moreover, the PDS emerged from the election as Italy's largest party—albeit by the narrowest of margins, and while polling a relatively modest 21 percent of the vote.[1] If it could not claim the office of prime minister, which went to Romano Prodi, the PDS did obtain the lion's share of cabinet positions, occupying 9 of the 20 ministries in Prodi's government, including the prestigious positions of Deputy Prime Minister, Finance Minister, and, most notable of all for ex-Communists, the Interior Minister.

These are unprecedented achievements that represent an historic turning point. But the victory of the *Ulivo* (and the PDS) hardly signal a massive shift of public opinion to the left side of the political spectrum. And no one is more aware of this than Massimo D'Alema, secretary of the PDS. It is useful to recall that the beginning of the year was marked by considerable political maneuvering to *avoid* elections, precisely because the outcome was not considered likely to clarify the political balance of power—and the chances of the Center-Left looked anything but solid. Antonio Maccanico's efforts to form yet another interim government (and, in so doing, to push Romano Prodi and the *Ulivo* into the background) had the full support of D'Alema and his closest collaborators. The goal, which has hardly been renounced by the PDS's leadership, was to produce a broad-based government to carry out a series of reforms that would, ideally, stabilize the "rules of the game" before the country went to the polls again in an atmosphere of division and uncertainty. Similarly, PDS overtures to Umberto Bossi and the *Lega Nord* only ended when Bossi decided to run against both the *Polo per le Libertà* and the *Ulivo*. These and other episodes indicate that the PDS was acutely aware of the *Ulivo*'s weakness, and likely fate in the event of elections. Prodi's victory may have been heartening and dramatic, but it did not change the underlying realities of Italian politics.[2] In strictly electoral terms, the left has, in fact, never been weaker. This victory owed far more to the vagaries of the electoral system, and to divisions in the opposing camp(s), than it did to any fundamental realignment of the party system or public opinion.

The much-heralded "Second Republic" is therefore still a long way from being realized — or, less dramatically and perhaps more accurately — the Italian transition is still far from complete. Italian politics in the post-*Tangentopoli* era has evolved in a bipolar direction, and has even witnessed, within a two-year span, the election of a center-right coalition followed by the election of a center-left coalition. But the two dominant poles of the political spectrum have not managed to coalesce into two distinctive political formations, or even two reasonably coherent coalitions. In fact, the number of parties represented in Parliament actually increased in both 1994 and 1996. Moreover, the extreme fragmentation of the party system and the fluid political situation it engenders has frustrated efforts to hammer out a broadly acceptable compromise about the rules of the game under which the transition can be completed.

Thus, at the end of 1996, the PDS and the left were by no means in as strong a position as a superficial reading of the year's events might suggest. Despite the impressive electoral victory, none of the fundamental problems or dilemmas facing the left at the beginning of the year had been resolved. Indeed, the victory added new problems to the old. What are these problems?

The Left's Dilemmas

1. The *Ulivo* hardly won a resounding victory. Its majority was extremely narrow in the Senate, and it obtained a majority in the Chamber of Deputies only with the external support of *Rifondazione Comunista*, with whom it had struck an electoral alliance. Thanks to this alliance, and the decision of the *Lega Nord* to run alone, the *Ulivo* took enough single-member seats to squeak by, even though the overall proportion of the vote going to the parties of the Center-Right was actually greater in

1996 than it had been in 1994 when, united, *Forza Italia*, the *Lega Nord*, and *Alleanza Nazionale* won the elections.

2. The PDS is the largest party in the governing coalition, and indeed the country. It is also by far the most solidly organized party in Italy, with 675,000 members.[3] But it still can only claim the support of 21 percent of the electorate, while no other party in the *Ulivo* even reaches double figures. This blunt numerical reality dictated the electoral strategy of 1996: the *Ulivo* had to be cobbled together from extremely heterogeneous forces that ranged from Greens to ex-Christian Democrats, and included fragments or remnants of nearly every political persuasion imaginable, not to mention high-profile former ranking officers of the Bank of Italy. Moreover, even this disparate grouping was unable to win a majority in the Chamber of Deputies.

3. As the major force on the left, the PDS is obviously indispensable to any recomposition or simplification of that part of the political spectrum. More than that: the success of any such transformation will require the PDS to take a clear lead. But as long as the left remains so fragmented, and even its leading party barely exceeds a fifth of the vote, no such lead will be possible: the smaller parties, concerned with their own survival (and relative weight within any new formation), can delay or drag out any process of change. Further complicating any such process is the fact that the PDS is divided internally over precisely what form this new political force of the left should take (see point 5 below).

4. The PDS is in an awkward position vis-à-vis the *Ulivo*, understood as the governing coalition. The PDS may have been instrumental in the creation of the *Ulivo*, and it is the government's most important source of parliamentary support. Yet, contrary to basic parliamentary practice, the leader of the government does not come from the largest party in the coalition: Romano Prodi, and not a *pidiessino*, is prime minister. This relationship creates tensions between the PDS and Prodi, and between the PDS and the smaller parties within the governing coalition (it also complicates the PDS's relationship with *Rifondazione Comunista*).

Throughout the year, the PDS resented the fact that it was forced, on issue after issue, to defend government policies, having to assume the burden of keeping the majority together, while *Rifondazione* stood back and played the role of defender of high-minded principles. *Rifondazione* enjoyed conditioning the government's choices, and it obviously enjoyed putting the PDS in a difficult position. As *Rifondazione*'s parliamentary leader put it, "They want to play the role of the moderate left? Fine. Let them pay for the policies they have chosen".[4] Nor did it help that Prodi often seemed perfectly content to let the PDS carry the brunt of defending policy choices against public attack. On such occasions, Prodi would often assume a detached attitude that angered the PDS, which suspected that there might be less detachment than calculation in this hands-off attitude. Far more often than seemed comfortable, it was the PDS, not Prodi, that exposed itself in an effort to build consensus.

5. The PDS is *also* in an awkward relationship with the *Ulivo* understood as a political formation of the center-left. Everyone in the PDS wants to create a more inclusive, broadly-based party to hasten the recomposition of the party system into two distinctive poles, superseding the current fragmentation. But considerable disagreement exists about the most desirable eventual array of political forces in the future. D'Alema and those closest to him want to create a single new party that would be distinctively of the left, along the lines of the more successful socialist and social-democratic parties of Europe. For this reason, they hold out the (at least theoretical) possibility of including *Rifondazione* in this new formation, and they have tended to view the *Ulivo* as an electoral alliance—not the harbinger of a very broad-based party of the center-left. D'Alema's critics within the PDS, and many elements of the *Ulivo* with roots in the Catholic or lay traditions outside of the historical socialist movement, hold quite a different view of the future of the Italian party system. Their future party would be much more of the center-left than of the left, and would in fact build on the *Ulivo*'s experience; it would also have nothing to do with *Rifondazione Comunista*.

6. Finally, because of the precarious political balance of power, PDS secretary Massimo D'Alema and his collaborators are aware that the Center-Right Pole will remain a force to reckon with for the foreseeable future. They therefore look to the Pole's most moderate elements for a broader agreement on the rules of the game, including constitutional reform. But this raises profound suspicion among its own allies, or among those on whose support the government must count, such as *Rifondazione*. These suspicions are based on disagreements in principle, political calculations, and suspicions and resentments. A PDS-*Forza Italia* compromise will inevitably push the smaller allies of both into a secondary role, and simple self-preservation frequently leads these allies to oppose, for self-interested motives, anything that is proposed. But genuine disagreements do exist among the allies on the advisability of the most likely institutional reforms to emerge from this sort of compromise. Considerable hostility exists—in *Rifondazione*, in the left wing of the PDS, and in the Popular Party—against the French-style two ballot electoral system that the PDS favors to force a more clear-cut bipolarization. Even greater hostility exists, including within the PDS itself, over any of the variations of presidentialism that have been put forward by the Pole as a desideratum of institutional reform. A broad compromise with the Pole is also opposed by many who feel that any such agreement would provide Berlusconi with a way out of his judicial problems, would allow him to

continue his near-monopoly of Italy's commercial TV networks, or both.

These issues are all quite clearly inter-related. Some of those mentioned above are beyond the scope of this contribution (see Simon Parker's discussion of the Prodi government in this volume), and limitations of space prevent a discussion of others issues, e.g., the relationship of the PDS with the more moderate components of the *Ulivo*, in the detail they deserve. But, having at least sketched in the major dilemmas, we can focus in more depth on the problems that face the parties of the left, and developments in this area, in 1996. Fortunately for our purposes, 1996 found both *Rifondazione* and the PDS engaged in preparations for national party congresses: *Rifondazione*'s was held in December, while the PDS's was scheduled to take place early in 1997, but preparations for this event were well underway by autumn. These congresses provide an excellent opportunity to examine how the parties confronted their problems, and how they collectively prepared to face the immediate future.

The "Two Lefts" and *Rifondazione Comunista*

If the greatest fragmentation in the party system is found among the centrist forces that incline toward the left, the greatest obstacle to any sort of consolidation on the left is undoubtedly its division into two parties that share a common heritage, but grow more diverse with each passing day. These are, of course, the PDS and *Rifondazione*, which, in the course of 1996 solidified their respective identities as the more moderate and governmental, and the more radical and antagonistic, faces of the Italian left.

Both parties have their origins in the Italian Communist Party (PCI). The bulk of the PCI went along with the founding of a new party—the PDS—that was supposed to represent the first steps in the reconstitution of the Italian left in the post-cold war era.[6] The purpose of this reconstructed left was to have begun to bring together the disparate progressive forces of Italian politics into an entirely new political formation, made possible by the end of the cold war, and made necessary by the challenges of a rapidly changing world. This new party would then be in a position to win the support of a majority of the population, ending the left's exclusion from government throughout the postwar period. Party Secretary Achille Occhetto dragged the PCI through its final dramatic period and the PDS through its trouble-ridden early years, but was in effect forced to resign following the left's defeat in the 1994 elections. The party has been led since then by Massimo D'Alema, recognized as far more politically astute than his somewhat impetuous predecessor. D'Alema's crowning achievement to date has undoubtedly been the construction of the *Ulivo* alliance in 1995 as a way of bringing the left out

88

Stephen Hellmann

of the seeming isolation into which it had been thrown by its defeat in 1994, and into a direct governing role. But the transition begun by Occhetto remains incomplete, and the victory of the *Ulivo*—a center-left alliance supported externally by the far left—did not really affect the underlying reality.

The center of gravity of (in its own words) the "radical," "antagonistic" left is *Rifondazione*, whose founding core was made up of nostalgic hard-liners and the most militant elements from the PCI, along with a considerable rank-and-file following; these ex-Communists were joined by several far-left groups who dissolved themselves and moved wholesale into a "new" communist party that continued to be committed to the radical transformation of capitalism. *Rifondazione* has been ably led since 1993 by Fausto Bertinotti, a trade unionist historically identified with the most radical, militant wing of the CGIL. Bertinotti replaced another militant unionist in what was initially seen as a triumph for the most hard-line former Communists, but he quickly revealed himself to be an imaginative leader, able to mix demagoguery, an appealing media image, and maneuvering skills both in Parliament and behind the scenes to exploit to the full his party's pivotal position.

Rifondazione's very *raison d'être*, from the beginning, was to stand apart from the major party of the left. It is therefore not surprising that *Rifondazione* has promoted the "two left" argument in its strongest form, i.e., that it and the PDS now represent a *permanent* division of the left. It has used this argument to refuse even to discuss joining the Center-Left government, or any process of the reunification of the entire left under a single banner. Its strategy is to outflank others from the left to maximize its own support and freedom of maneuver. Posing itself as the privileged referent for all who want truly radical change, *Rifondazione* has every interest in distinguishing itself from other established forces on the left. Its occasional ultra-radical posture has generally paid off, as the three point increase between the 1994 and 1996 general elections (from 5.6 to 8.6 percent), as well as its more-than-respectable ability to maintain a membership of 125,000 indicates. Above all, the fact that its support has been determinant, in the Chamber of Deputies, for the survival of the Center-Left's ambitions since 1995 has enhanced its visibility—and bargaining leverage.

It would, however, be a gross oversimplification to see *Rifondazione* as nothing more than a bunch of extremists and nostalgic die-hards, despite the communist label and the continued insistence that capitalism can be superseded. It has used its leverage to maximum advantage, but *Rifondazione* faces several of its own contradictions. While still in the opposition, it learned that intransigence has its costs: a *de facto* alliance with Berlusconi and Fini that seemed to doom Dini's government in 1995 re-

sulted in an embarrassed retreat when *Rifondazione* rank-and-file re-
belled at the idea of allying with conservatives to bring down a government supported by the Center-Left. This behavior also resulted in the
exit of a number of prominent leaders to form the *Comunisti Unitari*, who
promptly allied with the PDS and the *Ulivo* in 1996. Following Prodi's
victory, *Rifondazione* proved quite skilled at exercising "critical support"
of the *Ulivo*, making the government respond to its concerns on a variety
of issues, such as slowing down privatization, forcing more taxation and
less social spending cuts, protecting pensions, and so on.[7] This exposes
the *Ulivo* to savage attacks from the right, who accuse Prodi of being in
Bertinotti's thrall. But such behavior inevitably involves compromises
for *Rifondazione* as well, which produces fierce attacks on the leadership
from the party's small but very militant left wing, which would prefer a
return back to the purity of the opposition.

These internal challenges were proved negligible at *Rifondazione*'s
third congress in December 1996. But they do point to a genuine dilemma: his party can, after all, deny a majority to Prodi (or his successor) any time it likes. Yet being part of the majority, and responsible for
the government's survival, is uncomfortable for a party that styles itself
as Italy's radical opposition. One can threaten all sorts of dire actions,
but bringing down a "friendly" government is a very serious act—as the
Dini episode proved. Given that the very flimsy 1996 majority was less a
victory of the left than an artifact of the electoral system and divisions
on the right, new elections could well lead to a return to power of the
Center-Right. This might please the extreme left wing of *Rifondazione*,
but everyone else recognizes that it would be a disaster. Thus, as many
observers have noted, *Rifondazione* plays a pivotal role, but in some ways
it is as much a hostage to the *Ulivo* as the *Ulivo* is to it.

A desire on the part of the leadership to move *Rifondazione Comunista*
beyond simply outflanking everyone from the left was evident even before the party's solid showing in the April elections. Then, during the
summer, emboldened by the election results and sensing an opportunity
presented by the PDS's and the *Ulivo*'s difficulties, Bertinotti announced
that *Rifondazione* was going to move from a posture of resistance to one
of active political assertiveness, and that it also intended to launch a battle against "sectarianism" in its own midst.[7] From that point on, the
party's actions have revealed an ambition greater than that of merely
protecting its own space on the left fringe of the spectrum. Recognizing
its own weakness, *Rifondazione* was committing itself to enlarge that
space by building a mass political movement, made possible and necessary by the PDS's move to the center, embrace of neo-liberal doctrines,
and "abandonment of the working class and downtrodden". Far from
resigning itself to occupying limited terrain and ceding hegemony of the

left to the PDS, *Rifondazione* sees the issue as nothing less than a contest for that hegemony, posing itself as an alternative to what it sees as the PDS's passive acceptance of the most damaging consequences of capitalism's globalizing tendencies.[8]

It initially seemed as if the "mass political movement" Bertinotti was proposing would represent a radical reconfiguration of the area to the left of the PDS, a submerging of all groups' and political forces' identities into a genuinely new political subject. In this spirit, *Rifondazione* made explicit overtures to social movements and groups outside the sphere of the parties in Italian society—the unemployed and marginalized, as well as the more visibly organized gays, feminists, autonomous social centers, and activists of every stripe. Much of the criticism of sectarianism, as the pre-congressional campaign and documents made clear, is directed as much at old prejudices and ideological closure toward the outside (including sexist and anti-gay attitudes), as toward the more classical ideological dogmatism that still persists in *Rifondazione*. "It is a cultural and behavioral closure toward any confrontation with different positions, which impedes any relationship with [social] movements that is capable of recognizing that they are both autonomous and the bearers of a visible strategic alternative option", is how the leadership's document put it.[9]

As the congress approached, however, it became clear that *Rifondazione* was not going to carry this reaching-out initiative to the point where it would be willing to call its own identity into question. Observers speculated that the more enthusiastic manifestations of Bertinotti's 1960s movement orientation had been reined in by party president Armando Cossutta, the ex-PCI leader who has the firmest grip on the loyalties of the party organization. Others suggested that a five-year-old organization that had barely consolidated itself and that was plagued with considerable organizational problems (see below) was simply in no position either to lead or participate in such a radically ambitious project as Bertinotti had proposed. Thus, while *Rifondazione* continues to speak of reconstituting the antagonistic left, it is evident that it does not intend to depart dramatically from its existing organizational model. *Rifondazione* will anchor a revitalized, "true" left, but has no intention of dissolving itself into a totally new political subject in the foreseeable future.[10]

Since Prodi's victory, *Rifondazione* has become quite openly aggressive toward the unions, and particularly the CGIL, which is accused of having "lost its autonomy," i.e., becoming far too conciliatory toward Prodi now that the PDS is in the government. Bertinotti has sent messages to the militant minority of the CGIL close to *Rifondazione* that it might want to consider establishing its own organization if it felt it was being systematically marginalized in the larger organization.[11]

The third congress, held at the end of 1996, reiterated and developed these themes—and won endorsement from 85 percent of the party, isolating the "purist" left. Interestingly, in the congress, *Rifondazione* did not express implacable opposition to Italian membership in the European Union, but spoke of a European unity that would occur under more progressive, pro-labor, terms, breaking with the monetarism and neo-liberalism that are currently dominant.[12] This was not a retreat from its oft-repeated "Euroskeptic" position, but it was not a purely negative anti-EU position, either. Here, as elsewhere, *Rifondazione* is positioning itself to reap political benefits from government policies that might prove unpopular.

These are important developments, but not because *Rifondazione* poses an imminent, or even a realistic, challenge to PDS hegemony on the left. They are important because they show that *Rifondazione*'s aspirations are more ambitious than many observers had assumed. This is disappointing news for those—starting with Massimo D'Alema and many in the PDS—who held the hope of at least a possible reunification of the left, albeit only in the future (see the discussion of the PDS pre-congressional debate below). It also must be bad news for anyone who hoped that there might soon be some sort of simplification of the Italian party system, beginning on the left, where it is most needed. Instead, *Rifondazione* seems—for reasons that are perfectly understandable from its own perspective—to be doing everything possible to render permanent the major division that exists.

Ambitions, however, are often not very realistic. If *pidiessini*, with 21 percent of the vote and nearly 700,000 members, lament their lack of resources, what is one to say about a party as volatile, and in the final analysis, as weak, as *Rifondazione*, with barely more than a third as many votes and a quarter of the members as the PDS? Among the many interesting things that emerged during the congress was the astonishing turn-over rate of *Rifondazione* membership: roughly a quarter of each year's members consists of people who were not members the previous year; a similar proportion fails to renew their cards.[13] Thus, while the overall number had remained stable at around 125,000, fully 30,000 members were turning over every year—hardly an auspicious sign for a political force that wants to be the anchor for broad-based, movement-focused, coalition of the most progressive forces in society.

Planning for the Second Congress of the PDS

The PCI's transformation into the PDS was a painful, drawn-out process, marked by two extremely divisive party congresses in 1990 and 1991. Since there had also been a major congress in March 1989—seen, six months before the fall of the Berlin Wall, as a major turning point for the PCI—the party that became the PDS had actually experienced three congresses in just under two years. Racked by internal divisions and a seemingly unstoppable hemorrhage of members, militants, and electors until 1993, the fledgling PDS obviously had no stomach for further public airing of its seemingly incurable internal ailments. From late 1993 onward, the press of political events in which the PDS was a major protagonist made it relatively easy to put off—or, early in 1995, actually postpone—the stock-taking, debate, and election of leadership that a national congress is supposed to represent.[14]

Thus, by the time the more-than-overdue second congress was finally set in motion in 1996, scheduled for early 1997, the PDS had undergone dramatic transformations. It remains the best-organized party in Italy, but for some time, the PDS has born only a faint resemblance to a mass party.[15] Between 1991 and 1996, the local party leadership experienced extensive turnover (in some locales, more than once). At the very top of the party, Occhetto had been forced out, and was replaced by D'Alema after an unprecedented head-on competition with Walter Veltroni, the editor-in-chief of *L'Unità* who became Deputy Prime Minister in 1996.

The contest with Veltroni was, as such things always are, in part a clash between personal loyalties and styles, but it also served to crystallize the major division in the PDS after its traumatic earlier years. This division by no means exhausts all the viewpoints within the PDS, but it has tended to be the party's major strategic and ideological fault-line. As alluded to above, on one side of this division have been those, including D'Alema and his closest collaborators, who wish to build a new left-wing force that remains anchored within the tradition of European socialdemocracy, although they envision a pluralistic force that includes lay, Catholic, environmental, feminist and other backgrounds. While highly critical of *Rifondazione Comunista*, this group still considers *Rifondazione* an essential component of a future broad formation of the left. On the other side are those who consider the socialdemocratic tradition obsolete and inadequate: theirs is a broader vision that includes the above, but makes far more explicit reference to the liberal-democratic tradition and individual citizenship rights and is more aggressively anti-statist. For lack of a better term, I refer to this quite composite group as the PDS's liberal-democratic or "right" wing. These people are heir to the old *migliorista* wing of the PCI, i.e., those who wanted the fastest and most complete break with the communist tradition (and label), and the most thorough make-over of the PCI-PDS into a party of government. They see the center-left as the "natural" area into which the PDS should expand and transform itself, and are therefore the PDS's most unqualified supporters of the *Ulivo*, for they see in it a "rough draft" of the future political formation. Veltroni, who sees a party suited for the twenty-first century more in terms of Clinton's Democrats or Blair's Labour Party, is this group's leading exponent.

Until late in 1996, the differences within the PDS, and between the PDS and *Rifondazione*, remained roughly as they had since D'Alema became secretary in 1994. But toward the end of the summer, comments by D'Alema and his collaborators suggested an acceptance of ideas previously identified with the more pro-*Ulivo*, liberal-democratic wing of the party. Was this simply a tactical adjustment by D'Alema, a peace offering to Prodi and the *Ulivisti* to reassure them that the PDS was not going to strike too autonomous—or critical—a course vis-à-vis the government? Or was it simply an effort, with the PDS's congress scheduled for early 1997, to head off the most serious criticism within the party? There is at the moment no real challenge to D'Alema's leadership of the PDS: if anything, the central role he played in the *Ulivo*'s victory strengthened his already very firm grip on the party. But no one enjoys lacerating disagreements; it is always better to make some concessions to one's opponents in order to avoid alternative motions, or endless strings of amendments, during the congress itself. Lengthy and debilitating debates—as the PDS knows all too well from its own experience—usually weaken a party's image far more than they clarify issues.

Short-term political calculations undoubtedly played some role in the evolution of the party leadership's formal statements as preparations for the congress carried into the autumn of 1996. There certainly was considerable change in the leadership's formal statement of the PDS's broad vision and strategic aspirations: a comparison of D'Alema's original congressional motion, deposited on October 16, with the amended version that appeared in the first week of November, shows the incorporation of extensive parts of amendments and documents written by adversaries or critics of the secretary, as well as by many others.[16] In the best mediating tradition, proposals were adopted from all points of the spectrum: the left wing of the party (which identifies itself as such), feminists, environmentalists, and, the right or liberal-democratic wing.

In certain key areas such as institutional reform, there was more a reiteration of the PDS's established positions than any significant shift in the arguments presented. Of course, the PDS's positions as they have matured on institutional reform were already quite far-reaching in their implications: federalism, unicameralism and a "Chamber of the Regions," a chancellor-style democracy and a directly-elected head of state, among other things. And the PDS's final motion does adopt some of the right wing's anti-statist language—but the mainstream PDS positions on decentralizing powers and reforming and streamlining the bureaucracy were already quite well-developed. At any rate, the final document does

not go as far in its anti-statism and anti-party rhetoric as does the language of the right wing, which often implies that political parties are
outmoded, and inevitably invade the space of civil society.

The amended document met with a hostile reaction from Achille Occhetto. The former secretary apparently had believed that D'Alema
would be openly challenged by a contrasting motion put forward by
those most supportive of the *Ulivo* (and closest to his own ideas). He had
personal as well as more principled reasons to be dismayed at the resulting compromise, which many of his erstwhile supporters, starting with
Deputy Prime Minister Walter Veltroni, signed. Though few used words
as harsh as Occhetto's ("disgust"), critics from both left and right argued
that D'Alema had pre-empted any real discussion by accepting so many
(ten) amendments to the original document.[17] But for all the mediation,
and for all the complaints of the right wing that the final document was
too accommodating to the left wing[18], the congressional motion makes
more concessions, on the issues that really matter, to the right than to
anyone else.[19] Distinctions between D'Alema and the right remain, but,
in most cases, they have been diminished.

Contentious Issues

Three of these issues are especially important: *Rifondazione Comunista*,
the *Ulivo*, and reform of the welfare state. At times, the motion represents a clear departure from previously-expressed views; on other occasions, the change is more of a clarification.

Rifondazione Comunista. This shift is evident in the motion's discussion of *Rifondazione*. Well into 1996, D'Alema framed the PDS's relationship with *Rifondazione* in terms that came close to those of the left wing
of his party. *Rifondazione*'s insistence that the left had two components,
one more radical and one oriented toward government, was rejected.
And the common origins of both parties in the PCI was posed as one
more argument in favor of an eventual reunification of both, along with
many other forces, in a new party of the left. This was understood to be
a merely hypothetical proposition — for *Rifondazione* has vociferously rejected any consideration of such suggestions — but it was indicative of a
party that did not ignore (or scorn) its left flank when it looked to the future. By the time D'Alema presented his initial congressional motion,
"the existence, in Italy today, of two lefts is undeniable".[20] Ironically, the
acceptance of Rifondazione's language does *not* represent a shift to the
left, for to accept "two lefts" is to accept a profound division. The PDS
left wing's own document makes this very clear, and denounces "theo-
rizing and rendering permanent the division between a democratic, governing left counterposed to a purely oppositional left".[21] But the only

proposal from the left wing that was accepted in this part of the final document is a rather wishy-washy reference not to automatically exclude *Rifondazione* from an eventual recomposition of the entire left.[22]

In contrast, the right wing's amendments to the same section were accepted: these use quite intransigent language, and deny that the PDS and *Rifondazione* could ever share the same political goals. The discussion of "two lefts" is now framed much more critically than in D'Alema's original document. The amended PDS motion argues that the PCI was split into two essentially irreconcilable parts, one anti-system and "antagonistic," the other more reformist and government-oriented. This ambiguity, "probably inevitable and even useful for an entire historic period, became, with the passage of time, suffocating and paralyzing".[23] The transformation of the PCI into the PDS was meant to leave this ambiguity behind forever. But *Rifondazione* rejected this transformation, and became a party precisely to carry on the antagonistic, oppositional element within the old PCI. To present the PDS and *Rifondazione* as two parts of the same tradition—as D'Alema's original motion did—obscures this background and the two parties' fundamental incompatibility. It also means, "consciously or not, to put on the agenda, if not actively hope for, the reconstitution of the old, paralyzing mish-mash of reformism and antagonism," with consequences that would inevitably reproduce the consociational degenerations of the First Republic.[24]

The *Ulivo*. That the PDS's precongressional document would be strongly supportive of the *Ulivo*, understood both as a political project and as the government of Romano Prodi, should hardly come as a surprise. It would be politically suicidal for the principal supporter of the government to take an arm's length attitude toward it, especially since there was no lack of evidence of strained feelings between the PDS and the *Ulivo* (see above and also Simon Parker's chapter). Even if the PDS actually needed more freedom to maneuver vis-à-vis the government, and even if supporters of the *Ulivo* were fully aware that the coalition was a very long way from being an autonomous political movement, it would be inappropriate to dwell on these problems in the party's major strategic statement.

D'Alema had spent much of the year, i.e., well after Prodi took office, pointing out that the *Ulivo* was an electoral coalition, and the PDS's primary political priority was to reinforce itself as part of the reconstruction of the entire left. His very public effort through the summer to recruit former Socialists into this project shows that he was clearly trying to move along these lines—to the point of annoying some allies and members of his own party. But by the autumn, there was not very much to show for these efforts: former Socialists who had not long ago defected to the Pole had, for the most part, already allied with D'Alema or Prodi.

These efforts may well have convinced him that there was, in any event, precious little "submerged" public support whose loyalty these fragments of the old PSI still commanded.[25]

With this background in mind, it was immediately significant that D'Alema's initial motion spoke of the *Ulivo* as "a strategic, and not simply an electoral and transitory alliance." This is quite a concession, but it was not enough for the pro-*Ulivo* forces in his party. Their own document takes pains to define "strategic" with great care, noting that everyone uses this term with reference to the *Ulivo*, but avoids spelling out what this actually means. They argue that the *Ulivo* is weakened if viewed simply as an alliance, for that puts it constantly at the mercy of its component parts—the parties, who will treat it as a necessary evil produced by the electoral system and little more. The goal, in contrast to this party-centered approach, should be to build outward from the alliance itself, strengthening it. This is a substantial "correction" of D'Alema's earlier formulation—is incorporated in its entirety into the final document.[26] That document's acceptance of most of the right's language on the *Ulivo* was widely interpreted, by friends and adversaries alike, as evidence that an open confrontation with Veltroni and the right wing at the congress was going to be avoided.

But the final document does not uncritically incorporate all of the right's suggestions, even on this issue. For example, the right explicitly proposed abandoning the strategic idea of a Center-Left alliance, in favor of "a political subject of a new type" that could potentially win the support of a majority of Italians. The reference to the *Ulivo* here is rather blatant.[27] Instead, the final document reiterates that the *Ulivo* cannot be considered a party. Moreover, positive references in the final document to the Socialist International as the most advanced political forum in the world, the place where the true renewal of the left is taking place, underscores that the compromise with the right wing—which considers references to socialism obsolete—left important internal differences unresolved.

Welfare State Reform. This is the subject that is most fraught with real and potential conflict for the PDS and the *Ulivo*, for it is here that Bertinotti (and the unions) have drawn the clearest line in the sand. If the achievements of Italy's welfare state—explicitly, existing pension arrangements—are seriously threatened by austerity measures designed to meet the Maastricht convergence criteria, they will fight these measures. *Rifondazione* has threatened to withdraw support for the government if it tries to undermine existing pension arrangements, and has even defended the seemingly indefensible, the so-called "baby pensions" (awarded, in the past, to public-sector employees with less than 20 years' service).

It has been clear for some time that the PDS has a far less "protection-ist" attitude about many aspects of the Italian system of welfare, which it considers excessively corporatist, i.e., protective of entrenched interests at the expense of the weak and unorganized. During a trip to New York, D'Alema was challenged by a questioner, who said that it was hard to see how a party that challenged the welfare state could define itself as being of the left. His response was revealing: "What is more left-wing, to defend the rights of a fifty-year-old railroad worker who has taken early retirement, or those of a young person without a job?".[28] This critical at-titude has been increasingly articulated in terms of a more efficient econ-omy in which the role of the state, while not eliminated altogether, will primarily be regulatory. The PDS's emphasis on efficiency and on Italy's need to adjust to the phenomenon of globalization has been duly noted, and denounced, by *Rifondazione* as evidence of it becoming little more than an apologist for free-market forces. This criticism stings, especially when the major determinant of the *Ulivo*'s economic policies appears to be to bring Italy into line with the Maastricht parameters. Moreover, while the criticism is probably technically accurate only with regard to the PDS's right wing, it is close enough to the truth to put D'Alema (and Prodi) slightly on the defensive. Toward the end of 1996, their references to Maastricht started to include criticisms of the overly monetarist criteria that informed EU policy, with not enough attention paid to economic growth and employment.

This background helps us understand the ambiguities—and the un-happiness of the right wing—with the final document's discussion of the welfare state. The original motion was consistent with earlier PDS posi-tions, reflecting a party committed to a fundamental rethinking of the model of welfare, despite recognizing that it was "the most advanced form of social compromise" realized in the industrialized countries of the West in the postwar period. In the words of the original motion, which remained unaltered in the final document:

> We must be brave enough to think in terms of less guarantees and protec-tions, and more culture, work, and an expansion of individual opportu-nity on the basis of equal starting points. The passage from a welfare of guarantees to a welfare of opportunities is the way to win the support of those (young high-school and university graduates, women, some entre-preneurs) who feel excluded from the old system of guarantees... effec-tive equality of opportunity is also the strongest response to the argu-ment that limited public resources necessarily means the end of the wel-fare state.[29]

The right was so pleased with this that it did not even present amendments on the subject—although the inclusion of a left-wing amendment in the final document caused strong objections. This amendment avoids "equality of opportunity" language and explicitly warns against challenging the hard-won compromise hammered out with the unions over pensions. The left's amendment also echoes classical European welfare-statism: it speaks of extending universal citizenship rights and of committing Italy to an eventual *increase* in social spending, if only to bring it into line with spending levels in the most advanced European nations. But even the left acknowledges the inequities that exist under the current system, and speaks of the need for fundamental changes.[30]

Conclusions

Ambiguities persist in the PDS's final document, just as disagreements continue to exist within the PDS over how far to go in rethinking and re-shaping the welfare state. But these disagreements take place within a party that, on almost all issues, moved more toward the political center in the course of 1996. And, while *Rifondazione*'s third congress isolated the extreme left within its own ranks, there was a ring of truth in Fausto Bertinotti's comments that the major parties of the left had perhaps never been so far apart in the entire postwar period.[31] He was of course not referring simply to the ideological gulf between the two parties' congressional documents, but to their increasing tendency to take opposite sides on practically every issue of substance facing the governmental majority.

This situation might cheer those within the *Ulivo* and the PDS whose vision of the future excludes *Rifondazione* altogether. But in both the short and medium term, a left that barely obtains 30 percent of the vote can hardly afford to be so badly divided. Divisions within the *Ulivo* itself, whether based on principles or self-interest, only further serve to underscore how unlikely it is that a major reorganization and consolidation of the left will occur soon.

A more pressing question is not whether, but when, these divisions will prove so problematic that they make the continuation of Prodi's government—and perhaps any center-left coalition—impossible. There is an extremely powerful incentive on all sides to keep the Center-Left going: the lack of alternatives in Parliament, and the very uncertain electoral future of an *Ulivo* that lost *Rifondazione*'s support, or was so internally divided that elections became necessary. But keeping the coalition together has its own political costs, and the major price was paid in 1996 by the PDS. D'Alema's unhappiness over this situation was an open secret within a few months of the *Ulivo*'s victory, as is shown to by his persistent efforts to draw *Rifondazione* into the coalition, or at least into a "programmatic agreement" that would limit Bertinotti's ability to alter negotiating terms at will. Predictably, Bertinotti refused all such offers, arguing that the gulf between *Rifondazione* and the *Ulivo* was too great. By autumn, D'Alema was complaining that the PDS could not afford to hand Bertinotti a victory every three months.[32]

If 1996 created such difficulties between the two major parties of the left, then 1997 may provide a decisive test. Two issues have the greatest potential to usher in real change, but, for this very reason, are going to prove explosive. The first challenge will be to see if the *Ulivo* is able to put any significant part of welfare spending (particularly pensions) on the agenda in 1997. The second will be to see if D'Alema and Berlusconi's seemingly unending waltz around a left-right accord over institutional reforms is finally translated into action. If either of these events occurs at all, it will be notable. If they occur without a break between *Rifondazione* and the PDS and a crisis in the *Ulivo*, it will be nothing short of miraculous.

Notes

1. The exact figure is 21.1 percent of the proportional list vote, as opposed to 20.6 percent for Berlusconi's *Forza Italia*.

2. For more details on the elections and the outcome in Parliament, see the contributions of Luca Verzichelli and Alessandro Chiaramonte to this volume.

3. *Il Corriere della Sera* (29 November 1996). All citations from *Il Corriere della Sera* come from its website at http://globnet.rcs.it and therefore have no numbered pages.

4. S. Menichini, "Rifondazione scopre il gioco. Ma non lo cambia," *Il manifesto*, 14 December 1996. All references to *Il manifesto* were obtained at its website at http://www2.mir.it and therefore lack page numbers.

5. There is a vast literature on various aspects of this transformation. For some of the essential historical details and contextualization, see M.J. Bull, "The Unremarkable Death of the Italian Communist Party", in F. Sabetti and R. Catanzaro, eds., *Italian Politics: A Review*, vol. 5 (London: Pinter, 1991), pp. 23-39; S. Hellman, "The Difficult Birth of the Democratic Party of the Left", in S. Hellman and G. Pasquino, eds., *Italian Politics, A Review*, vol. 7 (London: Pinter, 1992), pp. 68-86.

6. See Simon Parker's contribution to this volume for more details.

7. A. Garzia, "Perché svolto", *Il manifesto*, 2 July 1996, and the extensive discussion of *Rifondazione*'s reactions to this development in *Il manifesto*, 3 July 1996.

8. For some of the flavor of these arguments, see the headings "Dalla critica anticapitalistica alla trasformazione della società. Il nostro progetto" and "Contro Maastricht per l'Europa dei popoli," in the Bertinotti-Cossutta "First Motion", *Rifondazione* Third Congress Documents (definitive versions dated 5 October 1996, obtained from the party's website: http://www.rifondazione.it.

9. See the heading, "Un nuovo partito comunista di massa" in the Bertinotti-Cossutta "First Motion,"*op. cit.*

10. For references to this discussion, see M. Notarianni, "La cosa 2 nascerà dal Prc?", *Il manifesto*, 30 November 1996; (G.f.b.), "Accordo tramontato", *Il Corriere della Sera*, 15 December 1996; S. Menichini, "Compagni per strada, Bertinotti non fa 'Cose'", *Il manifesto*, 15 December 1996.

11. M. Contini, "Il Prc sfida la Cgil: 'Ci siamo anche noi'", *Il manifesto*, 23 July 1996.

12. Based on newspaper accounts as this article was being completed.

13. G. Moltedo, "Il partito che c'è, le tessere che girano", *Il manifesto*, 13 December 1996.

14. In response to these criticisms, a "thematic" congress was held in July 1995, but its scope was quite limited, as the title suggests. For a discussion of this congress, see M. Gilbert, *The Oak Tree and the Olive Tree*, in M. Caciagli and D.I. Kertzer, eds., *Italian Politics: The Stalled Transition* (Boulder, Westview Press, 1996), pp. 101-117, esp. pp. 107-110.

15. P. Scalisi, "La dissoluzione delle strutture organizzative di base dei partiti", in *Polis*, no. 2, 1995, pp. 221-245.

16. The congressional documents are presented under several headings — amendments, contributions, and documents — and can be found at the PDS's website: http://www.pds.it/congresso_97.

17. For Occhetto's remarks, see *Il manifesto*, 6 November 1996. For representative comments from other critics, see G. Fregonara, "I fulmini di D'Alema sui ribelli del Pds", *Il Corriere della Sera*, 7 November 1996, and I. Dominijanni, "Troppo consenso fa male", *Il manifesto*, 6 November 1996.

18. See especially the "post-scriptum" to Item 5 — "Perché sul lavoro e stato sociale non proponiamo emendamenti", contributo n. 1, "Scelte precise, scelte democratiche", from the *Contributi al Congresso* on the PDS congressional website. Hereafter: Contributo 1 (Destra).

19. M. D'Alema *et al.*, "Unire ed innovare la sinistra italiana. Mozione Congressuale," located at the PDS congressional website. Hereafter: Final Motion (Amended).

20. Heading entitled "Una nuova forza della sinistra," in *Congresso nazionale del Pds. Unire ed innovare la sinistra italiana. Mozione congressuale di Massimo D'Alema* (deposited 16 October 1996), located at the PDS website. Hereafter: Original D'Alema Motion.

21. Heading entitled "Principio federativo e nuova unità della sinistra," contributo n. 2, *Contributi al Congresso della sinistra del PDS*, located at the PDS website's congressional documents page. Hereafter: Contributo 2 (Sinistra).

22. Emendamento 7. Primo firmatario Giorgio Mele. "Amendments" section of PDS congressional website.

23. Emendamento 9. Primo firmatario Augusto Barbera, "Amendments" section of PDS congressional website.

24. *Ibidem.*

25. In one of the more grotesque political developments of the year, some of Bettino Craxi's most loyal followers reconstituted the PSI, to general indifference (*Il Corriere della Sera*, 1-2 December 1996).

26. See, for comparative purposes, the first heading of the Original D'Alema

Motion; then "La sinistra e l'Ulivo," in D'Alema *et al.*, Final (Amended) Motion, comparing the latter with heading n. 6, "Rafforzare e far crescere l'Ulivo" in Contributo n. 1 (Destra).

27. Heading '"Proposta di governo" e "sinistra di governo"', in Contributo 1 (Destra).

28. S. Menichini, "Mela amara per D'Alema", *Il manifesto*, 13 September 1996.

29. Heading "La sinistra e la riforma del welfare," in Original D'Alema Motion and in Final (Amended) Motion.

30. Emendamento 3. "Un nuovo e più ampio stato sociale dei cittadini" Primo firmatario Gloria Buffo. "Amendments" section of PDS congressional website.

31. A. Garzia, "'Nessun patto con il Pds'", *Il manifesto*, 15 December 1996.

32. For a good summary of the situation in the summer, see F. Martini, "Il disagio all'ombra di D'Alema", *La Stampa*, 12 July 1996, located at *La Stampa*'s website, http://www.lastampa.it, and therefore unpaginated. For the autumn, see F. Saulino, "Ulivo, cresce il malumore verso il premier", *Il Corriere della Sera*, 3 October 1996.

6

Majoritarian and Proportional Electoral Systems: The Sicilian Case

Orazio Lanza and Riccardo Motta

On 16 June 1996, just sixty days after the general election, elections for the renewal of the Sicilian Regional Assembly were held. The political forces which had faced each other in two competing blocs shortly before each presented separate lists of candidates. The motivation for this choice lay in the region's proportional electoral system which discourages political alliances. In fact, the half-hearted attempts made to reconstitute the two opposing fronts before the election were abandoned almost immediately. In a region which traditionally voted for conservative-leaning and right-wing candidates, the victorious Center-Left had no interest in making the Sicilian elections a continuation of the general election campaign. Defeat in the general election exacerbated the Center-Right's existing internal difficulties, and the Sicilian vote was seen as an occasion to test the internal balance of forces rather than for revenge on the Center-Right's opponents.

Thus Sicilians voted twice in the space of sixty days with two very different electoral systems. Although the principal actors were essentially the same in both elections, what was on offer to the electorate was different. Caution is therefore required in analyzing the results of these elections. However, it is worth considering whether a common thread runs between the two despite the evident discontinuity in moving from a prevalently majority electoral system to a proportional one.

The Election Results

The superiority of the Center-Right over its Center-Left rival in Sicily was never in doubt before either election. With the exception of the

Lazio region, the *Polo del Buon Governo* had achieved its best result there, in terms of both votes and seats, in the 1994 general election, taking 43 of 55 seats in the Chamber of Deputies and 16 of 27 in the Senate. Thus the *Polo* was seeking to confirm and consolidate its position in a region fast coming to be considered a stronghold.

TABLE 6.1. 1996 Sicilian General and Regional Election Results (Percentage of Valid Votes)

		Chamber of Deputies		
	Senate	Majoritarian Segment	Proportional Segment	Regional Assembly
Polo per le Libertà	42.4	52.9		
Forza Italia			32.2	17.1
Alleanza Nazionale			16.4	14.1
Cristiani Democratici Uniti (CDU)			⎱ 8.1	9.2
Centro Cristiano Democratico (CCD)			⎰	9.8
Lista Pannella	6.8	0.3	2.9	
Total Center-Right	49.2	53.2	59.6	50.2
Ulivo	40.4	41.3		
PDS			16.6	14.1
Partito Popolare Italiano (PPI)			5.7	7.4
Lista Dini			4.4	4.9
Dini-PPI				0.6
La Rete				3.6
Greens (*Verdi*)			2.7	1.0
Rete-Verdi				0.6
Rifondazione Comunista			7.0	4.3
Rif. Com.-Verdi				0.5
Alleanza Democratica				0.7
Total Center-Left	40.4	41.3	36.4	37.7
Mov. Soc.-Fiamma Tricolore (MSFT)	5.3	3.1	1.6	1.2
Noi Siciliani	3.2	0.8	1.5	1.8
Cristiani Sociali	–	–	–	1.1
Socialisti Italiani	1.4	0.2	0.3	1.9
Others	0.5	1.4	0.6	6.1
Total Others	10.4	5.5	4.0	12.1
Total	100	100	100	100

Note : The *Polo* did not put up candidates in three Senate districts, the *Ulivo* in one Chamber district.

The clearly positive result obtained by the Center-Right is confirmed by Table 6.1, which summarizes the results for the Senate, Chamber of Deputies (in both majority and proportional sections) and the Regional Assembly. Considering only the two main blocs for the moment, it can be noted that, with the exception of the Senate (where it was not present in three of the fifteen electoral districts), the Center-Right took more than 50 percent of the vote, clearly distancing its Center-Left rival. At the same time, however, the distance between the two formations oscillated noticeably. Bearing in mind that the various elections all took place within the space of sixty days, moreover, the fluidity of the electorate was considerable. In particular, there is a gap of 10.4 percentage points between the Center-Right's most favorable and least favorable results (the proportional vote for the Chamber and the vote for the Senate, respectively) compared with the Center-Left's 4.9.

Even taking into account that Italy is going through a phase of high electoral volatility, these results are unusual. Two different lines of interpretation have been proposed. The first assumes that, since the general and regional elections were very close together in time, voters' preferences will have remained substantially the same. An explanation must therefore be sought in the differences between the electoral systems and in what was on offer to the electorate. In particular, the general election took place with a relatively strong electoral system and highly structured party situation while the opposite was true of the regional elections.

The second interpretation, on the other hand, emphasizes the characteristics of the Sicilian electorate. Two different versions of this interpretation can be distinguished. According to the first, the results of the elections were in line with past experience: Sicily has always demonstrated a higher degree of electoral volatility than the rest of Italy. The electoral behavior of Sicilians had merely confirmed its fundamental characteristics, bringing them out more clearly: the fragile moorings of the past having disappeared, the passage between one electoral arena and another produced discordant and at times almost schizophrenic results. The second version is concerned with the elements of discontinuity with the past. It notes that in general the Sicilian electorate supported the Center-Right to the detriment of the Center-Left. However, it emphasizes the existence (in line with the broader process of change) of a floating electorate which, situated in the area between the two main political formations, was responsible for a high degree of electoral instability.

Each of these interpretations probably places too much emphasis on particular aspects at the expense of others. As we shall see, the old and the new are closely intertwined in the difficult process of transition taking place in Italy, and it is not always an easy matter to attribute a determining influence to one factor rather than another.

The Elections for the Chamber of Deputies

Although in 1996 the *Polo per le Libertà* took a majority of the votes cast, a result it had failed to achieve in 1994, the number of seats it obtained in both the Chamber of Deputies and the Senate (38 and 14 respectively) was noticeably smaller.

The salient, and at the same time contradictory, aspects of the general election can be seen by comparing the results of the majoritarian-voting electoral districts, where the candidates of the *Ulivo* were successful, and the proportional segment. In all but one of the ten districts the same thing happened: the lists composing the *Polo* obtained a majority of the votes for the proportional segment, but it was the candidate of the *Ulivo* who won the corresponding majoritarian-vote district (see Table 6.2). These can be defined as "incongruent" districts. Although this is quite possible under the existing electoral system, the size of the phenomenon is nevertheless significant. In four districts the *Polo* was well ahead of the *Ulivo* coalition in the proportional segment, while the exact reverse occurred in the majoritarian component of the election. In the move between the proportional and majoritarian vote, the *Polo* lost 15 percent of its electoral support, or seven percent of the total votes cast, the equivalent of a medium to small-sized party in its own right.

TABLE 6.2. 1996 Distribution of Votes by Political Grouping in Districts Won by the *Ulivo* (Chamber of Deputies): Majoritarian (M) and Proportional Segments (P)

Electoral District		Center-Left			Center-Right		
		No.	%	Diff.	No.	%	Diff.
Mazara	M	24,732	43.0	+2.3	21,372	37.1	−15.2
	P	22,839	40.7		28,581	52.3	
Termini	M	32,839	48.7	+11.7	31,672	47.0	−12.0
	P	24,294	37.0		38,847	59.0	
Canicattini	M	29,573	50.1	+4.4	24,122	40.9	−7.1
	P	26,274	45.7		27,573	48.0	
Sciacca	M	29,356	48.8	+5.8	23,210	38.5	−14.4
	P	25,203	43.0		30,980	52.9	
Enna	M	35,054	52.4	+8.6	31,868	47.6	−4.8
	P	28,969	43.8		34,714	52.4	
Caltagirone	M	28,307	50.9	+2.8	23,247	41.8	−6.4
	P	26,674	48.1		26,783	48.2	
Augusta	M	31,364	45.3	−1.5	30,977	44.8	−5.3
	P	32,114	46.8		34,339	50.1	
Modica	M	35,939	51.3	−7.6	30,257	43.2	+10.1
	P	29,836	43.7		36,396	53.3	
Vittoria	M	30,820	54.2	+6.1	26,026	45.8	−3.3
	P	26,970	48.1		27,453	49.1	
Gela	M	35,347	55.4	+7.8	24,525	38.5	−8.5
	P	29,846	47.6		29,486	47.0	
Total	M	308,756	48.9	+4.1	267,996	42.4	−9.0
	P	274,779	44.8		315,252	51.4	

The phenomenon described above was present throughout Sicily, including the districts won by the *Polo* (see Table 6.3). With the exception of two districts, including one in which there was no *Ulivo* candidate, the *Polo* systematically lost support in the move between proportional and majoritarian voting while the *Ulivo* systematically did better (with two exceptions).

TABLE 6.3. 1996 Difference (in Percentage Points) between Proportional and Majoritarian Segment Voting in Districts Won by the *Polo* (Chamber of Deputies)

	Center-Left	Center-Right
Trapani	–	+13.6
Marsala	+4.0	–2.0
Alcamo	+5.4	–0.6
Cefalù	+5.3	–5.7
Bagheria	+8.1	–11.0
Partinico	+5.7	–1.8
Palermo–Capaci	+6.7	–3.0
Palermo–Resuttana	+5.4	–1.3
Palermo–Zisa	+9.1	–4.5
Palermo–Libertà	+6.2	–2.9
Palermo–Villagrazia	+8.1	–10.1
Palermo–Settecannoli	+8.8	–4.7
Caltanissetta	+5.7	–13.0
Licata	–0.2	–0.6
Agrigento	+0.3	+0.1
Messina Centro	+5.8	–6.9
Messina–Mata e Grifone	+6.9	–15.0
Taormina	+6.7	–9.6
Milazzo	+6.4	–9.1
Barcellona	+7.5	–8.7
Nicosia	+7.4	–7.8
Paternò	+4.9	–10.2
Giarre	+2.6	–10.6
Acireale	+5.9	–9.3
Gravina	+4.1	–5.4
Catania–Picanello	+4.8	–2.5
Catania–Cardinale	+3.9	–10.0
Catania–Misterbianco	+3.9	–7.1
Siracusa	+4.1	–6.9
Avola	+7.0	–10.0
Ragusa	+4.4	–2.7

A similar discrepancy between voting for proportional lists and in majority districts has been observed in connection with previous general elections and has been put down to "two types of voting behavior: strategic voting and ideological voting. When someone chooses not to vote for their preferred candidate in a uninominal districts because they think they will lose anyway, it is a strategic vote. When someone refuses to vote for the candidate of their own side because they do not like him for some reason and therefore abstain or even vote for an opposing candidate it is an ideological vote".[1] We can discard the first type, which is obviously not relevant to the present case, and concentrate on the second.

On the one hand, the concept of ideological voting furnishes a coherent and plausible interpretation of the divisions present in the vote. On the other, it agrees with post-election commentary attributing the defeat of the *Polo* largely to competition from minor groups, such as the *Movimento Sociale-Fiamma Tricolore* (MSFT), who presented their own candidates. This interpretation suggests a connection between votes for *Alleanza Nazionale* and for the MSFT and in particular that a certain section of *Alleanza Nazionale* voters who voted for that party's list in the proportional quota preferred, where they were present, to vote for MSFT candidates in the majority-voting electoral districts rather than for Center-Right candidates who were some distance from them in political terms. It would also explain the loss of votes from the center, suggesting that, in their turn, the more moderate of the *Polo*'s voters preferred to vote for the opposing side rather than for *Alleanza Nazionale* candidates in the electoral districts. This is certainly a plausible and coherent interpretation, ascribing the difference in votes between the proportional and majoritarian voting to voters on the two extremes of the *Polo*, in particular those from *Alleanza Nazionale* and from the CCD-CDU.

If the above hypotheses were true one would expect a correlation between the performance of MSFT candidates and the party to which the *Polo*'s candidate belonged. This was indeed the case, but in the opposite direction to that expected. Where the *Polo*'s candidates belonged to *Alleanza Nazionale* the MSFT took 5.3 percent of the vote compared with 4.9 percent where they were not. In neither case was there a difference in the MSFT's performance between the proportional and majoritarian votes. Moreover, on the whole *Alleanza Nazionale* candidates did better in majoritarian voting than other candidates of the *Polo* (–5.8 percentage points compared with –8.0 points), which would seem to suggest that any seepage of moderate voters to the opposing formation was not a result of candidates' party allegiances.

Besides lacking empirical confirmation, the interpretation of the divided vote as an expression of ideological voting clashes with the characteristics traditionally ascribed to the Sicilian electorate. Ideological voting depends on a voter being both ideologically inflexible and better informed than the average (since it is necessary to know the leanings of the candidates in competition—on both your own and the opposite side, if possible): in sum, a well informed and ideologically rigid voter. However, if this conclusion is put beside the premise that the divided vote in the 1996 general election was higher in Sicily (and the South) than in the rest of Italy, it would be necessary to conclude that there was a greater prevalence of such voters in these regions than elsewhere. This conflicts with much of the research conducted on voting behavior in Sicily and the South. While this last consideration is the least decisive and empirically founded, it contains a common sense indication of the direction which needs to be further investigated.

The first aspect which needs to be emphasized is that in 1994 also the *Polo del Buon Governo* gained less votes in the proportional than in the majoritarian component of the election. On that occasion also the phenomenon had been present in almost all of the electoral districts (38 out of 41), with a difference of –6.5 percentage points in western and –4.8 points in eastern Sicily.[2] Thus the divided vote cannot be attributed entirely to particular historical factors or fully explained by the character and content of the 1996 election campaign. It should also be borne in mind that the *Polo per le Libertà* took a staggering 60 percent of the votes in the proportional segment, a far greater success than it obtained in any other region of Italy. Finally, it is worth remembering that *Forza Italia* also scored a significant success (taking 32 percent in the proportional vote). The size of this achievement becomes apparent when it is remembered that in the areas which gave most votes to *Forza Italia* after Sicily — Lombardy and Campania — the party reached just a little over 23 percent.

TABLE 6.4. 1996 Differences (in Percentage Points) in Majoritarian and Proportional Segment Voting for the *Polo* and the *Ulivo* According to the Number of Candidates Presented (Chamber of Deputies)

	No. of Candidates			
	2	3	4	5 or More
No. of Districts	11	15	12	2
Polo	-2.9	-7.8	-8.9	-13.6
Ulivo	+6.5	+6.0	+4.3	+5.8

Note: The district of Trapani, in which there was no *Ulivo* candidate, has been excluded.

The picture which emerges from this and our earlier considerations is of a powerful political formation with certain weak points. These weak points proved decisive for the contest in the single-winner electoral districts. The difference in the results obtained by the *Polo* in proportional and majoritarian voting was undoubtedly due to a seepage of votes to the opposing front, but the larger part of that seepage would appear to have gone to minor parties and diversionary lists. Table 6.4 shows, in fact, that while the difference between votes received for single-winner district alliances and for proportional lists always worked against the *Polo*, it varied considerably according to the number of candidates standing in a given electoral district. Where only the *Ulivo* and the *Polo* were in competition, the difference was smallest. It increased considerably where candidates from smaller parties also stood. The same was not true for the *Ulivo*.

The general election results in Sicily confirm that the problems within the Center-Right coalition did not derive from ideological voting[3] but rather from a dispersion of votes between one electoral arena and the other. Further confirmation was provided by the regional elections sixty days later. The importance of the smaller lists was strengthened by the proportional electoral system, which weakened the internal solidarity of the political formations and placed each party in the position of having to defend its own, and only its own, interests.

The Regional Elections

Voting for the renewal of the Sicilian Regional Assembly took place on 16 June 1996 on the basis of pure proportional representation. The only change over preceding regional elections was that voters now had only a single vote.[4] With the collapse of the regional party system it was inevitable that an electoral system of this kind would accentuate a number of trends already present in earlier regional elections. The first was fragmentation, encouraged by an electoral law which required only 150 signatures for a list to be presented. In all, 146 lists representing 47 different political groupings were involved in the elections. In most cases they were present in only one province and were the expression of a multitude of local exigencies. The number of so-called "service lists" had fallen compared with the previous elections, but there were a number of "do-it-yourself" lists representing individual outgoing deputies. The number of autonomist lists, that Sicilian equivalent of *Lega Nord* support which had often been present in earlier regional elections, had also increased.

The number of lists obtaining seats increased compared with the regional elections of 1991 (see Table 6.5), and the lowering of the provincial quotient required for election due to high levels of abstention ensured that some lists won a seat with little more than 10,000 votes, or less than one percent of the vote at regional level. Overall, fifteen political groupings obtained seats, six obtaining a seat despite being present in only one province. The latter had taken place on only one previous occasion, and then it had been only one list.

Fragmentation in the presentation of lists was translated, therefore, into a fragmentation of the party system, both in terms of the number of parties and the dispersal of their support. In fact, the three leading parties obtained only 45 percent of vote between them; in the previous regional elections they had taken 70 percent.

TABLE 6.5. Seats, Lists, and Candidates and Elected Members in 1991 and 1996 Sicilian Regional Assembly

	No. of Seats Assigned		No. of Lists Presented		No. of Candidates	
	1991	1996	1991	1996	1991	1996
Agrigento	9	9	11	14	86	106
Caltanissetta	5	5	9	15	43	71
Catania	18	19	17	22	261	330
Enna	4	3	10	10	36	30
Messina	12	12	14	16	129	181
Palermo	22	22	14	22	270	434
Ragusa	5	5	14	13	68	56
Siracusa	7	7	12	16	76	108
Trapani	8	8	13	18	90	128
Total	90	90	114	146	1,059	1,444

	1991 Elected Members Standing in 1996	1991 Elected Members Re-elected in 1996	Newly Elected Members in 1996
Agrigento	4	2	7
Caltanissetta	2	1	4
Catania	10	7	12
Enna	2	1	2
Messina	6	4	8
Palermo	12	5	17
Ragusa	4	3	2
Siracusa	7	2	5
Trapani	3	3	5
Total	50	28	62

Note: The ex-deputies Nicita and Burgaretta are not included among the "1991 elected members standing in 1996": the former, elected in 1991 and then re-nominated but not elected in 1996, was forced to resign during the legislature; the latter had been a deputy in the 10th Legislature (1986-91) and then a substitute for a few days in the 11th (1991-1996). A number of ex-deputies to the national parliament who had not previously been elected to the Sicilian Regional Assembly are included among the "newly elected members".

Source: Elaborated from information supplied by the Sicilian Regional Assembly, drawn from the daily newspapers *La Sicilia, La Gazzetta del Sud* and *Il giornale di Sicilia,* 18 June 1996, or from P. Scaramozzino, "Un'analisi del voto del 16 giugno per l'Assemblea Regionale Siciliana", a paper delivered in a seminar of the Chair of Regional Law, Faculty of Law, and the Italian Electoral Studies Society, Palermo, 19 July 1996.

This indicates that a number of typical characteristics had been accentuated in 1996 compared with previous regional elections and helps to explain the changes which took place between the general and regional elections of that year. Electoral support for the two coalitions and for individual political forces was significantly different than it had been in the general election and it is interesting to observe to what extent votes shifted between and/or within the two coalitions.

Looking at the results of the two elections firstly from the point of view of the main coalitions, it can be noted that the changes which took place regarded primarily the Center-Right; the Center-Left remained more or less stable (see Table 6.1). It is more difficult to identify the direction of the shift in the vote, however, because there was a notable increase in votes for minor parties between the two elections. These parties did not constitute a single grouping, nor did they constitute a family of politically contiguous parties.

TABLE 6.6. Difference in Votes Received in 1996 General Elections (Chamber of Deputies, Proportional Segment) and Regional Elections

	Palermo Trapani	Caltanis- setta, Agrigento	Siracusa, Enna, Messina	Catania, Ragusa	Sicily
Center-Right	–12.9	–4.0	–8.3	–8.6	–9.4
Center-Left	+0.4	+4.8	–0.3	+1.2	+1.3
Others	+12.5	–0.8	+8.6	+7.4	+8.1

It can be seen from Table 6.6, which shows the percentage difference in the votes obtained by the coalitions in the two elections, that the Center-Left increased its share of the vote by 1.3 points in the regional elections compared to the general election. This trend was uniform throughout Sicily with the exception of the Agrigento-Caltanissetta area. The figures for the Center-Right are more interesting, particularly when they are considered together with those for the smaller parties: the Center-Right lost 9.4 points, the minor parties gained 8.1 points. Moreover, when the various territorial units are considered it is clear that the fall in the Center-Right's vote was not uniformly distributed throughout Sicily and was inversely correlated with gains by the smaller parties. Naturally these figures do not offer the certainty that a massive shift of votes from the Center-Right to the smaller parties took place in the regional elections. They do suggest, however, that the two trends were related, particularly since, as electoral research shows, voting for smaller parties in Sicily is traditionally associated with moderate or right-wing politics.[5]

The final aspect which needs to be noted is that the Center-Right parties were not equally susceptible to competition from the smaller parties. Only *Forza Italia*'s votes varied inversely with that of the smaller parties, while the changes in support for the CCD, the CDU and *Alleanza Nazionale* were uniform across the four geographical areas considered (Table 6.7).

TABLE 6.7. Difference in Votes Received by *Forza Italia*, CCD-CDU, *Alleanza Nazionale* and Minor Parties in 1996 General Elections (Chamber of Deputies, Proportional Segment) and Regional Elections

	Palermo Trapani	Caltanis- setta Agrigento	Siracusa Enna Messina	Catania Ragusa	Sicily
Forza Italia	–17.8	–9.2	–15.3	–14.7	–15.1
CCD-CDU	+10.3	+10.7	+10.3	+11.8	+10.9
All. Nazionale	–2.5	–2.2	–1.0	–2.8	–2.3
Minor Parties	+12.5	–0.8	+8.6	+7.4	+8.1

Coalitions, Parties, and Candidates

It was not only parties and coalitions of parties which fought for seats in Sicily on 21st April and 16th June. There were the candidates too: on 21 April, 119 of them contested 27 Senate seats and 179 the 55 seats for the Chamber. There was thus an average of less than four candidates fighting each seat and to win a (single-winner district) seat generally required at least 30,000 votes in a constituency with 120,000 inhabitants; on 16 June, 1,444 candidates contested the 90 Sicilian Regional Assembly seats (see Table 6.5). Thus there were 16 candidates per seat, and a few thousand votes in a district of over a million inhabitants might be sufficient to be elected.

TABLE 6.8. Levels of Preference Voting in Sicily: 1987 and 1992 General Elections and 1991 and 1996 Regional Elections (Percentage Values)

	1987 General (Chamber)	1991 Regional	1992 General (Chamber)	1996 Regional
Agrigento	54.8	63.4	81.8	86.8
Caltanissetta	44.0	53.5	75.6	82.8
Catania	40.4	51.2	74.8	76.8
Enna	48.6	46.3	74.9	80.2
Messina	58.6	68.8	79.6	82.5
Palermo	49.5	56.1	82.7	78.3
Ragusa	36.4	39.6	71.1	78.5
Siracusa	39.1	50.9	72.5	81.0
Trapani	46.4	50.1	78.5	79.8
Total	47.1	54.9	77.9	80.0

Note: In the 1992 and 1996 elections, the single preference voting rule was operative.

Sources: For the elections of 1987, 1991 and 1992, M. Morisi, ed., *Far politica in Sicilia* (Milan: Feltrinelli, 1993); for 1996, elaborated from information supplied by the Department for Local Entities of the Sicilian Region and/or from *La Sicilia*, *La Gazzetta del Sud* and *Il giornale di Sicilia*, 18 June 1996.

It is not surprising, then, that in the latter case competition between candidates was fierce both within and between parties (thanks also to the single vote rule) and that a dispersion of votes resulted not simply from competition between the parties but also between candidates from "fraternal" lists. In a relatively unstructured party system candidates were in fierce competition both with colleagues from their own lists and competitors from politically contiguous ones.

TABLE 6.9. Levels of Preference Voting in Sicily for Each Political Party: 1992 General Elections and 1991 and 1996 Regional Elections (Percentage Values)

Lists	1991 Regional	1992 General (Chamber)	1996 Regional
Partito Democratico della Sinistra (PDS)	47.9	66.8	77.7
Rifondazione Comunista	27.3	27.3	56.2
La Rete	45.4	82.7	85.8
Verdi	28.6	38.7	63.9
Partito Socialista Italiano	57.2	79.8	—
Partito Socialdemocratico Italiano	47.9	86.4	—
Partito Repubblicano Italiano	43.6	80.8	—
Democrazia Cristiana	64.8	86.6	—
Partito Liberale Italiano	45.7	83.1	—
Movim. Soc. Italiano / Alleanza Nazionale	41.5	59.9	77.7
Lista Pannella	—	22.0	—
Referendum	—	27.0	—
Lega Lombarda	—	31.7	—
Forza Italia	—	—	71.4
CDU	—	—	82.8
CCD	—	—	92.6
PPI	—	—	92.2
Lista Dini	—	—	89.1
Socialisti Italiani	—	—	82.2
Noi Siciliani	—	—	71.2
Movimento Sociale-Fiamma Tricolore	—	—	75.9
Other Lists	—	39.3	81.9
All Lists	54.8	77.9	80.0

Note: In the 1992 and 1996 elections, the single preference voting rule was operative.

Sources: For 1991 and 1992, M. Morisi, ed., *Far politica in Sicilia, op. cit.*; for 1996, elaborated from information supplied by the Department for Local Entities of the Sicilian Region and/or from *La Sicilia, La Gazzetta del Sud* and *Il giornale di Sicilia,* 18 June 1996.

Although it is difficult to make comparisons with the past, it is very likely that this contributed to the fact that on 16 June Sicilian voters improved upon a record they already held, making use of their preference vote for individual candidates within lists as never before. Only two voters in ten voted for a list without voting for a particular candidate (see Table 6.8).

Accepting D'Amico's hypothesis that preference voting should be considered as an indicator of the personalization of the voting process and that this was particularly evident in regional elections in Sicily, where "local factors and the personalization of the voter/party relationship found particularly strong grounds for coming to the fore",[6] then it would seem that the relationship between candidates and voters had a greater effect on the outcome of the vote of 16 June, despite the proportional electoral system, than it did on either 27 March 1994 or 21 April 1996, when a predominantly majoritarian system was in force. For many voters on the latter two occasions, at least at the local level, the choice of which side to support was more important than the choice concerning particular candidates.[7] On the other hand, it is reasonable to suggest that these criteria were reversed on 16 June and that where doing so did not conflict strongly with a voter's normal party loyalties choice of candidate was more important than choice of list.

Personalization of the voting process and widespread use of the preference vote are not new to Sicily, particularly where regional elections are concerned. On 16 June, however, both phenomena were present alongside the single preference vote and in the absence of the parties which had in the past been able to blunt its impact. The ability of parties organized in internal factions to neutralize its effects had been displayed during the 1992 general election, when they preserved their role in electoral organization through the application of strategies based on geographical subdivisions and the distribution of votes.[8] Single-faction, formally unitary parties such as the PDS were less able to adapt and were more exposed to the danger of internal fragmentation, particularly where the seats to be won were few in number.[9]

The evidence from Sicilian regional elections demonstrates that the single preference vote was able to bring about many of the objectives hoped for by its adherents after the main parties organized into internal factions had disappeared.[10] In fact, it is clear that:

1) differences in levels of preference voting between the various parties diminished (Table 6.9). A difference emerged, however, between *Forza Italia* and its customary allies in this respect;

2) the threshold for winning seats fell: Table 6.10, showing the number of votes obtained by each elected candidate per hundred voters in their electoral district, and Table 6.11, showing the number of votes per 100 votes for the list to which the elected candidates belonged, reveal very clearly the type of process taking place. In 1991 most of those elected had required the preferences of at least 5 per hundred voters; with the single preference vote in 1996 more than half those elected required less than 1 per 100 voters and only 14 out of the 90 elected obtained more than 10,000 votes. Only 10 had *not* done so in 1991, with 26

surpassing the 50,000 mark;

3) the role of the party machine and internal currents diminished: election in 1991 for a candidate meant "control" of at least a third of the votes obtained by his/her party's list (either directly or through the current to which he/she belonged) by those who were successful; in 24 cases of the 90 it represented "control" of at least half. Few of the candidates elected in 1996 obtained a third or more of the preferences of those voting their party's list (Table 6.11). Most candidates did not therefore require a strong hold on their local party machine;

4) in many cases the electoral hierarchies established by the parties were overturned by voters. In over 50 percent of the lists obtaining seats the head of the list was not elected.[11] This phenomenon was strongest for the parties who inherited the greater part of the ex-*Democrazia Cristiana*'s vote (the CCD, PPI, *Forza Italia* and the *Lista Dini* in particular) but the PDS and *Alleanza Nazionale* were not immune: in the former case this occurred in 3 cases out of 10, in the latter 3 out of 9).

TABLE 6.10. Percentage of Preferences Obtained by Individual Candidates, Calculated on the Total Number of Voters Cast in the District, in the 1991 and 1996 Regional Elections

	1991		1996	
% of Preferences	No. of Deputies	% of Deputies	No. of Deputies	% of Deputies
Less than 1	5	5.5	42	46.7
1 to 2	11	12.1	26	28.9
2 to 3	9	10.0	14	15.5
3 to 4	9	10.0	5	5.6
4 to 5	7	7.8	1	1.1
5 to 6	8	8.9	1	1.1
6 to 7	10	11.1	—	—
7 to 8	5	5.6	1	1.1
8 to 9	3	3.3	—	—
9 to 10	1	1.1	—	—
10 to 11	7	7.8	—	—
11 to 12	7	7.8	—	—
More than 12	8	8.9	—	—
Total	90	100	90	100

Sources: Elaborated from information supplied by the Department for Local Entities of the Sicilian Region and/or from *La Sicilia*, *La Gazzetta del Sud* and *Il giornale di Sicilia*, 18 June 1996.

Briefly, then, the role of internal party currents and the party apparatus had diminished, voting had become more personalized, and competition within parties had changed character. Certain kinds of party disappeared altogether without, however, any substitute organizations coming along to take their place. Thus part of the traditional political class was able to recycle itself at the same time as local administrators, certain interest groups (the trade unions particularly,[12] but also other organizations present locally[13]) and certain "junction" professions (doctors and lawyers, for example) saw their importance within the hierarchies of weakly-organized political parties increase.

TABLE 6.11. Percentage of Preferences Obtained by Individual Candidates, Calculated on the Number of Voters Voting Their Lists, in the 1991 and 1996 Regional Elections

% of Preferences	1991		1996	
	No. of Deputies	% of Deputies	No. of Deputies	% of Deputies
Up to 5	—	—	—	—
5 to 10	1	1.1	22	24.5
10 to 15	2	2.2	15	16.7
15 to 20	4	4.5	10	11.1
20 to 25	13	14.4	11	12.2
25 to 30	6	6.7	11	12.2
30 to 35	11	12.2	4	4.5
35 to 40	12	13.3	5	5.6
40 to 45	8	8.9	8	8.9
45 to 50	9	10.0	—	—
50+	24	26.7	3	3.3
Total	90	100	90	100

Sources: See Table 6.10.

A number of politically important facts which emerged from the June 16th elections—*Forza Italia's* defeat, the good showing of the CCD and CDU and the impasse reached by *Alleanza Nazionale* and the PDS—need to be considered in the above context. It seems reasonable to suggest that both the strategies adopted in compiling party lists and the performance of individual candidates had an important effect on the outcome of the electoral contest.

Flush with the successes obtained in predominantly bipolar contests at the general elections of 1994 and 1996 and in the European elections of 1994,[14] in which the party's leader, Silvio Berlusconi, had stood personally and competition for preference votes had been low, *Forza Italia* opted for a strategy which depended heavily on the symbolic value of its being a "new" party with "new" candidates, regardless of whether they had local links. The same strategy which had led to success in the prevalently majoritarian general election contests and in the European elections, in other words. Given its weak organizational framework *Forza Italia* may not have had much choice. However, it is clear that it did not produce the results hoped for on this occasion. *Forza Italia* was, at one and the same time, among the parties which lost most votes compared with the general election a few weeks earlier and one of those whose symbol produced the highest "added value" —support not tied to a particular candidate. In fact, as Table 6.9 shows, *Forza Italia*, along with the Communists, was the party with the lowest number of preferences compared to the overall vote obtained. It could reasonably be suggested, therefore, that: a) *Forza Italia*'s candidates did not have strong "control" of their own party electorate and were not in a position to make the best use of their list's electoral potential; b) the party found itself competing over its natural pool of electoral support with organizations which were better prepared, had firmer local roots and were in a better position to take advantage of the personalization of voting characteristic of regional elections.

TABLE 6.12. Previous Experience in Elected Assemblies of Regional Deputies Elected in 1996

	Member of Parliament	Regional Deputy	Never Elected to Local Council	No Previous Experience	Unknown	Total
Forza Italia	—	2	8	5	2	17
All. Nazionale	2	4	8	—	—	14
CDU	—	3	2	1	1	7
CCD	—	6	3	1	1	11
PDS	1	6	4	2	—	13
PPI	1	1	2	2	—	6
Rete	—	3	—	—	—	3
Socialisti	1	—	2	—	—	3
Rifond. Com.	—	—	3	3	—	6
Lista Dini	—	1	1	—	2	4
DIY Lists	—	3	—	—	—	3
Others	—	—	2	1	—	3
Total	5	29	35	15	6	90

Sources: Elaborated from information supplied by the Sicilian Regional Assembly.

There is empirical support for these hypotheses. For example, looking at the way in which the Center-Right's lists, particularly those of *Forza Italia*, the CCD and the CDU, were put together it can be noted that:

1) in addition to the fact that a large number of *Forza Italia* candidates were presumably involved in their first election contest (as the significant number of those actually elected who had no previous election experience would suggest; see Table 6.12), the party's lists in populous municipalities lacked local candidates. The party had privileged municipalities which were the seats of provincial government when selecting candidates. Messina is a typical example in this respect: a large number of *Forza Italia*'s candidates were municipal or provincial councilors from

the provincial seat, while there were no candidates from populous municipalities such as Barcellona Pozzo di Gotta or Milazzo. The results was that *Forza Italia* took 23.5 percent of the vote in the provincial seat, 17.7 percent in the province as a whole, 12.1 percent in Milazzo and only 9.9 percent in Barcellona. In the latter two municipalities the CCD, with local candidates, took 23.1 and 14.3 percent of valid votes cast respectively:

2) the CDU and CCD adopted a strategy relying on the tried and trusted personal organizational machines of the many ex-deputies (Christian Democrat or otherwise) who still sought election and who frequently subordinated their support for a list to being found a place on it.[15]

A significant number of retiring ex-Christian Democrats were candidates in the CDU lists. The CCD's lists were very open, on the other hand, ex-Socialists and ex-Social Democrats standing alongside ex-Christian Democrats. Judging by the results it would appear that the strategies adopted by the CDU and the CCD were rewarded with a certain success.

The figures in Tables 6.12 and 6.13 also allow some hypotheses to be formulated concerning the electoral "impasse" reached by the PDS and *Alleanza Nazionale*. Both parties were faced with a dilemma: should they open up their lists to candidates from outside the party in order to try and win new support or adopt a strategy of closure to try and safeguard the organization from exposure to the centrifugal tendencies unleashed by the single preference vote? It is reasonable to suppose that the latter strategy prevailed in both cases. The PDS counted on the re-nomination of outgoing deputies (a number of whom decided not to seek re-election, however) and also placed a number of party functionaries, leaders of traditionally allied organizations and local administrators in their lists. The single preference vote, however, resulted in internal competition, and the party bureaucracy was defeated in a number of cases, the most spectacular among them being the defeat of the outgoing leader of the PDS group in the Regional Assembly by a "new mayor" and the secretary of the Catanese party federation's defeat by a trade unionist.

In *Alleanza Nazionale*'s case, as indeed in that of *Forza Italia*, the "organizational dilemma" revolved primarily on the strategy to be adopted towards the organizational machines left behind by the collapse of the Christian Democracy, a necessary step for broadening or consolidating the party's electoral base. For *Alleanza Nazionale* excessive openness would have involved the sacrifice of party of its traditional leadership and the opening of electoral space for the MSFT; for *Forza Italia* sacrificing its image as a "new" party. *Alleanza Nazionale*, like the PDS, opted for a defensive strategy and sought to advance a number of local administrators in addition to re-nominating outgoing deputies.

Preliminary analysis would seem to show that strategies based on finding room for electoral machines which already existed at the local level were fruitful. *Forza Italia* obtained its best result in Catania, where it presented two outgoing deputies (Salvo Fleres and Filadelfio Basile), and the same was true of *Alleanza Nazionale* with Giuseppe Roberto Grippaldi, an ex-senator (originally a Christian Democrat and subsequently CCD) in Enna.

TABLE 6.13. Outgoing Regional Deputies Who Stood Again for Election (Columns A) and Were Re-elected (Columns B) in 1996

		List in Which Candidate Stood for Re-election in 1996									
		FI		CDU		CCD		AN		PDS	
Previous List	Seats	A	B	A	B	A	B	A	B	A	B
DC	39	2	1	10	3	3	2	—	—	—	—
PDS	13	—	—	—	—	—	—	—	—	9	6
PSI	15	—	—	—	—	1	1	—	—	—	—
Rif. Com.	1	—	—	1		—	—	—	—	—	—
MSI-DN	5	—	—	—	—	—	—	4	4	—	—
PRI	3	1	1	—	—	—	—	—	—	—	—
PLI	2	—	—	—	—	—	—	—	—	—	—
PSDI	6	—	—	—	—	3	1	—	—	—	—
Rete	5	—	—	—	—	—	—	—	—	—	—
DIY	1	—	—	—	—	1	1	—	—	—	—
Total	90	3	2	10	3	8	5	4	4	9	6

		List in Which Candidate Stood for Re-election in 1996											
		Rif. Com.		*Rete*		*Dini*		PPI		DIY		Total	
Previous List	Seats	A	B	A	B	A	B	A	B	A	B	A	B
DC	39	—	—	—	—	—	—	2	1	3	2	20	9
PDS	13	—	—	—	—	—	—	—	—	—	—	9	6
PSI	15	—	—	—	—	1	1	—	—	2	1	4	3
Rif. Com.	1	—	—	—	—	1	—	—	—	—	—	1	—
MSI-DN	5	—	—	—	—	—	—	—	—	—	—	4	4
PRI	3	—	—	—	—	—	—	—	—	1	—	2	1
PLI	2	—	—	—	—	—	—	1	—	—	—	1	—
PSDI	6	—	—	1	—	—	—	—	—	—	—	4	1
Rete	5	—	—	4	3	—	—	—	—	—	—	4	3
DIY	1	—	—	—	—	—	—	—	—	—	—	1	1
Total	90	—	—	5	3	2	1	2	1	7	3	50	28

Note: Nicita, an ex-PSDI deputy who stood with a "do-it-yourself" list and was not re-elected, is not counted (see note to Table 6.5).

Source: Elaborated from official data.

Conclusions

The general and regional elections in Sicily demonstrate that despite a great deal of electoral fluidity the supremacy of the Center-Right over the Center-Left remained intact and that leakage of votes from one side of the political spectrum to the other was not particularly marked. Thus Sicily showed its traditional, "moderate" face once more and even after the disappearance of the Christian Democracy, the Socialist Party (PSI) and the minor lay parties, the preferences of the electorate continued to lie within the political area these parties had occupied. However, despite being able to call on a deeper pool of electoral support, the Center-Right suffered due to the traditional fluidity of conservative-leaning voters; the different outcomes of the various elections can be explained by its tendency to dispersion, a tendency either checked or accelerated by the particular rules of the electoral contest, the stakes and the options available. In this situation *Forza Italia*, having been created and forged for a specific electoral contest and a long way from its electoral "home", displayed its weaknesses. When the old rules of the electoral game applied, on the other hand, the parties which had emerged from the dissolution of the Christian Democracy tended to have an advantage, while *Alleanza Nazionale* and the PDS took little profit from the highly fluid electoral situation.

The traditional weakness of the Sicilian party system was also accentuated, and the regional elections, which brought together a weak electoral system and a weak party system, resulted in fragmentation. The party organization which had suffered least in the judicial turmoil of the preceding years adopted a defensive strategy, more concerned with self-preservation than winning greater support, when faced with the centrifugal tendencies of the single preference vote. For *Alleanza Nazionale* and the PDS the party organization, however weak, proved to be both a resource and a limitation which it was difficult to ignore. Thus, with the end of the "archipelago" political parties, particularly the Christian Democracy, and their power of aggregation and mediation, and the lowering of the threshold for election, the space for those with personal organizational machines and interests seeking direct political access has been enlarged. However, neither these new organizational machines and parties nor those which emerged from the dissolution of the Christian Democracy appear to have either the capacity for aggregation of their predecessors or, most importantly, the ability to perform equally well in any type of electoral contest.

Although it is extremely difficult to make comparisons where the rules and arenas of competition are different, the general election results would appear to suggest that a partial and artificial reconstruction of the

political parties' capacity for aggregation and function in controlling political access could perhaps be helped by some institutional engineering.
A bipolar contest and a majoritarian electoral system seem to discourage
centrifugal tendencies and facilitate greater demand aggregation.

Translated by John Donaldson

Notes

1. See S. Bartolini and R. D'Alimonte, "La competizione maggioritaria: le
origini del Parlamento diviso", in *Rivista italiana di scienza politica*, no. 3, 1994, p.
677. The authors refer to ideological voting only in connection with the left coalition.

2. Figures referring to the *Polo del Buon Governo* and the *Polo per le Libertà* also
include the Pannella List.

3. See Bartolini and D'Alimonte, "La competizione maggioritaria", *op. cit.*.

4. Sicily is one of Italy's five "special status" regions. It therefore has wide
autonomy and legislative competence over local electoral rules. A number of
statutes amplify the Sicilian region's powers and increase its autonomy. This is
symbolized by the fact that the region's legislature is referred to as an
"assembly" rather than a "council" and its 90 members are called "deputies",
not "councilors".

The system of proportional representation used to elect the Regional Assembly is based on the natural quotient method. Electoral districts correspond with
provincial boundaries, and the number of deputies elected in each of them depends on the resident population at the last census. The quotient is calculated,
therefore, by dividing the total number of valid votes obtained by all the lists in
a province by the number of seats to which it is entitled. Lists are awarded as
many seats as the number of times the quotient is contained in the number of
votes it obtained. The residual seats in each province, not assigned with a full
quotient, are awarded to the lists with the largest remainder vote, including
those lists which did not make a single quotient. The latter has often led to parties presenting a second list (referred to by commentators as a "servant" list) in
order to win a further seat on the basis of the largest remainder vote. In 1991 the
PSI won two seats (one in Agrigento, the other in Trapani) by presenting such a
list, as did the PDS (in Palermo and Ragusa). In 1996 only the PDS presented a
second list, and only in Ragusa, and successfully won a second seat.

Until the 1991 election, Sicilian legislation on the election of regional deputies
gave voters the possibility of expressing three preferences in provinces with up
to 15 seats to be assigned and four in the others (in practice the provinces of Catania and Palermo, the only two electing more than 15 deputies).

5. See A. Anastasi, "Il voto siciliano nel lungo andare (1946-1992)", in M.
Morisi, ed., *Far politica in Sicilia* (Milan: Feltrinelli, 1993).

6. See R. D'Amico, "La 'cultura elettorale' dei siciliani", in M. Morisi, *Far
politica in Sicilia, op. cit.*, p. 250.

7. See O. Lanza, "Catania per esempio. Torna l'offerta di destra sulla piazza elettorale", in *Politica ed economia* , no. 3 (May-June), 1994, pp. 64-68.

8. See G. Pasquino, ed., *Votare un solo candidato. Le conseguenze della preferenza unica* (Bologna: Il Mulino, 1993) and A. Agosta, "Ceto politico e competizione elettorale alla prova della preferenza unica: le elezioni politiche del 1992 in Sicilia", in M. Morisi, *Far politica in Sicilia, op. cit.*, pp. 258-316.

9. Agosta's study of the impact of the single preference vote in Sicily reveals that it produces "different effects within the various parties. Those parties organized into factions, such as the DC, reacted best to the challenges imposed by this innovation, although having to make the necessary adjustments, belying predictions of collapse due to greater inter-personal competition for votes. Parties which tended towards the existence of only one single current, such as the PSI under Bettino Craxi, or which had only recently accepted the reality of internal divisions and in which factions were loosely organized, such as the PDS, demonstrated a lesser capacity of adaptation and risked an increase in fragmentation. In fact, the multiple preference mechanism allowed the hegemonic group within formally unitary parties to entirely control the outcome of voting, particularly when the number of deputies who could be elected was small" (A. Agosta, "Ceto politico e competizione elettorale", *op. cit.*, p. 305).

The "necessary adjustments" mentioned by Agosta refer particularly to the compilation of electoral lists. The internal party currents produced deft strategies for the selection of candidates and, above all, for their territorial distribution, avoiding damaging contests between candidates seeking to exploit the same pool of votes and at the same time seeking to "cover" the entire territory with locally connected candidates.

10. As is well known, supporters of the single preference vote sought to: 1) foster a closer bond between candidates and voters; in other words, to make voting a more personal affair; 2) break up the power of the internal party factions, which were able — in the multiple preference system — to create a multiplying effect on the vote, subordinating the possibility of being elected to possession of a high degree of "control" over the voters of one's own party and rendering possible the one of the classic paradoxes (the candidates preferred by voters were not always the ones to be elected); 3) lower the threshold of votes required for election, thus increasing the chances of weaker candidates, whether from minority currents within the parties or from "civil society" (A. Agosta, "Ceto politico e competizione elettorale", *op. cit.*, pp. 285-286).

Lowering the cost of election campaigns was also an objective. Not much information exists on this subject, but it does not seem to have been attained in Sicilian regional elections. There were rumors of candidates spending fortunes to obtain the few thousands votes necessary for election. In short, the unit price of preferences would appear to have risen.

11. In most of the case where this occurred voters did not respect the hierarchies established by the parties. Although it is true that a number of lists ordered there candidates alphabetically, it is also the case that the main parties (*Forza Italia, Alleanza Nazionale* and the PDS, but also *Rifondazione Comunista* and *La Rete*) designated an official head of the list in most provinces.

12. One of the themes brought out by the regional elections has been competition between the different categories within the trades unions, and within the

CISL in particular, who on occasion supported candidates from different parties (the PPI and the CDU, for example).

13. The various Catholic organizations played a major role, having a far more articulated grass-roots presence in society than the others (with the exception of organized crime, of course).

14. F. Longo, "Il voto in Sicilia fra arena europea e arene statali", in F. Attinà, F. Longo and S. Panebianco, eds., *Identità, partiti e elezioni nell'Unione Europea* (Bari: Cacucci, 1995) pp. 105-123.

15. One of the most striking example of this is Filadelfio Basile, an outgoing local administrator who was still expected to stand for "his" party, the CDU, hours before the lists were due to close. In fact, he stood as a candidate, and was first among the elected, for *Forza Italia*. Thanks in part to the electoral machine Basile brought with him, *Forza Italia* did better in Catania than elsewhere.

7

The Government
of the *Ulivo*

Simon Parker

The founding of the *Ulivo* alliance marked a sea change in the campaigning strategy of the parties of the Center-Left since the disastrous defeat of 1994. The victorious electoral coalition that Berlusconi succeeded in creating at that time, even though it was to end in acrimony and the fall of his government, proved that the old *Progressisti* alliance had to widen its horizons if it aspired to compete with the Right on equal terms. As elections loomed in the early months of 1996, it was equally clear to the *Popolari* who had opposed joining forces with the *Polo* that electoral salvation could only come from an alliance with the ex-PCI and the other forces of the Center-Left. What the neo-Christian Democrats could not accept, however, was that the PDS should lead the alliance. Ironically, the hierarchy of the PDS was of the same opinion, since they reasonably calculated that ex-Christian Democracy voters would not turn around 180 degrees in their voting habits, but they may be persuaded to support a trusted public figure who was identifiably part of the Catholic political tradition without necessarily being a political professional.

Romano Prodi had been a top candidate for prime ministerial office at the time of the fall of the Giuliano Amato government in April 1993. But at that time doubts were expressed on the left over his links with the Christian Democrat establishment, while Mario Segni only gave lukewarm support to Prodi's candidature since he was disinclined to accept the number two post in a future government.[1] This time the omens were far more encouraging. Walter Veltroni had risen to number two position within the PDS and he was a keen advocate of the *Ulivo* campaign which he carefully planned and managed. For example, PDS volunteers for the *comitati per Prodi* were joined by many young people with no previous political experience who were inspired by the anti-partitocratic, pro-European, and socially responsible vision of this unlikely youth hero.

A full analysis of the elections is provided elsewhere in this volume (see Chiaramonte's contribution), but it is worth reiterating that although the Center-Right polled 248,824 more votes than the *Ulivo* and *Rifondazione* combined, Berlusconi and Fini's coalition finished with 78 fewer seats in the Chamber of Deputies than their rivals. This was largely due to the fact that the Center-Left were better organized at the constituency level and their candidates had a stronger appeal to voters in the constituency races than their parties did in the proportional contest. Hence nearly one and a half million votes that had gone to the parties of the *Polo* in the proportional contest ended up electing rival candidates, or splitting the Right's vote (in the case of the *Lega Nord* and Pino Rauti's *Fiamma Tricolore* party) so that the Center-Left candidate could come through on the rails.[2] In other words, the *Ulivo*, by exploiting the anomalies of the electoral system succeeded in being more than the sum of its parts.[3] The *Polo* having been unilaterally divorced by the *Lega Nord* found it difficult to monopolize the center-right vote in Northern and Central Italy and paid a heavy penalty in the constituency elections.

All the President's Men: Romano Prodi's Ministerial Team

Like several of his cabinet colleagues Prodi was not a career politician but a professional initially called to public service in a "technocratic" capacity. He was born into a large family at Scandiano, a small town near Reggio Emilia in the north of Italy's "red belt" in 1939. Having studied economics at the University of Bologna under Beniamino Andreatta, an influential Catholic intellectual who became Defense Minister in his former pupil's government, Prodi later went on to pursue postgraduate studies at the London School of Economics and in the United States. After returning to Bologna to lecture he became director of the university's prestigious Center for Industrial Economics (Nomisma) in the mid-1970s. Prodi's expertise in public sector economics was first used by Giulio Andreotti when he appointed the professor as Minister for Industry for a brief period in 1978.

But it was with his appointment as director of IRI, the massive state industrial conglomerate, in 1982 that Prodi really earned his spurs — describing the experience of battling with politicians and entrenched business interests as "my Vietnam". Prodi's seven years at the helm of IRI were decisive. Although he succeeded in selling Alfa Romeo to Fiat, the sale of SME, the agro-food giant, to Carlo De Benedetti was blocked by

Bettino Craxi for political rather than commercial reasons. Prodi's success at IRI was reflected in the transformation of the company's balance sheet from a 3.056 trillion lire ($1.9 billion) deficit when he arrived to a 1.263 trillion lire ($789 million) surplus when he left in 1989. After returning to university life, Prodi was again called on to reorganize IRI by Prime Minister Ciampi in 1993 following the defenestration of the then-chairman Franco Nobili in the wake of *Tangentopoli*. The successful flotation of Credito Italiano and the Banca Commerciale Italiana, the steel firm Ilva, and SME (this time without Craxi's interference) provided the future Prime Minister with invaluable experience of the inner workings of the Italian state and raised his profile and credibility among domestic reformers and the business community as well as with foreign governments and investors.

In many respects Prodi's prime ministership represents a continuity with the technocratic governments of Carlo Azeglio Ciampi and Lamberto Dini. With Ciampi in charge of the Treasury and Dini at Foreign Affairs the top three posts in government were occupied by centrist reformers, none of whom had been vocational politicians until the 1996 elections. The most independent appointment was certainly that of the enigmatic Antonio Di Pietro, the former magistrate and best known *Tangentopoli* investigator, who was given the Public Works and Urban Areas portfolio for the very good reason that this major spending ministry had been the "locus classicus" of *Tangentopoli*. Who better to clean out the Augean stables of old corruption than the Hercules of *Mani Pulite* himself?

The Justice portfolio which was entrusted to the Turin criminal lawyer, Giovanni Maria Flick, was a more controversial appointment. D'Alema was known not to be enthusiastic, and a number of anti-corruption magistrates expressed misgivings when Flick proposed a "political solution" to *Tangentopoli* after initiating a dialogue with Berlusconi on how best to tackle the corruption crisis. Allegations that the minister was proposing an amnesty for those accused of bribery were, however, vigorously denied, and the minister's proposals to widen the use of domicilary detention for prisoners in *semi-libertà* and to clamp down on the public leaking of criminal investigations and private legal work by public magistrates have mostly been welcomed.[4]

Tiziano Treu at Labor and Augusto Fantozzi at Foreign Trade stood in Dini's *Rinnovamento Italiano* list in the April elections which, although allied to the *Ulivo* coalition, reflected the overlap between the moderates of the *Polo* and the Center-Left. Dini made no secret of his intention to steer the *Ulivo* into the dead center of Italian politics and complained at the "under-representation" of his party despite the fact that, with only 4.3% of the vote, Dini's men acquired a seventh of the ministerial posts — including Foreign Affairs, the number two job in the cabinet.

The Catholic center was well represented by the remnants of the ex-Christian Democratic Party, the progressive faction of which eventually won the battle for control of the PPI and stood as part of the *Ulivo* alliance in the parliamentary elections. The *Popolare* "pasionara" of the Veneto, Rosy Bindi, was awarded the important Health Ministry, former Foreign Minister Andreatta took over at Defense, and the old-style southern Christian Democrat Michele Pinto was given Agriculture. Antonio Maccanico, a former Republican and founder of *Unione Democratica* (a successor party to the PRI and "secular center") assumed the delicate task of overseeing the Rai as Minister for Post and Telecommunications. Maccanico's political background was regarded with suspicion by some on the left given that of all the new ministers Maccanico was the most identified with the old regime, having served in the governments of De Mita and Andreotti. After having served as president of the powerful Mediobanca, he was called upon by President Scalfaro to form a government for institutional reform at the end of the 12th Legislature, but the announcement of a general election cut short Maccanico's prime ministerial ambitions.

Although the PDS took the lion's share of government posts, D'Alema was criticized for not insisting on a greater number of senior cabinet positions for his party. Of these, only the Ministry of the Interior, long-considered a Christian Democrat fiefdom, went to the veteran leader of the reformist wing of the old PCI, Giorgio Napolitano. Other important cabinet level posts were filled by Luigi Berlinguer at Education, Vincenzo Visco at Finance, and Pierluigi Bersani at the Ministry for Industry. Two out of the three women in Prodi's government came from the PDS: Livia Turco took on the Family and Social Affairs brief, and Anna Finocchiaro became Minister for the new post of Equal Opportunities. Both declared their intention to put women at the center of the political agenda, but only Rosy Bindi was to find a place in the cabinet. Largely unknown outside their own party were the new and comparatively young ministers — Edo Ronchi at the Environment and Claudio Burlando, D'Alema's loyal lieutenant and a former mayor of Genoa who presided over Transport. Franco Bassanini, the former Socialist and scourge of Craxi, took on the key (but non-cabinet) brief of Public Administration and Regional Affairs.

On 31 May the new government won its first confidence vote by 322 votes to 299. It was not an overwhelming majority, and without the 35 votes of *Rifondazione Comunista* Prodi's government would have been virtually powerless to impose its will on Parliament. The crucial veto power of *Rifondazione Comunista* deputies was vividly apparent to Fausto Bertinotti when he offered a conditional endorsement to the government's refusal to make concessions to the right over institutional reform. But the *Rifondazione* leader declared himself to be unconvinced by the economic and financial program of the government which tied itself to the twin objectives of implementing the conditions of the Maastricht Treaty and reducing the size of the state budget at all costs.

The Program of the Prodi Government

The *tesi dell'Ulivo* which formed the program for Prodi's electoral campaign ran to 88 items and covered every area of policy from bioethics to judicial reform.[5] Some of its most significant features dealt with the new constitutional reforms which were to mark out the institutional framework of the "Second Republic" as conceived by the Center-Left. The program aimed at encouraging democracy while at the same time allowing democratic institutions to function more responsively and effectively. Stopping short of endorsing the direct election of the Prime Minister, Prodi's program did however propose making it obligatory for each list to indicate which prime ministerial candidate the party would support in the new legislature. No longer would the President of the Republic choose the Prime Minister but a majority of parliamentary representatives. A Prime Minister could only be removed on the basis of a constructive vote of no confidence. Elections to Parliament would be through single member constituencies elected on the basis of the double ballot system. The Senate would be transformed into a Chamber of the Regions organized on similar lines to the German Bundesrat with the regions enjoying the same federal powers as the German Länder with the right to raise taxes, pass laws, and exclusively manage the delegated powers of the state. The regions would also be entitled to their own representation within the institutions of the European Union. All functions other than the core functions of the nation-state (foreign affairs, defense, public order, justice, treasury) were to be devolved to the regions.

This was an impressive range of commitments, but other than the Bassanini law (discussed below), Prodi seemed content to leave the formulation of new institutional reforms to Parliament. In his first speech to the new legislature Prodi instead chose to emphasize the fight against unemployment as the government's key priority. It is therefore worth examining the *Ulivo*'s rather cautious employment policy when compared to former Prime Minister Berlusconi's famously unrealized promise to create a million new jobs.

The measures contained in the *Ulivo* election program centered on a combination of supply-side provisions in regard to education and training (particularly directed at the young unemployed), and a restructuring of welfare and unemployment benefits for the unemployed so that *cassa integrazione* would in future provide only temporary relief for those made redundant. On the demand-side there was a commitment to increasing employment opportunities especially in the tertiary sector, but the promise of new jobs through environmental improvement programs did not specify how many posts would be created or how soon. Of more significance was the carefully worded proposal to increase employment opportunities in weaker sectors of the economy "with the support of the trade unions" by introducing greater wage flexibility but without resorting to the imposition of the "wage-cage" straight-jacket .[6]

A particularly controversial measure was the proposal that the long term unemployed will be required to register with a new *Agenzia per il Lavoro* (Employment Agency) and will be obliged to accept the first offer of a job or undertake socially useful work on behalf of the community. Essentially this is a "workfare" program which is well established in the United States (and President Bill Clinton promised to toughen it still further on his re-election) and which has recently been piloted by the Conservative government in the United Kingdom with nods of approval from the Labor opposition. The fact that this could be included in the *Ulivo* government's program without provoking the veto of the PDS is an indication of the rather different conceptions of "social solidarity" that Prodi and Veltroni now share in contrast to the *no passaran* stance of *Rifondazione* and the trade unions.

There was no immediate cause for the traditional left to mobilize its supporters in defense of the *stato sociale* because Prodi's cabinet showed no desperate urge to blaze a legislative trail in the government's first hundred days or to dance on the corpse of the First Republic as the many who filled the piazzas of Italy brandishing *Ulivo* banners and the hammer-and-sickle on April 22 had hoped. As spring gave way to summer, the faithful were not alone in nurturing a certain disappointment at the lack of visible government achievements. The press which had been so favorable in the aftermath of the *Ulivo* victory soon began to talk of a crisis of leadership and a lack of direction. Ministers and party leaders gave briefings to journalists that pointed up tensions within the coalition and a lack of cohesion within the government.

This sentiment was not limited to the politicians and the lobby correspondents. Three months after its inception, the president of Confindustria, Giorgio Fossa, accused Prodi's government of inertia and a lack of ideas. It appeared not to matter that previous governments with far more solid majorities (e.g., Berlusconi's) had failed to pass any significant legislation, or that Montecitorio was notoriously a Bermuda Triangle into which draft bills disappeared and were never seen again. The *Ulivo* had promised concerted and coherent action, and instead the media were being treated to the familiar spectacle of the different ministries of the archipelago state acting quite independently and often in open conflict with one another. For example, Di Pietro's Ministry of Public Works was busy opening new motorways while Edo Ronchi (the ex-revolutionary communist-turned-Green) Environment Minister promised to put an end to the "cement culture" that had dominated state planning for the last 50 years.

Although many of these criticisms may have been justified, the government had not been as inactive as some of its critics claimed. The commitment to reform of the public administration which had been a key feature of the *Ulivo* election program found expression in a draft bill presented to the Senate in July under the joint authorship of Bassanini, Prodi and Napolitano.[7] This law aimed at "rationalizing and simplifying administrative activity" through "the speeding up, the reorganization and the replanning of administrative procedures".[8] For anyone that has had to stand in line for hours waiting for a residency certificate at a municipal registry office or who has been forced to take time off work to renew their driving license, bill no. 1034 constituted a small revolution against the grinding bureaucracy that is every day life for most Italians. Yet while Prodi's ministers continued to believe in the reformability of the institutions of state within the existing structures, the PDS hierarchy had a grander vision in mind which pointed at the reconstruction of the entire apparatus of the republican state.

The Constitutional Debate

One of the first declarations that Romano Prodi made as Prime Minister was to rule out proposals for a new "constituent assembly" which had nevertheless won support among some sections of the left and which the *Polo* had at least not positively opposed. However, encouraged by an apparent consensus on the need to reform the "Mattarellum" to allow for a greater correlation between constituency and proportional contests (assuming that the proportional element was to be retained) D'Alema began behind the scenes negotiations with the party leaders of the *Polo*.[9]

Talks between Massimo D'Alema and Silvio Berlusconi in late October constituted a preliminary attempt to identify common ground for the Bicameral Commission on Institutional Reform, and this "parliamentary solution" to the problem of institutional reform continued to gather pace in the months ahead. Yet talk of a possible "enlarged majority" involving elements of the opposition provoked a robust response from Bertinotti, who threatened to withdraw his party's support should the political architecture of the government change. Between Prodi and D'Alema a developing tension was revealed when D'Alema was quoted as saying that "reforms were more important than the government".

Clearly two distinct agendas were emerging: for D'Alema and most of the PDS the Prodi government should be seen as a government of transition which would oversee the entry of Italy into EMU, while Parliament (rather than a new constituent assembly) would devise the new institutional architecture that all parties could endorse and which would be followed by fresh elections. For Prodi and many of his ministers, the five year mandate was sacrosanct, and the *Ulivo* program offered the best prospect for the type of institutional reform that moderates and progressives alike could hope for. Prodi did not rule out bringing *Rifondazione* into the government, or even elements of the opposition, but he insisted that a German-style grand coalition would be a denial of the will of the electorate. This stalemate between "the man of the hour" and "the man of tomorrow" gave the press ample opportunity to exploit and exaggerate rifts between the two leaders, and it was a discord—real or imaginary—that the right was not slow to exploit.

Weathering the Storm

We could summarize Romano Prodi's difficulties in the first six months of government in four ways. The structural problem of the *"Rifondazione* factor"—or the potential veto power of the neo-communists over government legislation, and the "Dalemoni factor" which centered not only on the developing rapport between the leader of the PDS and Silvio Berlusconi over the issues of constitutional and judicial reform discussed above, but also on a rising tide of dissent within the PDS over the leadership style of the premier and the perception of the government as a weak policy-maker.

The other two difficulties were episodes rather than long-term causes of government instability, but both events had potential long-term implications for the stability of the nation as a whole. The first involved the new *polo escluso* of Italian politics, the *Lega Nord*, which although polling over 3.75 million votes in the April elections found itself effectively locked out of the Second Republic which Bossi's movement had been partly instrumental in bringing about. The second episode which threatened to provoke a political crisis was the resignation of Antonio Di Pietro following fresh allegations of abuse of public office when he was one of the leading investigators in the Enimont corruption scandal. Both events involving the *Lega* and the "rampant magistracy" indicated just how premature it was to see the *Ulivo* government as constituting a fundamental break with the dramatic conflicts that had brought about the demise of the First Republic. The challenge from the *Lega* is dealt with elsewhere in this volume (see Diamanti's contribution), but it is worth briefly discussing the background to the fall of Antonio Di Pietro, since for many Italians and foreign observers he had come to symbolize the "moral" crusade against the corruption of power in Italy.

Midway through the budget crisis, news of a further dramatic development in the internecine war between the magistrates of Brescia and the *Mani Pulite* investigators in Milan made headlines around the world. The Prosecutors' Office in Brescia let it be known that key members of the *Mani Pulite* team were to be investigated for abuse of public office including the ex-investigating magistrate Antonio Di Pietro.[10] Di Pietro also stood accused of *falso ideologico* for his investigations into the Enimont scandal which had led to the conviction of some of the most powerful business managers in Italy and resulted in the suicide of Raul Gardini.

The response of the Minister for Public Works was immediate: on November 14 he addressed a letter to the Prime Minister from Istanbul, where he was on a ministerial visit, announcing his resignation from the government and the need to rid himself of the "insidious accusations" that had been made against him. Despite a chorus of appeals from the Prime Minister and his government colleagues urging him to reconsider his decision, Di Pietro insisted that his decision was irrevocable. This was a major blow to the government, but as the accusations continued against the ex-minister, Di Pietro appeared increasingly isolated. No doubt some senior figures in the *Ulivo* coalition were even secretly relieved that this loose cannon had been rolled out of the stockade—even if it meant he was now free to fire at will.

With the arrest of the head of the state railways company (FS), Lorenzo Necci and the financier Francesco Pacini Battaglia for corruption and conspiracy by La Spezia magistrates in September, a new chapter opened in the complex story of *Tangentopoli*.[11] It was alleged that for financial motives or in order to protect their informants, certain judges and police officials had not pursued their investigations into suspected criminals as the law required. The hue and cry launched by *Tangentopoli* 2 not only brought an impressive list of powerful figures into the media spotlight, it also resulted in Brescia magistrates pointing the finger of accusation against the original *Tangentopoli* team for their alleged misconduct in the Enimont investigations.[12]

If the departure of Di Pietro, and the renewed attacks against his co-accused in *Mani Pulite* achieved anything it was to raise as an urgent priority the need to regulate a magistracy that was now engaged in a fratricidal war of score settling that threatened to destabilize not just the

political establishment but the administration of justice itself.[13] Even
Prodi was not spared the attentions of a lone magistrate, Giuseppe
Geremia, who (among other charges) wanted to indict the Prime Minister for the sale of the Cirio company on allegedly over generous terms to
a cooperative when he was director of IRI.[14] On this point at least,
D'Alema and Berlusconi appeared to be in full agreement, but when it
came to the primary purpose of government, namely the management of
the public purse, consensus soon gave way to open conflict.

The Battle of the Budget

The *manovrina*, or mini-budget, which was finally approved on June
19 constituted the first real test of the government's ability to steer vital
legislation through Parliament while maintaining the unity of the coalition forces and the support of *Rifondazione*. The measure which raised 16
trillion lire had been an exceptional effort according to Prime Minister
Prodi, and he characterized the measure as above all "equitable". Notably the provisions left out, for the time being, cuts in sensitive areas of
the public sector like the health system which would have provoked a
wave of protest. The *Alleanza Nazionale* leader, Gianfranco Fini, complained that the measures were superficial, not structural, and that the
government was merely buying time by deferring payment on its debt.
Even so, the *manovrina* failed to cover the "hole" in the current debt
which ran to at least 21 trillion lire, and the *manovrina*, as the government admitted, could only be considered a stop-gap measure.

Although the majority parties defended the measure for having protected the more vulnerable sections of the population, they knew only
too well that the real test would come in the autumn with the vote on
the annual budget (*Finanziaria*) for 1997. The budget bill was always
likely to be a source of potential conflict both inside and outside the
Ulivo coalition. In many ways Carlo Azeglio Ciampi had to reconcile the
irreconcilable—to bear down on public finances and to raise additional
tax revenue while ensuring that the financial pain was spread equitably
and without appearing to specifically punish the self-employed and
small business owners (the sector which was notoriously prone to fiscal
evasion).

It was to be a vain hope. In the same weekend in November separate
rallies were organized by *Rifondazione Comunista* in Naples against the
additional taxes on salaried employees, while in Rome, the *Polo* mobilized the small business owners, the self employed and other opponents
of the proposed consolidated property and business tax (IREP) in a demonstration which the organizers claimed involved more than 500,000

people. Bertinotti compared the Naples rally to the demonstration two years previously which had mobilized the largest demonstration in the post-war period against Berlusconi's attack on public pensions.

The *Polo* kept up the pressure on the government by withdrawing its parliamentarians in what was soon dubbed an "Aventine secession" of the Center-Right—recalling the protest of the Socialists against Mussolini in 1924. That Berlusconi should dub Prodi's government a "regime" had obvious connotations which were doubly ironic given the historical origins of *Forza Italia*'s main coalition partner. Government ministers and the group leaders of the majority party were still trying to persuade the *Polo* to return to the floor of Palazzo Madama in December when the *Finanziaria* should have begun the completion of its parliamentary passage—an indication of how big a rift now existed between the *Ulivo* government and the official opposition.

Until this point the government appeared to be on course for a successful budget when on 21 October Bankitalia reduced official interest rates. A move that was interpreted by Prodi and Ciampi as an injection of confidence and a recognition of the government's achievements in containing public expenditure. Relations with the trade unions were proceeding much less smoothly, however, with an inconclusive end to the meeting between the government and the main trade union confederations on the budget proposal at the end of October. Dissatisfied with the provisions announced by Ciampi in the budget, the leaders of the three main trade union confederations announced a general mobilization in defense of employment and against proposed taxes on housing and income that they claimed would hit salaried employees particularly hard. Although Prodi denied that there was a breakdown in relations between the government and the unions, the leader of the CGIL, Sergio Cofferati, warned that unless the government came up with a satisfactory response to the unions' grievances there would be no chance of further talks.

Sensing the isolation of the government from the public, Prodi announced that after the budget had been approved he would appear on television to explain its key provisions. Meanwhile the Prime Minister held face-to-face talks with the leaders of *Rinnovamento Italiano* (Dini) and *Rifondazione Comunista* (Bertinotti) on the IREP tax and the controversial "Eurotax" designed to yield 12.5 trillion lire in a one-off additional income levy. Despite these difficulties, the government could at least congratulate itself on the Chamber of Deputies Budget Committee's approval of a (somewhat pared down) Eurotax which was followed later in the week by approval of the remaining elements of the 62.5 trillion lire budget on the main floor of the Chamber.[15] When the bill reached the Senate, the government conceded further amendments on the Eurotax which removed nearly half of the self-employed tax payers from the levy. The *Ulivo* government had staked its credibility and its future on a fiscal and economic policy that it hoped would keep Italy within the small and exclusive first tier of the "two-tier" European Union that would emerge with the arrival of the euro in 1999. Given that Italy's application for membership of EMU was the single most important and defining policy objective of Prodi's government, it is worth examining the developments in some detail.

The Road to EMU

The publication of the government's economic and financial plan (DPEF) which was to form the basis of the 1997 budget provisions was the first major test of the *Ulivo* administration's economic competence in the eyes of domestic and foreign observers. The treasury team led by former Prime Minister Ciampi came under attack from Italy's own EU commissioner, Mario Monti, who predicted that Italy would not be among the first countries to form part of the Economic and Monetary Union if it adopted these budget proposals. From the left, *Rifondazione* disassociated itself with a policy that threatened significant cuts in public expenditure, as did the main trade union confederation, CGIL, which was worried at the prospect of public sector job cuts and a salaries freeze. Other eminent business figures such as Giovanni Agnelli, former head of Fiat, added fuel to the fire by insisting that "only a miracle" would permit Italy to join EMU in 1999.[16]

An important first step on the road to EMU was taken by Treasury Minister Ciampi in November when he promised that the lira would reenter the Exchange Rate Mechanism of the European Monetary System at "a little above 1,000 lire to the deutsche mark".[17] This was an important signal since earlier in the year the Italian Treasury had come under attack from German financiers who warned that, if Italy and Spain were allowed to join EMU with their present levels of debt, they risked immediately devaluing the new euro currency and thus scuppering the whole project. Ciampi's response was terse and uncompromising—Italy's right to participate in EMU could not be challenged by financial hawks, however well qualified they might claim to be. Neither did he welcome the public misgivings about Italy's membership credentials by other European leaders, a pointed reference to Jacques Chirac who made no secret of his concerns.[18]

Thus Ciampi's budget, as the *Financial Times* pointed out, was "tailor made to meet the Maastricht treaty criterion that requires countries to keep general government borrowing below 3% of gross domestic product".[19] But in a warning to the "Club Med" EU states, which include Italy, Spain, Portugal and Greece, the Bundesbank President Hans Tietmeyer cautioned against attempting to meet the criteria "in a breathless short-term effort.[20] This pronouncement seemed all the more prescient when Prodi's later announcement of an early review of Italy's generous state pension provisions was questioned by his own finance minister.[21] Given that the pensions burden has long been regarded by economists as one of the major causes of Italy's chronic public debt problems, this was not encouraging news for the fiscally austere watchdogs of EMU.[22] With a budget deficit that was expected to reach 130 trillion lire (£54.18 billion) in 1996, or 7 percent of GDP, the "Eurotax" introduced in the autumn budget of 12.5 trillion lire and the additional 13 trillion lire resulting from "treasury operations" even combined with spending cuts of 12.5 trillion lire seemed hardly adequate. But with a primary public surplus (revenue plus expenditure minus debt servicing) of around 5% percent of GDP, Italy's underlying economic performance continued to offer grounds for optimism.

Yet if the budget measures were merely "window-dressing" for the purposes of EMU, commentators wondered how sustainable this tight fiscal policy could be if combined with continuing downward pressure on interest rates. It is true that the cost of paying for the public debt (forecast to be 123 percent of GDP in 1997 as opposed to the 60 percent maximum required by Maastricht) would reduce borrowing by nearly 1 percent of GDP for every 1 percent cut in interest, but fiscal deflation resulting from increased taxation and reduced public expenditure would be bound to slow domestic growth. Giorgio Radaelli of Lehman Brothers doubted that given these factors Prodi's prediction of 2 percent growth for 1997 was sustainable: "You cannot have it both ways: either the cuts will be achieved, and the growth will be slower, or investors won't believe the cuts are credible".[23] Thus the "Made in Italy" lobby's discomfort at the disadvantageous ERM re-entry rate of 990 lire to the deutsche mark merely reflected the belt-tightening resentment of large sectors of Italian society at the sight of a big bill for what for too long Italians had seen as a free meal ticket.[24]

Certainly the re-entry of the Italian lira into the Exchange Rate Mechanism of the European Monetary System on November 25 gave an important morale boost to a government that was looking increasingly beleaguered in the face of internal and external pressures. Ciampi's successful negotiation for re-entry to the EMS gave a fillip to the chances of Italy participating in the first wave of EMU. With the budget successfully through the Chamber of Deputies where the government's majority depended on the support of *Rifondazione*, Prodi's main obstacle had been overcome. Inflation continued to fall and by the end of 1996 it had reached 2.5 percent which was in line with the EU average. With interests rates also declining appreciably and a 60 trillion lire (£23.7 billion) trade surplus (Italy experienced a 90 percent growth in exports following its exit from the ERM in 1992), the Italian economy has been far outperforming its "hard-core" rivals such as France.

However, this rosy picture was somewhat shattered when in an interview with Alan Friedman of the *International Herald Tribune* published at the end of November, Prodi admitted that Italy would not be able to reduce the national budget deficit to the 3 percent required by Maastricht and that the true figure was likely to be 3.3 percent, although his government's own finance bill declared as its objective a deficit of 3.1 percent of GDP.[25] Clearly the government's difficulties were compounded by the unknown factor of future economic growth that all EMU candidates had to factor into their budget calculations, but if Italy hoped to be saved from the tough entry test imposed by the deutsche mark area countries and France, finessing the rules at the last minute was not a strategy that many other European finance ministers were (at least publicly) prepared to endorse.

Conclusion

A far from convincing performance by the *Ulivo* in the Sicilian regional elections in June should have given Prodi pause to reflect on the risks of a "softly, softly" approach to the unveiling of government policy. [26] Although Prodi regarded his own leadership style as *incauto*, by which he probably meant to imply that it was spontaneous rather than incautious, he saw caution as a positive virtue when it came to general government policy. Prodi answered his critics by insisting that the German and Swedish governments had been even more restrained in their deflationary policies than Italy, whereas the mailed fist approach of the Chirac government against the public sector workers in December 1995 had provoked such strident protests that the government was forced to back down. In contrast, Prodi intended to enter Europe "without running people over". [27] This was a noble sentiment, but few even on the government benches believed that the bitter pill of fiscal retrenchment could be sweetened by the knowledge that the sacrifice was being shared by everyone.

Although Prodi encountered strong resistance from the trade unions over the cuts in public expenditure and tax rises, this was as nothing compared to the mass mobilization of organized labor against Berlusconi's attacks on pension entitlements that spelt the beginning of the end for his administration in December 1994. Berlusconi made a point of freezing labor out of the process of government[28], but in its first year the *Ulivo* administration proved to be very open (some would say too open) to representations from every sector of Italian economic and social life. This return to a leadership style, while not formally corporatist, nevertheless recognized the legitimacy of representatives of collective interests as institutional interlocutors. This represented a significant contrast with even the technocratic governments of the Second Republic (Amato, Ciampi, Dini) and could be considered a weakness in terms of an apparent indecisiveness in policy-making and a willingness to compromise too readily for fear of alienating powerful lobbies. The strength of this approach, however, lay in widening the responsibility of government beyond the Council of Ministers to Parliament as a whole and ultimately to the entire electorate.

If, as Lord Dahrendorf claims, virtually everything that the *Ulivo* government has tried or promised to achieve in Italy could have been done equally well by a "good government of the Center-Right" (such as Aznar's in Spain), then the traditional supporters of Italy's progressive parties could be forgiven for being disillusioned.[29] Yet the real significance of the *Ulivo* victory is that the polarized pluralism that long defined Italian politics has been replaced by a centripetal realignment of the party system which has seen both the far right (*Alleanza Nazionale*) and the far left (*Rifondazione*) throwing their support behind centrist governments.

Perhaps Prodi is right to argue that in Italy "the biggest revolution is [the restoration of] normality". But although the European Monetary Institute may eventually be convinced, it will take a lot more to persuade public opinion that "normality" translates into higher living standards and honest, effective and efficient public services.

Notes

1. G. Pasquino and S. Vassallo, "The Government of Carlo Azeglio Ciampi", in C. Mershon and G. Pasquino, eds., *Italian Politics: Ending the First Republic*, vol. 9 (Boulder: Westview Press, 1994), pp. 55-73 at p. 58.

2. In the single member constituency contests the *Ulivo* candidates polled 1,700,384 more votes than the *Polo* (*L'Espresso*, 10 May 1996).

3. On the *Ulivo*'s adept exploitation of the electoral law see G. Pasquino, "Il futuro dell'Ulivo", in *Il Mulino*, no. 3, 1996, pp. 494-501.

4. *L'Espresso*, 15 August 1996.

5. *Tesi per la definizione della piattaforma programmatica dell'Ulivo*, 6 December 1995.

6. *Ibid.*, p. 14. The "wage-cage" is a tool , abolished in the aftermath of the "Hot Autumn", which allowed a worker employed by the same company to re-

ceive a different wage whether the factory or office was located, for example, in Milan or Naples.

7. *Ibid.*, p. 6.

8. *Disegno di Legge* S1034 (Testo Presentato, Versione Provvisoria Non Revisionata), Senato della Repubblica, XIII Legislatura, 23 July 1996.

9. For a discussion of the 1993 electoral reform (known as the "Mattarellum" after Sergio Mattarella, its Christian Democrat architect) see S. Parker, "Electoral Reform and Political Change", *1991-1994*, in S. Gundle and S. Parker, eds., *The New Italian Republic. From the Fall of the Berlin Wall to the Rise of Berlusconi* (London and New York: Routledge, 1996), pp. 23-57.

10. *Il Corriere della Sera*, 14 November 1996.

11. "Il pendolino della giustizia", *Il manifesto*, 17 September 1996.

12. Di Pietro had also been under investigation by the Brescia magistrates for alleged misconduct in his activities as a magistrate prior to *Tangentopoli*. See M. Caciagli and D.I. Kertzer, "Introduction: The Stalled Transition", in M. Caciagli and D.I. Kertzer, eds., *Italian Politics: The Stalled Transition* (Boulder: Westview Press, 1996), pp. 25-40 at p. 37. The nature of Pacini Battaglia's allegation against Di Pietro were not made public when the investigation into the minister was first announced (*Il Corriere della Sera*, 11 November 1996). Subsequently the banker-turned-state's witness was reported to have admitted contacts with a large group of powerful figures in politics and business including Antonio Maccanico (Prodi's Minister for Posts and Telecommunications) and the opposition leader Silvio Berlusconi (*L'Unità*, 2 October 1996).

13. For a fuller discussion of this problem see D. Nelken, "Stopping the Judges", in M. Caciagli and D.I. Kertzer, "Introduction: The Stalled Transition", in M. Caciagli and D.I. Kertzer, eds., *Italian Politics: The Stalled Transition*, (Boulder: Westview Press, 1996), pp. 187-204.

14. "Iri-Cirio, ecco le accuse a Prodi. La difesa del premier: tutto falso", *Il Corriere della Sera*, 30 November 1996.

15. The budget was approved unanimously since the *Polo* deputies had boycotted the Chamber of Deputies.

16. *L'Espresso*, 11 July 1996.

17. In an interview with the Berlin newspaper, *Die Welt am Sonntag*, reported in *Il Corriere della Sera*, 4 November 1996.

18. After having failed to persuade Spain and the other Southern European members of the EU to form a united front in demanding softer convergence criteria (a request to which Germany and France were never likely to accede), Prodi was forced to increase the government's revenue provisions from 40 trillion lire to 80 trillion lire even to have a chance of meeting the deficit requirement. It was inevitable therefore that the government would be forced to return to Parliament in the new year to request further funds.

19. *Financial Times*, 21 October 1996.

20. *Ibidem.*

21. "Prodi calls for pensions debate", *Financial Times*, 25 November 1996. To give some idea of how big is the government's pension obligations: INPS, the state pension scheme required an injection of 72 trillion lire (£28.5 billion) just to cover one quarter of its commitments for 1996.

22. For a detailed analysis of this problem see F. Padoa Schioppa Kostoris,

"Excesses and Limits of the Public Sector in Italy: the Ongoing Reform", in S. Gundle and S. Parker, eds., *The New Italian Republic, op. cit.*, pp. 273-293.

23. *Financial Times,* 21 October 1996.

24. Some analysts believed that the Bank of Italy was intervening to the tune of $18 billion in the month prior to re-entry in order to prevent the lira appreciating too strongly against the deutsche mark. Had the lira gone back in at too much below 1 DM to 1,000 lire the government could expect strong protests from the business lobby. For example, Giovanni Agnelli warned that "anything above 1,000 lire is fine, anything below is bad" (*Financial Times,* 25 November 1996). In the end Italian businesses appeared to accept that its government had negotiated the best deal it could, and with a generous 15% margin within which the lira can float either side of its entry rate before the European central banks have to intervene, the 1,000 lire to the deutsche mark quota appeared to be essentially symbolic.

25. "Prodi says Italy faces uphill battle to Euro", *International Herald Tribune,* 29 November 1996.

26. The Catholic right CCD and CDU doubled its share of the vote with respect to the April general election, displacing *Forza Italia* (whose votes were cut in half) as the largest party in Sicily. The Catholic and liberal wing of the *Ulivo* (PPI and Dini) did somewhat better (up 2 points and 1 point respectively)

27. Interview in *Il Corriere della Sera,* 2 November 1996.

28. See M. Carrieri, "Industrial Relations and the Labour Movement", in S. Gundle and S. Parker, eds., *The New Italian Republic, op. cit.*, pp. 294-307.

29. Interview in *L'Espresso,* 14 November 1996.

8

The Majoritarian System, Act II: Parliament and Parliamentarians in 1996

Luca Verzichelli

When President Scalfaro, noting the failure of Antonio Maccanico's attempt to form a broad government coalition to complete the process of institutional reform, dissolved the 12th legislature before its natural term the crisis of identity of the Italian Parliament returned forcefully to the center of the political stage. The two-year existence of the first Parliament to be elected with a majoritarian electoral system had demonstrated all the limitations of an incomplete transition. Faced with a profound political crisis, electoral reform on its own had not been sufficient to bring about a reduction in the fragmentation of the political parties, let alone a stabilization of the government and its relations with the legislature.

Government instability was not the only sign of the failure of the legislature. The many uncertainties and frequent *coups de théâtre* seemed to suggest that a further period of adjustment (totally unforeseen even a few months earlier)[1] would be required in order to recompose the situation and allow a repositioning of the various actors. In reality the confusion which accompanied the long crisis of the Dini government, with the rise and rapid fall of the so-called *inciucio* (a cross-party compromise, entailing reciprocal advantages, aimed at expanding the government's support in Parliament but which ignores outstanding political and institutional problems) marked the end of a period of transition which had persisted since the fall of Berlusconi's government. This situation had permitted Dini's technocratic government to endure beyond all expectations, the leaders of the two blocs to slowly rebuild their respective alliances and the President of the Republic to continue to play a pivotal political role. Once more the price for all this was paid by the Parliament and the parliamentary class. Parliament as an institution was reduced to a secondary role, forced to wait on developments in the political crisis and paralyzed by the absence of a political majority. As a parliamentary class, those elected in 1994 were faced, in a situation which continued to be dominated by uncertainty, with yet another examination by the electorate.

The return to the ballot box brought with it new questions concerning the destiny of the Italian political class, therefore. In the first place, what consequences might be expected from any changes in support for the various formations which had taken place since March 1994? In other words, what effects would a loss of support for the *Polo per le Libertà*, or a Center-Left victory even, have on the turnover in and sociological profile of members of Parliament? Moreover, important episodes which occurred during the legislature, the *Lega Nord*'s abandonment of the *Polo* and the disintegration of the Popular Party (PPI) in particular, created the conditions, in the north of the country at least, for an electoral campaign completely different to that which had taken place two years earlier.[2] Thus expectations of a further redefinition in the parliamentary class were more than justified.

A number of questions unrelated to the balance of forces between the various political formations also remained, in particular whether or not the new élite which had emerged from the 1994 election would consolidate its position. Did the parliamentary newcomers of that year (70 percent of the total) have a concrete chance of being re-elected, presaging the beginning of a new cycle in Italian politics? Analysis of indicators such as parliamentary turnover and seniority in the various sections of the parliamentary class serves precisely to understand the degree of consolidation of an élite and the characteristics of the process.

Alongside doubts concerning the durability of the novice parliamentary politicians of 1994, however, were others relating to their desire to continue in that role. In particular, were those exponents of *civil society* who had been lent to politics in the vacuum created by the collapse of the First Republic truly willing to continue with their commitment to politics, offering themselves as "permanent" members of the new parliamentary élite? Many observers displayed a certain caution on the matter, and some went as far as to predict a return in numbers of the *professional politicians* momentarily excluded by the 1994 election result.[3] From this point of view, it became interesting to analyze not only the novelties produced by the new election but also the continuities. The spotlight was directed in particular at the personnel of the two political formations which, in a matter of years, had revolutionized the Italian party system: *Forza Italia* (FI) and the *Lega Nord*. At the same time, questions were asked concerning the likely physiognomy of the other parties, all tied in one way or another to the structures, political formations and élites of the past but all grappling also with problems of internal reorganization.[4]

Finally, the more complex problem of the *institutionalization* of the new Parliament appeared on the horizon after the 1996 election. The changes of recent years, brought about both by the introduction of the semi-majoritarian electoral system and stirrings within the party system, have had extremely "damaging" effects on the functioning and stability of Parliament, the most evident being precisely the continual recourse to early elections. Is it now possible, after the second run of the new electoral system, to verify the existence of effects pointing in the opposite direction, contributing to a recomposition of stable procedures and functions within the institution of Parliament? And if this is was indeed the case, in what ways would this "new institutionalization" be different to that which had characterized the first fifty years of the Republic?

The analysis which follows is intended to offer anyone seeking to answer these questions in a more comprehensive and pondered work the essential framework for doing so. The first point to be examined regards the changes produced within the parliamentary class by the 1996 election. The social and political profile of members of Parliament will then be considered, paying particular attention to the differences between the present Parliament and that elected two years ago, immediately following the introduction of the new electoral system. Finally, the prospects for a consolidation of the system of parliamentary groups and of the institutional leadership which has developed within Parliament will be analyzed. While other studies have preferred to use the party affiliations of those elected,[5] the data presented in the tables here has been aggregated on the basis of parliamentary groups (Table 8.1), the only exception being CCD and CDU senators who, for reasons of comparison, are grouped together in subsequent tables. This procedure favors analysis of the internal organizational units of Parliament, distinct both from structures of social articulation (parties and movements) and electoral aggregations (majority coalitions and proportional lists). In the text itself, on the other hand, data on parties in the strict sense will also given when necessary; for example, the PDS is "invisible" when it is incorporated within the larger *Progressista Federativo/Sinistra Democratica* (Federated Progressives/Democratic Left) grouping in the tables.

In this manner it is possible to obtain fresh indications concerning the degree of innovation and internal homogeneity within those groups constituting, in the second Parliament to be elected with the majoritarian electoral system, the nucleus of the parliamentary class which will have to meet the challenges of an important phase in the country's recent political history. Indeed the number and importance of the obligations, sym-

TABLE 8.1. Political Forces and Parliamentary Groups: Chamber and Senate, 1994 and 1996

1994			1996		
Parties Represented	Groups in Chamber	Groups in Senate	Parties Represented	Groups in Chamber	Groups in Senate
Rif. Com.	*Rif. Com.* (39)	*Rif. Com.* (19)	*Rif. Com.*	*Rif. Com.* (35)	*Rif. Com.* (11)
Greens *La Rete*		Greens-*La Rete* (13)	Greens		Greens (14)
PDS *Cristiani Sociali*	*Progressista Federativo* (143)	*Progressista Federativo* (76)	*La Rete** PDS *Comunisti Unitari Cristiani Sociali Laburisti*	*Sinistra Democratica* (172)	*Sinistra Democratica* (99)
PSI *Alleanza Democratica**		PSI (10)			
PPI*	PPI (33)	PPI (34)	PPI *Unione Democratica* PRI	*Democratici Popolari* (67)	*Democratici Popolari* (31)
Patto Segni*			*Lista Dini Patto Segni Socialisti Italiani* MID	*Rinnovamento Italiano* (26)	*Rinnovamento Italiano* (11)
Lega Nord	*Lega Nord* (117)	*Lega Nord* (60)	*Lega Nord*	*Lega Nord* (59)	*Lega Nord* (27)
CCD	CCD (27)	CCD (12)	CCD CDU	CCD-CDU (30)	CCD (15) CDU (10)
Forza Italia	*Forza Italia* (113)	*Forza Italia* (36)	*Forza Italia Federalisti Liberali P. Federalista*	*Forza Italia* (123)	*Forza Italia* (47)
Alleanza Nazionale	*All. Naz.* (109)	*All. Naz.* (48)	*All. Nazionale*	*All. Naz.* (92)	*All. Naz.* (44)
SVP* PVA*	Mixed (49)	Mixed (19)	SVP* PVA* MSFT*	Mixed (26)	Mixed (15)

* Parliamentarians belonging to Mixed group.

Note: For the connections between the various parties, majority coalitions and proportional lists see the tables in Chiaramonte's article in this volume. The size of each group refers to the situation at the beginning of each legislature and includes life senators (they are not included in later statistics). Significant variations in the composition of parliamentary groups took place during the 12th legislature, including the creation of new groups. Fuller analysis of this phenomenon can be found in L. Verzichelli, "I gruppi parlamentari dopo il 1994. Fluidità e riaggregazione", in *Rivista Italiana di Scienza Politica*, vol. 26, no. 2, 1996, pp. 391-413.

bolic and otherwise, which must be met by what is likely to be the final legislature of the century (barring recourse yet again to early elections, naturally) are sufficient to definitively establish the present members of Parliament as the core of the much-heralded (but still uncertain) political elite of the "Second Republic".

The Situation After 21 April: What Has Changed?

A changed parliamentary class emerged from the election of 1996: although distinctly lower than the exceptional peak reached in 1994, the percentage of parliamentarians who had been elected for the first time remained high, particularly in the Chamber of Deputies (44.8 percent, compared with 40.3 in the Senate). The whole of the political spectrum was involved, but renewal was particularly evident in the parties of the center.[6] Parliamentary turnover between 1994 and 1996 is captured in Figure 8.1, which aggregates the Chamber and Senate, and Table 8.2. The general tendency for the percentage of first-time parliamentarians to fall is clear. The sole important exception in the Chamber of Deputies was the PPI, whose parliamentary personnel changed profoundly in the wake of the well-known difficulties experienced in 1995. The party thus had a higher overall ratio of first-time parliamentarians than *Rinnovamento Italiano*, a newly-founded movement.

Other political forces also displayed significant change in their parliamentary personnel, however, only two years after the last election. Among them were the three formations with fewest ties to the traditional Italian parties: the Greens, who had always favored a conspicuous turnover in parliamentary personnel, *Forza Italia* and the *Lega Nord*. The parties (*Alleanza Nazionale* and *Rifondazione Comunista*) and political groupings (*Sinistra Democratica*) most closely linked to the old system, on the other hand, revealed the lowest ratios of first-time parliamentarians. Although falling, the level of parliamentary turnover nevertheless remained high when compared with the past: the 30 percent threshold, considered all but insurmountable during the previous thirty years, had become a "minimum" level of renewal for even the most stable groups in Parliament.

A further phenomenon noted by observers was the reappearance of parliamentarians who had fallen by the wayside in 1994. In reality, with the exception of the *Lega Nord*, the phenomenon was of limited proportions. The total number of such returns to Parliament was 40 (23 in the Chamber and 17 in the Senate), 12 of them concerning representatives of the *Sinistra Democratica* (4.4 percent of the entire grouping). However, the parliamentary groups with the highest percentage of such "recovered" personnel were the PPI (7 in all, or 7.1 percent of the group), *Rifondazione Comunista* (4, or 4.4 percent) and, particularly, the CCD-CDU (5, or 10.9 percent). Although only a small part of the parliamentary class was involved, the links between the new élite in these parties (or at least a significant part of them) and the old political leadership is worth emphasizing.

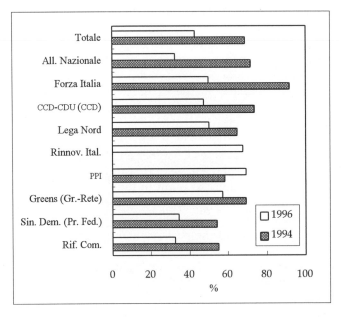

FIGURE 8.1. Newly-elected Parliamentarians (Deputies and Senators) by Parliamentary Group in 1994 and 1996

Data on parliamentary turnover is not enough, however, particularly in a period of frequent elections, to establish whether Italian parliamentarians are consolidating their role within representative institutions, transforming themselves into a significant and stable sector of the political class. It is useful, therefore, to consider electoral seniority in order to see which groups and parties are developing a category of "long-term" parliamentarians (Table 8.2). Today average seniority (understood as the number of times a parliamentarian has been elected prior the present legislature) is around two legislatures in both the Chamber and the Senate, higher than it had been in 1994. The only parties below that average were the PPI and *Rinnovamento Italiano* in the Chamber, *Forza Italia* in both Chamber and Senate and the *Lega Nord* in the Senate. However, with the sole exception of the PPI, average seniority in 1996 was higher than it had been in 1994. The groups with the highest average seniority were *Alleanza Nazionale, Rifondazione Comunista,* CCD-CDU and *Sinistra Democratica.* Disaggregating the PDS from the latter, the percentage of both parliamentarians with average seniority or above (8.3 percent in the Chamber and 10.2 in the Senate) and first-time representatives (40.4 and 27.6 percent respectively) stay at the same levels.

TABLE 8.2. Parliamentary Seniority by Group, 1994 and 1996

Chamber of Deputies	Newly Elected		3 or More Legislatures		Average Seniority (in Legislatures)	
	1994	1996	1994	1996	1994	1996
Rifondaz. Comunista	61.5	40.0	5.9	2.9	1.6	1.9
Sinistra Democratica						
(Fed. Prog.)	58.7	39.9	5.6	9.4	1.7	2.0
PPI	51.5	70.1	15.2	10.4	2.2	1.6
Rinnovamento Italiano		73.1		3.8		1.4
Lega Nord	69.5	50.8		1.7	1.3	1.7
CCD-CDU (CCD)	77.3	46.7	9.1	16.7	1.6	2.0
Forza Italia	90.5	47.2	3.4	4.1	1.5	1.6
Alleanza Nazionale	74.5	32.3	11.8	15.1	1.7	2.1
Total	70.8	44.8	6.0	8.9	1.6	1.9

Senate	Newly Elected		3 or More Legislatures		Average Seniority (in Legislatures)	
	1994	1996	1994	1996	1994	1996
Rifondaz. Comunista	38.9	9.1	27.8	9.1	2.4	2.5
Greens						
(Greens-*La Rete*)	69.2	57.1	7.7	7.1	1.4	1.8
Sinistra Democratica						
(Fed. Prog.)	45.5	27.6	5.2	10.2	1.8	2.2
PPI	45.2	40.7	6.5	18.5	1.9	2.2
Rinnovamento Italiano		54.5		18.2		1.9
Lega Nord	61.7	48.1			1.3	1.9
CCD-CDU (CCD)	66.7	48.1	16.7	12.0	1.8	2.0
Forza Italia	94.4	58.3	2.8	2.1	1.1	1.5
Alleanza Nazionale	64.6	32.6	12.5	16.3	1.8	2.2
Total	58.4	40.3	7.9	9.5	1.7	2.0

Note: Groups given in parentheses refer to 1994 (12th legislature).

A first point can be emphasized then: all of the parliamentary groups linked to formations from the past showed a significant increase in parliamentary seniority compared to 1994. In other words, they demonstrated a greater degree of stabilization in the parliamentary class than newer movements. Further variations emerge from a more detailed consideration. A lesser incidence of senior members (i.e., those present in three or more legislatures) is to be found in the two parties representing an organizational evolution from the traditional parliamentary opposition parties, the Communists (PCI) and the *Movimento Sociale Italiano* (MSI). In the three small formations which succeeded the *Democrazia Cristiana*, particularly the CCD,[7] on the other hand, the importance of long-serving parliamentarians—some of whom had survived successive waves of renewal, others being "recovered" after a longer or shorter absence[8]—was to some extent still felt.

In reality, having been elected for the first time in one of the last three elections, the length of the parliamentary experience of a great majority of the present parliamentary class has been limited. Only 62 deputies (9.8 percent) and 36 senators (11.4 percent) were first elected before 1990. The political class wiped out on 27 March 1994 has certainly not returned simply because the small group of politicians mentioned above have found their way back into Parliament. However, the transformation has been complex and slow. The victory of the Center-Left coalition (in terms of seats), for example, made an important contribution to the quantitative turnover in personnel. However, by substituting a number of newly-elected representatives of the *Polo* with a leadership whose party extraction was more evident than that of *Forza Italia* and the *Lega Nord*, it also set limits on the transformation set in motion in 1994. The re-selection of sitting members of Parliament, particularly marked in the case of some groupings in the victorious coalition, is an indication of the greater continuity in the *Ulivo's* parliamentary class.[9]

The *Lega Nord*, which had lost a conspicuous part of its parliamentary group in the course of the 12th legislature, *Forza Italia*, which failed to represent more than 25 percent of its outgoing deputies and 40 percent of outgoing senators, and the PPI, particularly where the Chamber is concerned, changed their personnel most drastically. New personnel also arrived with the *Lista Dini*, of course, although the latter was also formed in part by experienced politicians (from its Socialist and *Patto* components). Among what might be called the settled parliamentary class, on the other hand, we find the parties heir to the PCI and MSI. The PDS and *Rifondazione Comunista* in particular re-presented a large proportion of personnel already tested in the preceding two elections, although there was more change in the Senate where in the past a part of the old Communist leadership had congregated. Being more important in electoral terms than the old MSI, *Alleanza Nazionale* had a large number of first-time representatives, but at the same time a high percentage re-confirmed from the old parliamentary group.

In general terms, those elected returned to a fairly homogenous pattern as far as women's representation and age are concerned. Women made up 11.3 percent of those elected to the Chamber, compared with more than 15 percent in 1994, and 8.3 percent of the Senate. The lowest levels of female representation were in *Alleanza Nazionale* (with less than 5 percent of parliamentarians being women), the PPI and the CCD-CDU. The two parties of the left, on the other hand, had the highest levels of female representation (above 20 percent in both cases). With regard to age, the *Lega Nord* stands out: deputies' average age is about 40, senators' a little over 50. The difference between these figures and the global averages of 48.1 percent and 53.8 percent respectively, after the three rounds of elections which had seen the rise of Bossi's movement, are an evident sign of the different criteria used in selecting the *Lega*'s personnel.

A further indicator traditionally used for interpreting circulation and turnover within the parliamentary class is average age on entry to Parliament. In this respect the first-time parliamentarians of 1996 were a relatively "old" group, with an average of 47.3 years for the Chamber and 52.2 for the Senate. This brings the overall average (calculated on the basis of all parliamentarians) to 45.5 (Chamber) and 51.1 (Senate), the highest recorded since 1976. The first-time parliamentarians of the *Lista Dini, Forza Italia* and the PPI in particular contributed to raising the average, while the *Lega Nord* had the youngest group (39.4 years and 48.6 in Chamber and Senate respectively). The values for the other formations are all around the average, but a substantial difference emerges when the coefficient of variation is considered.[10] The latter demonstrates a far greater scattering for *Alleanza Nazionale* and *Rifondazione Comunista*. The distribution of the age of first election has a particularly high coefficient for the *Alleanza Nazionale* group in the Chamber (23.5 compared with an average of 20.5). In the Senate, on the other hand, it was the neo-Communist group which displayed the most dispersed distribution (19.4 as opposed to the 15.4 average). It is an important sign that in these two parties the parliamentary selection criteria had to meet the requirement of promoting candidates with very diverse social profiles. In *Rifondazione*'s case this arose as a result of the very different origins of the various groups within the leadership when the party was formed (older PCI exponents who had never before reached Parliament, leaders of the 1980s New Left, etc.). In *Alleanza Nazionale*'s, it might be suggested that a "mixed" selection, rewarding different generations of party exponents, was made.

If the tendency for the actual political class to consolidate confirmed itself and no further shocks were forthcoming from radical reforms of the electoral system, a medium-term scenario with a parliamentary class little different in terms of average age at first election, sex and seniority might be imagined. But there is another important factor to be considered: the stabilization of parties and movements such as *Forza Italia* and the *Lega Nord* who are in a position to strengthen their organization and maintain broad support. It is no accident that the stabilization of the new parliamentary class is much more visible in parties with solid and secure organizational foundations such as *Alleanza Nazionale*, the PDS and *Rifondazione Comunista*. However, the fluidity of the party system means that the situation is a great deal less certain concerning the center parties, from the Catholic parties of the *Polo* through to the PPI. Regarding the *Lega Nord*, meanwhile, the clear signs of renewal brought about by the innovative selection policy which produced a "second generation" political class within the organization, closely identified with the secessionist message and opposition to both of the main political blocs in Italy, have already been emphasized. A number of interesting questions also surround the durability and internal cohesion of the *Lega's* parliamentary personnel.

A Portrait of the Parliamentary Class

So far it has been noted that a particular configuration of the parliamentary class, due in part to the 1996 election, which overturned the political equilibrium created in 1994, in part to the ongoing restructuring of a number of important center parties, has been created. The changes in personnel have involved both the return to Parliament of certain individuals who had already appeared on the national political stage and, for varying motives, an authentic renewal in the representatives elected by some of the parties. In light of this, observation and interpretation becomes even more difficult. Firstly, it is necessary to compare the characteristics of this political class, "renewed" in two stages in 1994 and 1996, with those who dominated the institutional scene until only a few years ago in order to elucidate the differences between them, other than the mere "physical" substitution of parliamentarians. Thereafter it will also be necessary to establish whether or not these characteristics are really determined by selection patterns and career paths within parties and/or geographical areas.

Consideration of parliamentarians' occupational origins confirms what commentators following the 1996 election campaign claimed: a large percentage of parliamentarians elected for the *Ulivo* came from the public sector, while there was a clear predominance of private sector backgrounds among those elected for the *Polo* and the *Lega Nord*. The percentage of deputies from public-sector professions (including academics, the military and magistrates as well as public employees) was 34.3 for the *Sinistra Democratica* (38.6 for the PDS), 40.0 for *Rifondazione Comunista* and 46.3 for the PPI. Only 22.8 per cent of *Forza Italia* deputies were from the public sector, 19.4 per cent of *Alleanza Nazionale*'s and 13.6 per cent of those elected for the *Lega Nord*. The highest percentages of another interesting occupational category, full-time politicians and trade unionists, were to be found in the PDS and *Rifondazione Comunista*, along with *Alleanza Nazionale* (31.4, 17.1 and 15.1 percent respectively), the latter thus showing a rather different profile to both the other parties of the *Polo* and the *Lega Nord*. Looking in more detail (Table 8.3), it can be noted that changes in certain characteristics of the parliamentary class already discernible in 1994 were confirmed in 1996.[11] In particular, the lesser importance of party functionaries among parliamentarians was balanced by the growth of previously marginal categories such as high-ranking bureaucrats and teachers, but also entrepreneurs, managers and members of the non-legal professions. Academics were on the increase slightly compared with past years, lawyers on the decrease.

The occupational distribution within groups varies widely and certain characteristics of segments of the parliamentary class, corresponding to the most important parties and already evident in 1994, are confirmed. In particular, categories such as full-time politicians were concentrated within the left and *Alleanza Nazionale*, public functionaries and academics were strongly represented in the centre parties (but also significant within the *Sinistra Democratica*) as were the liberal professions, particularly lawyers, within *Alleanza Nazionale*. The parliamentary personnel of *Forza Italia* confirmed the party's particular links with the world of entrepreneurs and managers, although selection of candidates for both the Chamber and Senate appears to have shown greater favor towards individuals with public-sector backgrounds than had been the case in 1994. The various Catholic parties exhibited a fairly similar professional profile, with a strong presence of public functionaries but also many representatives of the professions. The small *Rinnovamento Italiano* group displays a similar occupational composition, but the role of the universities and higher ranking public and private administrators was greater, reflecting the particularly strong requirement for social visibility on the part of moderate candidates in the single-winner districts who did not have the support of an extensive party machine.

The *Lega Nord*'s representatives, on the other hand, increasingly rooted within the productive sector of the small and middling middle class, were of rather different extraction than the other sections of the parliamentary élite. Professionals, shopkeepers, artisans and entrepreneurs now constitute over half the *Lega*'s parliamentary representatives. They were from less "visible" professional groups than their colleagues

TABLE 8.3. Professional Origins of Parliamentarians, 1994 and 1996 (% Values)

	Rifondaz. Comunista		Sin. Dem. (Fed. Prog.)		Greens (Gr.- Rete)		PPI		Rinnov. Italiano	Lega Nord		CCD-CDU (CCD)		Forza Italia		Alleanza Nazionale		Total	
	'94	'96	'94	'96	'94	'96	'94	'96	'96	'94	'96	'94	'96	'94	'96	'94	'96	'94	'96
Chamber																			
Political Functionary	28.2	17.1	36.4	31.6	–	–	12.1	9.0	3.8	5.1	1.7	13.6	10.0	3.4	0.8	20.0	15.1	17.6	13.8
Trade-union Functionary	7.7	2.9	2.8	2.9	–	–	6.1	4.5	–	0.8	–	–	–	–	–	3.6	3.2	2.9	2.1
Worker	10.3	17.1	2.8	2.9	–	–	–	1.5	–	0.8	1.7	–	–	–	–	0.9	–	1.6	2.1
Commercial, Artisan	–	–	1.4	–	–	–	–	–	3.8	4.2	10.2	4.5	–	–	0.8	2.7	–	2.2	1.3
Entrepreneur	–	–	0.7	2.3	–	–	–	4.5	7.7	13.6	8.5	4.5	6.7	24.1	22.2	4.5	7.5	8.4	8.1
Manager	–	2.9	–	1.2	–	–	–	–	7.7	2.5	–	–	–	13.8	12.3	–	1.1	3.3	3.3
Lawyer	–	2.9	5.6	4.7	23.1	7.1	3.0	13.4	3.8	9.3	1.7	18.2	10.0	7.8	13.1	21.8	26.9	10.5	11.3
Other Liberal Professions	5.1	11.4	9.1	12.9	53.8	7.1	6.1	9.0	11.5	30.5	40.7	13.6	20.0	17.2	18.9	20.0	16.1	16.3	11.3
Teacher	17.9	20.0	12.6	11.7	–	21.4	21.2	17.9	–	10.2	10.2	4.5	16.7	5.2	1.6	9.1	3.2	10.5	9.4
University Professor	10.3	11.4	11.9	11.7	–	35.7	33.3	14.9	23.1	5.1	–	13.6	6.7	8.6	8.2	–	5.4	8.6	9.7
Public-sector Manager	2.6	2.9	8.4	4.7	15.4	7.1	12.1	10.4	15.4	1.8	–	4.5	6.7	5.2	10.7	2.7	5.4	4.9	6.0
Pubic-sector Employee	10.3	5.7	4.9	7.0	–	7.1	3.0	7.5	15.4	5.1	10.2	18.1	13.3	3.4	3.3	7.3	9.7	5.4	7.8
Other	7.7	5.7	3.5	6.4	7.7	–	3.0	7.5	15.4	3.5	15.3	4.5	10.0	9.5	8.2	5.5	6.5	7.8	8.6
Total	100	100	100	100	100	100	100	100	100	100	100	100	100	100	100	100	100	100	100
(N)	39	35	143	171	13	14	33	67	26	117	59	22	30	113	123	109	93	630	630
Senate																			
Political Functionary	11.1	18.2	9.1	12.2	–	–	3.1	3.7	9.1	–	–	–	–	–	–	2.1	2.3	4.5	5.4
Trade-union Functionary	5.6	–	7.8	9.2	–	–	–	–	–	–	–	–	–	–	–	–	2.3	2.0	3.8
Worker	5.6	–	1.3	2.0	–	–	–	–	–	–	3.7	–	–	–	–	–	2.3	1.0	1.3
Commercial, Artisan	–	–	2.6	–	–	–	–	–	–	6.8	3.7	–	–	–	10.4	–	2.3	0.6	0.6
Entrepreneur	–	–	–	2.0	–	–	12.5	11.1	9.1	23.4	14.8	15.4	–	22.9	6.3	2.1	2.3	10.5	5.7
Manager	–	–	1.3	2.0	–	–	3.1	–	9.1	1.7	–	–	–	14.3	14.6	2.1	2.3	2.9	2.5
Lawyer	5.6	18.2	6.5	5.1	–	–	9.4	14.8	–	6.8	3.7	13.4	–	8.6	12.5	27.7	23.3	10.2	14.4
Other Liberal Professions	16.7	–	10.4	10.2	–	–	15.6	3.7	18.2	22.0	25.9	30.8	–	8.6	4.2	17.0	20.9	15.0	13.3
Teacher	22.2	18.2	10.4	11.2	–	–	6.3	7.4	–	8.5	18.5	23.1	–	8.6	18.8	12.8	9.3	10.5	9.8
University Professor	5.6	9.1	26.0	22.4	–	–	15.6	22.2	27.3	8.5	3.7	7.7	–	17.1	18.8	8.5	9.3	17.2	18.1
Public-sector Manager	5.6	–	16.9	13.3	–	–	15.6	18.5	9.1	3.4	3.7	7.7	–	2.9	14.6	12.8	11.6	9.9	11.4
Pubic-sector Employee	–	18.2	3.9	6.1	–	–	12.5	11.1	9.1	6.8	11.1	–	–	–	6.3	4.3	11.6	4.1	8.6
Other	11.1	18.2	3.9	2.0	–	–	6.3	7.4	9.1	11.9	11.1	–	–	17.1	12.5	4.3	–	8.0	7.9
Total	100	100	100	100	–	–	100	100	100	100	100	100	–	100	100	100	100	100	100
(N)	18	11	77	98	–	–	32	27	11	59	27	13	–	35	48	47	43	315	315

in the *Polo*: artisans rather than big businessmen; white-collar employees rather than managers; shopkeepers or modest professionals rather than lawyers—a faithful reflection of that "local society" which is the backbone of autonomist/secessionist feeling and support for the *Lega*.

TABLE 8.4. Parliamentarians' Party and Local Government Experience Prior to Arrival in Parliament, 1994 and 1996

	Rifondaz. Comunista		Sin. Dem. (Fed. Prog.)		Greens (Gr.-Rete)		PPI		Rinnovam. Italiano
Chamber	1994	1996	1994	1996	1994	1996	1994	1996	1996
None	10.3	17.1	24.1	18.6			42.4	23.9	50.0
Party Only	43.6	42.9	26.6	22.7			30.3	26.9	11.5
Local Govt. Only	–	–	10.3	7.0			12.1	9.0	7.7
Both	46.2	40.0	39.9	51.7			15.2	40.3	30.8
Total	100	100	100	100			100	100	100
(N)	39	35	143	172			33	67	26
Senate	1994	1996	1994	1996	1994	1996	1994	1996	1996
None	5.6	–	26.0	31.6	23.1	28.6	12.9	14.8	36.4
Party Only	22.2	27.3	15.6	15.3	23.1	28.6	3.2	14.8	18.2
Local Govt. Only	5.6	9.1.	26.0	15.3	30.8	–	19.4	11.1	9.1
Both	66.7	63.6	32.5	37.8	23.1	42.9	64.5	59.3	36.4
Total	100	100	100	100	100	100	100	100	100
(N)	18	11	77	98	13	14	31	27	11

	Lega Nord		CCD-CDU (CCD)		Forza Italia		Alleanza Nazionale		Total	
Chamber	1994	1996	1994	1996	1994	1996	1994	1996	1994	1996
None	28.8	22.0	22.7	20.0	72.4	68.3	12.7	12.9	33.7	29.7
Party Only	39.8	23.7	22.7	30.0	11.2	12.2	8.2	18.3	24.0	21.9
Local Govt. Only	9.3	10.2	13.6	6.7	10.3	6.5	10.0	5.4	9.7	7.3
Both	22.0	44.1	40.9	43.3	6.0	13.0	69.1	63.4	32.7	41.1
Total	100	100	100	100	100	100	100	100	100	100
(N)	118	59	22	30	116	123	110	93	630	630
Senate	1994	1996	1994	1996	1994	1996	1994	1996	1994	1996
None	23.3	48.1	–	24.0	58.3	66.7	16.7	18.6	23.8	33.3
Party Only	33.3	14.8	8.3	24.0	8.3	10.2	8.3	18.6	16.8	16.8
Local Govt. Only	13.3	7.4	66.7	16.0	27.8	8.3	22.9	14.0	22.9	11.7
Both	30.0	29.6	25.0	36.0	5.6	14.6	52.1	48.8	36.5	38.9
Total	100	100	100	100	100	100	100	100	100	100
(N)	60	27	12	25	36	48	48	43	315	315

The second group of variables to be considered in this tentative portrait of the parliamentary class is the political-administrative experience of the members of the various groups (Table 8.4). Here only a rapid synthesis of members' political socialization prior to election can be given, concentrating on a comparison between the last two legislatures.[12] The most evident element to emerge from Table 8.4 in this respect is the greater experience of the parliamentary class in 1996. Overall, "complete" political experience (those having held both party and local elected office) returned to above 40 percent, concentrated within three parliamentary groups (*Alleanza Nazionale, Sinistra Democratica* and *Rifondazione Comunista*) which had two things in common: they represented solidly and formally organized parties and, secondly, they were more or less directly related to "historic" political formations.

The case of the *Sinistra Democratica* is particularly interesting. The level of political experience prior to entering Parliament was high overall, and even more so when only the representatives of the PDS are considered. In the latter case, those with both party and local government experience rises to 55.5 percent for the Chamber and 44.2 percent in the Senate. Clearly recruitment of "left-wing independents" without strong prior party socialization remained more typical of the upper chamber. It should also be remembered that many of the 26 *Sinistra Democratica* deputies not attributed to the PDS were also "out-and-out" politicians, hailing from other political formations (*Comunisti Unitari*, Valdo Spini's *Socialisti Italiani*, Social Democrats, Republicans and even some ex-Christian Democrats).

This difference between the Chamber and Senate, also characterizing the *Lega Nord*, CCD-CDU and *Alleanza Nazionale* groups, may be due in part to the difference in electoral procedure: with the proportional recovery mechanism based on voting for pre-arranged party lists, the larger parties could arrange relatively secure seats for particular candidates without having to find them a "stronghold" single-winner seat—a perfect mechanism, therefore, for placing key figures from the national party apparatus.

The groups representing the post-Christian Democrat parties confirm the tendency towards a reinforcement of pre-parliamentary "training". The PPI in particular greatly strengthened its group of politically socialized deputies, at the same time maintaining the robust presence of such individuals already evident in the Senate group in 1994. The representatives of the biggest opposition party, *Forza Italia*, were most clearly different from the others in terms of their pre-parliamentary experiences. Although the number of *Forza Italia* parliamentarians with a background in the party machinery doubled, almost two-thirds of their parliamentary personnel was composed of individuals arriving directly on the national political stage without previous political experience.

Observing the composition of the current Italian Parliament, the impression is that certain prerequisites in terms of political experience have reasserted themselves since 1994. This does not exclude the presence of a number of new and distinctive characteristics, however. Alongside the increasingly numerous group of political novices and representatives of "civil society" was another composed of a small minority of individuals with local administrative experience but no party-political position. To some extent this may be related to recent reforms introducing direct election of mayors and the provincial presidents, a phenomenon which has undoubtedly given this kind of political training greater prestige when compared with internal party life and offices than was the case in the past.

With the important exception of *Forza Italia*, whose recruitment is strongly oriented to the world of finance and production, selection of parliamentary candidates continues to be dominated by the party political dimension. The selection process for *Forza Italia* candidates remains just as centralized as in parties such as *Rifondazione Comunista*, the PDS and *Alleanza Nazionale*, however. Candidates at all levels are chosen by the national leadership and then form the object of negotiation within equally centralized coalitions. All studies conducted on the 1994 election results and initial studies of the most recent consultation confirm this. Although it is possible to interpret aspects of the social profile of Parliament as an attempt to adjust selection procedures in order to increase the representativeness of candidates running in single-winner districts, the degree to which those procedures are centralized and the control every party exercises over its own nominations have not been affected. The real protagonists of the selection process are party secretariats and coalition negotiators, who pay little heed to the local and intermediate levels. The majoritarian electoral system, therefore, has not produced decentralization in the selection of parliamentary candidates, nor has it favored the emergence of a truly alternative model of recruitment. Rather, the powerful role of national party élites has survived.[13]

Differences emerge from looking at those who are selected, as the present study does, and not at those who do the selecting. Although the personnel of the more organized among the political formations all demonstrated evident party-political experience (differing, however, in its intensity and in the "social roles" occupied by candidates), the "new" parties of the 1990s, *Lega Nord* and *Forza Italia* particularly, displayed this characteristic to a lesser degree. Indeed, it was insignificant in the case of *Forza Italia*. An important difference does exist between *Forza Italia*'s parliamentarians and those of the *Lega* in terms of their social "visibility", however. The first represented the "wider society" of the middling and higher strata of the productive sector and, when not "parachuted" in by the national leadership, had regional rather than local links. The latter are representatives of a "local society" identified with the party itself. The *Lega*'s present representatives in Parliament are predominantly long-serving militants already having political-administrative experience under their belts. The greater importance given to prior party-political involvement thus distinguishes them from their ex-allies and from *Rinnovamento Italiano*, the other "new" movement. A firm distinction nevertheless needs to be made between the pre-parliamentary political experience of the *Lega* parliamentarians, limited to the few years of the federalist movement's existence, and that of the parliamentary cohorts of the various small parties of the Center-Right and Center-Left, whose origins lay in the old "unitary" parties.[14]

The picture of the parliamentary class as it has emerged so far contains far fewer surprises than was the case even a couple of years ago. It could be suggested that the larger number of seats won by the Center-Left favored the return of a centralized and party-centered system for the selection of parliamentary candidates, largely due to the ability of the PDS and *Rifondazione* to impose candidates from their party apparatus on their allies and also to impose the professional politicians who compose the smaller parties' leaderships (and who are well represented in Parliament) on their own voters. The high levels of political experience registered in the PPI group would seem to suggest that the moderate wing of the *Ulivo* coalition also retains a party-centered model of parliamentary recruitment, although its organizational diversity from the PDS and *Rifondazione* remains, naturally. Given their continuity with the last generation of the Christian Democrat leadership, the CCD-CDU might be considered as persisting in a clientelist-party model based on a mixture central control and the power of local (party) personalities. This model is also applicable to *Alleanza Nazionale*, although arguably centralization within the party is stronger.

Alfio Mastropaolo has recently carried this reasoning to its limit, arguing that lack of change is more evident in the Italian political panorama in recent years than is change. From this point of view, the changes noted in the socio-political profile of the parliamentary élite are simply the latest stage in a long-term process beginning (but not sufficiently studied) in the late 1970s. The crisis of older generations of politicians, the decline in ideological polarization and the progressive disintegration of the social control exerted by the main parties are all considered factors explaining this process, the early indications of which can be seen in the parliamentary class of fifteen years ago (among the left-wing independents of the time who are now important members of the parliamentary and governing élite, for example).[15]

The evidence presented here contrasts somewhat with the notion of stasis which underlies this interpretation. It is probably overstating the case to consider the impetus for renewal of the 1990s as already exhausted, and it is necessary to emphasize the qualitative changes which have taken place in recruitment to the political élite. There are also other signs of change, however timid, partly as a result of the new electoral system. Although sparse, the evidence supporting such an interpretation merits attention and identifies two sub-groups within the parliamentary class which undoubtedly represent interesting departures from the past. The first is composed of parliamentarians with little experience in the party-political sphere, who were recruited at a relatively late age and who have considerable social status (generally *Forza Italia* but also, with certain variations, *Rinnovamento Italiano*). The second is centered on a class of politicians whose party-political training occurred essentially at local level (*Lega Nord*). At the moment these characteristics apply to limited sectors of the political class, but it is possible to envisage certain of them — over-representation of the "productive sphere" or "local society", for example — being exported to other formations. Naturally the debate on these questions needs to be developed further, considering both variants within the present parliamentary class and comparisons with other countries.[16]

The Institutionalization of the New Parliament

The second problem to be considered is the organizational consolidation of the majoritarian Parliament in the present transitional phase. It is an important problem and certainly cannot be resolved in a handful of pages, on the basis of impressionistic evidence. The very complexity of the issue, however, makes it worthwhile to begin the discussion of the significance of the second election held under the majority system immediately, focusing on the elements which suggest that a stabilization is taking place or, on the contrary, that a further period of adjustments is being experienced. More exactly, we are here concerned firstly with the prospects open to a parliamentary and party sub-system which continues to demonstrate extreme fragility in relations between the coalitions, parties and individuals composing it. Secondly, the role and degree of institutionalization of the new majoritarian parliamentary leadership needs to be considered.[17]

To begin with, returning to Table 8.1, the 1996 election results can be analyzed in terms of the changes taking place in the system of parliamentary groups. A recent attempt to evaluate the question in view of the impact of electoral reform suggested that, given the highly varied nature of Parliament, a relatively long period of realignment was to be expected.[18] The extremely fluidity of the situation in which the 12th legislature found itself from the very beginning, however, suggested that problems of cohesion would arise *within* as well as between parliamentary

groups. This promptly came about. The principal reason for this fragmentation is the persistence of the logic of proportionalism at all levels
of the parliamentary system, pushing parties towards the maintenance
of an independent representation in the two chambers. This was (and is)
abetted by the permissive nature of the regulations regarding the
formation of parliamentary groups. The minimum number of members
required to form of parliamentary group remains 10 in the Senate and 20
in the Chamber.[19] The consequence was that from the very beginning the
12th legislature saw an even greater proliferation of parliamentary
groups than had been the case under the "First Republic". The changes
linked to events between 1994 and 1996 then went to work on this initial
situation.[20]

What has taken place since the second vote held under the majority
system? It would appear, firstly, that the Italian Parliament remains in a
transitional phase, despite signs that the parliamentary party system is
stabilizing. The number of parliamentary groups remains the same as in
the previous legislature; higher, that is, than the average for the 1980s.
Considering the *Sinistra Democratica* group a "natural" progression from
the experience of the *Progressisti Federati* (and ignoring the change of
name demanded by the *Lega Nord* to emphasize its status as an independence movement), the present system of parliamentary groups
would appear unaltered from that of the 12th legislature. Although the
high level of fragmentation persists, the sub-system of parliamentary
parties would appear to be stabilizing.

The parties of the Center-Right are largely responsible for the high
number of parliamentary groups, following the same strategy of autonomy they adopted after the 1994 election. In the Senate the *Polo* is represented by four separate parliamentary groups. The CCD and CDU, who
even presented a joint proportional list, maintain separate parliamentary
groups. Attempts at aggregation have prevailed in the Center-Left, on
the other hand. The *Sinistra Democratica* group contains a larger number
of political formations than its *Progressisti Federati* predecessor.[21] With
the exception of a few members of *La Rete*, who joined the mixed group,
the *Sinistra Democratica* contains all those who stood under the
"European Left" banner for the Senate (PDS, *Comunisti Unitari, Cristiani
Sociali, Laburisti*, the Social Democrat Dante Schietroma and a number of
Republicans who arrived by way of *Alleanza Democratica*). Almost all of
the independents elected for the *Ulivo* coalition also joined the *Sinistra
Democratica* group in Parliament.[22] Two other groups were actually the
aggregations around a proportional list despite bearing the name of a
movement (*Rinnovamento Italiano*) and a party (PPI). Finally, the Greens
and *Rifondazione Comunista* preferred to maintain their autonomy or,
failing that, to join the mixed group.[23] The fall in the number of parlia-

mentarians joining the mixed group is itself a sign of stabilization. As Table 8.1 shows, the number of deputies who were automatically assigned to the mixed group fell from 49 in 1994 to 19 in 1996. A somewhat smaller fall took place in the Senate (26 to 15). In addition to the formations already mentioned, only the representatives of the *Partito Repubblicano Italiano* (PRI), a handful of regional parties and a few independents were part of the mixed group, evidence of a greater coherence between the logic of electoral coalitions and parliamentary groupings.

This initial description suggests that the political fragmentation within Parliament, an evident sign of the party system's imperfections, is not an impediment to the organizational stabilization of the legislature, however difficult that may prove. It may well create a party and parliamentary sub-system capable of surviving for the near future, or at least of avoiding the kind of upsets which have characterized recent years. A hint in this direction comes from the reduction in the instability of individual affiliations. Although there have been a number of important "defections" from one group to another in the early part of the 13th legislature,[24] the continuous stream of such defections which brought new parliamentary groups into (sometimes fleeting) existence in earlier years is no longer evident.

Reinforcement of the representative political class on the one hand, and the creation of an organic and stable relationship between government and parliamentary majority on the other is not, however, sufficient to measure the institutionalization of Parliament. The classic comparative studies have stressed the importance of intervening variables such as internal leadership formation and specialization in creating a stable institutional role within the political-constitutional system. Given the turnover of personnel, the whole of the country's institutional leadership could hardly seem other than completely new following the 1994 elections. The substitutions of Giorgio Napolitano and Giovanni Spadolini by Irene Pivetti and Carlo Scognamiglio were significant from more than a political point of view, but it was the parliamentary group presidencies which demonstrated the principal changes: with the exception of the leader of the PPI group in the Senate, Nicola Mancino, all the holders of this office were new and, as a result of the situation hinted at above and the continual turnover in the leadership of the various formations, would continue to change throughout the legislature.

Over and above "electoral" effects, the staying power of new leadership groups in Parliament needs to be assessed. Certainly, the victory of the *Ulivo,* and the consequent redefinition of the main institutional offices, produced leadership changes providing for greater political experience, as was already clear in the sittings to designate the parliamentary presidencies.[25] It is likely, however, that the parties now in opposition

have also managed to create groups of institutional representatives, reinforcing the higher echelons of their parties. For this reason the whole of
the parliamentary leadership in the past two legislatures is analyzed in
Table 8.5, considering a number of variables discussed earlier. This sector of the parliamentary class, composed of 111 deputies and 100 senators, includes the offices of president, vice-president, quaestor and secretary to the two chambers (the central leadership); presidents, vice-presidents and secretaries of parliamentary commissions (peripheral leadership) and the presidents and vice-presidents of parliamentary groups
(political leadership). The data presented refer to the situation at the beginning of each legislature.

TABLE 8.5. Characteristics of Parliamentary Leadership, 1994 and 1996

Chamber	Average Age		Average Parliam. Seniority		% Already Present in Leadership		% with No Experience		(N)	
	1994	1996	1994	1996	1994	1996	1994	1996	1994	1996
Central Leadership	45.2	49.9	1.4	2.8	38.9	56.3	11.1	17.0	18	16
Peripheral Leadership	47.2	50.0	0.6	1.3	7.7	20.0	29.2	26.2	65	65
Political Leadership	49.5	48.9	1.5	1.9	28.0	63.3	28.0	30.0	9	30
All	47.4	49.6	0.9	1.7	17.6	36.6	25.9	25.0	108	111

Senate	Average Age		Average Parliam. Seniority		% Already Present in Leadership		% with No Experience		(N)	
	1994	1996	1994	1996	1994	1996	1994	1996	1994	1996
Central Leadership	52.8	55.6	1.3	2.2	26.3	57.9	21.8	21.1	19	19
Peripheral Leadership	54.3	54.5	0.7	1.1	11.7	40.6	21.7	19.8	60	64
Political Leadership	54.7	54.7	1.7	1.7	30.8	64.7	15.4	0	26	17
All	54.1	54.8	1.0	1.4	19.0	48.0	20.0	17.3	105	100

Note: Age figures are expressed in years, seniority figures in legislatures. "No Experience"
means no party or political-administrative experience prior to election. "Central leadership"=president, vice-president, quaestor or secretary of a chamber; "peripheral leadership"=president, vice-president or secretary of parliamentary committee; "political leadership"=president or vice-president of parliamentary group.

The group which has imposed itself at the head of the legislature is
socially and politically more stable than the parliamentary class as a
whole. The average age of the three groups analyzed is particularly high
in the 13th legislature, as is the level of parliamentary seniority, the latter
particularly evident in the "central" leadership. Moreover, of those making up the three groups less than 30 percent had no political training
prior to entering Parliament, a fall in the already low level of the previous legislature and below the level of Parliament as a whole. But perhaps the most interesting thing as concerns reinforcement of institutional

leadership was that 36 percent of deputies and 48 percent of senators in the leadership group had already held such a position in the previous Parliament. The greatest continuity was demonstrated by the central and political leadership groups, confirming the prestige attached to holding offices "on the floor of the chamber" (presidency, vice-presidency, quaestor and secretary) and in political representation (president and member of the president's office) compared with positions in parliamentary commissions, the latter frequently allotted to individuals seeking institutional investiture as compensation for having been bypassed for promotion in other fields. The stabilization of the leading positions in Parliament is demonstrated by the re-appointment of a number of important figures and also the promotion of leading politicians to some of these roles in 1996.[26]

In reality the problems arising in each of the above arenas are different. In the parliamentary commissions each party represented requires "visibility" and the few positions available are therefore distributed first at coalition and then at party level. This is a complicated process which can have negative effects on both functional specialization among commission members and the institutionalization of commission leadership. Within the parliamentary groups, on the other hand, the quality of political leadership can be weakened through external control by party structures or élites, deliberately trying to maintain a low level of institutionalization on the part of the parliamentary party in order to exercise direct influence over "their" representatives. Weak parliamentary group organization is traditional in the Italian system, also recurring, in different forms, in the more recently formed political formations.[27] It is evident therefore that in both these sectors of the parliamentary élite the problem of institutionalization cannot be solved simply by a stabilization of personnel or reinforcing its leadership role. A simplification of the general political picture and a realignment of the party system in order to guarantee stability, on the other hand, become crucial. Simply put, only when a handful of "real" parties remain will the distribution of offices on the basis of merit and specialization be possible without too much conflict within and between the various political formations. The "federation" of various parties inside complex parliamentary groupings would also serve this purpose, certainly, but would require low levels of internal conflict in order to ensure a certain degree of continuity to parliamentary life as a whole.

The slow but clear consolidation of that sector of the parliamentary class which has been described here as the "central leadership", on the other hand, may be taken as indicating an institutionalization which bypasses the chaotic situation of the Italian party system. This is suggested by the speeded-up procedures for the selection and nomination of candidates for the various institutional roles agreed in 1996. As far as selection is concerned, a category of institutional representatives reproducing something of the generalized (but not specialized) political experience typical of the preceding historical phase would appear to be taking shape.[28] A solution to the other problem associated with the institutionalization of a parliamentary leadership, the consolidation of stable procedures for election to parliamentary offices which are also recognized by the opposition, is more complex. The entire phase of appointing presidents for the chambers, forming parliamentary groups and appointing their leaderships and selecting those to head them was certainly expedited more quickly than had been the case in 1994. There were problems nonetheless, with spirited protests aimed at the majority by the opposition and points of conflict within the various groupings themselves.[29] The other essential prerequisites for the emergence of a stable and autonomous institutional leadership are long and strife-free legislature and a style of conducting business on the part of the various parliamentary presidencies which is acceptable to all parties.[30]

A new institutionalization of the Italian parliament would appear to be under way, therefore, although many obstacles remain. In particular, the threat of party realignments persists, and the negative effects of the fragmentation caused by an electoral system which permits the survival of numerous political actors is still felt. However, besides the problems caused by the form and stability of the party system, the matter of institutional performance is also crucial. The analysis of the parliamentary leadership conducted here demonstrates that even the present legislature is capable of developing stable rules and procedures, the primary consequence of which would be to reinforce its leadership group but which would also influence its functioning as an institution. The signs are as yet contradictory. Discussion on matters such as the "Di Pietro case" or the legitimacy of the delegations of power included in the 1997 finance bill have been frequent and confused, debate on the country's real problems rare. Answers to the problem of institutional reform have been even less clear. The question of whether the process of reinforcing the institution of parliament progresses beyond the present, uncertain stage will be answered by the legislature itself as it proceeds.

Translated by John Donaldson

Notes

1. A reconstruction of the period of instability which led to the creation and then the continuation of Dini's technocratic government can be found in G. Pasquino, "Il governo di Lamberto Dini", in M. Caciagli and D.I. Kertzer (eds.),

Politica in Italia. Edizione 1996 (Bologna: Il Mulino, 1996), pp. 159-177.

2. A detailed reconstruction of these events and their consequences is offered by A. Di Virgilio, "Le alleanze elettorali: identità partitiche e logiche coalizionali", in *Rivista Italiana di Scienza Politica*, vol. 26, no. 3, 1996, pp. 519-584, and by Alessandro Chiaramonte's contribution to this volume.

3. See R. Brancoli, "Tornano i professionisti della politica" in *Il Corriere della Sera*, 16 April 1996.

4. The organizational and strategic innovations of the new Italian parties are already the subject of an extensive literature. For a thorough analysis of the paths taken by the political parties which have dominated the 1990s see particularly the contributions dedicated to the PDS, the post-DC parties, *Forza Italia*, the *Lega Nord* and *Alleanza Nazionale* in recent volumes of *Italian Politics*.

5. On this subject see L. Verzichelli, "La classe politica della transizione", in *Rivista Italiana di Scienza Politica*, vol. 26, no. 3, 1996, pp. 634-674.

6. 73.1 percent of *Rinnovamento Italiano*'s deputies and 54.5 percent of its senators were new to Parliament. Next was the PPI group with 70.1 and 40.7 percent, the *Lega Nord*, CCD-CDU, *Sinistra Democratica* and *Alleanza Nazionale* following. *Rifondazione*'s group showed the greatest degree of continuity with 40 and 9.1 percent respectively.

7. The data for 1994 already highlighted a greater continuity between the old Christian Democrat leadership and the CCD, a party strongly anchored in ex-DC "fiefs" in Southern Italy. That this is also the case of its ally, the CDU, is confirmed by the 1996 data. Disaggregating the data presented in Table 8.2, it emerges that long-serving parliamentarians accounted for more than 20 percent of CDU representatives in both Chamber and Senate.

8. Beniamino Andreatta, Sergio Mattarella, Nicola Mancino, Pier Ferdinando Casini, Clemente Mastella and Angelo Sanza in the first category, for example, and Ciriaco De Mita, Francesco Merloni, Franco Fausti, Mario Tassone, Agazio Loiero and Tancredi Cimmino in the second.

9. *Rifondazione Comunista*, the PDS and the Greens all re-presented over 70 percent of their deputies and well over 50 percent of their senators. The re-election rate for the *Lega Nord* (roughly 30 percent) and *Forza Italia* are both fairly low, on the other hand, although not for the same reasons. This question is given systematic treatment in L. Verzichelli, "La classe politica in transizione", *op. cit.*

10. The coefficient of variation is the percentage ratio between the standard deviation and the mean value of the distribution.

11. The comparison was made on the basis of data for the 1980s from the *Archivio sulla classe politica* of the University of Siena. For reasons of space the data is not presented in detail here.

12. Comparison over a longer period can be found in M. Cotta and L. Verzichelli, "La classe politica. Cronaca di una morte annunciata" in M. Cotta and P. Isernia, eds., *Il gigante dai piedi di argilla. La crisi della partitocrazia in Italia* (Bologna: Il Mulino, 1996), among others.

13. A not dissimilar argument is made in L. Mattina and A. Tonarelli, "I candidati. Visioni politiche e carriere", in *Rivista Italiana di Scienza Politica*, vol. 26, no. 3, 1996, pp. 483-517.

14. A fuller study would be required to further clarify this important issue.

On the basis of the information presently available, the continuity between the original party of reference of parliamentarians and their present parliamentary group is evident, however. The CCD-CDU group is composed essentially of ex-Christian Democrats. With the exception of a few independents and recent adherents (Nerio Nesi, Giuliano Pisapia and Lucio Manisco are among the better known), *Rifondazione Comunista*'s parliamentary personnel exactly reflects the party's political origins (the pro-Soviet wing of the PCI and extreme left-wing groups earlier absorbed by *Democrazia Proletaria*). Similarly, *Alleanza Nazionale*'s parliamentary group is heavily centered on ex-members of the MSI. On the whole, the groups with the most varied political origins continue to be the *Sinistra Democratica*, on the one hand, and *Forza Italia* on the other, although the reasons for this are obviously very different in each case.

15. A. Mastropaolo gives particular emphasis to the connection between the process of renewal under way in recent years and reactions to invasion over the last fifteen years by a party system centered on "business politicians" (or "political entrepreneurs"). See "Tra rivoluzione e restaurazione. Come cambia (e come non cambia) nel lungo periodo la classe politica", in *Italia Contemporanea*, forthcoming.

16. Empirical work on models of parliamentary selection is now somewhat dated. Useful information can still be found in M. Gallagher and M. Marsh, *Candidate Selection in Comparative Perspective* (Beverly Hills: Sage, 1988) and, naturally, in national studies. Although foreseen in the theoretical literature on changing party forms, the impact of recent institutional and electoral reforms and transformations in party organization require further consideration.

17. Here Huntington's classic definition of institutionalization as "the process by which organizations or procedures acquire significance and stability" (and which Cotta used in his various works on the Italian Parliament) is adopted. However, the analysis conducted below demonstrates that, in light of recent changes at both institutional and party levels, the indicators of parliamentary institutionalization need to be rethought.

18. See A. Manzella, "The First Majoritarian Parliament", in R.S. Katz and P. Ignazi, eds., *Italian Politics: The Year of the Tycoon* (Boulder: Westview, 1996), pp. 135-148.

19. See Article 14 of the both Senate and Chamber regulations, which also foresee a further reduction of this number where the new parliamentary group represents a political formation with national-level organization and widespread geographical presence. The inadequacy of these regulations given the new electoral system has been pointed out from a number of sides, but no modifications have as yet been introduced.

20. For a description of the fluidity of the situation during the 12th legislature, see L. Verzichelli, "I gruppi parlamentari dopo il 1994. Fluidità e riaggregazione", in *Rivista Italiana di Scienza Politica*, vol. 26, no. 2, 1996, pp. 391-413.

21. A group of the same name emerged in the Senate during the 12th legislature, but was composed entirely of a few *Progressisti* from *Alleanza Democratica*, a handful of independents and some life senators from the socialist area.

22. Two candidates who certainly did not have party affiliations, for example, are Federico Orlando and Furio Colombo.

23. As the Greens eventually did.

24. Between the formation of the parliamentary groups in the first week of June and December 1996, the following individuals changed group: Assunta Malavenda (*Rifondazione Comunista* to the mixed group), Gianvittorio Campus (*Forza Italia* to *Alleanza Nazionale*), Nicola Rivelli (*Alleanza Nazionale* to *Forza Italia*), followed by two important cases. Irene Pivetti joined the mixed Group following her expulsion from the *Lega Nord*, and Alessandra Mussolini temporarily left *Alleanza Nazionale* to join the mixed group. Another critical phase followed the presentation of the first budget of the Prodi government: Diego Masi (*Patto Segni*) resigned as president of *Rinnovamento Italiano*'s parliamentary group, which later led to the departure of members of the *Patto* and *Socialisti Italiani* segments. Lamberto Dini implemented a "buying campaign", after which members of CDU, *Sinistra Democratica* and *Forza Italia* joined his group. At the beginning of 1997 CDU and CCD parliamentarians "divorced", and Nicola Miraglia Del Giudice changed group four times in one month.

25. The actual presidents of the two chambers, Nicola Mancino and Luciano Violante were first elected in 1976 and 1979 respectively and always returned to Parliament thereafter. The presidents in office in the previous legislature, Scognamiglio and Pivetti, had only two years parliamentary experience at the moment of their election to the presidencies of Chamber and Senate. On the other hand, a little over two years ago the entire parliamentary contingents of *Forza Italia* and the *Lega Nord* had been newly elected or re-elected for the first time.

26. Differences between parties and in the stability of the leadership within each must be taken into account, naturally. It is undoubtedly the case, however, that the "political quality" of the personnel engaged in the management of parliamentary groups has always been fairly high. Examples can be taken from the past legislature, where many emerging personalities occupied such positions: future ministers such as Cesare Previti, Giuseppe Tatarella and Francesco Speroni; individuals like Cesare Salvi, Beniamino Andreatta and Nicola Mancino; and the *Lega Nord* parliamentarian Pierluigi Petrini (now in *Rinnovamento Italiano*). Mario Segni and Willer Bordon were also directly involved in the management of the *Sinistra Democratica*'s grouping after its formation. The *Sinistra Democratica*'s reappointment of Salvi in the Senate and promotion of Fabio Mussi in the Chamber in the current Parliament suggests the reinforcement of an influential parliamentary leadership, a phenomenon also observable in *Alleanza Nazionale* and *Rifondazione Comunista*. Influential personalities (Sergio Mattarella, for example) are to be found in charge of the PPI group, while *Rinnovamento Italiano* (struggling with internal problems) named Diego Masi and Ottaviano Del Turco to preside over its parliamentary groups, prestigious candidates even if neither is a long-serving parliamentarian. Finally, after the tumultuous events surrounding the parliamentary leadership during the 12th legislature, *Forza Italia* chose two of its most experienced representatives: Enrico La Loggia and Giuseppe Pisanu, both ex-Christian Democrats.

27. Berlusconi, for example, personally censured a number of *Forza Italia*'s parliamentary group leaders (among them Raffaele Della Valle and Vittorio Dotti). Faced with crises during the past legislature, *Rifondazione Comunista* and the *Lega Nord* promptly dropped their entire parliamentary leaderships.

28. See M. Cotta, *Classe politica e parlamento in Italia* (Bologna: Il Mulino, 1979).

29. Two examples: there were protests from the minor parties of the *Ulivo* coalition over the distribution of parliamentary offices; clashes took place within the *Polo*, particularly between the CCD-CDU and *Alleanza Nazionale*, over the choice of nominations for the presidency of the Commission on Rights and Privileges.

30. The problem had already been raised in 1994. After the bitter controversy surrounding the nomination of the president of the Senate both Scognamiglio and Pivetti repeatedly underlined their determination to guarantee equity and impartiality. The presidents of the chambers elected in 1996 have returned to the theme on a number of occasions, obtaining broad support across the political spectrum.

9

The Scalfaro Presidency in 1996:
The Difficult Return to Normality

David Hine and Emanuela Poli

The Constitution and Its Conventions

Whatever the outcome of the decade-long process by which Italy has been seeking to reform its institutions, Oscar Luigi Scalfaro's Presidency will undoubtedly go down in history as an important part of that process. Elected in 1992 by a Parliament still composed of First Republic politicians, Scalfaro had to preside over a series of profound, chaotic changes in political life which undermined old understandings and at least partially renewed the political class. The importance of the Presidency in these circumstances is self-evident. In all those areas in which the institution has hitherto been of significance, its role has been increased by the changes of rules and the questioning of long-standing conventions that have taken place since 1992.

In any case, long before 1992, the presidential role was an ambiguous one. The Constitution identifies the important duties of the President in articles 87, 88, 89, and 92. Had Italy after 1948 had a simple and stable party system based on electorally-endorsed alternation between competing parties or clear-cut coalitions, it is doubtful whether the President would, on the basis of these articles, have played a more controversial role than his counterpart in the Federal Republic of Germany. However, conventions can be as important to written constitutions as to unwritten ones, and where political life is complex and unpredictable, it is unlikely that written rules will be sufficient to define the role of institutions like the Presidency. This has certainly applied in post-war Italy, where there has frequently been a substantive as opposed to a merely formal role for the President in nominating prime ministers and dissolving Parliament, and this role has given rise to extensive constitutional debate about the conventions it has generated.[1]

The most important roles concern government formation, the dissolution of Parliament, and the making of public statements by the President. In these debates there is broad agreement that Presidents have on occasions acted to put pressure on prime ministers to form their governments in particular ways, or with particular programs. There is also agreement that the President of the Republic has often played some significant role in the dissolution process, at least in relation to the choice of who shall head the government in the run-up to the election, if not also in relation to the decision on dissolution.[2] Where there is much less agreement is on whether this form of behavior is legitimate, and whether it has occurred sufficiently often to have gelled into a set of constitutional conventions.

Similar ambiguity hangs over the presidential power of public utterance. Strictly, the Constitution limits the power of the President to making declarations to Parliament. In reality, unless he maintains a trappist silence on the many public occasions at which he is present and pressed by journalists to comment, the President is often likely to make his public declarations to a broader audience as well. As long as these utterances cannot be construed to breach the Constitution (in which case they would run foul of art. 90 of the Constitution and render him liable to impeachment), they can be judged politically unwise, but not unconstitutional. Although most commentators *assume* the President should be neutral in his public statements, there is no absolute constitutional requirement of such a condition, and at the margin no way of knowing what would fulfill it. And behind every judgment about the President's constitutional duty of political impartiality is the uncomfortable fact that Presidents are *elected* on a political basis at the outset of their term of office.

Debates among constitutional experts seeking to define a precise role for the President of the Republic have therefore inevitably been inconclusive. Strict constructionalists do not have enough to go on if they rely on the Constitution alone. But proponents of a "living Constitution" lack long-term, consistent, and stable patterns of presidential behavior which enable them to identify clear-cut conventions which fill out the written Constitution in each of the real-world situations in which a President may find himself. All of this was evident even before the Presidency of Oscar Luigi Scalfaro, but several factors have combined to make the debate about the presidential role even more sensitive and ambivalent since 1992.

The Significance of the Scalfaro Presidency

The most important is the way in which the electorate itself may have altered its attitude towards the Presidency as an institution. Some factors in this equation appear to have generated public support for a stronger role for the President, either as an *arbitrator* under broadly unchanged constitutional rules, or as a chief-executive President under (French-style) semi-presidentialism, or even an (American-style) fully separated presidential system. However, other factors in the equation point towards a public preference for a reduced presidential role, linked to a simplified and more clear-cut bipolar party system in which electoral choice leads directly to a definable parliamentary majority.

The former preference may be thought to be a direct consequence of a situation in which individual politicians, and whole parties, have been discredited by political corruption. In such circumstances, the institutions that guarantee the proper functioning of democracy have come to assume an uncharacteristically high profile in public life. As a result, some degree of public trust and some subconscious attribution of legitimacy have probably been transferred from parties and politicians to the holders of offices such as the Presidency of the Republic, the Presidencies of the two chambers of Parliament, the judges of the Constitutional Court, and the investigating judiciary. Moreover, when, as recently, institutional reform occupies an important place on the political agenda, it is easy to confuse rules for taking decisions with decisions themselves. If the rules are imprecise, or if the umpires start expressing preferences about new rules to be adopted, the boundary between constitutional guardian and partisan politician becomes even more indistinct. In such circumstances, it becomes less clear that, in a parliamentary democracy, the role of such office-holders is merely to ensure that the rules for taking decisions are respected, rather than to participate in the decisions themselves.

This consideration is reinforced in many voters' minds by, or perhaps more accurately it is confused with, a related one concerning the desirability of an outright change to a presidential or semi-presidential form of government. The debate over such a change predates the experiment with electoral reform ushered in by the 1993 referendum, but it may have been intensified by the perception that electoral reform has not, and on its own cannot, simplify the party system and produce cohesive governments. If electoral reform could not deliver, the case for adopting a form of presidential or at least semi-presidential government was bound to strengthen. It has been a complicating irony of recent years, therefore, that in being forced into a more visible and political role as President of the Republic in order to make an ailing parliamentary system workable, Scalfaro may have contributed to the belief that some form of presidential government would be desirable.

However, other considerations work in quite the opposite direction. It is true that contingent political events which have undermined the party system have legitimized increased presidential intervention in political life. On the other hand, the advent of an allegedly "majoritarian" electoral system — one of the most important bases of claims that Italy has moved from the

"First" to the "Second" Republic—would, if it could be ever be made effective, certainly work against presidential influence. Majorities that are agreed between the parties and then endorsed by voters in general elections should not subsequently not be remade by parliamentary bargaining or presidential mediation.

To the above considerations must, of course, be added a further, personal factor, linked to the potential controversy of Scalfaro's own political past. He was elected to the Constituent Assembly in 1946, and re-elected in every Parliament thereafter. He was under-secretary in six governments in the 1950s and 1960s, and Minister (of Transport, then Education, then the Interior) for various periods between 1966 and 1987, as well as Vice-President of the Chamber of Deputies from 1975 to 1983, and its President briefly in April-May 1992. His pedigree as a conservative figure in the Christian-Democrat establishment has thus been uncontestable, and it was as a Christian Democrat that he was elected President on 25 May 1992. Once in office, Scalfaro quickly sought to distance himself from his former party and its past, but in the frenetic world of claim and counter-claim generated by the judicial investigation of political corruption, a good deal of suspicion has inevitably been thrown in his direction. That he has survived when many political rivals, especially on the right, have had good reason to discredit him, may be strong circumstantial evidence that the suspicion had no foundation. Nevertheless, as a former occupant of the Ministry of the Interior, Scalfaro has been said to have had access to the same secret funds available to all holders of the office of Ministry of the Interior, and this accusation, however unfounded, has been a source of much speculative comment about his potential vulnerability as a political broker.

Scalfaro's Presidential Style

For all these reasons, it is inevitable that presidential duties and prerogatives have assumed a far higher profile under Scalfaro than under any of his predecessors, and have prevented him from reasserting the low-key and less controversial role for the Presidency that he would probably have preferred, particularly after the vicissitudes of his unpredictable predecessor Francesco Cossiga.[3] Furthermore, Scalfaro has not only had to *take* controversial decisions, but has had to defend them publicly. And he has had to use the artificially enhanced prestige of the Presidency in a more than usually political way in order to help governments to survive. This has been most marked in relation to the supposedly "weak" governments whose parliamentary majorities were at best ambiguous and at worst non-existent. In such cases Scalfaro has consciously offered the prestige, neutrality, and respectability of his office to governments which, at their formation, and at delicate moments thereafter, needed the authority and popularity of the President of the Republic to survive.

This was most in evidence in relation to the government of Lamberto Dini, formed after the collapse of the Berlusconi government in December 1994. The Dini government was controversial both for the manner in which it was born, and for the manner in which it was subsequently nurtured by the President. Scalfaro himself has acknowledged that there was no precedent for the decision he took in that crisis: to establish a government uncoupled from any specific parliamentary majority, entrusted with a very focused and pre-defined program, and explicitly designed to defuse the tension of a deteriorating political climate. By declining to dissolve in the face of a clear breakdown of a governing majority, which many thought had been chosen directly by the electorate the previous March, Scalfaro laid himself open to the charge that he was going against the majoritarian principle underlying the 1993 electoral reform. His critics demanded that voters be given an immediate chance to issue a verdict on the political responsibility for that breakdown, in order to cement the principle of a direct link between electoral majority and parliamentary majority. What they got was a government without a clear link to any identifiable electoral or parliamentary majority at all.

Scalfaro's decision in the crisis of December 1994 will no doubt continue to be debated for many years. The alternative to strong presidential support for Dini's government would have been the holding of a general election which — so the critics allege — could have produced a clear-cut verdict on the responsibility for the collapse of the outgoing Berlusconi government, and thus a more stable parliamentary majority in the future. By his action, so it has been said, Scalfaro bought enough time to obfuscate the simple but vital issues of parliamentary discipline and majoritarian cohesion that should have been put to the test once the *Lega Nord* abandoned the right-wing alliance under whose banner it was elected to Parliament. Instead, in a fog of party fragmentation and continuing exposures of political corruption, aimed at members of the emerging political class as well as the old one, voters lost sight of these "institutional" issues. As a result, the multi-party fragmentation present in March 1994 was no less marked in April 1996, and the resulting coalitions were no more cohesive or manageable. Had Scalfaro allowed a general election one year earlier, the operation of the parliamentary system could, so such an argument runs, have been entirely different. On this view, Scalfaro did much to prop up the old unstable parliamentary system.

Nor was it the case that having put the Dini government in office, Scalfaro was able to retire to the political shadows. Precisely because the government was initially a presidential one, it continued to need presidential support, even after acquiring more clear-cut political support in Parliament from the parties of the center and left. Far from down-playing the public pro-

file of the Presidency, Scalfaro therefore continued to play the role of mediator and broker deliberately and skillfully, maintaining a series of public utterances which kept the presidency in the limelight. He helped the Dini government develop its initially limited policy program towards a range of
more ambitious objectives, giving weighty moral support at each stage.[4] The
model, if there was one, looked much like the first years of the French Fifth
Republic, with an unelected President of the Republic steering the country
through a crisis, his support critical to any feasible government's survival.

Exactly how this behavior is interpreted depends on essentially-contested
interpretations of the alternatives available to the President, and the likely
outcomes. It has been argued, in the light of subsequent events (especially in
connection with evolving political relationships on the political right), that
the "choice" of Dini in preference to dissolution in December 1994 was less
decisive than it initially appeared. Scalfaro himself has argued that there was
no real "choice". As long as there was a possibility of keeping in existence a
Parliament so recently elected, it was the constitutional duty of the President
of the Republic, confirmed by long-standing republican convention, to pursue such a course.[5] Others have argued that even if one accepts that there
was scope for the exercise of presidential discretion, which is debatable, it is
far from clear that a dissolution would have resulted in the election of a
workable parliamentary majority better placed to restore financial-market
confidence than was the Dini government.

Identifying Scalfaro's deeper purposes in the 1994 Parliament is not easy,
and it is possible that most commentators have attributed greater long-term
purposiveness than is likely to be engendered in the heat of daily political
life. There is certainly little hard evidence that Scalfaro has ever formulated a
coherent plan through which to use the leverage of the Presidency to push
constitutional arrangements in any particular direction. As with most politicians, short-term exigencies have probably been more important than long-
term goals.

Those exigencies have centered for Scalfaro, as for his predecessors, on
governability in the most basic sense of ensuring that a government exists—
the very first duty of any President. If, in the post cold-war world, that has
become less necessary than in the past in purely political terms, it is, in a
world of global financial markets, a very great deal more necessary in economic terms. No one today expects a political vacuum—like that of 1964—to
threaten a coup d'état from left or right, as during Antonio Segni's presidency. However, the lack of a government can have a catastrophic effect on
an industrialized economy's money markets and exchange rates. The years
after 1992 coincided with a spectacular collapse in international confidence
in the Italian lira, the depreciation of which, at its peak in early 1995, was
well over 30% in relation to the German mark. Although it is difficult to link
financial-market pressure to any particular decision taken by Scalfaro, it is

important not to lose sight of this pressure as a background variable in several of the key crises he has faced.

Presidential Intervention as an Erodible Asset

Whatever interpretation is placed upon the events of the 1994-96 Parliament, it is difficult to avoid the conclusion that because of them, and after them, it would become increasingly difficult for President Scalfaro to play the same role, and with the same degree of authority, as in the early years of office. Presidential activism and political mediation were always likely to represent a gradually wasting asset for a president in Scalfaro's position. In the shock of the first wave of corruption exposures, it was relatively simple for the President to evoke popular loyalty and trust through simple public utterances encapsulating a mood of revulsion and moral outrage. This was at its peak during the 1992-94 Parliament, when an entire political class seemed to be disintegrating, and nothing had emerged to replace it. As the Giuliano Amato government gradually lost its key personnel, and the electorate got its chance to express a first verdict on events through the referendums on electoral reform, so the President had few rivals in the articulation of the public mood. This was most evident in Scalfaro's opposition to the ill-fated Biondi decree granting an amnesty to those accused of political corruption in March 1993, but it was infused throughout the subsequent government of Carlo Azeglio Ciampi, as the President took it upon himself, with considerable authority, to lay down the terms and conditions on which, once new electoral rules had been established, Parliament would be dissolved and fresh elections held.

The undermining of Scalfaro's unchallenged occupation of the moral high ground started with the election of 1994 and the establishment of the government led by Silvio Berlusconi. Albeit ambiguously, the outlines of a new political class began to emerge, as political regeneration started to take over from pure decomposition. Admittedly, the new government remained weak. It lacked a majority in the Senate, and it was led by a prime minister who was also a national business leader and monopolist-controller of the private television system. The low level of legitimacy this brought to the Berlusconi government, and the different, though no less tenuous legitimacy of its technocratic successor, left ample room for presidential guidance of a still quite public kind during the 1994-96 Parliament, especially on constitutional questions such as electoral law and media access.

However, the vacuum in political life was far less complete, and hence presidential mediation was less likely to be interpreted as disinterested and neutral. The clearest evidence of this was the inexorable tendency for Scalfaro himself, a man of unquestioned conservative credentials, to be pushed ever further into an unspoken alliance with the parties of the left. The Dini government may have started life as a government above party politics, but it ended its life as a government whose parliamentary support was drawn overwhelmingly from the ranks of the left, while critics of presidential activism, and of the probity of Scalfaro himself, were drawn overwhelmingly from the right. Scalfaro would no doubt have preferred to preserve a position of neutrality or at least centrality with respect to all parties in the spectrum, but as the parties themselves started to recover some legitimacy, that became far more difficult.

The Presidency in 1996

The events of 1996 fall squarely in line with this interpretation. The President has certainly not abandoned his high profile role, as we shall see below, but the efficacy of his interventions has continued to diminish, as has his ability to remain above party politics.

The General Election

This was evident even before the right launched its attack on Dini's government at the start of the year. The previous October, Dini had proposed a "seven-point program" for constitutional reform, implicitly suggesting that his own government be kept in being to push it through. Scalfaro himself immediately took up the same theme, proposing the reconstitution of the *Bicamerale* (the joint, bi-cameral commission) established in the previous Parliament. In December he took the idea further, proposing to send Dini's government back to Parliament for a new mandate once it had secured the passage of the 1996 budget and finance law. His clear implication was that with a broad-based majority of 85-90% of the two chambers behind it, such a government could then stay in being for up to two years while the *Bicamerale* did its work. To this argument for continuity was added a second argument, support for which was not of course limited to the President of the Republic and the government, to the effect that during Italy's six-month turn holding the Presidency of the Council of Ministers of the European Union, from January to June 1996, there were obvious interests of national prestige and credibility in not holding a general election campaign.

The determination of the parties of the opposition to ignore the President's proposals, and secure the immediate resignation of the Dini government, quickly undermined any hopes the President may have nourished for a speedy transition to a second Dini government and to the *Bicamerale*. Indeed, in the last weeks of 1995 and the beginning of 1996, the right intensified its pressure on Scalfaro's role, returning in particular to the issue of the

President's alleged betrayal, through his refusal to grant a dissolution, of the Italian electorate's clearly chosen parliamentary majority. Gianfranco Fini, Silvio Berlusconi, Marco Pannella, and Dini's volatile former Justice Minister Filippo Mancuso, all joined in the attack, accusing the President of abusing his powers of mediation and abandoning all pretense of political impartiality. Marco Pannella, in characteristically polemical mode, set about gathering 200,000 signatures to impeach the President of the Republic for abuse of his constitutional powers.[6] Gianfranco Fini expressed similar thoughts.

The purpose of the campaign was clearly to reduce the President's margin for maneuver in the forthcoming parliamentary debate on the Dini government's future. For those like Gianfranco Fini who were resolved to provoke an election, it was also intended to bring their allies (*Forza Italia* in particular) into line by polarizing the political atmosphere in a way which would prevent any possibility of a covert deal across the political divide.

In such circumstances, the impact of the "Scalfaro factor" that had worked well one year before in gathering parliamentary support for the Dini government was drastically reduced in scope. The parliamentary base which had sustained Dini in 1995 was no longer solid. Right and left were divided on the terms for a new parliamentary pact, both in terms of the name of a new prime minister, and in terms of the new institutional arrangements which all accepted such a pact had to be capable of delivering. The President—unwilling to send Dini back to Parliament to certain defeat in a confidence vote—did his best to extend the timetable. The Quirinale played an unusually engaged role in the inter-party talks that carried on through January, with hopes of progress being raised by talks between representatives of *Alleanza Nazionale, Forza Italia,* and the PDS on proposals for an Italian version of the semi-presidential republic. By the end of the month, however, there was still deadlock on a number of key issues, and more immediately on who should serve as prime minister if such a deal should come off.

The nomination of Antonio Maccanico as explorer-in-chief and hence potential prime-minister designate was in these circumstances another set-back for Scalfaro, whose strong preference was for continuity, with Dini remaining as Prime Minister at least until the end of the Italian presidency of the Council of Ministers. However, the prospect of a general election was rapidly becoming a serious risk for the President. An election victory for the right, and its version of plans for institutional reform, would seriously compromise his ability to remain in office in tandem with a government of the right. A Maccanico administration, for all its risks, including the possibility that it would be still-born, was preferable to an election, but even this plan, which for two weeks looked as if it might run, eventually fell on the unresolved ambiguities inherent in negotiations which had to achieve in a few days what the political system had for over a decade been unable to deliver. On February 16, Scalfaro was forced to admit defeat and dissolve Parliament. His one consolation was that Dini had avoided a confidence vote and could serve as caretaker prime minister.

Even this last factor was by no means without its edge, however, especially when Dini declared the foundation of his own party, and promptly aligned it with the *Ulivo* alliance. The last semblance of Dini's non-party technocracy—so important to the legitimacy of Scalfaro's original strong support for his government—was stripped away, and the parties of the right renewed their attack on Scalfaro's decision to allow Dini to continue in office as caretaker prime minister.

The Aftermath

Given the somewhat unpropitious background to the 1996 general election, at least from the President's perspective, the outcome must have been something of an unexpectedly pleasant surprise. Not only was the President's former prime minister on the winning side, and set to join the new government, but the very same financial markets that had reacted with such caution for over two years to the prospects of either a government of the right, or no government at all, now began to react with considerable optimism to the prospects of a government of the left, albeit one dependent in Parliament on *Rifondazione Comunista*. The risk of an overwhelming victory of the right, and of renewed tensions between a Berlusconi government and the Quirinale, made so much worse a second time around by the accumulated tensions of the 1994 Parliament, evaporated overnight.

Perhaps of greater significance for the institution of the Presidency of the Republic, however, was the possibility of a retreat to normality under conditions approximating to those of a government with a clear and stable parliamentary majority. And to a limited degree this is what the remainder of 1996 brought. The parties of the right, chastened by an unexpectedly heavy political defeat and divided over who was responsible, were for many months reduced to a state of relative quiescence. When they resurfaced in the late autumn, it was at least initially the tax policies of the new Prodi government that were in their sights far more than the perceived failings of the President of the Republic. The clear victory of the left, and the quasi-automatic inauguration of its prime-minister designate, Romano Prodi, made the process of government formation easier than for some years. Scalfaro began his consultations on May 15, and the new government was sworn in only three days later. The election of presiding officers in the new Parliament and the mechanisms of selecting Prodi's ministerial team even gave the President opportunities to show some quite visible institutional even-handedness between government and opposition, and to offer Prodi a mild rebuke for presuming to start assembling his government before being sworn in.

Despite the change in political context, however, the return to normality was never going to be easy for a President whose utterances had become a staple diet of the political press corps, and who had himself internalized a vision of the President as a paternal, but engaged, participant in the country's political renaissance. Perhaps more importantly, despite the swift establishment of the Prodi government, the extent of the return to "normality" remained, for a number of reasons, rather unclear.

The first factor of ambiguity in the new situation was the shadow of the negotiations over institutional reform which had preceded the 1996 general election. The failure of the leaders of *Forza Italia* and the PDS to reach agreement could not conceal the fact that they had come very close to doing so, and both Massimo D'Alema and Silvio Berlusconi continued to have their reasons for resuming negotiations at some point in the future. Such a development would entail a new governing formula, a new prime minister, and the possibility that in 1996 as in 1994, the initial quasi-majoritarian governing formula would be set aside within a fairly short period of time in favor of something very different. The role for the President of the Republic in such circumstances was again likely to be controversial.

A second factor of continuing "abnormality" was the surprising strength exhibited by the *Lega Nord* in the 1996 election. This, the *Lega's* complete self-imposed political isolation, and its leader's determination to raise the political stakes by returning to a strategy of secession, placed the issue of Italian national unity, and its counterpart the issue of federalism or at least greater regional autonomy, firmly back at the center of the political debate. And the *Lega's* tactics, however histrionic and absurd in the short term, posed a not insignificant constitutional and political danger in the longer term. It was a challenge to which a President of the Republic used to giving the lead in difficult constitutional areas could hardly resist rising, particularly when he felt a strong institutional duty to remind his countrymen of their common citizenship and common duties of solidarity.

Finally, of course, whatever return to normality had been achieved on the political front, the country continued to be many years away from a return to normality of the judicial front. The issue of political corruption would not go away. Indeed, in the autumn it was revived with a new intensity by firstly the discovery of a new tier of corruption among public officials involved in state contracting in the railways and other utilities, and then by new charges against Antonio Di Pietro, which led directly to the latter's resignation. And because the issue of corruption would not go away, nor would the related issue of judicial impartiality, where the President of the Republic, through his constitutional role of head of the Higher Council of the Judiciary, was at least indirectly involved.

Whether that role required, or was strengthened by, the regular stream of public utterances which emerged from the President during the course of the year will remain a matter of delicate judgment. Perhaps the best that can be said is that the variations on his theme were sufficient to leave an impression of at least a degree of even-handedness between on the one hand vigorous criticism of judicial excess (telephone-tapping, over-use of preventative detention, regular leaks from judges to the media, etc.) and on the other encouragement to continue in the rooting out of corruption in the face of extensive political intimidation. What was clear, however, was that the President was having great difficulty in restraining himself in this area, and the frequency of his interventions portrayed a picture of a President with a very clear belief in his right and duty to set the tone of debate in relation to the behavior of the judiciary.

It was perhaps a spill-over of that belief that led to one public utterance of the President during the course of the year which *was* widely agreed to be close to if not beyond the limits of acceptability. This concerned the issue of referendums and the use of decree-laws. Scalfaro may have supposed that he was merely articulating a widespread constitutional concern in criticizing the number of referendums being promoted, and the extent of governmental use of decree-laws, but to do so, as he did on 5 June 1996 in a speech to the Constitutional Court—whose duty was to judge the constitutional correctness of such measures—could have been interpreted—or misinterpreted—as an attempt to influence the behavior of the Court in ways which were unquestionably beyond the limit of the presidential prerogative.

Conclusion

By the end of 1996 Oscar Luigi Scalfaro was well into the second half of his term of office. In his four-and-a-half year period he had, without doubt, taken presidential intervention in daily political life beyond the limits which seemed prudent to most of his predecessors. Yet it is difficult to believe that many of those predecessors, had they faced the turmoil of the years after 1992, could have acted very differently. A neutral Presidency in times of extreme political uncertainty and upheaval is a fixed point of stability. As long as its occupant behaves with apparent decency and good-will, it is likely that the moral status of his office will rise as that of others within the political class falls. He will then almost certainly come under pressure to use that enhanced authority to help stabilize the political system. This is what happened in Scalfaro's case, and it is no surprise that by deploying his moral authority, he also made himself controversial. The choices he faced were acutely difficult ones, and the pressure to participate in public discussion was almost impossible to avoid. There can be questions about particular utterances, or about the appropriateness of the choice of particular locations or moments to intervene. The pressure of business will always affect the quality of judgments of this type. There can also be debate about particular decisions, and how they relate to both formal constitutional duties and informal conventions.

However, the one truly momentous personal decision made by Scalfaro in the period in question remains a negative one — the decision not to dissolve Parliament in December 1994 — and on this neither the Constitution, nor any identifiable convention developed by long-standing constitutional iteration and debate, can provide any guide to the correctness or otherwise of Scalfaro's decision. If there was any convention already in existence it was that the President's prime duty was to assist Parliament, especially a recently-elected Parliament, to survive. If it is argued that such a convention died with the First Republic, then it has to be demonstrated that it was the duty of the President himself to decide that the era of the First Republic was over, and then, even before anything other than electoral reform had reached the statute book, to make the first iteration of a quite new convention. It would certainly have been a brave President that did so, and more significantly, it would have been a President who exposed himself to just as much constitutional criticism as Scalfaro actually did by deciding that his duty was not to dissolve.

In fact, what emerges most clearly from Scalfaro's Presidency is that he faced a decision from which the institution was bound to emerge in a more constrained form. By choosing to keep the 1994 Parliament in being, and by sustaining a weak government, he may have slowed the descent from presidential power, because if a clear-cut majority had emerged from an immediate general election early in 1995, there would have been less need for Scalfaro to throw his weight behind the incoming government. On the other hand, precisely because Scalfaro had to become so engaged in support of Dini, his position, once the Dini formula was exhausted, was increasingly compromised. The events of 1996, in which Scalfaro sought to prolong the formula he had himself created, fall squarely in line with this trajectory.

Ultimately this is because the current form of government, whether it is deemed to be the First Republic or the Second, remains a parliamentary form. A decision in favor of a self-conscious shift towards French-style semi-presidentialism would require direct election of the President, and endorsement of the consequent constitutional change by Parliament and probably also the electorate in a referendum or at least a general election. Until this occurs, the presidential role must therefore normally be one of constitutional arbitrage rather than direct political engagement. Constitutional arbitrage may, however, in difficult circumstances give way to a degree of political engagement for a limited period, but such engagement is an easily erodible resource, as the events of 1996 demonstrate. What they do not necessarily demonstrate, however, is that at some point in the future Italy may not again need presidential mediation of the type experienced between 1993 and 1995. Of course, circumstances are unlikely to repeat themselves in the same form on a second occasion, and it is difficult to imagine that an entire political class will again be as delegitimized as in the early 1990s. But if presidential mediation is required, it will be an acid test of whether Scalfaro's own political engagement went so far as to discredit presidential engagement more generally—a matter on which for some time yet the jury will necessarily remain out.

Notes

1. For a representative sample of this literature (excluding some of the more politicized critiques of presidential behavior which have emerged in recent years) see especially: S. Merlini, "I presidenti della Repubblica", in G. Pasquino, ed., *La politica italiana* (Rome-Bari: Laterza, 1995), pp. 93-119, and A. Baldassare, "Il Capo dello Stato", in G. Amato and A. Barbera, eds., *Manuale di diritto costituzionale* (Bologna: Il Mulino, 1994), pp. 463-502.

2. Clearly, the power here is not an absolute one: if there is a majority set on dissolution, it will vote down any possible government. Moreover, the President probably has more influence in keeping in office a divided Parliament than in dissolving one where there is a clear majority willing to support a government. However, if the situation is finely balanced, with key groups inclined to prefer a dissolution, the President may be able to manipulate circumstances and choices in ways which make it difficult for those groups to incur the public opprobrium of causing a dissolution.

3. Scalfaro's election as President of the Republic was linked to a very clear-cut repudiation of the openly-expressed "presidentialism" of his predecessor Francesco Cossiga, and this repudiation was reaffirmed by Scalfaro in his inauguration speech on 28 May 1992.

4. The support Scalfaro offered was for a precise parliamentary program which included guarantees of political neutrality in the media, and regional electoral reform. On these issues, at a stretch, it could be suggested that the President's support fell into the realm of constitutional arbitrage, but support for Dini also included open espousal of financial measures to restore confidence in an unprecedentedly weak lira, which look much more straightforwardly political, and there is little doubt that by espousing such measures, Scalfaro descended further than any previous President into the political realm.

5. For an extensive rehearsal of the complex interpretations that can be placed on Scalfaro's opposition to dissolution in 1994, see C. De Fiores, "Il presidente della repubblica nella transizione", in *Democrazia e diritto*, vol. 35, no. 3-4, 1995, pp. 313-318.

6. Even *Il Corriere della Sera* commentator Ettore Rotelli supposed that the grounds for impeachment of Scalfaro were stronger than they had been for his predecessor (*Il Corriere della Sera*, 11 January 1996). For a comparison of Scalfaro's predisposition to make public utterances on constitutional and political matters, in comparison to that of his predecessor, Francesco Cossiga, see "Scalfaro esterna più di Scalfaro", in *MF*, 11 October 1995, p. 9.

10

Politics and Consumption: The Four Revolutions of Spectator Football

Nicola Porro

Football, it is said, represents much more than a sport for Italians. It is a social tradition, a collective passion, a custom which conditions other customs, a response to the need for expression and for identity. It is also an important employment sector: according to statistics from CONI (the Italian National Olympic Committee), at the end of 1994 those employed in the sector numbered 219,787. In recent years, football has also acted as a sensor to political change, going far beyond both its traditional image portrayed by celebrities and management, as well as the use, and not always just an ironic one, of language and iconography of extremism on the part of vocal supporters. Dal Lago has described the "footballization of politics". The experience of the Milan football club, following Berlusconi's decision to "take the field", represented a fundamentally symbolic and organizational paradigm in the transition from the corporate model of Fininvest to the political one of *Forza Italia*.[1]

Considering the social scope of the phenomenon, 1996 is a year to remember for reasons which go beyond the sporting dimension. The disappointments suffered for the unsuccessful performances of the national "blue" teams at the European Championships in England and the Atlanta Olympics and, conversely, Juventus' reconquest of the European title for club football, were just part of the background to four genuine revolutions.

1. The Bosman judgment delivered by the European Court of Justice on the 15 December 1995, opening up the professional sportsmen market, has applied to performance sport a principle of supranational regulation which until then had been firmly blocked by forms of "special legislation" and by various national jurisdictions. This has had immedi-

ate effects on the economic order of the clubs and on the actual structure of the European clubs.

2. Another acceleration in the processes of internationalization and commercialization of continental football has come from the European Union of Football Associations (UEFA). At the end of September 1996, UEFA made a further, decisive drive towards the transformation—set in motion five years earlier—of the old European Cup into a true and proper European Championship for club teams (the Champions League). By means of consecutive steps and regulatory developments prompted by the lobby of the big continental clubs, that which once represented a prestigious supplement to the national competitions has thus come to assume the form of an area of experimentation of a game totally identified as a product of television commercialization. The European football organization and the sporting federations of the less influential countries have only been able to take tentative measures to contain and delay the process, rather than opposing this trend completely.

3. The battle of the airwaves between the public broadcaster (Rai) and private broadcaster (Telemontecarlo, or TMC), over rights to the uncoded broadcasting of football matches, has been followed by the start in Italy also of the pay to view experience. A model destined, as the experiences of other countries demonstrate, to change the times, forms, and styles of football consumption, that is, of the most widespread collective entertainment for the Italians.

4. The impressive changes introduced in the production and the consumption of professional sport , and the even more radical ones heralded, have basically led to a fundamental revision of the legal and financial status and of the professional associations, beginning with the football clubs.

These are momentous changes, the foreseeable consequences of which are at the root of the leadership crisis which has assailed the FIGC (the Italian Football Federation) with the resignation of its president, Antonio Matarrese. He resigned the day after the Italian team was knocked out in the first round of the European Championships in England. The dismissal of the Italian team coach, Arrigo Sacchi, by the new federation management, which took over in the middle of December, constitutes the symbolic epilogue to a conflict not only of leadership, but also of policy, which plagues Italian professional football.

Sports: Supranational Regulation and Globalization

On 8 September 1996 the first football championship of the Bosman era opened. The European football clubs can draw on an open market, without having to shoulder the financial burdens resulting from the transfer of players (the price-tag payment). In theory, every team can employ as many foreigners as it wishes at the same time, even if a gradual application of the judgment is envisaged. In the first division of the Italian championship, the provisional number of foreign professional players is 83; only in the Piacenza line-up are there none. No less than 41 are new transfers, a mere 10 of whom are forwards, the experts preferring tactically and athletically fit men to the goal-scoring artistes for taking on the long and arduous sporting seasons.

Since it has become easier and relatively inexpensive to draw on the international market, it is no longer advantageous for the clubs to invest in the uncertain career prospects of young players. The extensive network of club training-grounds which constituted the hinterland and the cultural humus of professional football itself thus risks being destroyed.

Almost simultaneously, the launching of the Champions League is the forerunner to a European Super League for the big clubs. The approved system, in force from 1997-98, will reduce the risk of an accidental elimination of the most reliable clubs in the early stages of the competition with predictable damage to the television audience and to the related profits. Furthermore, clubs of the second division of the eight European footballing powers, which includes Italy, will also be able to take part in this, as well as playing in the national championships. The commercial and television rationale was the need to increase the marketable events and to plan their direction. Consistent with this philosophy is the idea of introducing into the national competitions *play-offs* for the awarding of the championship shield and *play-outs* to determine relegations. This would imply "sudden death" matches, with extraordinary entertainment value. At the same time, the practice of bringing forward matches to Saturdays becomes wider, as it is more practical for the demands of a packed international calendar and, above all, of television consumption.

For the big clubs, the new Champions League will devalue all the other traditional international competitions (the various UEFA Cups, Cup Winners Cup, etc.), and alter the very nature of the national competitions along the lines already seen in English professional football for some years. In Great Britain, by means of a policy of ownership with tax incentives, almost everywhere the clubs have become owners of the whole works. The stadiums, which have been privatized and to a large extent rescued from the plague of violence—due also to the drastic measures taken after the publication in 1990 of the alarming report by Lord Taylor—have multiplied and reappraised their offer of services for the paying public. The profit motive, in turn, has selected the viewers; something which has certainly contributed to eradicating the aggressive groups of fans, but also in transforming the traditional popular identity of football. Through the expansion of *merchandising*, which allows the clubs to market scarves, flags, caps, gadgets and souvenirs of every kind with the emblem and the colors of the team, profits are made which are not much lower than ticket sales returns. In this way, the clubs' transformation into businesses is also accelerated, as they independently manage the whole production of memorabilia and the marketing of specialized services , such as magazines and videos.

Brand loyalty acquires a quantifiable market value, to which the fans' sense of belonging confers a kind of supplementary value. The free market revolution in British football becomes evident to Italian fans in the summer of 1996 when the English clubs sign players of the caliber of Gianluca Vialli, Fabrizio Ravanelli, Roberto Di Matteo, Benito Carbone and, a few months later, Gianfranco Zola. Traditional importers of footballing talent from the whole world, the Italian clubs become exporters of a special work force such as the stars of spectator football and popular coaches, from Fabio Capello to Giovanni Trapattoni and Gigi Maifredi.[2] The exodus of Italian players and specialists, which is the direct consequence of the opening up of the football market, is in no way an exceptional phenomenon when compared to other cases. In fact, the Bosman judgment has unleashed similar dynamics to a certain extent everywhere, and in some cases (France, Norway and Holland) the number of idols of local clubs leaving to go abroad is decidedly higher. What, however, is far different and more dramatic is the psychological effect which such flights from national clubs have on the Italian public; a public used to considering itself the privileged importer of other people's talent.

As a popular and widespread subculture, club football—a blend of affection, traditions and prosaic commercial interests—witnesses a kind of symbolic shattering of its own traditional identity. Forced to navigate the open sea of a market with no restraints, the clubs are suddenly having to consider a form of disenchantment on the part of the star and of his fans. The ease and the frequency of transfers break the old sentimental ties between the fans and their standard-bearers on the pitch and lays bare the crudely contractual and utilitarian aspects of a relationship which has always been cultivated principally, not without some hypocrisy, in realms of fantasy ("Give us a dream!"). At the same time, the diaspora at the end of 1996 makes plain the vulnerability of a corporate system, such as that of Italian professional football, which for too long acquiesced to steer an ambiguous middle course, gaining from popular sentiment and the loyalty of the fans whilst failing to direct with any resolution the transition to possible new paradigms of an organizational and business nature. It could be maintained, therefore, that the crisis is one of the football substructure as a whole and that the very dominance assumed by the big clubs and by their circuit of alliances is nothing but one aspect of this singular crisis of leadership.

Television Wars

Nineteen-ninety-six is also the year in which spectator football becomes contested on the battlefield of the television war. The revolution of pay-to-view, which started with the 1996-97 championship, was preceded by the agonizing issue of broadcasting and uncoded TV rights which challenges Rai and private broadcasters. On the 20 October 1995 the league of divisions A and B had considered Rai's offer (157 billion lire a year for three years for uncoded broadcasts) and Telepiù's (55 billion a year to encode A games played before Sunday and those postponed in B, plus a guaranteed minimum of 70 billion lire for the nascent pay-to-view). A few days later a decree with the force of law allowed the use of coded transmissions from other authorized broadcasters as well.

On 15 December the financial sum was divided up into twelve different packages relating to the rights to uncoded and coded broadcasting. In the middle of February six companies (Rai, Fininvest, Cecchi Gori Communications, Direct TV International California, Telepiù and CNR) put forward their offers. The *coup de théâtre* takes place on 29 February 1996 with the disclosure of these offers. As expected, Telepiù wins the rights to coded transmission, but it is Cecchi Gori (patron of the Fiorentina club) who obtains the rights to broadcast uncoded programs. For the first time the public utility loses its most popular banner, despite the fact that the victorious group's actual technical capability to guarantee the quality of the sports programs and their reception by the whole country is debatable. The political stage, which sees the pre-electoral positioning of party and government men (the same Cecchi Gori is a political member of the PPI) and the deterioration of Letizia Moratti's administration of the Rai, feeds insinuations and suspicions of the behind-the-scenes intrigue involved in the affair.

Less than a month later, on 20 March, the situation is suddenly turned upside-down: Cecchi Gori refuses to produce the required surety, and the issue of control over the league of divisions A and B returns. On 13 April a Milan court rejects the appeal lodged by Cecchi Gori's lawyers, who dispute the consequences of not providing the surety. Two days later, Rai regains possession of the broadcasting and uncoded TV rights for the championship and the Italian Cup. The pay out, guaranteed by the Banca di Roma, amounts to 185 billion lire for the first year, 193.4 for the second, and 202 for the third, and this does not include the "advertising package" agreed upon by the ranked divisions league and Sacis, a franchise of the Rai.

However, the corporate transformation of professional football arrives at the real point of no return in the advent of a new kind of paid television, the so-called "pay-to-view": a distributor of scrambled broadcasts accessible to those subscribing to production and distribution circuits (Telepiù). In the minds of its promoters, pay-to-view is intended to supersede the pay-TV already in operation. The system enables consumers to follow all the matches of their favorite team live from home, according to a model of consumption which exists in some European countries, but which is established above all in the United States, where the four major sports (baseball, basketball, American football and ice hockey) are financed mainly through sponsorship and television rights.[3]

The new big business, tied to television's use of digital technology, is imminent. Digital television has already been tested in Germany with programs devoted to Formula 1 Grand Prix motor-racing and experimentally used for football in Great Britain at the beginning of 1996. It opens up enormous possibilities for the consumption of competition sport (it allows the viewing of stages of the game simultaneously or in succession, of interviews from the side of the pitch, of statistical updates, and so on) and, with such possibilities, its publicity marketability.[4]

In Italy as well, the income attached to television rights, boosted by the advent of the various forms of paid TV, has already been for some time the principal source of financing for the clubs. Furthermore, it was the criteria for its division which sparked off the conflict within the FIGC in the summer; the conflict which was made even more tense by Matarrese's resignation. The failure of the national team, especially at the European Championships in June, was only a pretext for a grand reckoning between the classified leagues and big clubs. And it is this reckoning which reveals the main clubs' desire to secede, due to their intolerance of the constraints and controls imposed by federation statutes. Apparently, what is wanted is a shaping of division A according to the model provided by the British Premier League which comprises twenty superclubs and operates completely independently of the secondary leagues. It thus corners the considerable profits which accompany all the possible forms of the spectator football product's marketing.

In Italy such dynamics, strongly demanded by the market, come up against several problems. Unlike the British sports organization, a public body does actually operate (i.e., CONI). It is a body furnished with far reaching powers for the management and regulation of the whole system. Whilst it is formally in charge of performance sport, the 1942 founding law gives it authority which in theory covers its whole area of activity—both competitive and non-competitive. Furthermore, through the betting connected to football (Totocalcio and Totogol), CONI manages a large part of the resources available for the financing of the whole of the varied national sporting movement. CONI is, moreover, a significant part of an interorganizational network which is far closer to the government and to the political system than happens in Britain's free market.

So it plays an institutional role, a role which is so influential and jealously guarded that this body often comes into conflict with the unruly and complex system of professional football. Affiliated *de jure* to CONI through the sporting membership federation, the football-as-spectator-sport circuit is in fact exposed to increasing demands for specialization and enticed by lucrative business opportunities. The organizational complexity and the growing differentiation of interests generate contradictions also within the umbrella structure (FIGC, commonly known as "Federcalcio"), which comprises the 38 clubs of the major leagues (divisions A and B), the 90 professional clubs of divisions C1 and C2—in large part sustained by the contributions of CONI—and the archipelago of the non-professional clubs.

Governmental Problems

Facing a classic problem of allocation of resources and legitimization of institutional roles, the federation experienced a crisis which highlights the anachronism of a legal structure which denies the chance to medium-sized professional football clubs to pursue profit-oriented goals. To have an idea of the economic impact of the issue, see Table 10.1 which summarizes the main sources of income for the clubs of divisions A and B, and demonstrates how, whilst there is a fundamental "egalitarianism" regulating the resources which come from public contributions (betting and CONI transfers), there is also a strict meritocratic selection for the television profits.

This is clearly a purely market-based logic, which favors the richest clubs, calls into play the role of the institutions, the responsibilities of CONI, the power relations between the federation leagues and even the club relations within the main league where the clubs from the Central and Southern Italy fear the exertion of influence by a clandestine management lead by the superpowers of the North (Juventus, Milan and Inter). On 6 August, an interplay of cross-vetoes prevented the federation assembly from electing Matarrese's successor. The competing candidates were the leader of the main league, Luciano Nizzola, and the head of the C league, Giancarlo Abete, with the president of the amateurs, Elio Giulivi, in the role of grand elector. The stalemate was caused by a regulation which grants veto power to each of the three leagues, since a reform based on the institution of the "minority bloc" and the granting of a weighted vote to the clubs had not been approved in time; this reform should rescue the federation leadership from a permanent state of blackmail and vulnerability. Confronted with the risk of paralysis, the CONI presidency nominates the secretary general of the body, Raffaele Pagnozzi, commissioner of Federcalcio. He takes office on 12 August in a climate strained by the lack of any settlement on the calendar of the 1996-97 championship.[5]

TABLE 10.1. Profits of A and B Division Football Clubs (Millions of Lire)

	Toto-calcio	Totogol	TV	Uncoded Pay-TV	Pay-to-view	Total
A Division	32,850	28,116	90,500	82,600	67,664	301,730
%	10.9	9.3	30.0	27.4	22.4	100
B Division	32,850	9,384	90,500	25,600	22,000	180,334
%	18.2	5.2	50.2	14.2	12.2	100
A and B	65,700	37,500	181,000	108,200	89,664	482,064
%	13.6	7.8	37.5	22.5	18.6	100

Source: Figures published in *Panorama*, 19 September 1996.

At the end of September, with the situation of friction now over thanks also to intensive diplomatic efforts, an agreement is reached—although it is not made official until the federation assembly of 14 December—which gives Nizzola the presidency and makes Abete vice-president with important areas of authority (refereeing and youth football). The return effects of the Bosman judgment thus enter into the complex negotiation. An 8-10 billion lire sum from Totogol's capital gain is considered by the C league as compensation for damages due to the smaller clubs for the reduced remuneration from youth training camps. The amateurs, on the other hand, claim an exemption from costs resulting from referee expenses, with an estimated saving of around 25 billion lire a year. There are, however, also structural reforms of professional football on the table. Such reforms aim to alter the organization of the B and C championships by reducing the total number of clubs. Abete's election platform provided for the creation of two subdivisions of Division B and three subdivisions with 18 teams each in Division C, thus obliterating twenty clubs; Nizzola's left the two major divisions unchanged and envisaged three subdivisions with 20 teams each for Division C and the disappearance of the current C2 Division, thus eliminating thirty clubs.

However, the ultimate question remains that of a redefinition of the legal status of the clubs which allows the large clubs to legalize and increase the business profile of their activities. Football clubs, subject to the federation statute of the FIGC, had been made joint-stock companies by Law no. 91 of 23 March 1981. They could not, however, distribute dividends amongst the shareholders, and the financial year was set on the basis of the sporting year, according to a special regulation suspected of discouraging fiscal transparency and honesty. The same body of shareholders became bound to the holding with subjective conditions in a way which was at variance with the regulations for other economic enterprises run in the form of a joint-stock company.

Deputy Prime Minister Walter Veltroni, responsible for sport, unveiled the contents of a legislative reform, begun with the Decree-law no. 485 of the 20 September 1996, which authorizes the clubs to pursue "profit goals", abolishing the disputed second subparagraph of Article 10 of Law 91. The clubs will no longer be obliged to reinvest profits "for the exclusive pursuit of sporting activity". They will also be granted a widespread shareholding and even allowed to be quoted on the stockmarket, the latter being limited to clubs which can boast three consecutive years in the black. Again, in this case, the example comes from England where the profit goal has been recognized since 1980 and where seven clubs are already duly quoted on the London Stock Exchange.[6]

Professional footballers, who, with a mixture of candor and hypocrisy, Law 91 equated with normal employees, will be subject to different administrative and stricter tax conditions. The common recourse to debt will also become less profitable, and the whole activity of the new joint-stock companies will be subject to the civil courts' jurisdiction and no longer to the sporting federation's (COVISOC) board of control. For the immediate future, the measures promise the clubs some breathing space, spreading the losses caused by the economic effects of the Bosman judgment over three financial years. As a corollary to the reform of the professional clubs, a further bill is heralded on tax relief for amateurs — a measure which affects over sixty thousand sports clubs, a fifth of which are football clubs — and on the establishment of a mixed committee (Ministry of Finance and Federcalcio), chaired by the head of the Department for Sport at the Prime Minister's office, Mario Valitutti, to reconcile the fiscal system with European regulations.

A Fragile Balance

So, the massive growth of commercial interests, the new balances of power corresponding to the changes in the clubs' structure and legislative innovation conditioned by the extension of supranational regulation act as interactive dynamics. The *Ulivo* coalition government and CONI find themselves at the crossroads of the need for realistic regulation of the sector and the need to curb the "strong powers". Thus, they can no longer avoid defining a new administration, which is the only means of checking the separatist tendencies of spectator football in relation to the wider system of performance sport. By means of legal betting, football finances a great deal of the activities of the whole sporting movement and represents, therefore, a resource which is difficult to replace within an institutional framework such as the Italian one. However, it is up to the institutional bodies to execute a complex role of both management and mediation within a system which does not want to surrender itself to private bargaining between the powerful.

So, it is understandable that, together with the announcement of the club reform, Veltroni issued a kind of letter-manifesto, addressed to the president of CONI, to Commissioner Pagnozzi and to the presidents of the three leagues, underlining the two crucial aspects of the problem: the protection of training grounds after the disruptive Bosman ruling and stadium violence, including the worrying resurgence of a rough and ill-mannered game on the pitch which was seen at the beginning of the championship, despite the new regulations.[7] It is a matter of a political statement which is intended to claim back a regulatory role for the institutions (and for CONI), a role which is legitimized by the very scope and the social dimension of the football phenomenon.

Football really constitutes a *political arena* in which the bargaining power held by individuals requires negotiation strategies, and, at the same time, demands powers of arbitration. It is not an abstract problem of status or of mutual jurisdiction recognition. Very concrete interests are at stake, the management of which creates much anxiety for the government. The match is concerned primarily with the constantly growing returns from the television market (Table 10.2) which have accelerated the transformation of football clubs into specialized holding companies.

For the 1996-97 championship (see also Table 10.1) the professional clubs will share out, according to a defined system, 482 billion lire gained from the revenue from Totocalcio (falling by 17% compared to the previous financial year) and Totogol (which registers a slight growth) and from the rights corresponding to uncoded television broadcasts, pay-TV and pay-to-view for the two league competitions (Divisions A and B) and for the Italian Cup. More than 50 billion lire must be added to these profits for the two top teams (Milan and Juventus) for their participation in the Champions League, and 7 billion for each team playing in the UEFA Cup and the Cup Winners Cup. On the other hand, the clubs earn only 282 billion lire from season tickets holders and ticket sales (Table 10.3).

So, appetites whet by television earnings nourish the roots of the superclubs, in the name of an aggressively *profit*-oriented philosophy which has difficulty in coexisting with the principle of public support of the sporting movement.

TABLE 10.2. Income from Televised Football

Period	Figure Paid (Thousands of Lire)	TV Channel(s)
1978-81	5,816,174	Rai
1981-84	42,714,561	Rai
1984-87	79,153,644	Rai
1987-90	180,450,000	Rai
1990-93	324,999,000	Rai
1993-96	571,850,510	Rai and Telepiù
1996-99	1,209,050,000	Rai and Telepiù

Note: In 1993-96, 423.1 billion lire were paid by Rai for uncoded broadcast rights, 148.7 billion lire by Telepiù for coded broadcasts.

Source: Il Corriere della Sera, 16 April 1996.

TABLE 10.3. Attendance and Income from the Championship

	Paying Spectators	Season-Ticket Holders	Total
1994-95 Attendance	1,551,028	3,003,715	4,554,743
1994-95 Income (Millions of Lire)	57,383	81,620	139,003
1995-96 Attendance	1,499,781	3,110,351	4,610,132
1995-96 Income (Millions of Lire)	57,789	87,570	145,359
Difference in Attendance from 1994-95 to 1995-96	−51,247	+106,636	+55,389
Difference in Income from 1994-95 to 1995-96	+405	+5,949	+6,354

Source: La Repubblica, 5 April 1996.

The profits from Totocalcio and Totogol, administered by CONI, and the direct payments to the clubs by the Rai are indeed, in the main, shared out equally between the 18 clubs of Division A and the twenty of Division B. What is rather different is the division of the profits supplied by commercial television (pay-TV and pay-to-view) and their negotiation by the leagues of A and B.[8]

Meanwhile, Italian football fundamentally enters into the area of action of multinationals. The Italian Cup, the competition linked to the "best championship in the world" and, over the last few years, subject to a depressing decline, will be sponsored by Coca-Cola. Fifteen billion lire will be assigned to the Divisions A and B, to be divided according to an inflexible meritocratic rule which will reward the strongest clubs. This is further confirmation of the crisis of that old principle of mutual aid among clubs, a principle which had permitted the survival of a far-reaching network of smaller clubs and teams, which were often representative of local situations without financial resources and unattractive in business terms.

Conclusion

A number of reflections are prompted by the four revolutions in Italian professional football. Firstly, the complex organizational structure, on which the impressive sphere of interests is based, depends on the clubs entering into commercial competition. The market dimension is altered by a growing segmentation of spectators: television viewers; the public of the stadiums who are encouraged to become season ticket holders (see figures in Table 10.3) and, soon, shareholders; significant groups of supporters, tamed through negotiation procedures (which are not always clear) between the club management and the organizational leadership. The figure of the casual fan, drawn by the sporting event itself and reluctant to be constructed within a network of strictly structured roles, is in decline.

The developing crisis of the youth training grounds is an omen of progressive depletion of the human reserves of football clubs. With new forms of domestic consumption of the event asserting themselves, it is probable that the stadiums will soon seem like oversized monuments for collective rites which have been made obsolete by individualized television consumption. But the very footballization of politics, triumphant in the symbolic-practical paradigm of Berlusconian Milan (loyal supporters clubs, charismatic leadership, myth of success, broad and flexible organizational networks with synergetic skills), could perhaps be analyzed subsequently as a response of the whole system, which is subject to operative problems created by institutional change and the crisis of traditional party forms. The political party-club is an original invention, but an ephemeral one. The political reports present a *Forza Italia* in search again of a structure which becomes, every day, increasingly similar to the detested traditional models and increasingly distant from the longed-for passive party and from its football-television form.

The segmentation of audiences and the commercial expansion of the market are both the effect of an important innovation of supply. The classic centrality of the national championship is being substituted by television supremacy in spectator football, with the European clubs rapidly going towards the creation of the continental Super League to follow the Champions League. With the end of the war of the airwaves (despite the fact that on the 11 December 1996, with a surprise sentence, a Florence court partially accepted the Cecchi Gori appeal against the revocation of rights to TMC), it is the expansion of technological supply and the forms of consumption (pay-TV, pay-to-view, digital systems) which combine, as the economists say, new product developments and new process developments, already with visible results. Entertainment products, which require both technical adaptation (a game which is increasingly faster, enjoyable, and "televisable") and suitable sporting capability in order to deal with packed-calendar seasons (drives for the purchase of foreign defenders), dictate a change in organizational models reaching as far as the structure of the clubs and their management structure.

The Bosman judgment, stimulating professional players' mobility, threatens the social humus of the game. Television football tends to challenge the system of public support negotiated between leagues, the CONI federation and public powers—within a framework of solidarity and mutual assistance—with market interests, that is the saleability of the entertainment product. Thus, even the football clubs become differentiated and conflicts appear inside the organs of government. Furthermore, the tendency towards the shedding of the professional spectator football substructure from the official system of performance sport (governed by CONI and supported by the state) becomes more marked.

The persistence of political and institutional links which characterize the organization of Italian sports means that it is less easy than elsewhere to make the big clubs completely autonomous. This, in turn, makes complex and constant negotiation between those involved necessary. Spectator sports—an exemplary intersection of the dual rationale of contemporary sport (a system of rules and a system of symbols)—thus demonstrates all of its intrinsically political nature: a political nature which no longer pertains simply to the traditional propaganda or representation policies of political leaders, local celebrities or businessmen in search of the limelight. Indeed, it now goes further with the transition from the politicization of football to the footballization of politics. The dismissal of Matarrese, the last big celebrity of the old Federcalcio, Sacchi's sad return to his stricken Milan, and Nizzola's entrustment of the national side's coaching to a pragmatic man of the pitch such as Cesare Maldini—very far from the high expectations and the aspirations of his predecessor—all represent the exemplary epilogue to an agonizing period of change in Italian football.

Translated by Katherine Davies

Notes

1. See A. Dal Lago, "Il voto e il circo", in *Micromega*, no. 1, 1994, pp. 138-145. For a model of political action in which the traditional philosophy of *membership* (the activists of a broadly-based party) is replaced by the organization and mobi-

lization of loyal fans (*supportership*), see N. Porro, "L'innovazione conservatrice. Fininvest, Milan Club e Forza Italia", in *Quaderni di Sociologia*, no. 9, 1994, pp. 6-18.

2. The diaspora of Italian football players is not limited to Great Britain alone. The phenomenon, which involves both athletes thrust out of the hyper-competition of the Italian championships and former winners wishing to secure a respectable end to their career, concerns Austria (Giannini, Gambaro, Onorati), Germany (Rizzitelli), Spain (Longhi), France (Malusci), Switzerland (Gualco), Scotland (Bruno, Salvatori, Di Canio) and even the United States (Donadoni and Galderisi) and Japan (Massaro and Schillaci). An exceptional case is that of Franceschini, Parma's young promise who was sent to a French club (Marseilles) governed by Parmalat and concerned with the "business synergy" promoted by the Tanzi group.

3. In Italy the "pay-to-view" concessionaire, Telecalciopiù, offers various subscriptions: from five hundred thousand lire for all 34 matches of the championship, for those who live outside the province in which the club is based, to three hundred thousand lire required from subscribers, resident in the province, who are only concerned with seeing the 17 away matches. Since January 1997 it has also been possible to buy single matches for 20-30 thousand lire, and there has been an expansion of subscription possibilities for the Division B competition (with costs varying from two hundred and fifty to one hundred and fifty thousand lire, with the same conditions applied to the higher division). To access the coded matches one needs a dish aerial, a digital receiver (different to the one used for pay-TV) and a smart card. The starting costs, hardly trivial for the typical subscriber, and some difficulties with the availability of the decoders have somewhat dampened the initial enthusiasm for the new product. However, observers predict a progressive expansion in demand and a large mid-term financial return.

4. In the British case, the principal negotiators of this enormous deal were the executives of the cartel of the major football clubs (the Premier Division) and one of the leading companies in digital technology, B-Sky-B. However, even in laissez-faire Great Britain, moves towards a complete autonomy of the system provoke active resistance when a new kind of public welfare, spectator sport, is at stake. In March the Conservative government denied the private directors (in this particular instance, Rupert Murdoch) exclusive rights to the eight most important sporting events of the year, bringing the traditional broadcasters (the public BBC channel and the two private networks, ITV and Channel 4) back into play to the detriment of the "lords of the coded broadcast". In a statement in the *Gazzetta dello Sport* of 28 August 1996, Commissioner Pagnozzi shows that he is well aware of the connection between the crisis in Federcalcio and the growth in television profits: "In eight years the income related to TV rights has increased almost tenfold. And from 1997 profits will be three times higher than those made up until last June, if the figures of the championship, the cups and the national competition are added together. So, the crisis is not due to the failure of electoral agreements, but to an extremely rapid growth".

5. On 29 July the clubs had blocked the completion of the calendar in order to force the conversion into law of the measures promised to limit the effects of the Bosman judgment: 200 billion lire's worth of redemption, owing to losses for the resetting of the parameters to zero, were at stake. This demonstrative gesture, deemed an intimidating one by the President Pescante, triggered off controversy and problems.

6. "Be a fan, buy the stock" is the advertising slogan coined to back the

popular share issue. A club such as Manchester United, moreover, boasts profits of 48 billion lire, and the price of its shares has risen from the nominal value of 4,800 to 11,300 lire. A survey, published in *La Repubblica*'s "Affari & Finanza" supplement (7 October 1996), reports that a good four and a half million of Italian sports fans would be prepared to invest in the football shareholding, but that the propensity to invest is accompanied by a clear demand for a role in the club management (electing the club president, participating in the selection of the trainer, even expressing opinions on the purchase and transfer of players). They are demands which cannot be proposed legally, since the preference shares guarantee dividends but do not grant their holders the right to vote. On the other hand, the three year constraint dampens much of the enthusiasm. According to the 1995 budgets of Division A, only Roma was in credit, by little more than five billion lire. Inter's deficit, on the other hand, amounted to no less than 32 billion lire, that of Napoli to 17 billion lire, Fiorentina's to 15 billion and Lazio's to 13 billion. Juventus' and Milan's deficits were smaller, at around 4 billion. Overall, Division A's debt amounted to 104.8 billion lire, Division B's to 38.9 and Division C clubs' to 66.7. The figures for the 1996 budgets, disclosed at the beginning of November, are even more worrying. The professional clubs together produce a deficit of over 250 billion lire. Above all, it is the big clubs who are in the red: Milan's deficit has risen to 44.3 billion lire, Inter's to 21 billion and Juventus' to 14 billion. Rome's budget is also 13 billion in the red (only its rival Lazio shows an improvement in its accounts). These are figures which entitle McKinsey's analysts to consider the clubs' entry onto the stock exchange questionable, at least for the next three to five years.

7. The extent of supporter violence during the 1995-96 championship (inside and outside the stadium) can be summarized in a few official figures: 131 arrests, 989 cautioned, 871 injured, more than a thousand restrictive measures, half of which provide for the " Sunday signing in" in police stations for the extremists banned from going to the stadium. As regards match violence, 1996-97 sees the introduction of an increasingly strict repression of foul play as well as the extension to the Italian championship of the international principle which automatically disqualifies for at least one round players sent off during the match.

8. Every club in Division A earns 1.825 billion lire from Totocalcio, 1.562 from Totogol and 5.028 from Rai TV rights. For the clubs in Division B the figures are slightly lower for Totocalcio and television rights (1.642 and 4.525 billion lire, respectively), while Totogol yields around 470 million. Pay-TV provides for the division of the club profits according to the final position of the teams: 8.4 billion lire will go to the top two in division A, 7.0 to those in third to fifth place and progressively decreasing sums for the remaining clubs (the last four places receive a total of 1.4 billion lire). An analogous principle regulates the profits of Division B: the sum of 2 billion lire for the top four places in the league decreases to 800 million for the bottom five. This trend is accentuated by pay-to-view, which earmarks 6.610 billion lire for the winner of the championship shield and only 2.181 billion to the bottom four of the league. This mixed system guarantees profits close to 23 billion lire for the championship side in Italy and little more than half (11.995 billion) for those at the bottom of Division A, while in Division B the top four share slightly more than 40 billion lire (10 each), as compared to little more than 8 million for the teams the 17th to 20th positions.

11

Italian Intervention in Bosnia and the (Slow) Redefinition of Defense Policy

Paolo Bellucci

On 18 December 1995, the first fifty soldiers of the Garibaldi regiment disembarked at the port of Ploce from the Italian Navy ship *San Giorgio,* and two days later arrived in Sarajevo. This force formed the vanguard of the Italian contingent involved in the "Joint Endeavor" operation, led by and mainly composed of NATO troops. By the end of January 1996, 2 549 Italian soldiers would be deployed in Sarajevo and South-East Bosnia-Herzegovina within the multinational division (along with French, Spanish, Portuguese, Belgian and Luxembourg troops) under French tactical command.

On 15 December 1995 the UN Security Council had adopted Resolution 1031, authorizing member states to form a multinational task force (IFOR, or Implementation Force) under NATO command, for the implementation of the peace agreements in Bosnia, elaborated in Dayton in November, but formally signed on 14 December in Paris. The IFOR operation constituted the first "outer zone" mission for NATO since its formation in 1949[1] and in which Italy participated for the first time with a contingent composed exclusively of volunteer soldiers from the Garibaldi and Folgore regiments.[2]

Italian participation in NATO intervention in Bosnia was the result of what could be described as a two-level game.[3] The attempt of Italian governments to enhance their role in the international arena[4]—within the context of the Alliance's mission and of its European component after the end of the cold war—encountered internal and external obstacles, and in particular the uncertainties of political elites and military leaders (the latter being hostile to any possible intervention in the Balkans) with respect to changes in the international context and to necessary adjustments of their own military and security policies. Italian policy in the context of the Balkan crisis fluctuated between *solidarity* (with the participation in WEU humanitarian aid operations and the subsequent death of 4 soldiers in a humanitarian aid plane which was shot down en route to Sarajevo from Spalato), *assertiveness* (request for participation in international forums, and in particular in the Contact Group) and *reprisal* (refusal to grant access to Italian bases for US Air Force Stealth bombers). Thus Italy participated in the 1992 Adriatic naval operation enforcing the embargo against Serbia (NATO-WEU operation); but only contributed to the NATO "Deny Flight" operation on a logistical level. It subsequently took part in the NATO bombing of Bosnia in the summer/autumn of 1995 but it refused to send ground troops to protect the withdrawal of UN forces planned for December 1994 and May 1995. It than took part in IFOR operations on December 1995.

Italian Involvement in Bosnia

The development of the Yugoslavian crises has obviously influenced, and restricted, the sphere of Italian foreign policy. Above all, the failure of EU diplomatic efforts—the principal, if not the sole forum in which Italy could have successfully promoted initiatives to protect its own interests in the area, as a nation particularly vulnerable to the military and social risks deriving from the conflict—has greatly reduced national capacities to influence events. The withdrawal of Europe from crisis management—it restricted itself from then on to ratifying *ex post* decisions made by the Contact Group—leads to the growing importance of informal multilateral diplomacy. Leaving aside for the moment the last resort of armed intervention, the Italian role underwent a political reshaping: excluded from the Contact Group, and uncertain about whether to contribute directly to military action, or simply to put its own military bases at NATO's disposition, it carved itself a valuable niche for autonomous humanitarian aid to the affected population.[5] In this context, the decision to participate in IFOR concludes a policy towards the Balkan crisis which has passed through four distinct phases, each with its own political style or prevalent tendency: Western solidarity; assertiveness; realism, and reprisal.

The Yugoslavian crisis interrupted a policy of cooperation with the Eastern countries which had been particularly active since the end of the 1980s. At the outbreak of the crisis, the Italian position coincided with the official position of the EC, being to facilitate the transition of the Yugoslavian Republics and avoid potentially explosive divisions. Similarly, after the German initiative for the diplomatic recognition of Slovenia and Croatia, which was also supported by the Vatican and as a result by the majority of the Christian Democrat party, Italy changed its position in harmony with the EC realignment.[6] During the succession of the Andreotti, Amato and Ciampi governments, the western phase of humanitarian solidarity (1991 to March 1994) encompassed participation in WEU humanitarian missions, as well as support and inclusion in WEU-NATO arms embargo missions against ex-Yugoslavia in the Adriatic. As concerns bilateral relations, Italy signed a memorandum with the new Croatian Republic, subsequent to its diplomatic recognition, protecting the resident Italian minority.[7] From November 1991 onwards, at the internal level, the Andreotti government implemented an asylum policy for the acceptance of Slovenian and Croatian refugees in the Friuli-Venezia Giulia region, in addition to providing economic assistance to counteract the regional economic effects of the Yugoslavian crisis. The Amato government which succeeded it supported the asylum policy and, ever mindful of the Albanian refugee crisis of 1991, remained actively involved in the humanitarian field, strengthening the transfer and distribution of aid in the former Yugoslavian territories.[8] As a result, Italy made substantial contributions for humanitarian assistance, and simultaneously provided logistical support for the shipping of personnel and resources to Bosnia.

The meeting of the Council of Ministers on 25 August 1992 to define the Italian position before the London Conference of 26-28 August reaffirmed the importance of a political solution to the crisis and the willingness of Italy to play an active role under the aegis of the UN towards peace in ex-Yugoslavia.[9] Within this framework, Italy engaged itself as a member of the WEU military force for the protection of humanitarian aid, as defined at the London Conference. The government's policy was greeted with strong internal political approval, with the exception of Marco Pannella, of the Radical Party, and the newly-formed PDS. The latter remained supportive of the deployment of WEU troops, but expressed concern about the possibility of Italian participation as a border country, violating standard UN practice.[10] The favorable opinion shown towards intervention changed dramatically after the shooting down of an Italian humanitarian aid plane in Bosnia at the beginning of September revealed the risks of military intervention and exacerbated Italian uncertainties. The UN decision, adopted shortly before the incident, to exclude Italy from peacekeeping operations, on the basis of its status as a border country and aggressor during the Second World War, was consequently almost welcomed (in fact, this decision, which amended Resolution 776, extending UNPROFOR presence to the whole of Bosnia, removed the reason for the veto of the Bosnian Serb Karadzic, and the subsequent one of Slovenia and Croatia.[11] Foreign Minister Colombo may have expressed regret at this decision; Defense Minister Salvatore Andò, however, appeared less concerned, and Italian soldiers, who had been worried by the difficulties and dangers of the mission[12], appeared relieved. Moreover, in the meantime, Somalia had emerged as a new arena in which Italy intended to contribute humanitarian aid.

The handover from the Amato government to Ciampi in the spring of 1993 did not alter the Italian policy of engagement in Western solidarity towards tackling the Balkan crisis. In April, Italy contributed to the NATO "Deny Flight" operation at the logistical level by allowing the use of its air-bases, but did not participate directly in Bosnian missions. This position was consolidated by UN Security Council Resolution 958 in November, which authorized the use of military aircraft to monitor protected zones. After the Atlantic Council consent of January 1994 to possible bombing against Serbs, as requested by UNPROFOR, Italian bases no longer simply provided logistical monitoring aid, but also a starting-point for war operations. This exposed Italy to possible Serb reprisals, as occurred after the ultimatum given by NATO to the Bosnian Serbs to withdraw all heavy weapons from Sarajevo, when Belgrade threatened to attack NATO installations in Italy.[13] The Italian government was still convinced of the preferability of a political solution over armed intervention, wary as it was of public hostility, in the West and Italy, to the recourse to military force. In Vienna, at the beginning of January 1994, the Italian Foreign Minister Beniamino Andreatta clearly supported this position[14], in addition confirming that many failures in Bosnia had been caused by public opposition in Italy and the West in general.[15] Nonetheless, pressured by such events as the killing of three Italian journalists in Mostar, the Pope's request for intervention in Bosnia, and the Sarajevo market massacre, Andreatta hastened to change his position, declaring the urgency of Western military intervention[16], and thus following the new US policy which was itself favorable to NATO intervention. Notably, in a subsequent pre-electoral interview, the Italian Foreign Minister emphasized the importance and influence of public opinion on national foreign policy.[17]

In reality, Italian public opinion was the opposite of the minister's perception. This was not a uniquely Italian mistake, and was common to most Western countries; indeed, this false perception has been interpreted as a partial explanation of the hesitation shown by the US and Europe towards military intervention.[18] Since the end of 1992, American, French, British, German and Italian public opinion had been favorable to armed intervention in ex-Yugoslavia. In March 1993 and February 1994, 65 percent of Italians approved of multilateral European intervention in Bosnia to secure peace.[19] It is certainly true that Italian troop involvement in a multilateral force would have caused a decline in public support, but it is also significant that, in January 1994, in the absence of any political discourse or national debate, 35 percent of Italians favored armed Italian participation in Bosnia (see Figure 10.1).

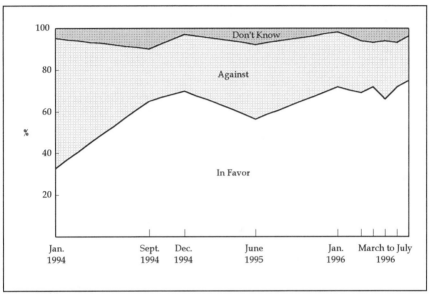

Source: Difebarometro

Question formats:
Jan. 1994: Concerning Bosnia, are you in favor or against armed Italian intervention in a country with serious internal problems?
Sept. 1994: If a peace agreement were signed in Bosnia, would you be in favor or against towards participation in a UN contingent by the Italian armed forces?
Dec. 1994 and June 1995: Would you be in favor or against participation by the Italian armed forces in a NATO contingent designed to end the conflict in Bosnia?
Jan. to July 1996: Recently a peace agreement has been signed in Bosnia. The Italian government has decided to send a troop contingent to uphold it. Are you in favor or against this decision?

FIGURE 10.1. Public Opinion Towards Italian Intervention in Bosnia

In December 1994, national public opinion strongly supported (70 percent) the participation of Italian armed forces with NATO in securing peace in Bosnia. This level changed over time: between December and June, it dropped to 57%, reflecting the impasse in negotiations and the growing intensity of the conflict. But, after the signing of the Dayton Agreement, support for the dispatching of troops to Bosnia returned to its December level. Overall, support shows a slight decline during the spring of 1996, with the consolidation of IFOR affected by various external factors—stagnation of the peace process, little success in international cooperation, and the focus of public opinion on national problems during and after the Italian electoral campaign—but a subsequent rise in the summer.[20]

The phase of solidarity ended in March 1994 with the opening of a short-lived debate on possible Italian military participation in UNPROFOR. Boutros-Ghali's request for raising the number of "blue helmets" in Bosnia—where the situation had deteriorated and where, for the first time since 1949, NATO had opened fire killing four Serb militia—pushed Britain to propose to the Security Council an intervention by Turkish and Italian troops. Andreatta's favorable bent towards participation contrasted with the more cautious attitude of Defense Minister Fabio Fabbri, who voiced the doubts of the Italian Armed Forces' chiefs about Italian involvement in the Balkan crisis, taking into account the small number of professional soldiers in the army. With its best troops still in Somalia, and the Garibaldi regiment, which had been envisaged since just before the November 1993 budget law as being composed entirely of professional soldiers, not yet in service, Italian participation was not yet feasible. Paradoxically, the strongest support for the dispatch of troops came from the Pacifist movement—long active in Sarajevo—whilst little attention was paid to the issue by political parties, who were currently engaged in the electoral campaign.[21] Minister Fabbri's declaration of the inappropriateness of the UN request for troops from Italy, whose Parliament had just been dissolved, closed the debate, despite Croatian and Slovenian openness towards a possible Italian intervention.[22]

Italian policy towards the Bosnian crisis entered its phase of *assertiveness* during the short-lived Berlusconi government, and continued throughout that of Dini. In the framework of traditional politico-military alliances, the new Foreign Minister Antonio Martino sought to enhance the position of Italy on the international scene during his first visit to Washington in May 1994 and—at the time of the reformulation of the Vance-Owen peace plan—requested that Italy join the Contact Group. As such, this constituted a recognition of the Italian engagement, from whose bases NATO aircraft had been flying missions into Bosnia.[23]

Minister Martino's overall objective of giving Italy a higher international presence—with the display of "a more muscular policy [after the internal crises of the previous two] had weakened the Italian profile in many areas"[24]—may have been evident, but the choice of the Bosnian crisis as an arena (even if a limited one) was not particularly appropriate. The participation in government of *Alleanza Nazionale*, which had included in its electoral program a redrawing of the borders defined by the Treaty of Osimo, and the consolidation of territories already belonging to Italy, significantly characterized Italian foreign policy towards

Slovenia and Croatia, making Italy an inappropriate partner for the negotiating role of the Contact Group. The following veto by Italy of the
association agreement of Slovenia with the EU confirmed this conclusion.
But assertiveness also led to a policy of *realism*, evident in Italy's self-
limitation as regards military involvement. In December 1994, when the
possibility of UNPROFOR withdrawal from Bosnia emerged, and NATO
launched a plan for the safe withdrawal of its contingent, Italy preferred
not to engage its troops. This choice was determined by some international hostility to the foreign policy of the Berlusconi government[25], as
well as the usual UN doubts about intervention by a border country and
doubts about the Italy's military capability for a highly risky ground operation.[26]

Self-limitation associated with assertiveness — but also with *reprisal* —
also characterized the policy of the Dini government which followed.
The fall of Sreberenica and Tuzla in the spring of 1995 determined the
deterioration of prospects for UNPROFOR. The choice facing the troop-
contributing countries (mainly France and Britain) was between
strengthening the peace contingent so that it could effectively combat the
Bosnian Serbs, or withdrawing once and for all. Whilst France and Britain, together with the Netherlands, placed a well-armed rapid intervention force in readiness, NATO launched another military plan to facilitate
an eventual withdrawal of UN forces, with the possible participation of
Italy. Direct Italian involvement in the Bosnian crisis returned to the political agenda. Foreign Minister Susanna Agnelli declared to the Chamber of Deputies that the government did not approve of extreme hypotheses on the fate of UNPROFOR, but neither did it support the prospect
of Bosnian rearmament; however, she made no clear stance on the subject of Italian involvement. This attitude was shared by the political parties: *Alleanza Nazionale* stated that the UN had to choose between serious
intervention or withdrawal, and even the *Partito Popolare* under the former minister Andreatta limited itself to warning against intervening too
readily, declaring "it is necessary to avoid a situation where Bosnia becomes the Vietnam of Europe; public opinion calls for intervention without being ready to shoulder the burden."[27]

At the meeting of the Council of Ministers on 18 July to define the
Italian position for the London Conference (which saw the participation
of the Contact Group and troop-contributing countries, and Italy as part
of the "European Troika") the government did not take any explicit position, but only affirmed the necessity of the peace negotiations in Geneva,
and confirmed that Italian involvement would continue within the
framework of the UN operation.[28] In reality, Ministers Agnelli and Corcione's policy of intervention by ground troops and a contribution by
Italian aircraft to the "Deny Flight" operation, had prevailed. According

to some media reports, the new technocratic Defense Minister Domenico Corcione, a former Chief of Staff, underlined the concrete risk of Serbian reprisals against Italy in case of direct intervention, advising against participation due to the inadequacy of Italian troops as compared to the type of mission required.[29]

Nevertheless, the government's refusal to make a decision provoked criticism, especially from within its own majority, and in particular from the PDS—from the president of the Senate Foreign Affairs committee denounced delaying tactics and the refusal to face problems; and also from Piero Fassino, the party's foreign affairs spokesman, who openly supported Italian intervention. From the opposition, Senator Cesare Previti of *Forza Italia* and its former defense minister, limited himself to declaring that the government's decision reflected what everyone already knew, namely that Italy was not ready to intervene with its military, and at the very most could only offer the use of its bases.

The London Conference defined the participation of Italian aircraft in NATO missions, as effective from their involvement in the bombing of Bosnia in September, thus enlarging the contribution of Italy which until then had been only logistical, though expensive (27 billion lire per month). In this context, the participation of Italy in the Contact Group meetings was also negotiated, thus confirming an Italian presence in the sessions where the medium-term structure of the territory and the plans for the economic reconstruction of the ravaged area were to be defined. Nonetheless, as Minister Agnelli subsequently affirmed[30], Italian participation in the Geneva meetings turned out to be within a consultative rather than negotiating group. The government's reaction to what was perceived, rightly or wrongly, as a deception, led to a reprisal when Italy refused to open its military bases to US Stealth bombers.

The aim of the government was to convince the US to put pressure on the two main opponents to Italian participation in the Contact Group, namely France and Britain, by emphasizing the Italian record of strong transatlantic loyalty. After the firm US refusal and the abstention of Germany, the government, supported in its "blackmail" by all main political parties, could only accept the settlement of the crisis without achieving any positive outcome for itself. The US offered to withdraw its request for the use of air-bases[31], not least because the Croat-Muslim offensive and NATO bombardments had bowed the Bosnian Serbs in the meantime.

The Italian request for a stronger political and diplomatic involvement in Bosnia was reiterated on the occasion of the US-Italy meeting for the definition of the multinational intervention for peace implementation.[32] Italy was invited to participate in the New York meetings of the enlarged Contact Group, but direct NATO responsibility for the peace-keeping operation in Bosnia redefined the operative and diplomatic context of intervention, through a redirection towards the classic decision-making procedure of the Atlantic Alliance, which weakened the Italian objective. The NATO (and US) request to participate in the mission in Bosnia was therefore welcomed by the Italian government[33], with a broad consensus in Parliament. In November 1995, in the debate of the Parliamentary Foreign Affairs and Defense Committees, Italian participation was thus approved—supported as it was by the framework of a peace accord, popular support, and with an Italian presence in all political forums managing the peace agreements. The Greens and *Rifondazione Comunista* found themselves alone in opposition.

The Slow Emergence of a Defense Policy

Not only did the Balkan crisis highlight the inadequacies of the current position of common security and the distance of the EU from being a unified and influential actor on the international stage: it also revealed the limits of Italian defense policy and the inadequacy of Italian military forces, in the framework of internal policy and with a clearly strong impact on foreign policy. The historical and political elements that determined Italian defense policy until the end of the 1980s have been noted. The question is whether the change in the world order, and the simultaneous and partially consequential change in the Italian political system, could actually lead to a redefinition of Italian defense policy. A change in policy had seemed imminent as a result of the hasty proposal for a reform of the armed forces—with the presentation before Parliament of the so-called "New Defense Model" (*nuovo modello di difesa*, or NMD), elaborated by the General Staff for Defense Minister Virginio Rognoni—but from which a coherent body of legislation had never emerged.

This proposal was later re-elaborated, in both its legislative and financial aspects, but not in its guidelines and fundamental concept, during the 11th Legislature by Minister Andò and the 12th Legislature by Ministers Previti and Corcione, but only in 1995 were relevant legislative measures implemented: the Chamber of Deputies approved the reform of the Armed Forces General Staff, the Senate did likewise for conscientious objection (which, although not being an integral part of the NMD, is regarded from a political and technical point of view as such, being closely linked to troop recruitment), whilst the project of organic reorganization of the Armed Forces remained under discussion. The dissolution of Parliament interrupted the legislative process, but not the functional-organizational one: the 1995 budget law already allowed the Defense Ministry to recruit a higher number of volunteers (to form a unit entirely composed of professional soldiers, of the type such as the Garibaldi regiment currently serving in Bosnia). Subsequently, the 1996 budget law granted the right to issue legislative decrees for the functional reorganization of defense to the government (as recently reiterated in the 1997 budget law). Since 8 August 1996, and the Chamber of Deputies' approval of a law for the reorganization of the military High Command, the process seems to have been revived.

The general guidelines of the Italian NMD are now, in short, the following:

— Firstly, a new definition of operational roles of the Armed Forces, which were reduced from five (1995 *Libro Bianco*) to three: presence and monitoring with task of military deterrence towards possible threats; defense of overseas interests and contribution to international security; integrated defense of national areas to protect national and allied integrity and sovereignty.

— Secondly, a significant reduction in personnel (from the present level of 360,000 soldiers to 250,000 as proposed in the Corcione Plan), divided into "active forces" (composed of a core of professional soldiers, characterized by high mobility and transportation capacities, as well as long range capability for the defense of national interests and peace-keeping and enforcing operations), "second phase forces" and "reserve and demobilized forces". From this stems the mixed recruitment system, based on conscription (limited in number) and volunteers (motivated by economic and professional considerations). The number of troop volunteers should rise from the present 15, 000 (4.2% of total forces) to approximately 70,000 (30%), causing conscription to contribute about 30% of personnel to the Armed Forces (compared to the current 60%).

— Thirdly, to ensure a unified command structure, a reform of the military hierarchy has been proposed, with a centralization of operational responsibilities to the Chief of Staff under the authority of which are the heads of the three Armed Services (instead of the present combined collegiate command structure).

— Finally, in order to enhance the qualitative and technological improvement of the defense structure, investment in the modernizing of equipment, to a level of 67,000 billion lire within 15 years, is envisaged. The costs of such a system would raise military expenditure to 1.2% of GDP, a proportion still below the rate of other European countries.

Such a proposal was of course criticized at both the political and strategic level.[34] From the second perspective, the question is again whether to choose a self-sufficient defense model which is still consistent with the international placement of Italy, and therefore seek military autonomy at the regional level, or conversely opt for a functional specialization with the other partners in the alliance.[35] The latter seems to have been encouraged both by the recent Atlantic Summit in Berlin, which established the European Defense Identity, with European forces distinct though not separate from their American counterparts, and also by previous WEU attempts to integrate different national forces in the so-called "Eurocorps" or "Euroforce".

Defense Policy and Party Depolarization

The delay in the approval of NMD can certainly be explained by the slow and woolly national policy style and with the exceptional political situation caused by the transition from the First Republic to the so-called "Second Republic". But this delay could be in some part due to the same national political culture which, in the field of foreign and defense policy, has traditionally been deeply divided, both at the level of the political elite and of the electorate. In the past, the Italian spectrum of shared foreign policy preferences has been particularly narrow. Foreign policy has traditionally been the cause of strong political conflict, with a polarization of party groups along the left-right axis. In order to understand whether Italy will ever achieve a new structure for its armed forces, it is necessary to verify if the current ideological depolarization has attenuated the traditional differences among political groups in matters of defense policy. If bipartisan consensus on the "New Defense Model", and in particular on strategic aspects such as the use of soldiers for peace-enforcing operations abroad and for the defense of national interests, and the scrapping of a conscription army, is forming, then this represents a sharp discontinuity in the Italian political tradition. This means it is necessary to verify if a broadening of the national spectrum of preferences amongst decision leaders has changed towards greater consensus, checking whether there have been substantial changes in public opinion orientation as far as defense is concerned.

During the 1992 elections, the last of the First Republic and the first of the post-cold war era, the parties still appeared to be distant from each other. On the basis of electoral programs, the hypothesis as to the emerging of a bipartisan consensus relating to defense and military policy consequent to ideological depolarization does not appear to be confirmed. The PDS, for instance, was opposed to the NMD and favored a numerically reduced defense structure with the sole task of territorial defense.

The 1994 elections were held within a totally transformed national and international scenario. At the internal level, the majoritarian electoral system, the disappearance of traditional parties and the rise of new political forces determined a complete reformulation of interparty competition. At the international level, the succession of local crises raised again the urgent question of defining an international security body, in which Europe, and consequently Italy, would be able give a more substantial contribution than in the past.

What were the parties' positions relating to security policy? An examination of electoral programs shows on the whole an attenuation in the differences in formulation. It is also noticeable how differences *between* the coalitions were far smaller in comparison with the differences *within* coalitions. For example, the difference between *Forza Italia* (FI) and the PDS was smaller than the difference between either of them and their allies.

As far as the strategic framework is concerned:
— FI wanted to see a reinforcement of European defense, *Alleanza Nazionale* proposed a revision of NATO and EU roles (together with, as already mentioned, a revision of Second World War treaties, and territorial claims regarding Istria, Fiume and Dalmatia).
— Whilst the PDS asked for a reinforcement of the NATO role within Europe, and its absorption by the UN, the Greens simply proposed a reform of the UN.

As far as the Armed Forces are concerned:
— FI and the *Lega* wanted to see mixed conscription/volunteer recruitment, while *Alleanza Nazionale* wanted professional soldiers only; FI was the sole party to propose voluntary female recruitment, and the *Lega*, at the time within the *Polo*, was the only one to propose a reform of the policy concerning conscientious objection.
— The PDS wanted a mixed recruiting system, but favored progressive professionalization; *Rifondazione Comunista* favored a reduction in military expenditure and a law concerning conscientious objection, as did the Greens.

The 1994 elections therefore outlined, on the basis of new political proposals in electoral programs, a new consensus on the fundamental principles of security policy. There was in fact a general agreement among the main parties on the issue of integrating the national military within NATO, with a tendency to emphasize the European component. At the same time, all the main political forces agreed on the necessity of progressively abandoning conscription as the sole means of recruitment within the Armed Forces, with a view to establishing a mixed conscription/volunteer system: the only dissenting voice came from *Alleanza Nazionale*, which proposed an entirely professional recruitment. However, the most radical differences only affected the extremes, with *Alleanza Nazionale* on one side and *La Rete*, *Rifondazione Comunista* and the Greens on the other.

These differences could have produced an asymmetrical political impact, as right and left showed differences at the ideological-symbolic level: from *Alleanza Nazionale* invoking the reappropriation of territory assigned to Yugoslavia after the Second World War, to the adhesion by the left parties to an idealistic vision of international relations. As has already been remarked, the *Alleanza Nazionale* position had a strong influence on the foreign policy of the Berlusconi government. Nonetheless, a pragmatic attenuation of this symbolic component could have plausibly been expected, as this party gradually shifted towards the center. The traditional issue could have remained salient for activists, notwithstanding its fading amid the growth of other party themes. In such a situation, the difference between *Alleanza Nazionale* and *Forza Italia* could have been limited to a stronger engagement towards military professionalism, without causing substantial damage in terms of the overlapping of their respective electorates. On the other hand, the ideological evolution of smaller leftist parties, for whom the idealistic vision of international relations—from pacifism to North-South cooperation—appeared to be a central part of their political identities, seemed more uncertain: this vision was difficult to dilute but equally difficult to integrate into the offer of the other parties successively allied to the electoral cartel of *Ulivo*, PDS and PPI. These considerations had a direct impact on the positions taken in the case of Italian participation in IFOR.

The 1996 elections witnessed a significant increase in bipartisan consensus among parties in the field of security policy (Table 10.1). The *Polo per le Libertà* and the *Ulivo* presented programs which were almost identical and which included the reform of the UN Security Council, national military integration within NATO opened to the East, and with an increased emphasis on the European component (favoring the integration of WEU within the EU common foreign and security policy). The only differences, more in emphasis than in substance, regard the recruitment model and conscientious objection. The *Polo per le Libertà* clearly favors professional armed forces (including female recruitment), whilst the *Ulivo* opts for a mixed system of conscription and volunteers, with a strong presence of the latter; on the other hand, the *Polo per le Libertà* recognizes the right to conscientious objection, whereas the *Ulivo* proposes national civil service open to women, to be formed by objectors and all those that prefer civil service to conscription.

Besides a reduced distance between the coalitions, an attenuation of differences within them has been observed. Within the *Polo*, FI and *Alleanza Nazionale* experienced a clear convergence in ideas. The former accepted *Alleanza Nazionale*'s strong tendency towards a professional army, while the latter agreed upon full integration within NATO (and a subsequent strengthening of ties between Europe and US, for which the

Alleanza Nazionale had traditionally shown no enthusiasm) and dropped any question of borders. More problematic was the situation within the *Ulivo*, whose program overlapped with the PDS and PPI's ideas (with the Greens following, although with some hesitation), but not with *Rifondazione*'s convictions, which remain anchored to its traditional opposition to NATO and any notion of professionalizing the armed forces. In terms of future legislation, this will involve a diversification and opposition of roles among the party coalitions in the Prodi government.

TABLE 10.1. Foreign and Military Policies in 1996 Party Election Programs

	Foreign Policy	National Security
Polo per le Libertà	Reform of UN Security Council. Greater Italian participation in NATO. NATO enlargement to include Eastern Europe. Integration of Eastern Europe and Mediterranean countries in EU.	Professionalization of armed forces, including female recruitment, and progressive reduction in conscription. Recognition of right of conscientious objectors to serve in credible and viable civil service. Maintenance of current levels of expenditure, with modernization of equipment and organization. Development of defense industries.
Ulivo	Broadening of EU to include Southern and Eastern Europe. Closer ties between EU and WEU. European pillar within NATO. NATO expansion to the East. Reform of the UN Security Council.	Integration in NATO, to adequate European armament levels. Mixed system of recruitment: professional and conscription. Construction of civil service, open to women, conscientious objectors and those not choosing conscription.
Rifondaz. Comunista	Discontinuation of NATO. Promotion of a conference on Mediterranean security and cooperation. Nuclear disarmament of Europe and the Mediterranean.	Reduction in conscription without professionalizing Armed Forces. Reform of conscientious objection; reduction in military expenditure and conversion of defense industries. Overseas missions exclusively under UN command.
Lega Nord		Integrated European defense; reduction in conscription; distinction between technologically advanced national defense, and preventive and peace-keeping intervention.

Let us now verify whether the process of ideological depolarization that produced substantial bipartite consensus on security policy as iterated in the 1996 electoral programs also characterized the attitudes and opinions of members of Parliament between the years 1993-1995.[36] The answer appears to be substantially positive. If we consider the tendencies of involved members of Parliament, in other words the members of the Chamber and Senate Committees for Defense, the necessity of granting the Italian Armed Forces a new operative and organizational structure emerges.[37] Since the NMD proposal is based upon an analysis of risk situations for Italy, which is different from the one adopted in the past (due to the disappearance of Eastern threats, Eastern and Mediterranean instability, *inter alia*), it is useful to evaluate the positions of members of Parliament on actual risks. These are reduced, in 1995, to two socio-political factors, namely Islamic fundamentalism and economic differences between the North and South of the world. Strangely enough, there is no significant mention of the situation in the Balkans (see Figure 10.2). Finally, the favorite alliance structure is that of Italy remaining part of NATO, but for 65% of members of Parliament this means constituting, within NATO, a Western European force with a European leadership. Seventy percent of PDS members of Parliament, 80% of *Alleanza Nazionale* members of Parliament and 57% of *Forza Italia* members of Parliament favor this option.

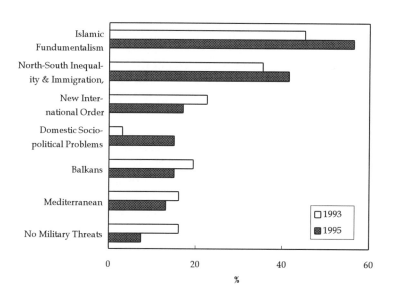

FIGURE 10.2. Threats to Italian Security
According to Members of Parliament, 1993 and 1995

Considering the preferred recruitment model between the years 1993-1995, the consensus for a mixed conscription/volunteer system decreases (from 74% to 58%) and, accordingly, consensus for a professional army grows (20% to 26%). Entirely professional armed forces are favored by 70% of *Alleanza Nazionale* members of Parliament, 57% of *Forza Italia* members of Parliament and surprisingly, 23% of PDS members of Parliament. Finally, in 1995, half of the members of Parliament favored an increase in military expenditure. This is the only issue where distinct political polarization is noticeable: the expenditure increase is favored by 15% of PDS members of Parliament (50% want it to remain unchanged) as opposed to 86% of *Forza Italia* members of Parliament and 60% of *Alleanza Nazionale* members of Parliament.

The final issue to be considered regards the relationship between public opinion and elaboration of political choices which, as is clear in the case of Bosnia, has a direct influence (and rightly so) on choices of foreign policy according to some, whilst for others it is highly advisable that such influence be avoided (the reason given being that public opinion's reaction to events is primarily emotional, and thus must not determine the choices of political leaders). Still considering consensus for the relevant choices in the field of defense policy (not in a time of crisis) and comparing the structure of preferences of the political elites with those of the voters, the result is some homogeneity but also significant differences. The perception of threats to Italian security is similar while, conversely, the difference between members of Parliament and voters is stronger in terms of the recruitment model: the volunteer system is favored by the majority of voters (43%), while the mixed one is favored by 34% — a complete inversion of the structure of parliamentarians' preferences. The differences among parties faithfully reflect such heterogeneity: 49% of *Alleanza Nazionale* voters favor an army of professionals (against 70% of their representation); in contrast, a quarter of Green and *Rifondazione* voters favor a professional army against a total rejection of this possibility by their representatives. It should be noted, nonetheless, that the overall tendency of members of Parliament and public opinion between the years 1993-1995 is towards homogeneity. Preferences for professional recruitment rise by 6 percentage points among members of Parliament and 8 percentage points among voters, while those favoring a mixed system decrease by 16 points among the former, and 13 points among the latter. We therefore witness significant consistency in the change of preferences between voters and members of Parliament (see Figure 10.3).

A comparative analysis of the structure of preferences for voters and their parliamentary representatives, and especially of Defense Committee decision-makers, reveals a stronger homogeneity of preference among voters of the different parties as compared to their parliamentary representatives. In other words, the representatives are more radical and polarized than their voters, both at the level of single parties and of the respective electoral coalitions. These party differences should not be overly stressed as they take place in a context characterized by greater homogeneity in political forces than in the past, and where differences regard more procedure and emphasis (how to do it) than proposals and objectives (what to do).

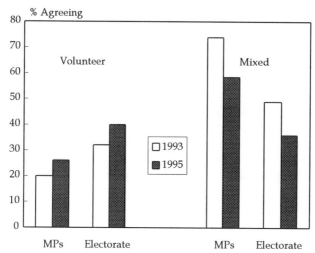

FIGURE 10.3. Evolution of Public Opinion and Members of Parliament's Preferences Concerning Type of Military Recruitment, 1993 and 1995

Italians now seem to pay considerable attention to the issue of security; but that does not mean that this interest is stable or that the perception of a national interest for Italy is clearly defined. The Difebarometro survey no. 3/1996[38] reveals that for the majority of Italians, the primary national interest is "internal political stability"; only 20% think of strengthening the image of Italy abroad as a priority objective, and only 7% mention the security of borders and defense of fellow nationals abroad. This highlights how, rightly, an effective foreign policy requires a stable and authoritative government. On the other hand, this result might imply a tendency for the Italian public to emphasize domestic problems versus international issues. In fact, the available data seem to suggest that Italian public opinion, after a phase of interest and open support for a stronger projection of Italy in the international arena between 1989 and 1994, is currently undergoing a phase of introspection and disillusionment about any possibilities of securing world peace after the bipolarization of the cold war. Between January 1994 and June 1996 a systematic decrease in the percentage of Italians oriented towards a multilateral foreign policy (the "internationalists", who wish foreign policy to be characterized by intense coordination with allies) can be observed. At the same time the number of those who feel that Italy should adopt an isolationist attitude, concentrating instead on domestic problems, rises. This tendency reversed in July 1996, and can be plausibly explained as a drop in uncertainty caused by the election campaign which had focused attention on internal policy. The expectation of greater internal political stability allows them to support greater involvement of Italy in international affairs.[39]

To conclude: in the middle of the 1990s, Italian public opinion is characterized by a political culture open to international issues, where innovative dimensions coexist with traditional aspects. Amongst the former are the ideological depolarization of voters and their subsequent homogeneity of preferences in the field of foreign and security policy, and a greater attention to international policy; amongst the latter are the uncertain perception of a national interest and an attitude favoring delegation in matters of international policy. The number of "isolationists", as well as support for a professional volunteer recruitment system, is greater. This attitude towards delegation shows both continuity and change: in line with the past, and especially the 1960s and 1970s[40], delegation shows a desire to hand over the defense of Italy to international organizations, such as NATO; and innovation can be perceived in the choice of delegating defense to a national army of professional soldiers.

Translated by Jocelyn Evans

Notes

1. The IFOR mission is also the first joint NATO-Partnership for Peace operation, involving non-aligned countries, such as Russia. Thirty countries are included with a total contingent of 60,000 troops, including 20,000 Americans, 12,00 British, 8,000 French and 4,000 Germans. The IFOR mission—to enforce the military agreements elaborated in the peace treaty—states the following as its main objectives: the upholding of the end of hostilities and the control of Bosnian airspace; the collection of heavy weapons and the demobilization of remaining forces; the identification and separation of factions; the definition and surveillance of the separation zone; the monitoring of the return of factions to their designated zones. To help the implementation of these measures in their entirety, according to the Conference of London on the civil and political reconstruction of Bosnia (8-9 December 1995), IFOR is responsible for the safety and control of the local population, collaborates in mine-field clearance and the dismantling of local military residues from the conflict, and ensures assistance for

intergovernmental and non-governmental humanitarian aid organizations. The initial duration of the mission, originally set at 12 months, has recently been extended for a further 18 months, with a reduced troop contingent of 31 000. See *Il Sole-24 Ore*, 5 December 1996.

2. The military contingent in the previous Italian mission in a multinational context — to Somalia in 1992 — was composed of conscripted troops who had to a greater or lesser extent volunteered. For an analysis of the motivating factors for soldiers involved in the peace-keeping operation, within a broader discussion of conscripted volunteers in the modern army, see F. Battistelli, *Soldati. Sociologia dei militari italiani nell'era del peace-keeping* (Milan: Franco Angeli, 1996). On Italian intervention in Somalia, see O. Croci, "The Italian Intervention in Somalia: A New Italian Foreign Policy After the Cold War?", in C. Mershon and G. Pasquino, eds., *Italian Politics: Ending the First Republic* (Boulder: Westview Press, 1995).

3. P. Isernia, "Bandiera e risorse: la politica estera negli anni ottanta", in M. Cotta and P. Isernia, eds., *Il gigante dai piedi di argilla* (Bologna: Il Mulino, 1996).

4. For analyses of the attempts to increase the assertiveness of Italian foreign policy in the 1990s, see J.W. Holmes, "Italian Foreign Policy in a Changing Europe", in S. Hellmann and G. Pasquino, eds., *Italian Politics: A Review, Vol. 8* (London: Pinter, 1993); O. Croci, "The Italian Intervention in Somalia", *op. cit.*; P.M. Neal, "The New Foreign Policy", in R.S. Katz and P. Ignazi, eds., *Italian Politics: The Year of the Tycoon* (Boulder: Westview Press, 1996). For an analysis of Italian foreign policy in the context of two-level game theory, see P. Isernia, "Bandiera e risorse", *op. cit.*

5. This role was confirmed after the end of the conflict. Italy, with a contribution of $50 million is, together with Holland, the most generous EU country in terms of Bosnian aid.

6. See J.W. Holmes, "Italian Foreign Policy in a Changing Europe", *op. cit.*

7. See *Presidenza del Consiglio dei ministri*, minutes of the meeting of 16 January 1992, in *Vita Italiana*, 1992.

8. See interview with Amato in *Il Corriere della Sera*, July 19, 1992.

9. See *Presidenza del Consiglio dei ministri*, minutes of the meeting of 25 August 1992, in *Vita Italiana*, 1992.

10. *La Repubblica*, 26 August 1992.

11. *Il Corriere della Sera*, 13 September 1992.

12. *La Repubblica*, 12 September 1992.

13. *Il Corriere della Sera*, 11 February 1994.

14. *Il Corriere della Sera*, 8 January 1994.

15. *La Repubblica*, 26 January 1994.

16. *La Repubblica*, 6 February 1994.

17. *La Repubblica*, 13 February 1994.

18. See R. Sobel, "US and European Attitudes toward Intervention in the Former Yugoslavia: *Mourir pour la Bosnie*?", in R.H. Ulman, ed., *The World and Yugoslavia's Wars* (New York: Council of Foreign Relations, 1996), pp. 145-181.

19. *Ibid.*, p. 178.

20. For an analysis of Italian public opinion on foreign policy, see P. Isernia, *Dove gli angeli non mettono piede. Opinione pubblica e politiche di sicurezza in Italia* (Milan: Franco Angeli, 1996).

21. *Il Corriere della Sera*, 6 March 1994.

22. *La Repubblica*, 8 March 1994.

23. *Il Sole-24 Ore*, 25 May 1994.

24. *La Repubblica*, 22 June 1994.

25. See P.M. Neal, "The New Foreign Policy", *op. cit.*

26. As transpired in a subsequent interview with Chief of Staff Venturoni, who bemoaned the lack of resources, but above all of a defense policy, which exposes the Italian armed forces to the risk of becoming outdated. See *La Repubblica*, 9 February 1995.

27. *Il Sole-24 Ore*, 13 July 1995.

28. See *Presidenza del Consiglio dei ministri*, minutes of meeting of 18 July 1995, in *Vita Italiana*, 1995.

29. Il *Corriere della Sera*, 19 July 1995.

30. Speaking in a debate at the PDS "Festa dell'Unità" in September; see *Il Corriere della Sera*, 13 September 1995.

31. *Il Sole-24 Ore*, 17 September 1995.

32. *Il Corriere della Sera*, 3 October 1995.

33. See *Presidenza del Consiglio dei ministri*, minutes of meeting of 2 November 1995, in *Vita Italiana*, 1995.

34. For an analysis of political reactions to the NMD proposals, see P. Isernia, *Politica militare e sistema politico: i partiti ed il nuovo modello di difesa* (Rome: CeMiSS, 1994). For a critique of the strategic installation of the model, see C.M. Santoro, ed., *Modello e modelli difesa* (Bologna: Il Mulino, 1992).

35. See C. Jean, *L'uso della forza* (Rome-Bari: Laterza, 1996).

36. On the basis of the two surveys carried out on members of the Chamber of Deputies and Senate Committees for Defense during the 11th and 12th Legislatures. The initial findings are presented in P. Bellucci, *La politica di difesa in Italia tra professionismo ed obiezione di coscienza*, paper presented at a conference promoted by the Italian Association of Sociology's Sociology and Politics Section, Turin, 8-10 May 1996.

37. Whilst in 1993, the criticisms of the constitutionality of the proposed NMD (with the possibility of military intervention outside national boundaries for active contributions to international security and to the defense of national interests) were supported by 30% of parliamentary members of the Defense Committee, in 1995 the criticisms only accounted for 15%, to be found in the Green-*La Rete* and *Rifondazione Comunista* political grouping. Seventy-seven percent of deputies and senators in the PDS held that the NMD does not in fact breach constitutional principles (see P. Bellucci, *La politica di difesa in Italia, op. cit.*).

38. See *Difebarometro*, report no. 3 (January), 1996.

39. See *Difebarometro*, report no. 4 (September), 1996.

40. See P. Isernia, *Dove gli angeli non mettono piede, op. cit.*

12

Statesman or Godfather?
The Andreotti Trials

Percy Allum

What Italian commentators have not hesitated to call the "trial of the century", in other words the trial for "mafia conspiracy" of Life Senator Giulio Andreotti, alias the "divine Giulio", seven-time prime minister and member of 34 of the 48 governments between 1946 and 1992, opened before the seventh section of the Court of Palermo on 26 September 1995. It was a trial that looks like lasting longer than any before, given the mass of documents (over 100,000 pages), the number (over 500) and quality (ministers and mafiosi, Sicilians and foreigners) of the witnesses called to appear, and the anticipated length (150 hearings planned, verdict expected in 1998). It was no surprise therefore that the opening in the bunker-courtroom of the Ucciardone Prison was invaded by the world media (50 television chains, 300 reporters, including 150 foreigners and their interpreters), the more so since "mafia" is one of the Italian words to have been round the world. Further, on 5 November 1995, the judge at the preliminary hearing in Perugia found that Andreotti had a case to answer for the murder of Mino Pecorelli, shot in Rome on 20 March 1979 and sent him for trial at the local Assize Court on 11 April 1996.

If the charge against Andreotti at Perugia is the more serious—he faces a life sentence—it is in one way simpler to face in the sense that the prosecution must prove that Andreotti's actions were personally intended to commit a specific crime (Pecorelli's murder). In the charges at Palermo, on the other hand, according to Article 416 bis of the Penal Code (introduced in the Rognoni-La Torre Law of 10 September 1982) simple relations between members of associations having certain "mafia" characteristics are sufficient for the crime of "mafia conspiracy"[1]. According to the Palermo Prosecutor's Office, in fact, there was evidence to believe that Andreotti had:

> made available to the mafia association named Cosa Nostra for the defense of its interests and the attainment of its criminal goals, the influence and power coming from his position as the leader of a political faction, as well as relations developed in the course of his actions and in this way he participated in the support, strengthening and expansion of the same association.[2]

In short, the judges claim that Andreotti had an organic relationship with the leadership of Cosa Nostra for at least twenty years; he furnished the bosses with political and legal support, and the latter, in exchange, secured votes and power for his political faction. To sustain the charges, the prosecution made use of numerous depositions of repentant mafiosi who turned state's witness (*pentiti*) and concrete, verified evidence. The defense naturally contested the veracity of both the dispositions and the evidence. Andreotti repeated that he had never helped the mafia; that he had never met mafia bosses, nor had any relation whatsoever with them. Indeed, he rejected out of hand the existence of a mafia-politics chain ("Buscetta theorem") formulated by the prosecution. It was up to the latter, argued his lawyers, to demonstrate his links with the mafia, something which they claimed it had singularly failed to do hitherto.

The Case for the Prosecution[3]

Arlacchi has pointed out that the prosecution's case consists of four elements:
1) the statements of 16 *pentiti* (including Tommaso Buscetta, Antonino Calderone, Francesco Marino Mannoia, and Gioacchino Pennino) which form the core of the prosecution case. Indeed, it was only in 1992 that a mafioso (Salvatore Messina) named Andreotti[4] personally for the first time. Subsequently, they spoke of a series of meetings between Andreotti and mafia bosses (Stefano Bontade, Toto Riina) as well as Salvo Lima's (the leader of Andreotti's faction in Sicily) role as intermediary between Cosa Nostra and Andreotti since 1969;
2) the evidence of businessmen, civil servants and Christian Democrat colleagues on the relations of Andreotti not only with Lima, but also with Corrado Carnevale, (the famous "sentence-killer" judge of the Court of Cassation, the court of ultimate appeal), with the mafia Salvo cousins (notorious and powerful "tax-farmers" from Salemi) and other exponents of Cosa Nostra;

3) the investigations and verification of witnesses' statements;
4) the examination of the enormous documentation of the numerous parliamentary enquiries (Antimafia, Sindona, P2) and judicial investigations (Aldo Moro, Mino Pecorelli, General Carlo Alberto Dalla Chiesa, Salvo Lima murders).

The episodes which the prosecution examined are many and complex, and their verification extremely difficult: suffice it to note that the prosecution developed 36 points in its reconstruction of Andreotti's relations with the mafia which cover a period of over twenty years, that went from Lima's (member of parliament and former mayor of Palermo) adherence to Andreotti's faction in 1969, to the meetings between the defendant and the bosses thanks to the Salvo cousins, Nino and Ignazio, to the Moro kidnapping, the Pecorelli murder and the friendship with the bankrupt financier Michele Sindona[4]. Naturally, it is not possible to outline all the episodes here. However, they all have one thing in common: the development of Andreotti's faction which, thanks to the Sicilians' support, was transformed from a simple Lazio faction to a faction of national importance (from circa 2 percent to 10 percent of the DC membership). At the time, Lima was one of the politicians most strongly supported by Cosa Nostra (and in particular by the boss Stefano Bontade); he enjoyed also very close ties to the Salvo cousins.

In 1976, Andreotti and Lima made a political pact with Vito Ciancimino (another former mayor of Palermo), who had close ties to the Corleonesi family, ratified at Palazzo Chigi; in 1978 Andreotti activated Bontade (and through him Buscetta) to attempt Moro's liberation and then halted the attempt; later the same year through Franco Evangelisti (his lieutenant and junior minister at the Prime Minister's Office) and the P2 leadership, he exerted pressure on the Bank of Italy to try to save Sindona's Banca Privata Italiana from collapse and through diplomatic channels to prevent Sindona's extradition from the United States to Italy to face charges.

In 1979, the Piersanti Mattarella (a Christian Democrat, President of the Sicilian Region) affair occurred. Up to that moment Mattarella had respected the Lima-Ciancimino pact, but in the spring, after the murder of DC Provincial Secretary, Michele Reina, he initiated a new policy hostile to the mafia. Andreotti came to Sicily to be briefed on the situation at a meeting with Bontade, Lima and the Salvo cousins. On 6 January 1980 Piersanti Mattarella was shot in Palermo on the decision of the "Cupola", and a few months later Andreotti returned to Sicily for another meeting with Bontade, Lima and the Salvo cousins at a villa on the outskirts of Palermo to protest at the killing. When Bontade threatened to withdraw his electoral support for Andreotti's faction, Andreotti was forced to accept the situation.

The prosecution's thesis is, thus, that Andreotti, having used the mafia organization for his own political ends, was unable to withdraw from
a criminal pact with it. On the contrary, he was obliged to strengthen it,
and this explains not only his very close ties with Lima, but also with the
Salvo cousins. From here, his probable involvement in several "Italian
mysteries" with even more serious implications: the Pecorelli (through
another lieutenant, Claudio Vitalone) and General Dalla Chiesa assassinations. In the mid-1980s, with the victory of the Corleonesi family
within Cosa Nostra, Andreotti's relations with the criminal organization
became more difficult. But, when the Andreotti faction failed to commit
itself sufficiently against the "maxi-trial" of 1986 or was unable to prevent the approval of the Mancini-Violante Law no. 29 of 7 February 1987
(which modified the terms of preventative custody, hence the liberation
of defendants), Cosa Nostra switched its votes in Palermo and elsewhere
to the PSI. Lima's and the Salvos' position became dangerous, and Andreotti was obliged to meet Riina—the occasion of the famous "kiss"
during a lull in the DC Festival of Friendship in Palermo—to save Lima's
life and with it his faction's power.

In this way, we come to the final episode which ended with Lima's
assassination and the *pentiti*'s accusations against Andreotti. The cause
was the maxi-trial appeal: it began in 1987 with a gradual dismantling
thanks to a long series of measures of the first penal section of the Court
of Cassation (presided over by Judge Corrado Carnevale), which used a
special technique for assessing the evidence with the result of undermining the *pentiti*'s statements. The mafia bosses expected the annul-
ment of the life-sentences thanks to the intervention of Andreotti and
Lima, who would have drawn Carnevale's attention to the problem as
he was close to Andreotti. However, the expected happy outcome did
not materialize because Carnevale was no longer in control of the situation, despite the violence unleashed by Cosa Nostra[6]: in fact, thanks to
the intervention of the Higher Council of the Judiciary, neither Carnevale nor his allies were appointed to hear the case, and consequently the
verdict was confirmed on 30 January 1992. A verdict which, according to
Pino Arlacchi, "sanctioned the historic defeat of Cosa Nostra, Buscetta's
and the other *pentiti*'s final reliability and the solidity of the judicial edi-
fice constructed by Judge Giovanni Falcone and his collaborators". The
consequences were almost immediate: the successive assassinations of
Lima (12 March 1992)[7], Falcone (23 May), Judge Paolo Borsellino (19
July), and Ignazio Salvo (17 September); and the naming of Andreotti by
the *pentiti*: Messina (3 August 1992), Gaspare Mutolo (17 December
1992), Mannoia (3 April 1993), Buscetta (6 April 1993).

With regard to the Pecorelli trial, the sources of the evidence are once
again the *pentiti*'s statements and the whole investigation which, ac-

cording to the judge at the preliminary hearing, "offers a coherent and convincing framework... This is particularly true of those who are named as the instigators of the murder" (i.e., Andreotti). In short, according to the *pentiti*, Pecorelli was killed because he was in possession of secrets about the Moro case, which, if revealed, would have damaged Andreotti very seriously indeed. It was a question of the missing pages of Moro's statement to the Red Brigades — discovered only in 1990, but the contents of which Pecorelli seems to have already known in 1978 — which poured light both on Andreotti's dealings with Sindona as well as his involvement in the biggest scandal of the time, that of the Italcasse. The investigation into Pecorelli's killing had progressively reduced the possible causes of the crime to the events surrounding Moro's statement and the Italcasse scandal. Indeed, the publication in 1979 of Moro's authentic statement could have damaged Andreotti to the extent of ending his political career because it would have become known that Andreotti had quietly collected the Italcasse billions and assigned a part to a Roman criminal group linked to the mafia's financial interests. According to the reconstruction of the investigating magistrates, Pecorelli was shot by two killers, one belonging to the "Magliana gang" and the other to Cosa Nostra. In addition, several *pentiti* accused Claudio Vitalone (a Roman judge before becoming a DC senator in Andreotti's faction) as one of the instigators of the killing. Thus, the Perugia Prosecutor's Office asked for Andreotti, Vitalone and three others to be sent for trial for concurrence in murder which was granted at the preliminary hearing in November 1995[8].

The Case for the Defense[9]

Andreotti's defense technique was simple: undermine the credibility of the *pentiti*'s statements which formed the basis of the prosecution's case. For this reason from the moment of his committal for trial, Andreotti used his access to the media (TV, press, books) to oppose the image of the statesman who had dedicated forty years of his life to the service of the national and international communities with that which appeared in the Sicilian mafia bosses' and killers' statements: his word against theirs. It was no coincidence that he cited in his defense the "gotha" of international diplomacy: the former American ambassadors to Italy, Peter Secchia and Maxwell Rabb; former German Foreign Minister Hans Deitrich Genscher; former US Secretary of State, Henry Kissinger, etc.[10] The prestige that he enjoyed abroad is an important symbolic element in his defense: it demonstrates of itself his extraneousness to the whole affair along the lines of the communiqué which he released on 23 March 1993, giving notice of the opening of the investigation into his activity:

> To accuse me of mafia is paradoxical. As a government and also personally I have adopted strong measures and proposed very severe and efficient laws against the mafiosi. I should have expected their vendetta and in a certain sense it is better like this than with the *lupara* [sawn-off shotgun].[11]

This line was strengthened by his criticism of the basis of the prosecution's case: "a basic defect of the investigation lies in confusing — a more or less accurate — historical reconstruction of the island DC with a criminal trial against me". It is Sicilian history ("personally", Andreotti claimed, "I have never been engaged in the administration of political matters concerning Sicily") while he is a political actor who has been playing on the national and international stage; hence Andreotti's refrain is: "What has this got to do with me?"[12].

In this situation, for him the basic thesis of the prosecution is simply ridiculous: to wit, that his political power had anything whatsoever to do with the strength of his Sicilian faction in the DC. His counter is based on two elements: 1) "I have never had appointments... from the party"; 2) he was already well placed politically before Lima's group joined his faction, having been Minister of Defense for six years and Minister of Finance for three. Hence, he had no need of the Sicilians' support: "he who imputes", he has said, "a determining role to these factional arrangements is on the wrong track". One can note, however, that if is true that the take-off of Andreotti's political career owed everything to his relations with Alcide De Gasperi and his links with the Vatican which initially secured his Lazio base, it is also true that the support of a faction became essential in the Cencelli Code[13] era, if one was to remain one of the DC's top leaders[14]. One can also add that his access to the premiership occurred only after the Sicilian group joined.

Naturally, this line of defense requires that he deny all the charges en bloc, that is to say the knowledge of any person or any fact that could link him in any way with Cosa Nostra, and he did it in a deliberately tough and merciless manner: "the accusation is nil".[15] But, as the Palermo prosecutors observed:

> Instead of furnishing plausible explanations regarding the facts about which he was questioned — he was often obliged to have recourse to the most improbable statements, and occasionally even to obvious untruths, most disconcerting in a man of his intellectual standing.[16]

So, Andreotti plays down, softens, denies: he claims that he never had the least suspicion that Lima had contacts with the mafia, "even if this reply might appear unconvincing".[17] Indeed, he specified that their twenty-year relationship was only political and not personal and that Lima had never mentioned them to him. Similarly, to the question, "is it possible for you to say that you alone never knew the Salvo [cousins]?" (the powerful and notorious mafiosi, Lima's friends—referred to as the "political and financial lungs of Andreotti's faction in Sicily"[18]), he replied: "It is not only possible, it is a fact." And naturally, he has never seen Riina: "that kiss... is a hypothesis that floats in the rarefied atmosphere of the absurd. For the rest, the shadows of the ridiculous grow".

Even as regards Corrado Carnevale, the "sentence-killer" judge, who was said to be close to him, Andreotti claims that he only had "relations of the good morning and good evening kind" with him; of Claudio Vitalone, considered his political creature, he denied that he was even part of his entourage. Finally, he dismissed his relations with Sindona, whom he had proclaimed in 1973 "the Savior of the Lira", with the statement: "there was a Sindona 1 and a Sindona 2. I had relations with Sindona 1, not with Sindona 2..."; in other words, there was a good financier before the 1974 crash whom half of Italy admired; and a fraudulent bankrupt with whom he had broken all relations, despite evidence to the contrary.[19]

Andreotti's reply to the specific facts which, according to the *pentiti*, involved him with Cosa Nostra, was even more drastic and blunt in its denial: for example, his meetings with mafiosi (Bontade, the Salvo cousins, Lima) in Sicily before and after the assassination of Mattarella are "an absolute pack of lies"; the meeting with Riina, Lima and Ignazio Salvo in Palermo in 1987 "another great pack of lies"; at this point he resorted to the thesis of his escort which follows his every step; that is, given his ministerial posts, all his movements in Italy and abroad are not only monitored but also recorded. Hence, it is impossible for him to make unsupervised movements. However, as a result of the prosecution's investigations, it appears that his movements were often not recorded and that it was easy for him in Sicily, even on official visits, to escape temporarily from the control both of the local escort and those who accompanied him from Rome.[20]

Finally, in the case of the documents and statements of persons "above suspicion", like Aldo Moro and General Dalla Chiesa, or his faithful lieutenants, like Franco Evangelisti and Vittorio Sbardella, Andreotti always finds a means to decry the sincerity of their statements. In his view, their testimony is vitiated by personal circumstances: if Moro wrote those things about me it was due to the conditions of his kidnapping by the Red Brigades and in any case, everybody knows that the letters were not true; if General Dalla Chiesa narrated those things in his personal diary, they were his existential problems that put him "in a

very particular spiritual state", inducing "mental confusion"; if Evangelisti confirmed circumstances that he denies it was because "he was very
debilitated... which... could make him reconstruct past events without
the proper accuracy."; if Sbardella made those statements, "they must be
assessed... in the light of the conflicts... in my faction." Finally, when
Claudio Martelli, the former Justice Minister in his last government, disputed his claim to the exclusive paternity of the antimafia legislation of
the 1980s, he offers a poisoned confession:

> Martelli's behavior saddened me, but I do not hold it against him. He was
> worried that the Prosecutor's Office might draw conclusions from the many
> *pentiti* statements on the pro-PSI electoral mobilization in Sicily in 1987... In
> the official record there is a grudge of his against me because unnamed
> lawyers, friends of mine, had promoted the affair of the protection fund.
> That I should investigate my ministers, and give credence to their denigra-
> tions is absolutely absurd. If anything... *I made the mistake of not keeping my
> eyes open enough.*[21]

This confession on the part of the most experienced politician in Italy
who had participated in nearly all the political combinations of the last
fifty years is nothing less than astonishing![22]
    In short, for Andreotti the whole case is the result of a conspiracy
against him. In his testimony to the Palermo investigating magistrates,
he formulated the vague hypothesis of an "unknown prompter", probably of American origin, given that the two most important *pentiti*, Buscetta and Mannoia, were interrogated in the United States. In support
of this hypothesis—which in pre-trial interviews, he called a "plot" and
pointed to an FBI official, Dick Martin—he published a letter from Abra-
ham Soafer (former aid to George Schultz at the US State Department in
the 1980s), a lawyer whom he had charged to look after his interests in
America:

> In the last three days, three reporters have called me... to have my reaction
> to a statement of yours in which you accuse the US government of being
> party to a sort of conspiracy against you... I replied that I had never heard
> you say anything of the kind... However, I said that the American govern-
> ment had treated you most unjustly, denying you access to the two *pentiti*
> who had given evidence against you... I added that it was possible that the
> Justice Department prosecutors had recalled resentfully the position that
> you had taken long ago in favor of dialogue with the PLO as well as the deci-
> sion to authorize Abu Abbas' departure from Italy after the Achille Lauro
> affair.[23]

He added that the straw that broke the camel's back, as it made the
English furious, was his decision to make public in Parliament the exis-

tence of the military apparatus, Gladio, without even warning them in advance.

The Trials in Progress

In Palermo the first great procedural battle engaged at the outset concerned territorial competence: the defense argued that Andreotti could not be tried in Palermo, but that the proper place was Rome or, failing that, Perugia where he was charged with murder, a much more serious crime than mafia conspiracy. The substantial point that lay behind this request was to establish whether Andreotti had committed the crimes he was accused of as a member of the government or simply as a politician. In the first case, the defense argued, the Ministers' Tribunal would be competent; in the second Rome or, as an ultimate hypothesis, Perugia. The prosecution countered that Andreotti's responsibility did not concern his activity as a member of the government, but that as leader of a faction that became important when Lima joined, given that Andreotti never acted directly, but always through intermediaries. Hence, Palermo was the natural place for a mafia trial because the massacres occurred in Sicily and the power and business center of Cosa Nostra still was to be found there[24]: "to transfer the trial", argued Public Prosecutor Guido Lo Forte, "is tantamount to not holding it".[25] After a week's suspension, the Court decided in favor of the prosecution. The Perugia judges followed suit a week later, committing Andreotti to stand trial in April 1996 for Pecorelli's murder. And this, despite the defense's argument that "there is no evidence and above all no motive, and if there is no motive, there can be no charge"[26]; the reason: Pecorelli, a cheap hack, was too insignificant to worry a man of Andreotti's stature. The distance between the two was far too great to think that Andreotti could give orders to his faithful lieutenant Vitalone to have Pecorelli silenced.

From December 1995 in Palermo (with audiences in Rome and Padua), and from May 1996 in Perugia, the *pentiti* have taken their stand in the witness box to testify. It will apparently need a further two years to hear all the witnesses who grow as the trials proceed and new evidence is entered. Up to now, there have not been any sensational revelations or *coups de théâtre*: the *pentiti* have more or less confirmed their earlier statements with one or two small novelties here and there. In this regard, it should be pointed out that the *pentiti* present a problem for the judges. Everybody, including Andreotti, agrees on the importance of the *pentiti* in the fight against, the mafia as a criminal organization. However, the question of their judicial credibility remains.

Firstly, the *pentiti* often recount facts and events of which they do not have direct knowledge; their sources are other mafiosi, bosses and simple "men of honor". Thus, for example, the sources of Buscetta, the best known of the *pentiti*, are the bosses Stefano Bontade and Gaetano Badalamenti. But, after Buscetta's testimony at the Perugia trial on 9 September 1996, in which he confirmed that it was Badalamenti who had told him that he (Badalamenti) and Bontade had "executed" the Pecorelli killing, decided by the Salvo cousins at Andreotti's request, Badalamenti made it known from United States (where he is prison on a 45 year sentence for his part in the Pizza Connection), through his American lawyer, that "he was prepared to return immediately to Italy for a confrontation with the liar Buscetta", but on a series of serious conditions.[27]

Secondly, the greater part of the *pentiti* are members (i.e., simple "men of honor") and not leaders of the mafia organization, thus the information that they have is that which the leaders judge convenient to communicate to their associates, and it is done in a very special cultural code, to wit the mafia code. Hence, in their statements the *pentiti* often have recourse to deductions, for them logical, but for outsiders pure conjecture. Indeed, none of the *pentiti* has claimed to have taken part in a meeting of the Commission (or "Cupola"), that is the core decision-making body. Further, it is necessary to bear in mind that the mafia is composed of rival families that need to keep themselves informed of the activities of the other families, but at the same time to transmit signals which are favorable to their own families and unfavorable to their enemies. Hence, they are not readily understandable to those on the outside.

Thirdly, *pentitismo*, or collaborating with the judicial authorities, appears to be evolving. Palermo Chief Public Prosecutor Gian Carlo Caselli has recently argued[28] that since the massacres of Judges Falcone and Borsellino, the phenomenon has begun a new phase because the number of *pentiti* has multiplied (now one a day), and hypothesizes that Cosa Nostra has changed tactics and ordered many mafiosi to collaborate with the aim of confusing the situation and leading the judges astray. Certainly, the number of "protected" persons (1,240 *pentiti* and their relatives) now exceeds 5,000, creating enormous judicial and financial problems (the cost is over 100 billion lire) for their administration. With regard to the judicial problem, it was raised by Giovanni Brusca (the boss of San Giuseppe Jato, arrested on 20 May 1996), who immediately declared his readiness to collaborate and then launched a series of provocations — including that of suggesting that Luciano Violante (then President of the Parliamentary Antimafia Commission) was the instigator of an alleged plot in 1991 (decided in the fifty minutes of the Rome-Palermo flight!) intended to incriminate Andreotti for mafia conspiracy[29]. This has contributed to raising doubts about the *pentiti*'s reliability, undermining public confidence in their testimony.

All this goes to show that the *pentiti* mechanism is a double-edged weapon: the information supplied by the *pentiti* is vital to break the *omertà* (conspiracy of silence) with which the mafia as a criminal organization has always known how to surround its criminal activity, and therefore needs scrupulous verification to corroborate it, so as not to fall into any traps or commit judicial errors.[30] Moreover, the possibility, raised by the Brusca affair, that Cosa Nostra is capable of defaming any politician, manipulating the *pentiti* can only undermine their credibility as reliable witnesses. In this they play the defense's game: Andreotti, as we have seen, has always claimed that he is the victim of a mafia plot.

Sans Conclusion

As we have seen, the weak point of the prosecution is that it is necessarily based on the *pentiti*'s statements in which they speak for the most part of facts of which they were not eyewitnesses, but heard second-hand.[31] Since Andreotti never acted in first person but always by means of third parties[32], his designs seldom leave traces; hence, the verification must be done through other mafia *pentiti*'s statements, with all the difficulties in terms of the reliability of such cases.

On the other hand, the weakness of the defense is, as the prosecution has stressed, its incredibility (*sic*) because Andreotti wants to deny the evidence in the little things as much as in the big. "He never furnishes a credible interpretation of the facts which he has taken part in, in which his responsibility is at stake, or in which he was more or less a witness."[33] Thus, Andreotti appears before the judges as the worst informed politician in Italy, that is to say that he does not know what all Italians who read the papers or watch the television news know. The fact that, as Salvatore Lupo has shown, a reasoned defense of his actions exists and that the former Communist Emanuele Macaluso has supplied it; in other words, he could have argued that he defended Sindona to protect Italy-Vatican relations; that he knew the Salvo cousins for electoral-financial reasons; that he left Lima to get on with his business in Sicily without understanding what it was; that he met and spoke with Dalla Chiesa without attaching much importance to the matter. But, at the same time, to be credible he would have to admit that he failed to take account of how much Lima, the Salvo cousins and company were conditioned and in consequence his own entourage too.[34]

In this way, he would not have prejudiced his penal position, only the judgment of his political actions. The fact that he does not do it—according to Lupo, this is perhaps the best indicator of his culpability—signifies that he has decided on a political defense, either because of his own arrogance—confident in a complete absolution—or because his political image is more important to him: the statesman, concerned with the world's destiny, has no time for the petty and vulgar goings-on in distant provinces. Thus, a veil is still left obscuring many "Italian mysteries".

It is impossible at this juncture to predict the outcome of the trials: but, in view of the silences and lack of material clues, it is difficult to believe in Andreotti's penal conviction. In this situation, the evidence of his penal responsibility is very tenuous; thus a verdict of "unproven" would not be surprising. However, whatever the outcome of the trial, there still remains his political and moral responsibility for the misdeeds of the postwar decades. We should never forget that Andreotti was one of the leading political figures of the First Republic. The corrupt clientelist system at the basis of Italian politics, dissected in so many political science studies and now documented in so many trial proceedings, had him at its core as one of its principal artificers. Of course, his story is not the whole history of Italy of these years, but it is still a significant part of it.

The author warmly thanks the archivist of *Il Gazzettino* of Mestre (Venice) and her staff for having made available material in the newspaper's archive.

Notes

1. The crime in Italian is: "associazione a delinquere di tipo mafioso".

2. *La vera storia d'Italia. Interrogatori, testimonianze, riscontri, analisi. Gian Carlo Caselli e i suoi sostituti ricostruiscono gli ultimi vent'anni di storia italiana* (Naples: Pironti, 1995), p. 874.

3. The principal sources from which the quotations are taken are: *La vera storia d'Italia, op. cit.*; P. Arlacchi, *Il processo. Giulio Andreotti sotto accusa a Palermo* (Milan: Rizzoli, 1995); A. Bolzoni and G. D'Avanzo, "I processi a Giulio Andreotti: Palermo", in L. Violante, ed., *Mafia e antimafia. Rapporto '96* (Bari: Laterza, 1996), pp. 72-87; C. Bonini, "I processi a Giulio Andreotti: Perugia", in *Mafia e antimafia. Rapporto '96, op. cit.*, pp. 88-99.

4. It should not be forgotten that, writing in 1985, Andreotti congratulated himself on the fact that all of the 26 complaints made against him between 1969 and 1983 had regularly been dismissed (P. Arlacchi, *Il processo, op. cit.*, p. 22).

5. *Relazione introduttiva* of Public Prosecutor Guido Lo Forte at the hearing of 18 November (*Il Gazzettino*, 19 November 1995).

6. Public Prosecutor Antonio Scopelliti was murdered on 9 August 1991 on his way home from the beach in Calabria, and the businessman Libero Grassi (a man who had never yielded to mafia extortion demands and who had invited his colleagues to rebel) on 29 August 1991 in Palermo.

7. After the confirmation of the verdict Riina said that "even that bugger Lima had done him down" (*La vera storia d'Italia, op. cit.*, p. 30).

8. The Pecorelli case is extremely complicated, and a more detailed treatment is found in the sources.

9. Added to the above sources: G. Andreotti, *Cosa Loro. Mai visti da vicino* (Milan: Rizzoli, 1995).

10. The former UN Secretary General Perez De Cuellar denied that he had been called as a witness: "I will limit myself to writing to the Court telling the truth. This is all I can do. It is not for me to make a judgment" (*Il Gazzettino*, 27 September 1995). One can ask what concrete knowledge of intra-party relations in Italy these illustrious foreign persons can have. It is clear that calling these people is a sort of challenge to the Palermo judges founded on an external, and so-called superior, legitimization to delegitimize them; if the international community hold Andreotti in such high esteem — Henry Kissinger called him "the leader who has made the biggest contribution to the postwar history of his country" — it cannot be wrong because it is the highest concourse in the world.

11. *Il Gazzettino*, 24 March 1993.

12. In this connection, it should be noted that Andreotti has always cultivated this image of himself as a figure on the international stage, as can be seen from the vignettes of world leaders in the series *Visti da vicino*; it is no coincidence that the title of his defense-book is *Cosa Loro. Mai visti da vicino*, because it is intended to mark his extraneousness to the Sicilian mafia world.

13. The Cencelli Code was a system of weighting of ministerial posts invented by a civil servant to decide their distribution among DC factions according to their representation on the party's National Council, in vogue in from the 1960s to 1990.

14. The historian of the DC Gianni Baget Bozzo has noted: "Andreotti was a [powerful Christian Democrat] because he combined many powers in his person... Spanish has a fine expression, *poderes facticos*, that expresses very well who ' Andreotti is, the point of convergence of the *poderes facticos* in Italy, both internal and external... Andreotti was the first to realize that true power is transversal in the sense that he is powerful who is able to have power in all the powers..." (*Panorama*, 5 October 1995, p. 15).

15. *Il Gazzettino*, 12 February 1995.

16. *La vera storia d'Italia, op. cit.*, p. 135. "Moreover, this is a habitual line of defense of his: already at the Sindona Commission (1981), a party colleague, Armando Sarti, exclaimed: 'You deny repeatedly nearly or all of the questions on which testimony and assessments have been established...'" (*Ibid.*, p. 431).

17. This despite the resignation of Paolo Sylos-Labini from the Planning Technical Committee in 1974 in protest against the appointment of Lima as Junior Minister at the Finance Ministry headed by Andreotti (*Ibid.*, pp. 147-149).

18. The expression was used by the boss Gaetano Badalamenti.

19. Judge Giorgio Ambrosoli's (the receiver of Sindona's Banca Privata Italiana who was shot on 12 July 1979) comment, after receiving intimidatory telephone calls at the beginning of 1979 warning him of the danger that Andreotti saw him as the principal obstacle to Sindona's salvation: "I did not think that Andreotti could sink so low" (*Panorama*, 28 September 1995, p. 23).

20. For example, there were the names of Carabinieri who had never accompanied Andreotti in certain places as claimed in the official records (*La vera storia d'Italia, op. cit.*, p. 196).

21. G. Andreotti, *Cosa Loro, op. cit.*, p. 161; italics added.

22. M. Franco wrote in 1989: "Truth is for him a relative concept. He claims to hate lies and not to tell them. But, in the mean time, he theorizes a curious concept... between truth and falsehood there is a middle way, which means telling only a part of the truth..." (P. Arlacchi, *Il processo, op. cit.*, p. 23). Without prejudice to the right of a defendant to keep silent or lie to save his skin, one cannot not compare this with the replies of British politicians and civil servants at the Scott Inquiry into Arms Sales to Iraq where the same conception was defended: "Half the picture may be true. It is not a question of lying, but of telling a part of the truth" (I. Adams and R. Pyper, "A Guide to the Scott Enquiry: An Exposition of Truth, Half-Truth and Nothing like the Truth", in *Talking Politics*, no. 2, 1994-95, pp. 87-94); in other words, being "economical with the truth".

23. Letter of 2 February 1995 in G. Andreotti, *Cosa Loro, op. cit.*, p. 67.

24. *Il Gazzettino*, 27 September 1995.

25. *Il Corriere della Sera*, 28 September 1995.

26. *Il Corriere della Sera*, 5 November 1995.

27. *La Repubblica*, 21 October 1996; the conditions included, among others, that his stay in Italy should only be temporary and only for a confrontation on the Pecorelli murder; that he should not be arrested or subjected to other measures regarding other investigations; that he return immediately to New York, etc.

28. *La Repubblica*, 3 September 1996.

29. *Il Corriere della Sera*, 28 August 1996.

30. The most notorious case of judicial error due to dubious testimony by a *pentito* was the Tortora case in 1980s; for details and comments see R. Lumley in *The Italianist*, 1986, 1987 and 1989.

31. Something which one of the few eyewitnesses, Mannoia, seemed to have understood, as is clear from the last exchange of his cross-examination at the trial on 5 November 1996. Lawyer Cappi: "You claim to have a monopoly of the truth"; Mannoia: "No sir, I do not claim to have a monopoly of the truth. I know that I have a monopoly of knowledge" (*L'Unità*, 6 November 1996).

32. A personal anecdote: the only time Silvio Gava got in contact with me to propose a meeting, the message passed through at least five intermediaries. I made it known that all that was necessary was to write a letter to my English address; naturally I have never received a letter. In consequence, there is no trace of this invitation. Only my word.

33. S. Lupo, "Mafia, politica e storia d'Italia a proposito del processo Andreotti", in *Meridiana*, no. 25, 1996, pp. 19-45, at pp. 32-33.

34. *Ibid.*, p. 42.

13

The Italian Presidency of the European Union

Philip Daniels

The Italian Presidency of the EU in the first semester of 1996 was confronted with a number of challenges in both the European and domestic arenas. At the European level, in addition to the day-to-day coordination and management of EU affairs, the Presidency was also responsible for the formal opening of the intergovernmental conference (IGC). The final weeks of the presidency were disrupted by the "beef crisis" when the British government's policy of non-cooperation obstructed the EU's decision-making processes. In the domestic arena, parliamentary elections in April 1996 threatened to undermine the continuity and effectiveness of the Italian presidency. More generally, the Presidency took place against the background of an ongoing national debate about the likelihood and desirability of Italy keeping pace with the moves towards a single European currency.

The Priorities of the Italian Presidency

The Italian Presidency coincided with an important juncture in the EU's development. The opening of the IGC in Turin in March 1996 gave the Italian government the opportunity to play an important role in shaping the agenda for a new phase of integration. At the same time, Italy's continued efforts to meet the convergence criteria for participation in the single currency gave it a chance to reaffirm its *communautaire* credentials.

Following consultations with its European partners, the government's priorities for its tenure of the presidency were agreed by Lam-

berto Dini's cabinet on 1 December 1995 and debated in the Chamber of
Deputies on 5 and 7 December 1995.[1] Foreign Minister Susanna Agnelli
outlined the program for the Presidency in her address to the European
Parliament at Strasbourg on 17 January 1996. To some extent, the program of any presidency represents a "wish list" and an affirmation of
national priorities in European policy. The time constraints of a six-
month tenure, the incursion of unforeseen crises and developments, and
the positions of other member states all limit a presidency's scope for
ambitious new initiatives. The principal task of the presidency, as the
Italian government recognized, is to provide continuity and coherence in
the conduct of EU affairs. Nevertheless, the control of the EU's day-to-day
business does give the presidency an opportunity to make an impact and
shape the agenda for the EU's development. The success or failure of a
presidency is measured in terms of the efficiency and skill with which it
handles routine EU business, and how it deals with inherited long-term
problems and unforeseen crises and emergencies.

The Italian government's program for the presidency focused on
three priority areas: to make the EU more effective and visible as an integrated economic area, as a community of citizens and as a leading player
in the international arena.

An Integrated Economic Area

The government's program highlighted the need for the EU to create a
stable economic environment and to implement effective employment
policies. According to the program, in order to achieve these objectives,
it would be necessary for the EU to coordinate and monitor the economic
policies of member states; to prepare the legal and technical instruments
for the move into the third phase of monetary union; to coordinate national policies for reviving employment; to implement the Commission's
program of social action; and to set in motion a comprehensive EU strategy to sustain growth and to prepare for the third millennium, including
investment in trans-European networks, the completion of the single
market, the liberalization of public services and the strengthening of the
framework research program.

The problem of unemployment in the EU developed as a central
theme of the Italian presidency. While acknowledging that the national
authorities were primarily responsible for employment policies, the Italian government wanted the EU to play a more prominent role in coordinating strategies and taking its own initiatives to stimulate employment.[2] The Italian government's approach to the EU's unemployment
problem shared much in common with the Commission's policy proposals in this area. At the European Council in Turin in March 1996, Jacques

Santer, the president of the Commission, submitted the policy initiative, "Action for Employment in Europe: A Confidence Pact". The initiative aimed to achieve a more consistent and coordinated strategy among the EU's institutions, the member governments and the two sides of industry. The European Council welcomed the initiative and agreed to give high priority to the issue of job creation at the next meeting in Florence in June 1996. In the run up to the Florence summit, the Italian presidency organized a Tripartite Conference (of the Commission, member governments and social partners) to address the issues of growth and employment in Europe.

At the Florence summit meeting (21 and 22 June 1996) the European Council broadly followed the Commission's proposals for tackling · Europe's unemployment problem and reflected an emerging consensus among member governments. It agreed that the EU should aim to create a macroeconomic framework favorable to employment, with high and sustainable non-inflationary economic growth seen as the key to job creation; it should fully implement the single European market, including greater liberalization of the electricity and telecommunications markets; it should accelerate reforms to achieve a more flexible European labor market; and it should make better use of its own policies to stimulate growth, employment and competitiveness, giving priority to sectors with the highest employment potential including the development of trans-European transport networks, the strengthening of scientific and technical research programs and support to small and medium-sized enterprises. No additional funding was agreed, however, by the European Council. Foreign Minister Lamberto Dini reported that the EU's approach was in line with the Italian government's desire to achieve a more flexible labor market and wage moderation in order to encourage investment to create jobs.[3]

The Italian presidency also made progress in the preparations for moves towards the creation of the single currency in the third stage of Economic and Monetary Union (EMU). In particular, the informal Ecofin Council in Verona (May 1996) made significant progress over the difficult questions of strengthening budgetary discipline in the third phase of EMU (in line with the German proposal for a "stability pact") and the relationship between the Euro and the currencies which remain outside the single currency area.[4]

A Community of Citizens

A second priority of the Italian Presidency was the commitment to develop the EU as a "community of citizens". The Presidency outlined a number of policy proposals designed to bring the EU closer to its citizens. These included the strengthening of the EU as a guarantor of free-dom and security, greater democratic participation and transparency in EU decision-making, full use of the principle of subsidiarity and more ef-fective EU action in areas (such as culture, education, tourism and health care) which contribute to shared community values.[5] The main focus of the Presidency's attention was the Third Pillar of Justice and Home Af-fairs (JHA) where it advocated a streamlining of the decision-making process, a shift away from intergovernmentalism towards the Commu-nity method and greater cooperation in areas such as extradition and the fight against international organized crime. The Presidency made some tangible progress in this area, most notably with the establishment of Europol by the deadline of 30 June 1996: the British government's oppo-sition to the proposal to give the European Court of Justice the right to interpret the Europol Convention had prevented agreement in the Jus-tice and Home Affairs Council, but the issue was finally resolved at the Florence European Council. In addition, the Italian Presidency's initia-tive to set up a European observatory for racism and xenophobia was welcomed and agreed in principle at the Florence European Council, al-though further examination of the judicial and financial conditions would be required before its establishment.

The EU as a Leading Actor in International Relations

The third priority area highlighted in the presidency program was the development of the EU's external dimension, and in particular a more effective common foreign and security policy (CFSP). According to the Presidency, a strengthening of the external dimension would ad-vance the process of European integration and enable the EU to play a much more incisive role in the promotion of international stability and security. The presidency program indicated a number of areas for action: these included an active EU role in the stabilization of former Yugoslavia, the development of the Euro-Mediterranean partnership, the involve-ment of the EU in the Middle East peace process, the preparation for fu-ture enlargement of membership, a strengthening of the trans-Atlantic dialogue and the consolidation of the World Trade Organization.

The results of the Presidency in this sphere of activity were mixed. In the case of former Yugoslavia, the Presidency succeeded in projecting a high European profile in the application of the Dayton Peace Accords. The Interministerial conference of the Peace Implementation Council (PIC) held in Florence on 13 and 14 June 1996 reaffirmed the commitment of the international community to the consolidation of peace and stabil-ity in post-war Bosnia. Agreement was reached on the control and re-duction of arms and a date was fixed for elections in Bosnia. The follow-

ing week, the Florence European Council pledged economic and political
support to Bosnia and EU assistance in the elections. The Italian government highlighted continued progress in the peace process in the former
Yugoslavia as an important achievement of its presidency.

The presidency had little opportunity to give substance to the New
Transatlantic Agenda which had been signed by the EU and the US in
Madrid in December 1995. The annual Transatlantic Summit, which was
held in Washington on June 12 1996, reviewed the progress made in the
transatlantic dialogue and set the priorities and objectives for the following six months. According to the Italian Presidency, the New Transatlantic Agenda provides an ideal framework for the strengthening and continuity of EU-US dialogue.[6] The largely positive picture was eclipsed,
however, by the transatlantic tensions provoked by the passage of the
Helms-Burton Act and the analogous D'Amato Bill which would permit
the United States to boycott foreign firms investing in Cuba, Iran and
Libya. The Italian Presidency condemned the legislation as damaging to
the multilateral trading system and the Conclusions of the European
Council in Florence promised a European response to the American action.

The Italian government claimed significant progress in the construction of the Euro-Mediterranean Partnership during its presidency. A series of meetings, seminars and ministerial conferences on culture and
education, new information technologies, industry, energy, tourism and
the environment represented an important legacy for future presidencies.[7] Progress in the development of the Euro-Mediterranean Partnership was hindered, however, by the Greek government's blocking of a
new EU program of technical and financial assistance to Mediterranean
countries. The Italian Presidency attempted but failed to unblock the
stalemate which was rooted in the ongoing Greek-Turkish dispute.
European Union relations with Turkey were a difficult issue for the Italian Presidency and it proved impossible to organize the proposed meeting of the EU-Turkey council of association.

Italy and the Intergovernmental Conference

The opening of the Intergovernmental Conference (IGC) in Turin in
March 1996 represented one of the key tasks of the Italian Presidency.
The broad themes of the IGC had been indicated in the Maastricht Treaty
and in the work of the Reflection Group which had been set up in June
1995 and reported to the Madrid European Council in December 1995.
The main task of the negotiations would be to meet the challenge of diversity posed by an enlarged Union, and this would require revision of

the legislative process, adaptation of the institutional framework and closer cooperation in the spheres of Justice and Home Affairs and a Common Foreign and Security Policy. The conclusions of the Turin European Council outlined the main objectives of the IGC negotiations; these were to construct a European Union which would be closer to its citizens, with a more democratic and efficient institutional framework and a strengthened capacity for external action.

The Italian Presidency was responsible for the opening of the IGC in Turin in March 1996 and presided over the initial negotiations. Italy viewed the IGC as an opportunity to overcome the deficiencies and inadequacies in the Maastricht Treaty and to create the institutional framework necessary for future enlargements and further integration in the EU.[8] In addition, it would give the EU a chance to get "closer to its citizens" and to recover public support for the European construction by focusing on themes relevant to the citizen, such as their rights and their physical and economic security. The Presidency's program outlined the government's priorities in its approach to the IGC negotiations:

1) A key objective should be a treaty which is comprehensible to ordinary citizens (with an amalgamation and simplification of the existing treaties), strengthens the democratic nature of the Union and enhances the effectiveness of the decision-making procedures in readiness for enlargement. It should clarify the operation of the institutional mechanisms and delineate the functional responsibilities of the EU in relation to national and regional authorities. Specific institutional reforms proposed by the Italian government included an extension of the Commission's right of initiative to include the sphere of Justice and Home Affairs; a reduction in the number of Commissioners; the generalized use of majority voting in Council with the exception of constitutional provisions; a change to the weighted votes of member states to reflect population sizes; a greater role for the European Parliament (EP) in the areas of CFSP and JHA and a move towards co-decision between the Council and the European Parliament in the legislative process.

2) The EU should develop its capacity to play a coherent and responsible leading role on the international stage. The Italian government proposed an overhaul of the institutional mechanisms of the CFSP to improve planning, strategic capabilities, the effectiveness of implementation and the visibility of EU actions both internally to European public opinion and externally in all international arenas. In order to achieve a stronger European security and defense identity, Italy favors the full integration of the West European Union (WEU) structures into the EU.

3) The EU should improve co-operation in the area of Justice and Home Affairs as a way of meeting the specific interests of citizens in relation to freedom and security and giving greater substance to European

citizenship. In addition, Italy favored the incorporation of fundamental civil and social rights in the treaty.

The Italian government argued that the IGC must be sensitive to public opinion from the outset since this would be vital to the acceptance of a new treaty. This would require more transparent procedures and the involvement of national parliaments, associations and individuals during negotiations and not just at ratification stage. More specifically, Italy supported the full participation of the European Parliament in the IGC negotiations, but this was strongly opposed by some member states, including France. A compromise was agreed at the Turin European Council which provided for the European Parliament to have regular and detailed information on the progress of IGC negotiations and allowed it to offer its views on issues under discussion. The Italian Presidency took a broad interpretation of the European Parliament's role, maintaining regular contact with the Parliament's President (and two other nominated members of the European Parliament) and ensuring that the European Parliament was supplied with the documentation of the IGC's work.

The Italian Presidency prepared an interim progress report on the IGC negotiations for the Florence European Council, indicating areas of agreement and controversial political issues where compromise was difficult.[9] Foreign Minister Lamberto Dini noted the divergent priorities and visions among member states and called on the heads of government at Florence to give a strong and unequivocal signal to accelerate the negotiations and progress beyond the phase of mere reiteration of national positions. In his report to the European Parliament on 19 June 1996[10], Dini highlighted the most controversial themes which included the definition of fundamental rights and the substance of citizenship, the adaptation of the EU's institutional system, the proposal to include a specific article on employment in the new treaty, and the strengthening and enlarging of the scope of European cooperation in the spheres of JHA and the CFSP.

The Conclusions of the Florence European Council called on the IGC to turn its attention to the main political issues so that a general draft outline of the revision of the treaties could be presented to the Dublin European Council in December 1996 and the work of the IGC completed by mid-1997.[11] The Conclusions at Florence reiterated the principal objectives of the IGC negotiations, which should aim to bring the EU closer to its citizens, to strengthen and enlarge the scope of the CFSP, and to ensure the good functioning of the institutions and the efficiency of the decision-making process.[12] While each of these objectives would require difficult political negotiation and compromise, the Italian government could be satisfied that many of the Council's substantive proposals

closely matched its own priorities for the IGC. As in the earlier IGC negotiations for the Single European Act and the Maastricht Treaty, Italy was
once again at the forefront of those countries favoring further integration
and a strengthening of EU institutions. In contrast to the earlier IGCs,
however, the Italian government's proposals for reform in 1996 showed
a greater political realism and were therefore more likely to find support
among other member states.[13]

The BSE Crisis

The Italian Presidency was confronted with the BSE crisis midway
through the semester. In late March 1996 the British government announced a possible link between bovine spongiform encephalopathy
(BSE) and the human variant, Creutzfeld-Jacob disease. The EU re-
sponded to this potential danger with the immediate imposition of a total ban on the export of British beef and its derivatives. Under pressure
from farmers' groups and the Euroskeptic wing of the Conservative
Party, the British government demanded an easing of the EU restrictions
on beef exports and a timetable for the phased lifting of the ban. The EU
refused to back down, however, and on 21 May 1996 the British government adopted a policy of non-cooperation designed to disrupt EU
business.

The impasse was broken when the Italian Presidency successfully negotiated an agreement shortly before the Florence European Council.
The agreement, included in the Conclusions of the Presidency, represented a climbdown by the British government despite Prime Minister
Major's best efforts to portray it as a "victory". The framework agreement provided for a phased lifting of the ban but did not include a timetable or a date for its complete removal. In addition, Britain would need
Commission approval, on a case-by-case basis, before it would be permitted to sell beef in non-EU markets and any easing of the ban was conditional on the British authorities proving that measures to eradicate BSE
were working. The British policy of non-cooperation was strongly criticized by the Italian government[14] and its European partners and
prompted calls for Treaty reforms to make such disruptive tactics impossible in the future.

Slovenia

The signing of the EU-Slovenia Association Agreement in Luxembourg on 10 June 1996 represented an important breakthrough by the
Italian Presidency and opened the way for Slovenia to join the list of po-

tential new EU members. The Association Agreement had been blocked for four years by Italy which was in dispute with Slovenia over the issue of the restitution of property belonging to Italians expelled from Yugoslavia at the end of the Second World War. The new Prodi government moved quickly to clear the way for the Association Agreement and Piero Fassino, the new number two at the Ministry of Foreign Affairs, negotiated a bilateral deal with Slovenia. The deal makes provision for foreigners to buy property in Slovenia and secures special rights for Italian exiles. In response to criticisms in parliament, the government acknowledged that there were still unresolved issues such as outstanding claims for compensation. Nevertheless, the government offered a number of justifications for its accord with Slovenia: first, Italy was isolated and its European partners were pressing for an agreement; second, in holding the Presidency of the EU, Italy was obliged to subordinate its legitimate national interests to the resolution of a multilateral problem; third, the unresolved issues, such as redress, could now be approached in a more favorable bilateral climate; and fourth, the dispute with Slovenia risked damaging Italy's attempts to develop its interests in Central and Eastern Europe.[15]

The Domestic Political Background
and the Debate About Italy's Role in Europe

In the months before Italy assumed the Presidency of the EU, it was feared that the uncertain domestic political situation would disrupt or undermine the government's performance during the semester.[16] Proponents of early parliamentary elections argued that the "technocratic" government, led by Lamberto Dini, lacked the necessary stability and political authority to provide effective leadership to the Italian Presidency. In spite of frequent indications that his government would resign, Dini was still in office when Italy assumed the presidency in January 1996. The government was not to survive the full semester, however: unable to secure cross-party agreement on constitutional and institutional reforms, President Scalfaro dissolved Parliament and called elections for 21 April 1996.

Some of Italy's European partners expressed concerns that the national elections and the formation of a new government would disrupt the presidency and undermine continuity. In the event, the attention given to the election campaign and the turnover in government had no evident impact on the conception and the direction of the presidency.[17] Three factors explain this continuity: first, there was broad political and parliamentary consensus on the priorities of the Italian semester; second, consistency in European policy was facilitated by the appointment of Lamberto Dini as foreign minister in Romano Prodi's new government; and third, much of the work of the presidency was carried out competently by Italian diplomats who were largely unaffected by the turbulence in the domestic political arena.[18]

During the parliamentary debate on the vote of confidence, the prime minister-designate, Romano Prodi, committed his government to continue a consistent pro-European policy. The commitment to the European Union and the integration process is widely shared across the political spectrum in Italy. In recent years, however, the European issue has become a more prominent theme in domestic political debate and a source of political division. This was most evident during 1994 when Silvio Berlusconi's short-lived government, and in particular Foreign Minister Antonio Martino, adopted a more critical stance towards the EU. More recently, the issue of Italy's participation in the single currency has been at the heart of domestic political debate and provoked significant political disagreement.

A number of factors account for the growing politicization of the European issue in Italian politics. First, the pace and direction of political and economic integration since the mid-1980s has placed increasing demands on the Italian politico-administrative system and undermined longstanding clientelistic practices. Second, the traditional distinction between domestic and European politics has blurred as the process of integration has gathered pace and impinged more directly on policy spheres (such as economic management) which were once the domain of the nation-state. Third, Italy's difficulties in keeping pace with the integration process, particularly in the spheres of monetary and fiscal policy, have given rise to fears that it would be relegated to the sidelines of the EU.

The salient issue of Italy's readiness for EMU came to the fore during the final weeks of the Italian Presidency and remained a key theme of political debate throughout the remainder of 1996. EMU poses a difficult challenge for Italy and compliance with the Maastricht convergence criteria requires painful and unpopular political choices.[19] Opposition to the EMU project emanates from two principal sources: first, those who question the benefits of EMU and fear that the competitiveness of the Italian economy would be seriously undermined if it were locked into a rigid, single currency area; and second, those critics who oppose the cuts in public expenditure and/or the increases in taxation required to bring the budget deficit and public debt in line with the Maastricht parameters. Any hopes that the timetable for EMU could be delayed or the convergence criteria relaxed have failed to materialize.[20]

The Prodi government made clear its commitment to Italian participation in the single currency, arguing that the fiscal and monetary disciplines would stimulate growth, competitiveness and employment. Nevertheless, political necessity dictated that the painful taxation and expenditure measures designed to cut the budget deficit would have to be introduced in a phased program. The Prodi government's three-year economic and financial plan, approved at the end of June 1996, provoked domestic political opposition and was criticized by Mario Monti, the Italian commissioner responsible for the internal market.[21] Monti claimed that the government's limited package of measures indicated a lack of commitment to EMU and that the three-year timetable to cut the budget deficit threatened to delay the introduction of the single currency.[22]

The government's economic and financial plan indicated a budget deficit for 1997 of 4.5 percent (later revised to 5.4 percent following a Constitutional Court ruling on pension entitlements), falling to 2.8 percent in 1998. These targets appeared to be excessively optimistic, however, particularly in the light of the 1996 budget deficit of almost 7.5 percent of GDP compared to the 5.9 per cent originally projected by the Dini government. Two principal factors account for the failure to meet the targets: first, lower growth rates than anticipated led to a shortfall in government revenue; and second, interest rates did not come down as fast as expected, leading to higher debt service costs. Although Italy has achieved a healthy primary surplus (government receipts exceeding expenditure), the problem of the budget deficit derives in large measure from the interest payments required to service an accumulated public debt equivalent to approximately 125 per cent of GDP.

The controversy over Italy's readiness to join the single currency erupted again in early October 1996 when French President Jacques Chirac was reported to have said that Italy would not be ready to comply with the Maastricht convergence criteria for entry into the single currency in 1999. In an attempt to avert a serious deterioration in diplomatic relations between Rome and Paris, President Chirac issued a hasty denial, alleging that there had been a misunderstanding and praising the efforts of the Prodi government to tackle the budget deficit. At the heart of the dispute was the longstanding French grievance that the devaluation of the lira, following its exit from the Exchange Rate Mechanism (ERM) in September 1992, had given Italy an unfair competitive advantage, particularly in the textile and automobile sectors.

The government's commitment to take Italy into the single currency was given added credibility when the lira reentered the ERM on 25 November 1996 at a central parity of 990 lire to one German mark. This central parity, agreed following nine hours of negotiation in the European Monetary Committee, represented a compromise between the Italian position which favored a rate of 1,000 lire to one German mark and the Franco-German preference for a stronger lira. Membership of the ERM is a prerequisite for participation in the single currency, and the government hopes that reentry will boost the credibility of the lira on the money markets, thereby permitting a reduction in interest rates and lower public debt servicing costs. Doubts persist, however, about Italy's chances of making the first wave of members expected to be admitted on 1 January 1999: the larger than projected deficit for 1996 means that the government will be obliged to introduce additional budgetary measures to meet its deficit targets for 1997 and 1998.

The decision on which countries will be allowed to join the single currency at the outset will be based on political considerations as well as economic indicators. Germany, for example, is reluctant to admit member states which may find it difficult to survive over the long term in a "hard Euro" zone and wants to see a durable, structural improvement in Italian public finances rather than one-off measures (such as the "Eurotax") designed to meet the Maastricht criteria.[23] The German government's insistence on the "stability pact" represents an attempt to ensure fiscal discipline for countries which join the single currency area. France is more likely to push for Italian membership of the single currency, fearing that Italy would be able to take advantage of competitive devaluations if it were to remain outside.

The end of the 1990s are crucial years for Italy in its relationship with the European Union. To keep pace with the integration process requires significant political and economic adjustments to the Italian state: most importantly, the emerging economic model in Europe challenges key features of the post-war Italian political economy such as the state's involvement in industry, the use of public expenditure to buy political consent and devaluation as an economic tool to achieve competitiveness. In Italy, as in many other EU member states, the budgetary constraints imposed by the Maastricht convergence criteria have provoked political opposition. This opposition is not a coherent or united anti-Maastricht coalition but rather a number of disparate interests and groups threatened by the EMU project; these include welfare recipients and public employees hit by cuts in public expenditure, taxpayers faced with increased tax demands, and enterprises threatened by a loss of competitiveness when currency devaluation will no longer be a policy option.[24] The Prodi government has insisted that it is crucial for Italy to restore its credibility in Europe[25], and this will require painful economic and political adjustments. The alternative is possible exclusion from EMU and the prospect of Italy being sidelined in the EU while an inner core of member states presses ahead with economic integration.

Notes

1. See *Presidenza italiana del Consiglio dell'Unione Europea*, Chamber of Deputies, Servizio Studi, XIII Legislatura, no. 21, June 1996, pp. 92-218.

2. See the report on the conclusion of the Italian Presidency of the EU given by Lamberto Dini, the Minister of Foreign Affairs, to the Third Commission (Foreign and Community Affairs—Affari Esteri e Comunitari) of the Chamber of Deputies on 18 June 1996, reproduced in *Presidenza italiana del Consiglio dell'Unione Europea: Documentazione conclusiva*, no. 21/2, Chamber of Deputies, Servizio Studi, XIII Legislatura, June 1996, pp. 1-36.

3. See the audience with the Minister of Foreign Affairs, Susanna Agnelli, before the Third Commission of the Chamber of Deputies on 7 February 1996, reproduced in *Presidenza italiana del Consiglio dell'Unione Europea*, no. 21, *op. cit.*, pp. 219-230.

4. See the government's communication on the Italian Presidency to the Third Commission (Foreign and Community Affairs) of the Chamber of Deputies on 8 May 1996, reproduced in *Presidenza italiana del Consiglio dell'Unione Europea*, no. 21, *op. cit.*, pp. 274-288.

5. See the Minister of Foreign Affairs, Susanna Agnelli, before the Third Commission of the Chamber of Deputies on 7 February 1996, reproduced in *Presidenza italiana del Consiglio dell'Unione Europea*, *op. cit.*, pp. 219-230.

6. See report by Lamberto Dini, the Minister of Foreign Affairs, to the Third Commission (Foreign and Community Affairs) of the Chamber of Deputies on 18 June 1996, reproduced in *Presidenza italiana del Consiglio dell'Unione Europea: Documentazione conclusiva*, *op. cit.*, pp. 1-38.

7. *Ibidem*.

8. On the Italian government's priorities for the IGC see the debate in the Chamber of Deputies reproduced in *Presidenza Italiana del Consiglio dell'Unione Europea*, no. 21, *op. cit.*, pp. 11-91. Italy rejects proposals for an "inner" and "outer" core of member states, preferring instead differentiated integration or "flexibility in unity" within a unified institutional structure.

9. See the *Bulletin of the European Union*, no. 6, 1996, pp. 43-57. In an addendum to the progress report on the IGC, the Italian Presidency presented draft treaty texts to illustrate some of the options presented to the IGC. On the divergent national positions see F. Gallo, "Maastricht Watch", in *The International Spectator*, no. 1, 1996, pp. 95-114, and G. Mather and W. Himes, *Britain's Relationship With the EU* (London: European Policy Forum, 1996).

10. See Dini's speech to the plenary session of the European Parliament in Strasbourg, 19 June 1996, reproduced in *Presidenza italiana del Consiglio dell'Unione Europea*, no. 21/2, *op. cit.*, pp. 31-61.

11. See the *Bulletin of the European Union*, no. 2, 1996, p. 58.

12. *Ibid.*, pp. 13-14.

13. This political realism was noted by Foreign Minister Susanna Agnelli who said that the Italian government would approach the treaty revision on the basis of "a realistic, but certainly not minimalist, mandate". See her report to the Third Commission, 7 February 1996, reproduced in *Presidenza italiana del Consiglio dell'Unione Europea*, no. 21, *op. cit.*, p. 221.

14. See Dini's remarks to the Third Commission of the Chamber of Deputies on 18 June 1996, reproduced in *Presidenza italiana del consiglio dell'Unione Europea*, no.

21/2, *op. cit.*, pp. 7-8.

15. *Ibid.*, pp. 28-30.

16. See the debate in the Chamber of Deputies reproduced in *Presidenza italiana del Consiglio dell'Unione Europea*, no. 21, *op. cit.*, pp. 92-218.

17. *Ibid.*, p. 4.

18. For contrasting views of the performance of the Italian Presidency see A. Manzella, *La Repubblica*, 1 July 1996 and S. Romano, *La Stampa*, 22 June 1996.

19. On the implications of EMU for Italy see E. Espa, "L'Italia e l'Unione monetaria", in *Europa/Europe*, no. 1, 1996, pp. 83-103. Also see L. Bernardi, "La finanza pubblica tra dinamiche recenti e prospettive europee: premessa e sintesi del Rapporto", in L. Bernardi, ed., *La finanza pubblica italiana: Rapporto 1996* (Bologna: Il Mulino, 1996), pp. 9-32.

20. The Maastricht criteria have produced tensions within the Center-Left · government coalition over their potential negative impact on employment. Minister of Foreign Affairs Dini warned that the parameters were non-negotiable but that the timetable for the introduction of the single currency could be modified by the Heads of State (see *La Repubblica*, 27 August 1996).

21. See the interview with Monti in *Il Corriere della Sera*, 28 June 1996.

22. The Ecofin meeting of 8 July 1996 welcomed the measures but called on the government to correct the "excessive deficit" more rapidly.

23. See *The Financial Times*, 26 November 1996.

24. On this theme see P.-C. Padoan, "Can Italy Keep Up to Europe?", in *The International Spectator*, no. 2, 1996, pp. 17-35.

25. See the interview with Romano Prodi, "'Non faremo i satelliti di nessuno'", in *LiMes*, no. 3, 1996, pp. 23-28.

Documentary Appendix

compiled by Marzia Zannini

This documentary appendix is a precious aid for comprehending the events that are described in this volume. Inasmuch as the appendix is a rare collection of economic, political, and social data on the Italian context, its value becomes increasingly important in the long term.

The statistical tables offer a profile of the complex economic, political, and social changes which have occurred in Italian society. The first section contains historical series of data which represent the social and economic background which helps one understand the second and more important section, that lists the year's election results.

In 1996 there were fewer electoral appointments than in 1995, when both administrative voting (regional and municipal elections) and 12 referenda took place. Nevertheless, 1996 was a year of great electoral and political change: the Center-Left won the political elections for the first time. The tables in second section show that, due to the new electoral system, the winners received less votes than their main competitor but conquered more seats in Parliament due to their coalition-making capability. The results of the national parliamentary elections are followed by data on the 284 municipal elections and the Sicilian regional elections.

This appendix, as in previous editions, contains three sections of data. The first, which includes tables A1 to A7, refers to population, labor force, crime and national economic statistics. The second section (tables B1 to B11) provides the various elections results. The third section reports the evolution of membership in the main political parties during the fifty years of the Italian Republic.

TABLE A1. Resident Population by Age Group and Sex (in Thousands[a])

	Age Group			Total Population
	0-14	15-64	65 and Over	
Both Sexes				
1986	10,877	38,854	7,470	57,201
1987	10,541	39,085	7,664	57,290
1988	10,218	39,293	7,887	57,398
1989	9,924	39,467	8,112	57,503
1990	9,620	39,620	8,335	57,575
1991	8,993	38,991	8,773	56,757
1992	8,856	39,110	8,995	56,961
1993	8,725	39,210	9,203	57,138
1994	8,620	39,247	9,401	57,268
1995	8,678	39,090	8,872	56,640
Males Only				
1986	5,578	19,209	3,003	27,790
1987	5,408	19,348	3,076	27,832
1988	5,245	19,482	3,162	27,889
1989	5,096	19,586	3,255	27,937
1990	4,941	19,678	3,349	27,968
1991	4,600	19,373	3,575	27,548
1992	4,534	19,450	3,671	27,655
1993	4,468	19,508	3,762	27,738
1994	4,415	19,528	3,848	27,791
1995	4,465	19,460	3,634	27,559

[a] Rounded figures

Sources: Istat, *Annuario statistico italiano* (Rome, 1986-1995); for 1995: Istat, *Forze di lavoro* (Rome, 1996).

TABLE A2. Present Population by Position on the Labor Market (in Thousands)

	Labor Force							Total
	Employed				Seeking Job			
	Agri-culture	Industry	Other	Total	Unem-ployed	Seeking First Job	Others Seeking Job	
Both Sexes								
1986	2,241	6,821	11,794	20,856	501	1,296	814	23,467
1987	2,169	6,716	11,952	20,837	547	1,354	932	23,670
1988	2,058	6,788	12,256	21,102	537	1,412	937	23,988
1989	1,946	6,753	12,305	21,004	507	1,405	954	23,870
1990	1,863	6,940	12,593	21,396	483	1,357	912	24,148
1991	1,823	6,916	12,853	21,592	469	1,285	898	24,244
1992	1,749	6,851	12,859	21,459	551	1,370	878	24,258
1993	1,669	6,725	12,073	20,467	845	1,005	485	22,802
1994	1,574	6,587	11,959	20,120	983	1,048	529	22,680
1995	1,490	6,494	12,025	20,009	1,005	1,150	570	22,734
Males Only								
1986	1,442	5,194	7,317	13,953	289	617	209	15,068
1987	1,413	5,111	7,322	13,846	313	665	251	15,075
1988	1,345	5,155	7,489	13,989	305	687	248	15,229
1989	1,261	5,103	7,487	13,851	286	676	257	15,070
1990	1,197	5,233	7,586	14,016	264	667	246	15,193
1991	1,165	5,259	7,678	14,102	256	645	241	15,244
1992	1,105	5,214	7,626	13,945	297	692	238	15,172
1993	1,045	5,145	7,141	13,331	490	518	90	14,429
1994	999	5,022	7,036	13,057	593	552	105	14,307
1995	956	4,934	7,043	12,933	597	599	115	14,244

Note: In 1993 new defintions of "labor force" and "people seeking a job" were introduced. Since then these groups include people who are at least 15 years old (whereas the prior defintions applied to 14-year-olds as well). In addition, individuals who lose their job for reasons other than dismissal (resignation or end of temporrary employment) are now excluded from "others seeking job".

Source: Istat, Compendio statistico italiano 1996 (Rome, 1996).

TABLE A3. Labor Conflicts: Number and Impact of Contractual and Non-Contractual (i.e., Political) Disputes

	Conflicts	Thousands of Participants	Thousands of Hours Lost
		Contractual Disputes	
1986	1,462	2,940	36,742
1987	1,146	1,473	20,147
1988	1,767	1,609	17,086
1989	1,295	2,108	21,001
1990	1,094	1,634	36,269
1991	784	750	11,573
1992	895	621	5,605
1993	1,047	848	8,796
1994	858	745	7,651
1995	545	445	6,365
		Non-Contractual Disputes	
1986	7	667	2,764
1987	3	2,800	12,093
1988	2	1,103	6,120
1989	2	2,344	10,052
1990	—	—	—
1991	7	2,202	9,322
1992	8	2,557	13,905
1993	7	3,536	15,084
1994	3	1,868	15,967
1995	—	—	—

Note: The figures for participants and numbers of hours lost are in thousands. "Non-contractual coflicts" concern political economic measures, social reform, and national and international political events.

Source: Istat, Compendio statistico italiano 1996 (Rome, 1996).

TABLE A4. Births and Marriages

	Births		Marriages			
	Total Births	% Variation	Total Marriages	% Variation	Religious Marriages	% Variation
1986	555,445	–3.79	297,540	–0.33	255,407	–0.59
1987	551,539	–0.70	306,264	+2.93	261,847	+2.52
1988	569,698	+3.29	318,296	+3.93	266,534	+1.79
1989	560,688	–1.58	321,272	+0.93	267,617	+0.41
1990	569,255	+1.53	319,711	–0.49	266,084	–0.57
1991	562,787	–1.14	312,061	–2.39	257,555	–3.21
1992	575,216	+2.21	312,348	+0.09	255,355	–0.85
1993	552,587	–3.93	302,230	–3.24	248,111	–2.84
1994	536,665	–2.88	285,112	–5.66	230,573	–7.07
1995	526,064	–1.98	266,795	–6.42	216,435	–6.13

Sources: Istat, *Annuario statistico italiano* (Rome, 1986-1995); for marriages in 1995, data refer to the Jan. 1-Nov. 30 period and are drawn from Istat, "Bollettino mensile di statistica", July 1996.

TABLE A5. Classification of Officially Recorded Crimes

	Against Persons	Against Family or Morality	Against Property	Against Economy or Public Trust	Against the State	Other	Total
1986	125,192	14,118	1,355,507	410,934	41,734	82,688	2,030,173
1987	138,272	14,826	1,507,040	394,360	47,093	103,395	2,204,986
1988	136,685	14,228	1,529,876	416,387	46,158	90,597	2,233,931
1989	125,769	13,073	1,573,805	422,166	41,968	97,314	2,274,095
1990	103,039	7,363	1,575,016	223,740	21,550	67,366	1,998,074
1991	121,881	10,256	2,255,918	326,584	35,590	66,834	2,817,063
1992	202,149	11,552	2,032,579	378,331	43,297	72,983	2,740,891
1993	183,072	12,694	1,980,831	373,155	54,034	76,182	2,679,968
1994	193,990	13,731	2,059,864	387,784	59,678	77,635	2,792,682
1995	195,025	14,338	2,185,742	342,041	64,348	81,324	2,882,818

Note: For 1990 and subsequent years, the data are no longer fully comparable with those for earlier years. For criminal accusations against a person already subjected to investigations, the new Code of Criminal Procedure (Article 405) identifies the start of judicial action as the moment at which the person is formally charged with a crime. Unlike previous years, then, the statistics no longer include cases closed without trial for lack of evidence or other causes. In comparing 1990 and 1991 data, it should be kept in mind that organizational difficulties linked to the implementation of the new Code have caused delays in judicial action and in the transmittal of information to Istat. Thus, for most classifications above, the Istat data register decreases in 1990 and then increases in 1991.

Sources: Istat, *Annuario statistico italiano* (Rome, 1986-1995); for 1994 and 1995: Istat, "Bollettino mensile di statistica", July 1996.

TABLE A6. Gross Domestic Product (in Market Prices) and the Consumer Price Index: Yearly Values and Percentage Variations over the Previous Year

	Gross Domestic Product				Consumer Price Index (1990=100)	
	Current Prices	% Variation	1990 Prices	% Variation	Index	% Variation
1986	898,289	+11.02	1,164,465	—	80.3	+5.80
1987	982,763	+9.40	1,200,523	+3.10	84.1	+4.73
1988	1,090,023	+10.91	1,246,966	+3.87	88.4	+5.11
1989	1,191,961	+9.35	1,282,905	+2.88	93.9	+6.22
1990	1,310,659	+9.96	1,310,659	+2.16	100.0	+6.50
1991	1,427,571	+8.92	1,325,582	+1.14	106.3	+6.30
1992	1,502,493	+5.25	1,333,072	+0.57	111.7	+5.08
1993	1,550,296	+3.18	1,317,668	−1.16	116.7	+4.48
1994	1,638,506	+5.69	1,345,674	+2.13	121.4	+4.03
1995	1,770,949	+8.08	1,385,618	+2.97	127.7	+5.19

Source: Banca d'Italia, Relazione annuale (Rome, 1996).

TABLE A7. National Debt and Annual Budgetary Deficit, in Absolute Terms and as a Percentage of the Gross Domestic Product

	National Debt			Budget Deficit		
	Billions of Lire	% Variation	% of GDP	Billions of Lire	% Variation	% of GDP
1986	793,583	+16.2	88.2	116,826	+14.9	11.7
1987	910,542	+14.7	92.6	128,226	+9.8	11.4
1988	1,035,812	+13.8	94.9	124,986	−2.5	11.2
1989a	1,169,869	+12.9	98.0	119,466	−4.4	10.4
1990	1,318,798	+12.7	100.5	122,471	+2.5	11.4
1991	1,487,399	+12.8	104.1	118,620	−3.1	10.6
1992	1,674,349	+12.6	111.3	107,189	−9.6	10.2
1993	1,864,319	+11.3	119.5	139,466	+30.1	9.9
1994	2,044,801	+9.7	124.6	124,406	−10.8	9.0
1995	2,196,384	+7.4	124.0	142,338	+14.4	7.0

a Some methodological innovations in banking statistics determine a discontinuity in the data series concerning the national debt, starting from 31 December 1988.

Source: Banca d'Italia, Relazione annuale (Rome, 1996).

TABLE B1. Elections to the Chamber of Deputies, 21 April 1996, Majoritarian Ballots. Regional and National Returns (Absolute Number of Votes Cast)

Lists	Piemonte	Valle d'Aosta	Lombardia	Trentino-Alto Adige	Veneto	Friuli-Venezia Giulia	Liguria	Emilia-Romagna	Toscana	Marche
Polo per le Libertà	1,067,156	15,810	2,300,984	147,845	1,013,811	313,692	439,565	984,594	904,602	400,026
Ulivo	1,190,936	-	2,276,159	170,143	-	270,398	534,008	1,591,408	1,294,051	407,249
Lega Nord	588,527	6,223	1,733,114	57,767	1,031,155	205,920	136,763	199,143	55,463	15,489
Progressisti	33,821	-	-	-	64,324	18,699	41,080	149,534	199,796	121,795
Ulivo-Lega Auton. Veneta	-	-	-	-	998,343	-	-	-	-	-
Mov.Soc. Fiamma Tricolore	-	-	19,473	-	4,459	11,725	-	6,698	20,488	26,139
Ulivo-Part. Sardo d'Az.	-	-	-	-	-	-	-	-	-	-
Sudtiroler Volkspartei	-	-	-	156,973	-	-	-	-	-	-
Lega d'Azione Meridionale	9,157	-	-	-	-	-	-	-	-	1,842
Pannella-Sgarbi	9,353	-	-	-	2,029	6,581	-	-	-	-
Mani Pulite	-	-	-	-	11,609	3,462	-	-	8,137	-
Rifondazione Comunista	-	5,593	-	-	-	-	-	-	-	-
Others	51,688	49,398	45,663	75,451	16,334	9,472	999	5,444	5,755	4,317
Total Valid Votes	2,950,638	77,024	6,375,393	608,179	3,142,064	839,949	1,152,415	2,936,821	2,488,292	976,857
Entitled to Vote	3,685,438	101,392	7,535,249	756,092	3,788,226	1,082,618	1,471,089	3,419,993	3,035,195	1,246,758
Voters	3,177,538	84,456	6,731,997	659,628	3,336,045	930,867	1,236,201	3,121,756	2,685,357	1,070,914
Invalid Votes	226,634	7,432	355,239	51,132	193,297	88,175	83,238	184,429	196,817	93,969
Blank Ballots	93,833	2,862	165,424	26,629	92,643	21,586	35,885	100,452	104,129	53,829
Contested Votes	266	-	1,365	317	684	2,743	548	506	248	88

TABLE B1 (continued)

Lists	Umbria	Lazio	Abruzzo	Molise	Campania	Puglia	Basilicata	Calabria	Sicilia	Sardegna	National Total
Polo per le Libertà	236,167	1,697,402	362,548	83,460	1,451,709	1,074,594	141,277	481,168	1,423,128	456,239	14,995,777
Ulivo	286,421	1,624,290	358,248	64,862	1,402,566	1,086,703	145,344	478,424	1,083,868	155,905	14,420,983
Lega Nord	8,947	–	–	–	–	–	–	–	–	–	4,038,511
Progressisti	41,307	72,897	26,026	–	102,808	–	28,865	24,156	–	57,140	982,248
Ulivo-Lega Aut. Veneta	–	–	–	–	–	–	–	–	–	–	998,343
Mov. Soc. Fiamma Tric.	–	151,364	44,711	13,810	126,423	53,322	13,558	47,033	83,906	6,413	629,522
Ulivo-Part. Sardo d'Az.	–	–	–	–	–	–	–	–	–	269,340	269,340
Sudtiroler Volkspartei	–	–	–	–	–	–	–	–	–	–	156,973
Lega d'Az. Meridionale	–	–	–	–	–	82,279	–	–	–	–	82,279
Pannella-Sgarbi	–	–	21,940	6,955	–	7,939	3,361	–	7,771	2,370	69,945
Mani Pulite	–	–	–	–	–	31,358	3,899	–	–	–	67,818
Rifondaz. Comunista	–	–	–	–	12,403	–	–	–	–	–	17,996
Others[a]	–	9,799	–	5,093	122,152	23,302	–	15,160	93,031	41,340	574,398
Total Valid Votes	572,842	3,555,752	813,473	174,180	3,218,061	2,359,497	336,304	1,045,941	2,691,704	988,747	37,304,133
Entitled to Vote	708,642	4,433,163	1,162,550	320,056	4,656,488	3,359,517	524,317	1,782,686	4,384,108	1,392,661	48,846,238
Voters	622,960	3,803,181	895,271	216,881	3,541,358	2,603,240	393,975	1,203,400	3,102,091	1,079,322	40,496,438
Invalid Votes	50,080	246,458	81,655	42,281	318,849	243,115	57,630	154,217	409,175	89,601	3,173,423
Blank Ballots	24,121	102,905	39,545	23,989	151,884	108,061	24,755	70,727	152,812	36,817	1,432,888
Contested Votes	38	971	143	420	4,448	628	41	3,242	1,212	974	18,882

Source: Calculated from data provided by Ministero dell'Interno–Direzione centrale per i servizi elettorali:Camera dei deputati:Elezioni politiche 21 aprile 1996 (Rome, 1996).

TABLE B2. Elections to the Chamber of Deputies, 21 April 1996, Majoritarian Ballots. Regional and National Returns (Percentage of Votes Cast)

Lists	Piemonte	Valle d'Aosta	Lombardia	Trentino-Alto Adige	Veneto	Friuli-Venezia Giulia	Liguria	Emilia-Romagna	Toscana	Marche
Polo per le Libertà	36.2	20.5	36.1	24.3	32.3	37.3	38.1	33.5	36.4	41.0
Ulivo	40.4	–	35.7	28.0	–	32.2	46.3	54.2	52.0	41.7
Lega Nord	19.9	8.1	27.2	9.5	32.8	24.5	11.9	6.8	2.2	1.6
Progressisti	1.1	–	–	–	2.0	2.2	3.6	5.1	8.0	12.5
Ulivo-Lega Auton. Veneta	–	–	–	–	31.8	–	–	–	–	–
Mov. Soc. Fiamma Tricolore	–	–	0.3	–	0.1	1.4	–	0.2	0.8	2.7
Ulivo-Part. Sardo d'Azione	–	–	–	–	–	–	–	–	–	–
Sudtiroler Volkspartei	–	–	–	25.8	–	–	–	–	–	–
Lega d'Azione Meridionale	0.3	–	–	–	0.1	0.8	–	–	–	0.2
Pannella-Sgarbi	0.3	–	–	–	0.4	0.4	–	–	0.3	–
Mani Pulite	–	–	–	–	–	–	–	–	–	–
Rifondazione Comunista	–	7.3	–	–	–	–	–	–	–	–
Others	1.8	64.1	0.7	12.4	0.5	1.1	0.1	0.2	0.2	0.4
Total Valid Votes	100.0	100.0	100.0	100.0	100.0	100.0	100.0	100.0	100.0	100.0
Voter Turnout (Voters x 100/Entitled to Vote)	86.2	83.3	89.3	87.2	88.1	86.0	84.0	91.3	88.5	85.9
Invalid Votes x 100/Voters	7.1	8.8	5.3	7.8	5.8	9.5	6.7	5.9	7.3	8.8
Unexpressed Votes[a] x 100/Entitled to Vote	19.9	24.0	15.4	19.5	17.0	22.2	21.6	14.1	18.0	21.6
Blank Ballots x 100/Invalid Votes	41.4	38.5	46.6	52.1	47.9	24.5	43.1	54.5	52.9	57.3

TABLE B2 (continued)

Lists	Umbria	Lazio	Abruzzo	Molise	Campania	Puglia	Basilicata	Calabria	Sicilia	Sardegna	National Total
Polo per le Libertà	41.2	47.7	44.6	47.9	45.1	45.5	42.0	46.0	52.9	46.1	40.2
Ulivo	50.0	45.7	44.0	37.2	43.6	46.1	43.2	45.7	40.3	15.8	38.7
Lega Nord	1.6	–	–	–	–	–	–	–	–	–	10.8
Progressisti	7.2	2.1	3.2	–	3.2	–	8.6	2.3	–	5.8	2.6
Ulivo-Lega Aut. Veneta	–	–	–	–	–	–	–	–	–	–	2.7
Mov. Soc. Fiamma Tric.	–	4.3	5.5	7.9	3.9	2.3	4.0	4.5	3.1	0.6	1.7
Ulivo-Part. Sardo d'Az.	–	–	–	–	–	–	–	–	–	27.2	0.7
Sudtiroler Volkspartei	–	–	–	–	–	–	–	–	–	–	0.4
Lega d'Az. Meridionale	–	–	–	–	–	3.5	–	–	–	–	0.2
Mani Pulite	–	–	–	–	–	–	1.2	–	–	–	0.2
Pannella-Sgarbi	–	–	2.7	4.0	–	0.3	1.0	–	0.3	0.2	0.2
Rifondaz. Comunista	–	–	–	–	0.4	–	–	–	–	–	0.0
Others[a]	–	0.3	–	2.9	3.8	1.0	–	1.4	3.5	4.2	1.5
Total Valid Votes	100.0	100.0	100.0	100.0	100.0	100.0	100.0	100.0	100.0	100.0	100.0
Voter Turnout (Voters x 100/Entitled to Vote)	87.9	85.8	77.0	67.8	76.1	77.5	75.1	67.5	70.8	77.5	82.9
Invalid Votes x 100/Voters	8.0	6.5	9.1	19.5	9.0	9.3	14.6	12.8	13.2	8.3	7.8
Unexpressed Votes[a] x 100/Entitled to Vote	19.2	19.8	30.0	45.4	30.8	29.7	35.9	41.1	38.6	28.9	23.6
Blank Ballots x 100/Invalid Votes	48.2	41.8	48.4	56.7	47.6	44.4	43.0	45.9	37.3	41.1	45.2

Source: Calculated from data provided by Ministero dell'Interno–Direzione centrale per i servizi elettorali–Camera dei deputati: Elezioni politiche 21 aprile 1996 (Rome, 1996).

[a] Unexpressed votes= non-voters+invalid votes

TABLE B3. Elections to the Chamber of Deputies, 21 April 1996, Proportional Ballots. Regional and National Returns (Absolute Number of Votes Cast)

Lists	Piemonte	Lombardia	Trentino-Alto Adige	Veneto	Friuli-Venezia Giulia	Liguria	Emilia-Romagna	Toscana	Umbria	Marche
PDS	501,713	964,979	52,274	374,468	109,460	299,318	1,065,361	883,856	194,677	286,839
Forza Italia	643,524	1,509,820	80,522	542,635	178,093	224,902	450,886	363,911	96,875	173,717
Alleanza Nazionale	357,697	574,830	65,855	371,231	127,873	159,209	343,516	401,247	116,259	162,617
Rifondazione Comunista	306,149	436,791	20,487	166,777	62,786	119,682	249,083	316,885	71,986	103,811
Lega Nord	540,820	1,636,346	74,586	928,182	195,864	119,188	216,217	46,006	33,936	14,614
Pop-SVP-PRI-UD-Prodi	198,442	397,953	99,723	257,782	75,262	62,136	237,956	145,279	27,563	60,384
CCD-CDU	130,907	297,674	28,342	171,801	47,540	48,231	144,526	121,173	25,678	79,824
Lista Dini	88,316	266,989	50,095	165,661	–	68,068	115,511	109,828	12,608	53,291
Federazione dei Verdi	72,771	151,675	27,792	79,380	33,075	28,859	74,570	50,248	–	26,988
Pannella-Sgarbi	71,577	133,055	–	29,908	–	31,299	68,438	48,831	–	18,694
Mov. Soc. Fiamma Tricolore	–	30,253	–	9,775	9,169	–	13,859	17,364	–	11,943
Socialista	6,896	–	–	–	–	7,054	–	20,894	–	–
Lega d'Azione Meridionale	–	–	–	–	–	–	–	–	–	–
Unione Nord Est	–	–	–	63,951	–	–	–	–	–	–
Union für Sud Tirol	–	–	55,499	–	–	–	–	–	–	–
Others	46,247	5,961	8,302	9,498	4,963	–	8,371	17,855	–	5,545
Total Valid Votes	2,965,059	6,406,326	563,477	3,171,049	844,085	1,167,946	2,988,294	2,543,377	585,545	998,267
Entitled to Vote	3,685,438	7,535,249	756,092	3,788,226	1,082,618	1,471,089	3,419,993	3,035,195	708,642	1,246,758
Voters	3,177,670	6,731,601	659,688	3,334,770	933,589	1,236,221	3,114,749	2,684,367	618,615	1,070,903
Invalid Votes	212,358	322,654	96,137	163,111	89,431	67,753	126,090	140,632	33,051	72,470
Blank Ballots	89,269	130,459	73,555	72,853	20,420	26,449	59,008	63,622	14,693	37,250
Contested Votes	253	2,621	74	610	73	522	365	358	19	166

TABLE B3 (continued)

Lists	Lazio	Abruzzo	Molise	Campania	Puglia	Basilicata	Calabria	Sicilia	Sardegna	National Total
PDS	844,778	170,768	35,339	641,264	520,620	80,816	222,474	445,622	202,418	7,897,044
Forza Italia	579,996	159,310	32,367	751,675	579,253	62,357	193,784	864,290	227,425	7,715,342
Alleanza Nazionale	1,041,256	174,309	35,789	600,751	421,843	49,213	248,151	440,829	182,916	5,875,391
Lega Nord	–	–	–	–	–	–	–	–	–	3,777,786
Rifondaz. Comunista	373,519	90,225	16,944	292,942	176,203	34,050	106,131	187,832	83,677	3,215,960
Pop-SVP-PRI-UD-Prodi	189,976	61,470	22,615	260,923	123,492	42,363	71,845	152,442	61,103	2,555,082
CCD-CDU	168,724	60,870	21,150	257,165	178,383	33,290	95,527	217,111	60,218	2,190,019
Lista Dini	169,948	36,337	7,183	132,532	87,740	18,874	44,351	117,085	69,704	1,627,191
Federazione dei Verdi	90,509	27,028	4,219	97,583	40,378	7,665	18,709	72,902	20,725	937,684
Pannella-Sgarbi	63,756	24,410	4,217	49,622	36,132	4,847	19,735	75,903	20,609	701,033
Mov. Soc. Fiamma Tric.	57,096	18,397	5,424	54,451	37,027	6,853	18,761	42,097	6,252	338,721
Socialista	14,590	–	2,414	41,207	29,292	–	17,605	9,624	–	149,576
Lega d'Az. Meridionale	–	–	–	–	72,152	–	–	–	–	72,152
Unione Nord Est	–	–	–	–	–	–	–	–	–	63,951
Union für Sud Tirol	–	–	–	–	–	–	–	–	–	55,499
Others	3,497	–	3,826	34,227	50,514	2,303	4,090	56,073	61,262	322,534
Total Valid Votes	3,597,645	823,124	191,487	3,214,342	2,353,029	342,631	1,061,163	2,681,810	996,309	37,494,965
Entitled to Vote	4,433,163	1,162,550	320,056	4,656,488	3,359,517	524,317	1,782,686	4,384,108	1,392,661	48,744,846
Voters	3,803,309	895,274	217,722	3,540,231	2,608,424	393,986	1,200,784	3,100,675	1,079,196	40,401,774
Invalid Votes	204,027	72,078	25,656	321,264	254,674	51,337	138,436	418,169	82,009	2,891,337
Blank Ballots	70,791	32,841	13,418	150,517	108,873	20,992	62,588	159,469	34,431	1,241,498
Contested Votes	1,637	72	579	4,625	721	18	1,185	696	878	15,472

Source: Calculated from data provided by Ministero dell'Interno–Direzione centrale per i servizi elettorali–Camera dei deputati: Elezioni politiche 21 aprile 1996 (Rome, 1996).

TABLE B4. Elections to the Chamber of Deputies, 21 April 1996, Proportional Ballots. Regional and National Returns (Percentage of Votes Cast)

Lists	Piemonte	Lombardia	Trentino-Alto Adige	Veneto	Friuli-Venezia Giulia	Liguria	Emilia-Romagna	Toscana	Marche	Umbria
PDS	16.9	15.1	9.3	11.8	13.0	25.6	35.7	34.8	28.7	33.2
Forza Italia	21.7	23.6	14.3	17.1	21.1	19.3	15.1	14.3	17.4	16.5
Alleanza Nazionale	12.1	9.0	11.7	11.7	15.1	13.6	11.5	15.8	16.3	19.9
Lega Nord	18.2	25.5	13.2	29.3	23.2	10.2	7.2	1.8	1.5	1.0
Rifondazione Comunista	10.3	6.8	3.6	5.3	7.4	10.2	8.3	12.5	10.4	12.3
Pop.- SVP-PRI-UD-Prodi	6.7	6.2	17.7	8.1	8.9	5.3	8.0	5.7	6.0	5.8
CCD-CDU	4.4	4.6	5.0	5.4	5.6	4.1	4.8	4.8	8.0	4.7
Lista Dini	3.0	4.2	8.9	5.2	–	5.8	3.9	4.3	5.3	4.4
Federazione dei Verdi	2.5	2.4	4.9	2.5	3.9	2.5	2.5	2.0	2.7	2.2
Pannella-Sgarbi	2.4	2.1	–	0.9	–	2.7	2.3	1.9	1.9	–
Mov. Soc. Fiamma Tricolore	–	0.5	–	0.3	1.1	–	0.5	0.7	1.2	–
Socialista	0.2	–	–	–	–	0.6	–	0.8	–	–
Lega d'Az. Meridionale	–	–	–	–	–	–	–	–	–	–
Unione Nord Est	–	–	–	2.0	–	–	–	–	–	–
Union für Sud Tirol	–	–	9.8	–	–	–	–	–	–	–
Others	1.6	0.1	1.5	0.3	0.6	–	0.3	0.7	0.6	–
Total Valid Votes	100.0	100.0	100.0	100.0	100.0	100.0	100.0	100.0	100.0	100.0
Voter Turnout (Voters x 100/Entitled to Vote)	86.2	89.3	87.2	88.0	86.2	84.0	91.1	88.4	85.9	87.3
Invalid Votes x 100/Voters	6.7	4.8	14.6	4.9	9.6	5.5	4.0	5.2	6.8	5.3
Unexpressed Votes[a] x 100/Entitled to Vote	19.5	14.9	25.5	16.3	22.0	20.6	12.6	16.2	19.9	17.4
Blank Ballots x 100/Invalid Votes	42.0	40.4	76.5	44.7	22.8	39.0	46.8	45.2	51.4	44.5

TABLE B4 (*continued*)

Lists	Lazio	Abruzzo	Molise	Campania	Puglia	Basilicata	Calabria	Sicilia	Sardegna	National Total
Pds	23.5	20.7	18.5	20.0	22.1	23.6	21.0	16.6	20.3	21.1
Forza Italia	16.1	19.4	16.9	23.4	24.6	18.2	18.3	32.2	22.8	20.6
Alleanza Nazionale	28.9	21.2	18.7	18.7	17.9	14.4	23.4	16.4	18.4	15.7
Lega Nord	–	–	–	–	–	–	–	–	–	10.1
Rifondaz. Comunista	10.4	11.0	8.8	9.1	7.5	9.9	10.0	7.0	8.4	8.6
Pop.-SVP-PRI-UD-Prodi	5.3	7.5	11.8	8.1	5.2	12.4	6.8	5.7	6.1	6.8
CCD-CDU	4.7	7.4	11.0	8.0	7.6	9.7	9.0	8.1	6.0	5.8
Lista Dini	4.7	4.4	3.8	4.1	3.7	5.5	4.2	4.4	7.0	4.3
Federazione dei Verdi	2.5	3.3	2.2	3.0	1.7	2.2	1.8	2.7	2.1	2.5
Pannella-Sgarbi	1.8	3.0	2.2	1.5	1.5	1.4	1.9	2.8	2.1	1.9
Mov. Soc. Fiamma Tricolore	1.6	2.2	2.8	1.7	1.6	2.0	1.8	1.6	0.6	0.9
Socialista	0.4	–	1.3	1.3	1.2	–	1.7	0.4	–	0.4
Lega d'Az. Meridionale	–	–	–	–	3.1	–	–	–	–	0.2
Unione Nord Est	–	–	–	–	–	–	–	–	–	0.2
Union für Sud Tirol	–	–	–	–	–	–	–	–	–	0.1
Others	0.1	–	2.0	1.1	2.1	0.7	0.4	2.1	6.1	0.9
Total Valid Votes	100.0	100.0	100.0	100.0	100.0	100.0	100.0	100.0	100.0	100.0
Voter Turnout (Voters x 100/Entitled to Vote)	85.8	77.0	68.0	76.0	77.6	75.1	67.4	70.7	77.5	82.9
Invalid Votes x 100/Voters	5.4	8.1	11.8	9.1	9.8	13.0	11.5	13.5	7.6	7.2
Unexpressed Votes[a] x 100/Entitled to Vote	18.8	29.2	40.0	30.9	29.9	34.6	40.4	38.8	28.4	23.0
Blank Ballots x 100/Invalid Votes	34.7	45.6	52.3	46.9	42.7	40.9	45.2	38.1	42.0	42.9

Source. Calculated from data provided by Ministero dell'Interno–Direzione centrale per i servizi elettorali–*Camera dei deputati: Elezioni politiche 21 aprile 1996* (Rome, 1996).

[a] Unexpressed votes= non-voters+invalid votes

TABLE B5. Elections to the Senate, 21 April 1996. Regional and National Returns (Absolute Number of Votes Cast)

Lists	Piemonte	Valle d'Aosta	Lombardia	Trentino-Alto Adige	Veneto	Friuli-Venezia Giulia	Liguria	Emilia-Romagna	Toscana	Marche
Ulivo	974,677	–	1,929,519	143,835	938,783	276,942	430,796	1,373,013	1,130,597	482,698
Polo per le Libertà	902,722	14,810	1,853,547	127,133	840,604	288,233	396,011	829,900	727,279	353,235
Lega Nord	504,821	6,458	1,376,761	59,464	839,097	180,534	123,718	215,522	51,635	24,293
Progressisti	62,617	–	50,234	–	–	–	84,454	175,024	160,777	–
Mov. Soc. Fiamma Tricolore	–	–	84,256	–	39,058	–	–	–	43,954	–
Pannella-Sgarbi	–	–	142,045	–	–	–	–	57,832	35,806	–
Ulivo-Ps d'Azione	–	–	–	–	–	–	–	–	–	–
Socialista	22,471	–	50,172	–	–	–	–	–	33,979	–
L'Abete SVP PATT	–	–	–	178,415	–	–	–	–	–	–
Mani Pulite	24,070	–	–	–	35,359	–	–	–	24,872	–
All. Lombarda Autonomia	–	–	106,337	–	–	–	–	–	–	–
Unione Nord Est	–	–	–	–	72,559	–	–	–	–	–
Noi Siciliani Frs	–	–	–	–	–	–	–	–	–	–
Lega d'Az. Meridionale	–	–	–	–	–	–	–	–	–	–
Verdi-Verdi	61,675	–	–	–	–	–	–	–	–	–
All. Pensionati Europei	60,687	–	–	–	–	–	–	–	–	–
Democrazia Sociale	–	–	55,957	–	–	–	–	–	–	–
Fed. Liste Civiche Italiane	–	–	–	–	–	–	–	–	–	–
Rifondazione Comunista	–	5,682	–	–	–	–	–	–	–	–
Others	27,102	39,908	–	25,179	2,898	2,411	5,144	–	18,568	10,687
Total Valid Votes	2,640,842	66,858	5,648,828	534,026	2,768,358	748,120	1,040,123	2,651,291	2,227,467	870,913
Entitled to Vote	3,295,340	90,646	6,671,148	666,005	3,347,455	972,193	1,335,149	3,077,905	2,720,385	1,112,911
Voters	2,825,459	74,937	5,938,707	577,907	2,925,662	828,564	1,112,106	2,791,858	2,395,067	946,769
Invalid Votes	184,427	8,079	289,109	43,809	156,729	80,310	71,605	140,346	166,978	75,715
Blank Ballots	81,925	3,941	146,705	24,948	79,004	18,693	33,975	79,647	89,550	43,308
Contested Votes	190	–	770	72	575	134	378	221	622	141

TABLE B5 (continued)

Lists	Umbria	Lazio	Abruzzo	Molise	Campania	Puglia	Basilicata	Calabria	Sicilia	Sardegna	National Total
Ulivo	239,117	1,458,502	269,089	82,194	1,155,814	739,173	151,197	322,009	918,429	–	13,016,384
Polo per le Libertà	206,596	1,393,028	327,154	64,553	1,154,564	865,721	108,991	393,223	964,259	375,935	12,187,498
Lega Nord	12,224	–	–	–	–	–	–	–	–	–	3,394,527
Progressisti	50,958	–	63,112	–	98,128	110,963	–	79,031	–	–	935,298
Mov. Soc. Fiamma Tric.	–	131,161	46,637	10,164	126,731	82,279	11,663	51,828	121,028	–	748,759
Pannella-Sgarbi	–	80,064	–	–	–	–	–	–	154,048	–	511,689
Ulivo-Ps d'Azione	–	–	–	–	–	37,841	4,053	–	–	421,636	421,636
Socialista	–	43,349	–	2,553	74,601	–	–	28,840	32,645	–	288,610
L'Abete SVP PATT	–	–	–	–	–	–	–	–	–	–	178,415
Mani Pulite	–	–	–	–	–	19,853	4,868	–	–	–	109,022
All. Lomb. Autonomia	–	–	–	–	–	–	–	–	–	–	106,337
Unione Nord Est	–	–	–	–	–	–	–	–	–	–	72,559
Noi Siciliani Frs	–	–	–	–	–	–	–	–	72,070	–	72,070
Lega d'Az. Merid.le	–	–	–	–	–	63,665	–	–	–	–	66,583
Verdi-Verdi	–	–	–	–	–	–	2,918	–	–	–	61,675
All. Pens. Europei	–	–	–	–	–	–	–	–	–	–	60,687
Democrazia Sociale	–	–	–	–	60,064	–	–	–	–	–	60,064
Fed. Liste Civiche Ital.	–	–	–	–	–	–	–	–	–	–	55,957
Rifondaz. Comunista	–	–	–	–	–	–	–	–	–	–	5,682
Others	–	10,089	–	4,434	17,980	54,796	5,688	2,178	11,474	44,607	283,143
Total Valid Votes	508,895	3,116,193	705,992	163,898	2,687,882	1,974,291	289,378	877,109	2,273,953	842,178	32,636,595
Entitled to Vote	634,704	3,900,203	1,030,126	284,755	3,948,214	2,850,740	452,973	1,536,959	3,768,806	1,187,734	42,884,351
Voters	549,428	3,305,928	779,667	189,576	2,960,445	2,202,869	337,682	1,019,522	2,631,696	914,648	35,308,497
Invalid Votes	40,512	186,978	73,495	25,018	265,496	228,136	48,282	136,340	356,924	71,918	2,650,206
Blank Ballots	21,924	83,661	38,132	14,268	140,348	113,907	20,768	68,690	141,171	31,453	1,276,018
Contested Votes	21	2,757	180	660	7,067	442	22	6,073	819	552	21,696

Source: Calculated from data provided by Ministero dell'Interno–Direzione centrale per i servizi elettorali–*Senato della Repubblica: Elezioni politiche 21 aprile 1996* (Rome, 1996).

TABLE B6. Elections to the Senate, 21 April 1996. Regional and National Returns (Percentage of Votes Cast)

Lists	Piemonte	Valle d'Aosta	Lombardia	Trentino-Alto Adige	Veneto	Friuli-Venezia Giulia	Liguria	Emilia-Romagna	Toscana	Marche
Ulivo	36.9	–	34.2	26.9	33.9	37.0	41.4	51.8	50.8	55.4
Polo per le Libertà	34.2	22.2	32.8	23.8	30.4	38.5	38.1	31.3	32.7	40.6
Lega Nord	19.1	9.7	24.4	11.1	30.3	24.1	11.9	8.1	2.3	2.8
Progressisti	2.4	–	0.9	–	–	–	8.1	6.6	7.2	–
Mov. Soc. Fiamma Tricolore	–	–	1.5	–	1.4	–	–	–	2.0	–
Pannella-Sgarbi	–	–	2.5	–	–	–	–	2.2	1.6	–
Ulivo-Ps d'Azione	–	–	–	–	–	–	–	–	–	–
Socialista	0.9	–	0.9	–	–	–	–	–	1.5	–
L'Abete SVP PATT	–	–	–	33.4	–	–	–	–	–	–
Mani Pulite	0.9	–	–	–	1.3	–	–	–	1.1	–
All. Lombarda Autonomia	–	–	1.9	–	–	–	–	–	–	–
Unione Nord Est	–	–	–	–	2.6	–	–	–	–	–
Noi Siciliani Fns	–	–	–	–	–	–	–	–	–	–
Lega d'Azione Meridionale	–	–	–	–	–	–	–	–	–	–
Verdi-Verdi	2.3	–	–	–	–	–	–	–	–	–
All. Pensionati Europei	2.3	–	–	–	–	–	–	–	–	–
Democrazia Sociale	–	–	–	–	–	–	–	–	–	–
Fed. Liste Civiche Italiane	–	–	1.0	–	–	–	–	–	–	–
Rifondazione Comunista	–	8.5	–	–	–	–	–	–	–	–
Others	1.0	59.7	–	4.7	0.1	0.3	0.5	–	0.8	1.2
Total Valid Votes	100.0	100.0	100.0	100.0	100.0	100.0	100.0	100.0	100.0	100.0
Voter Turnout (Voters x 100/Entitled to Vote)	85.7	82.7	89.0	86.8	87.4	85.2	83.3	90.7	88.0	85.1
Invalid Votes x 100/Voters	6.5	10.8	4.9	7.6	5.4	9.7	6.4	5.0	7.0	8.0
Unexpressed Votes[a] x 100/Entitled to Vote	19.9	26.2	15.3	19.8	17.3	23.0	22.1	13.9	18.1	21.7
Blank Ballots x 100/Invalid Votes	44.4	48.8	50.7	56.9	50.4	23.3	47.4	56.8	53.6	57.2

TABLE B6 (continued)

Lists	Umbria	Lazio	Abruzzo	Molise	Campania	Puglia	Basilicata	Calabria	Sicilia	Sardegna	National Total
Ulivo	47.0	46.8	38.1	50.1	43.0	37.4	52.2	36.7	40.4	—	39.9
Polo per le Libertà	40.6	44.7	46.3	39.4	43.0	43.8	37.7	44.8	42.4	44.6	37.3
Lega Nord	2.4	—	—	—	—	—	—	—	—	—	10.4
Progressisti	10.0	—	—	—	—	—	—	—	—	—	2.9
Movim. Soc. Fiamma Tricolore	—	4.2	8.9	6.2	3.7	5.6	4.0	9.0	5.3	—	2.3
Pannella-Sgarbi	—	2.6	6.6	—	4.7	4.2	1.4	5.9	6.8	—	1.6
Ulivo-Ps d'Azione	—	—	—	—	—	1.9	—	—	—	50.1	1.3
Socialista	—	1.4	—	1.6	2.8	—	—	3.3	1.4	—	0.9
L'Abete SVP PATT	—	—	—	—	—	—	—	—	—	—	0.5
Mani Pulite	—	—	—	—	—	1.0	1.7	—	—	—	0.3
All. Lomb. Autonomia	—	—	—	—	—	—	—	—	—	—	0.3
Unione Nord Est	—	—	—	—	—	—	—	—	—	—	0.2
Noi Siciliani Frns	—	—	—	—	—	—	—	—	3.2	0.0	0.2
Lega d'Azione Meridionale	—	—	—	—	—	3.2	1.0	—	—	—	0.2
Verdi-Verdi	—	—	—	—	—	—	—	—	—	—	0.2
All. Pensionati Europei	—	—	—	—	—	—	—	—	—	—	0.2
Democrazia Sociale	—	—	—	—	2.2	—	—	—	—	—	0.2
Fed. Liste Civiche Italiane	—	—	—	—	—	—	—	—	—	—	0.2
Rifondazione Comunista	—	—	—	—	—	—	—	—	—	—	0.0
Others	—	0.3	—	2.7	0.7	2.8	2.0	0.2	0.5	5.3	0.9
Total Valid Votes	100.0	100.0	100.0	100.0	100.0	100.0	100.0	100.0	100.0	100.0	100.0
Voter Turnout (Voters x 100/Entitled to Vote)	86.6	84.8	75.7	66.6	75.0	77.3	74.5	66.3	69.8	77.0	82.3
Invalid Votes x 100/Voters	7.4	5.7	9.4	13.2	9.0	10.4	14.3	13.4	13.6	7.9	7.5
Unexpressed Votes[a] x 100/Entitled to Vote	19.8	20.0	31.4	42.2	31.7	30.7	36.1	42.5	39.6	29.0	23.8
Blank Ballots x 100/Invalid Votes	54.1	44.7	51.9	57.0	52.9	49.9	43.0	50.4	39.6	43.7	48.1

Source: Calculated from data provided by Ministero dell'Interno–Direzione centrale per i servizi elettorali–*Senato della Repubblica: Elezioni politiche 21 aprile 1996* (Rome, 1996).

[a] Unexpressed votes= non-voters+invalid votes

TABLE B7. Municipal Elections, 9 June 1996: 33 Municipalities with over 15,000 Inhabitants. Summary of National Returns

Lists	Valid Votes	%	Seats
Partito Democratico della Sinistra	134,328	17.1	203
Alleanza Nazionale	81,884	10.4	77
Forza Italia	77,200	9.8	90
Partito Popolare Italiano (PPI)	65,251	8.3	83
Rifondazione Comunista	49,648	6.3	49
Centro Cristiano Democratico (CCD)	42,695	5.4	28
Cristiani Democratici Uniti (CDU)	35,896	4.6	28
Other Leagues	34,897	4.4	17
Lega Nord	30,273	3.9	19
Civic Lists	22,947	2.9	11
Ulivo	19,853	2.5	24
Federazione dei Verdi	14,693	1.9	7
Lista Dini	12,996	1.7	12
Polo per le Libertà	12,245	1.6	6
Forza Italia-CCD-CDU	10,957	1.4	9
CCD-CDU	6,705	0.9	7
Socialists	4,659	0.6	1
Si-Socialisti Italiani	3,777	0.5	7
Movim. Sociale Fiamma Tricolore	3,653	0.5	0
Partito Repubblicano Italiano (PRI)	2,719	0.3	1
Federazione Laburista	2,910	0.4	1
Comunisti Unitari	2,945	0.4	0
Other Green Lists	1,571	0.2	0
Left Mixed	4,671	0.6	6
Center-Left Mixed	47,050	6.0	65
Center Mixed	21,028	2.7	10
Center-Right Mixed	4,844	0.6	4
Right Mixed	2,298	0.3	1
Others	30,925	3.9	22
Total	785,518	100.0	788

A total of 880 seats were assigned; 91 seats were reserved for lists the mayoral candidates of which were not elected.

Entitled to Vote	1.200.584
Voters	904.463
Voter Turnout (Voters x 100/Entitled to Vote)	75.3
Invalid Votes	38,308
Invalid Votes x 100/Voters	4.2
Blank Ballots	12,008
Blank Ballots x 100/Invalid Votes	31.3
Mayor Votes Only	80,637

Source: Calculated from data provided by Ministero dell'Interno-Direzione centrale per i servizi elettorali.

TABLE B8. Municipal Elections, 9 June 1996: 130 Municipalities with up to 15,000 Inhabitants. Summary of National Returns

Lists	Valid Votes	%	Seats
Civic Lists	71,531	20.1	493
Partito Popolare Italiano (PPI)	36,742	10.3	131
Lega Nord	17,510	4.9	53
Left Mixed	12,468	3.5	70
Polo per le Libertà	8,074	2.3	19
Rifondazione Comunista	3,850	1.1	5
Ulivo	2,478	0.7	14
Partito Democratico della Sinistra	2,330	0.7	19
Alleanza Nazionale	2,211	0.6	3
Progressisti	1,028	0.3	2
Movim. Sociale Fiamma Tricolore	806	0.2	1
Cristiani Democratici Uniti (CDU)	710	0.2	1
Other Leagues	225	0.1	0
Forza Italia	205	0.1	0
Other Green Lists	65	0.0	4
Autonomist Lists	52	0.0	0
Center-Left Mixed	82,620	23.2	445
Center Mixed	47,228	13.3	284
Center-Right Mixed	62,404	17.6	289
Right Mixed	2,449	0.7	15
Others	374	0.1	0
Total	355,360	100.0	1,848

Total seats=1,896; 4 seats were not assigned.

Entitled to Vote	478,093
Voters	371,445
Voter Turnout (Voters x 100/Entitled to Vote)	77.7
Invalid Votes	12,493
Invalid Votes x 100/Voters	3.4
Blank Ballots	4,395
Blank Ballots x 100/Invalid Votes	35.2

Source: Calculated from data provided by Ministero dell'Interno-Direzione centrale per i servizi elettorali.

TABLE B9. Municipal Elections, 17 November 1996: 15 Municipalities with over 15,000 Inhabitants. Summary of National Returns

Lists	Valid Votes	%	Seats
Forza Italia	33,994	12.9	39
Partito Democratico della Sinistra	32,470	12.3	47
Alleanza Nazionale	29,497	11.2	38
Partito Popolare Italiano (PPI)	21,092	8.0	23
Rifondazione Comunista	17,056	6.5	33
Rifond. Comunista with Others	1,420	0.5	0
Cristiani Democratici Uniti (CDU)	12,789	4.9	18
Centro Crist. Democratico (CCD)	12,710	4.8	11
Civic Lists	11,728	4.5	17
Ulivo	11,299	4.3	25
Lista Dini	10,825	4.1	16
Lega Nord	5,347	2.0	2
Lega Nord with Others	7,512	2.9	4
CCD-CDU	5,907	2.2	4
Federazione dei Verdi	2,356	0.9	4
Movim. Sociale Fiamma Tricolore	1,133	0.4	1
Other Leagues	629	0.2	0
Partito Repubblicano Italiano	365	0.1	1
Autonomist Lists	176	0.1	0
Left Mixed	5,173	2.0	7
Center-Left Mixed	15,944	6.1	19
Center Mixed	13,384	5.1	15
Center-Right Mixed	10,001	3.8	17
Others	716	0.3	1
Total	263,523	100.0	342

A total of 380 seats were assigned; 38 seats were reserved for lists the mayoral candidates of which were not elected.

Entitled to Vote	389,495
Voters	303,072
Voter Turnout	
(Voters x 100/Entitled to Vote)	77.8
Invalid Votes	14,817
Invalid Votes x 100/Voters	4.9
Blank Ballots	2,879
Blank Ballots x 100/Invalid Votes	19.4
Mayor Votes Only	24,732

Source: Calculated from data provided by Ministero dell'Interno-Direzione centrale per i servizi elettorali.

TABLE B10. Municipal Elections, 17 November 1996: 106 Municipalities with up to 15,000 Inhabitants. Summary of National Returns

Lists	Valid Votes	%	Seats
Civic Lists	40,468	15.8	396
Ulivo	24,938	9.7	72
Lega Nord	15,226	5.9	62
Lega Nord with Others	2,487	1.0	6
Polo per le Libertà	9,348	3.6	23
Alleanza Nazionale	2,941	1.1	21
Cristiani Democratici Uniti (CDU)	1,359	0.5	2
Rifondazione Comunista	634	0.2	0
Partito Popolare Italiano (PPI)	633	0.2	1
Progressisti	540	0.2	2
Autonomist Lists	301	0.1	6
Movim. Sociale Fiamma Tricolore	220	0.1	0
Left Mixed	5,823	2.3	24
Center-Left Mixed	63,353	24.7	430
Center Mixed	33,336	13.0	216
Center-Right Mixed	50,122	19.6	196
Right Mixed	2,221	0.9	4
Others	2,390	0.9	5
Total	256,340	100.0	1,466

Total seats=1,484; 18 seats were not assigned.

Entitled to Vote	335,628
Voters	267,221
Voter Turnout (Voters x 100/Entitled to Vote)	79.6
Invalid Votes	10,881
Invalid Votes x 100/Voters	4.1
Blank Ballots	3,590
Blank Ballots x 100/Invalid Votes	33.0

Source: Calculated from data provided by Ministero dell'Interno-Direzione centrale per i servizi elettorali.

TABLE B11. Sicilian Regional Elections, 16 June 1996

Lists	Valid Votes	%	Seats
Forza Italia	456,125	17.1	17
Alleanza Nazionale	376,122	14.1	14
Partito Democratico della Sinistra	375,293	14.1	13
Centro Crist. Democratico (CCD)	261,830	9.8	11
Cristiani Democratici Uniti (CDU)	245,351	9.2	7
Partito Popolare Italiano (PPI)	198,392	7.4	6
Lista Dini	131,355	4.9	4
Rifondazione Comunista	115,138	4.3	6
La Rete	94,818	3.6	3
Socialists	50,369	1.9	3
Noi Siciliani	46,606	1.7	1
Mov. Sociale Fiamma Tricolore	31,606	1.2	0
Cristiani Sociali	30,276	1.1	0
Verdi	26,079	1.0	0
Alleanza Democratica	17,608	0.7	1
Rete-Verdi	16,347	0.6	1
Dini- PPI	16,119	0.6	0
Rifondazione Comunista-Verdi	14,093	0.5	0
Others	164,053	6.1	3
Total Valid Votes	2,667,580	100.0	90

Entitled to Vote	4,389,923	
Voters	2,892,968	
Voter Turnout		
(Voters x 100/Entitled to Vote)	65.9	
Invalid Votes	225,388	
Invalid Votes x 100/Voters	7.8	

Note: data for valid votes are definitive; figures concerning entitled to vote, voters and invalid votes are provisional.

Source: Calculated from data provided by Ministero dell'Interno-Direzione centrale per i servizi elettorali.

271

TABLE C1. Membership of the Main Italian Parties in the Post-War Period

Year	PCI/PDS	DC/PPI	PSI	PSDI	MSI/AN	PLI	PRI
1945	1,770,896	537,582	700,000	–	–	–	–
1946	2,068,272	602,652	860,300	–	–	–	–
1947	2,252,446	790,771	822,000	–	–	–	–
1948	2,115,232	1,095,359	531,031	–	–	–	–
1949	2,027,271	766,023	430,258	–	–	–	–
1950	2,112,593	882,674	700,000	–	–	–	–
1951	2,097,830	917,095	720,000	–	–	–	–
1952	2,093,540	954,723	750,000	–	–	–	–
1953	2,134,285	1,141,181	780,000	94,443	–	–	60,939
1954	2,145,317	1,252,524	754,000	–	–	–	51,911
1955	2,090,006	1,186,785	770,000	–	–	147,000	53,656
1956	2,035,353	1,377,286	710,000	128,553	–	–	47,093
1957	1,825,342	1,295,028	477,000	150,985	–	–	50,611
1958	1,818,606	1,410,179	486,652	123,618	–	173,722	56,166
1959	1,789,269	1,608,609	484,652	121,513	–	–	53,258
1960	1,792,974	1,473,789	489,837	119,167	191,397	–	–
1961	1,728,620	1,565,185	465,259	129,125	200,348	–	55,354
1962	1,630,550	1,446,500	491,216	153,717	198,995	–	49,307
1963	1,615,571	1,621,620	491,676	150,717	240,063	–	52,499
1964	1,641,214	1,633,003	446,250	165,980	227,214	–	54,526
1965	1,615,296	1,656,428	437,458	185,269	191,029	–	45,492
1966	1,575,935	1,592,134	700,964		161,890	–	56,570
1967	1,534,705	1,621,866	633,573		160,043	–	58,591
1968	1,502,862	1,696,182	–	–	199,950	148,562	84,280
1969	1,503,816	1,745,632	–	–	175,709	–	68,476
1970	1,507,047	1,738,996	506,533	–	188,878	–	95,368
1971	1,521,642	1,814,578	592,586	250,181	205,794	135,000	103,105
1972	1,584,659	1,828,998	560,187	284,772	239,075	139,725	–
1973	1,623,082	1,747,292	465,183	303,026	225,030	–	–
1974	1,657,825	1,843,515	511,741	279,396	210,018	–	–
1975	1,730,453	1,732,501	539,339	308,211	212,120	–	–
1976	1,814,262	1,365,187	509,388	–	217,110	–	–
1977	1,814,154	1,201,707	482,916	149,610	160,339	25,819	108,859
1978	1,790,450	1,355,423	479,769	148,131	152,234	37,951	107,000
1979	1,761,297	1,384,148	472,544	217,212	174,157	29,282	104,000
1980	1,751,323	1,395,584	514,918	108,470	165,810	44,966	106,536
1981	1,714,052	1,385,141	527,460	199,588	176,417	41,445	106,000
1982	1,673,751	1,361,066	555,956	126,015	159,169	43,417	106,000
1983	1,635,264	1,384,058	566,612	207,493	165,308	59,296	108,201
1984	1,619,940	1,382,278	571,821	165,733	180,688	39,180	96,207
1985	1,595,281	1,444,565	583,282	165,733	141,623	61,818	97,839
1986	1,551,576	1,395,784	593,231	133,428	156,520	36,931	117,031
1987	1,508,140	1,812,201	620,557	133,428	165,427	26,439	107,949
1988	1,462,281	1,693,346	630,692	110,000	151,444	17,768	99,386
1989	1,421,230	1,862,426	635,504	110,000	160,960	19,121	83,498
1990	1,264,790	2,109,670	660,195	–	142,344	44,732	72,175
1991	989,708	1,390,918	674,057	–	150,157	50,327	71,886
1992	769,944	–	51,224	–	181,243	18,731	71,200
1993	690,414	813,753	–	–	202,715	–	76,000
1994	698,287	233,377	43,052	–	324,344	–	20,916
1995	682,290	160,000	44,485	–	467,539	–	22,000
1996	675,114	172,701	38,472	–	486,911	–	–

TABLE C1 *(continued)*

	Partito Radicale	Demo-crazia Proletaria	Rifondaz. Comunista	Lega Nord	Forza Italia	CDU	CCD
1972	1,300	–	–	–	–	–	–
1973	1,500	–	–	–	–	–	–
1974	1,200	–	–	–	–	–	–
1975	1,635	–	–	–	–	–	–
1976	3,827	–	–	–	–	–	–
1977	3,280	–	–	–	–	–	–
1978	1,900	–	–	–	–	–	–
1979	2,455	2,500	–	–	–	–	–
1980	2,981	3,000	–	–	–	–	–
1981	2,904	3,500	–	–	–	–	–
1982	2,176	3,800	–	–	–	–	–
1983	3,660	4,235	–	–	–	–	–
1984	3,353	5,818	–	–	–	–	–
1985	2,984	6,466	–	–	–	–	–
1986	10,862	8,387	–	–	–	–	–
1987	11,645	9,153	–	–	–	–	–
1988	5,006	10,310	–	–	–	–	–
1989	2,429	–	–	–	–	–	–
1990	3,150	–	–	–	–	–	–
1991	2,860	–	112,278	–	–	–	–
1992	10,474	–	119,094	140,000	–	–	–
1993	42,676	–	121,055	–	–	–	–
1994	5,281	–	113,495	–	5,200	–	–
1995	3,995	–	115,537	–	–	205,923	4,000
1996	11,000	–	126,600	100,000	116,000	140,000	–

Sources and notes:

PCI/PDS Until 1985: "Statistiche ufficiali pubblicate in un supplemento speciale sul diciassettesimo congresso", in *L'Unità*, 26 January 1986; from 1986 to 1990: P. Ignazi, *Dal Pci al Pds* (Bologna: Il Mulino, 1992), p. 101; from 1991 to 1995, M. Caciagli and D.I. Kertzer, eds., *Italian Politics. The Stalled Transition* (Boulder: Westview Press, 1996).

DC/PPI Until 1988: C. Danè, "La Democrazia cristiana: strutture centrali e organi dirigenti dal 1943 al 1989", in F. Malgieri, ed., *Storia della Democrazia cristiana* (Rome: Cinque Lune, 1989), vol. 5; from 1989: various editions of *Italian Politics*. No data are available for 1992. The figure for 1995 is an estimate.

PSI Until 1967: F. Cazzola, *Il partito come organizzazione: studio di un caso. Il Psi* (Rome: Tritone, 1970); from 1970 to 1979: L. Bardi and L. Morlino, "Italy", in R.S. Katz and P. Mair, eds., *Party Organizations* (London: Sage, 1992), pp. 479-485; from 1980 to 1992: A. Di Virgilio, *Le metamorfosi del centro. Da Craxi ai "cespugli"*, forthcoming; for 1994 and 1995: official data supplied by Lillo Delfino; 1966 and 1967 membership refers to the unified Psi-Psdi party (Centro Italiano di Ricerche e Documentazione, ed., *Annuario dell'economia, della politica e della cultura*, Milan: Etas Kompass, 1967).

PSDI For 1953, 1956, 1957 and 1958: E. Bizzardi and C. Piazza, "L'organizzazione dei socialdemocratici 1948-1958", in C. Valluari, ed., *L'arcipelago democratico* (Rome: Bulzoni, 1981); for following years: L. Bardi and L. Morlino, *Italy, op. cit.*; 1966 and 1967 membership refers to the unified PSI-PSDI party (Centro Italiano di Ricerche e Documentazione, ed., *Annuario dell'economia, della politica e della cultura*, Milan: Etas Kompass, 1967).

MSI/AN	Until 1963: L. Bardi and L. Morlino, "Italy", *op. cit.*; from 1964: official data supplied by party. Figures include members of FDG and FUAN youth organizations.
PLI	Until 1987: L. Bardi and L. Morlino, "Italy", *op. cit.,*; from 1988 to 1992, R.S. Katz and P. Ignazi, eds., *Italian Politics: The Year of the Tycoon* (Boulder, Westview Press, 1995).
PRI	Until 1987: L. Bardi and L. Morlino, "Italy", *op. cit.,*; for 1978, 1979, 1981, 1982, 1992, 1993 and 1995: estimates supplied by party administration.
P. Radicale	Until 1991: L. Bardi and L. Morlino, "Italy", *op. cit.*; from 1992: official data supplied by party.
Dem. Prol.	L. Bardi and L. Morlino, "Italy", *op. cit.*
Rif. Com.	Official data supplied by Antonella D'Angeli on behalf of the party secretariat.
Lega Nord	*Il Messaggero*, January 18, 1997. The party does not supply official figures.
Forza Italia	Official data. The party was founded in 1994, and in that year there were 5,200 members; organizational enrollment was suspended in 1995.
CDU	Official data supplied by Gianni Campisi on behalf of the party's organizational office.
CCD	Official data; the figure does not include the party members in six of Italy's twenty regions and is therefore significantly lower than the real figure.

About the Editors
and Contributors

Percy Allum is Professor of Political Science at the Istituto Universitario Orientale of Naples.

Paolo Bellucci is a senior lecturer in the Department of Economic, Management and Social Sciences at the University of Molise.

Alessandro Chiaramonte is research fellow at the London School of Economics and Political Science.

Roberto D'Alimonte is Professor of the Italian Political System at the University of Florence.

Philip Daniels is a lecturer in European Politics at the University of Newcastle upon Tyne.

Ilvo Diamanti is a senior lecturer in the Department of Sociology of the University of Padua.

Stephen Hellmann is Professor of Political Science at York University of Toronto.

David Hine is Senior Censor and Official Fellow of Italian Politics at the Christ Church College of Oxford.

Orazio Lanza is a senior lecturer in the Department of Analysis of Political, Social, and Institutional Processes at the University of Catania.

Patrick McCarthy is Professor of European Studies at the Bologna Center of the Johns Hopkins University.

Riccardo Motta is a senior lecturer in the Department of Analysis of Political, Social, and Institutional Processes at the University of Catania.

David Nelken is Professor of Sociology at the University of Macerata and Distinguished Research Professor of Law at the University of Wales at Cardiff.

Simon Parker is Professor of Political Science at the University of York (United Kingdom).

Emanuela Poli is a Ph.D student in European Politics and Society at the St. Antony's College of Oxford.

Nicola Porro is Professor of Sociology at the "La Sapienza" University of Rome.

Luca Verzichelli has a research doctorate in political science and works in the Department of Historical, Legal, Political, and Social Sciences of the University of Siena.

Marzia Zannini participates in research activities at the Istituto Cattaneo in Bologna.

Index